The *Real* Greatest Show on Earth

The *Real* Greatest Show on Earth

By Sergeant (Ret.)
Bert "Maverick" Gonzalez
Metro-Dade Police Department

ISBN: 979-8-9877174-0-0

First Edition: December 2023

Printed in the United States of America by Ingramspark

Published by JEBWizard Publishing, LLC.

"Real heroes die serving the law, not resisting it."

Miami-Dade Police Memorial Wall of Honor

DEDICATION

I dedicate this book to my parents, Norberto and Noemi. They both gave me my work ethic that I found later in life. My father, Norberto, gave me my desire to be perfect, though I couldn't always live up to that, and my temper, which sometimes I did. On the other hand, as a schoolteacher, my mother, Noemi, taught me to follow through and put forth the effort. Although she did my book reports for me when I didn't. How proud do you think she would be now? And to both for showing me their love in their own way. I miss them....

To my brother, Pete, and sister, Marisa, who are part of me and helped make me who I am. I am their big brother and will always look out for them.

To my children Cristina, BJ, and Lauren, who filled my life with hope and helped me to see the best in people.

To Carlos, who taught me about life and how to stand up for myself.

To my wife, Rosy, whom I met much later when I was ready to come full circle. She made me better than I was and continues to do so. She set my life's journey on calm waters, and I can't wait to sail off into the sunset with her.

And finally...

To all of our police officers, firefighters, and military personnel worldwide who put it on the line daily so we can live safely, pursue our happiness, and live freely, as we were meant to do. Without you, there wouldn't be an America.

Stay safe wherever you are.

The happiest sound in life is that of a child laughing.

The saddest sound in life is that of a child crying.

Let's all come together to keep our children safe and happy....

ACKNOWLEDGMENTS

I would like to thank and offer my great appreciation to those who encouraged and helped me write this book. Without them, it would have been impossible to convey and express my thoughts and experiences about my career and police work. I want to start with my longtime tennis and now business partner, Mike Gokel. He helped from the beginning and handled logistical hurdles when I needed it. To his artist, Neil Burden, who is a wiz with graphics and put together my website and pictures.

Thanks to all of my fellow *cops*, who graciously contributed their own *War Stories* for the book: Tim Adams, my niece Alina Alvarenga, Milton Arias, Kerry Bathe, Danny Christie, Allen Cockfield, Anthony "Tony" Corbin, Jose De Leon, Carlos Devarona, Angel Dovale, Jose "Gonzo" Gonzalez, my brother Pete Gonzalez, my son Norberto "BJ" Gonzalez II, Mario Gutierrez, Mike Kelly, K. King, Carlos Labrada, Robert "Bobby" Longworth, Raul "Chewy" Martinez, Danny Narcisse, Adejimi "Jimi" Obadeyi, Al Perez, Frankie Rivera, Frank Rodriguez, Christopher Rodriguez, Nelson Rodriguez, Mike Santos, Craig Sciortino, James "Pappy" Slack, & Tony V. I'm honored to tell your stories.

Thanks to Habsi Kaba, my first instructor and then mentor in Crisis Intervention working with the mentally ill, for contributing to this book and her friendship.

To my *Sounding Board*, who helped me bounce off ideas throughout this book's genesis and development: Joey Giordano, Tom Porteus Sr., Alan Graham, & Tom Gilligan. You kept me focused and on track.

And last, I want to give my deepest appreciation and thanks to Joe Broadmeadow from JEBWizard Publishing, my publisher. Being a first-time author and a *Nobody* in the literary world and writing a book about police work in these "troubled times" surrounding our profession, no mainstream publishing house or literary agents would touch me. Though the turndowns were polite, the message was clear.

Joe saw something in me and *our* story to take me on and give me a chance, and just for that, I will be forever grateful. Thank you, Joe!

Table of Contents

INTRODUCTION

There are many reasons why people decide to write a book. They may have a story idea, such as a fictional novel. They may have had a specific event in their lives that motivated them to write about or needed to move past it, or they may write about someone else's life. Some ran for office, didn't make it, and now believe that others want to hear about their failed attempt and somehow remain relevant.

I especially find interesting those who were involved in some scandal and then wrote a **Tell All**, trying to cash in. Or perhaps it is nothing more than a preemptive strike providing an affirmative defense should they be prosecuted or sued to save their career and protect themselves.

This does not include any of our military or first responders, who should tell their stories to help the public understand what we do and go through.

At the time I was writing this book, I had been a police officer for thirty-seven years as a member of the Miami-Dade Police Department, formally known, when I began in 1983, as the Metro-Dade Police Department. I have held the rank of sergeant for the last twenty-two which I'll get into more in upcoming chapters. But many times during my career, I've been told by people I met that I must have so many stories to tell and could or should write a book.

So I started thinking about that as I neared the end of my career and said to myself, "Yeah, why the hell not!" I have many stories about things I've seen, done, or experienced. But let me say these stories are not necessarily unique to me. Every police officer everywhere has experienced events that are all too common in police work. Any busy police department, and most are, has a fast-paced variety of incidents that would fill volumes from any of its officers.

So, I decided to tell my story primarily chronologically as my career has evolved. It lets me portray the development of a police officer from his first moments in the training academy to the moment they retired. So this is not only my story but *"our"* story. You will read about events in the lives of many of my brothers and sisters.

I contacted colleagues from different agencies and cities to send me "their" stories to share, as there are so many, and it would be much more interesting than just reading mine.

Police Work is one of those things that few have the courage to do, yet everyone sees and hears about. You cannot turn on the television without seeing an incident we are involved in or handling. I have always said that two people are always in the news: the President of the United States and the police from *Any Town USA* and beyond.

In deciding on the book's title, I thought about what would best describe what the average police officer sees, hears, and does daily. All those crazy things that happen have forever been popular subjects of many TV shows and movies.

Well, a circus came to mind, and we are the *Ringmasters* called to direct this circus, so the title seems to fit what we do. In keeping with the circus theme, I prefer to call the chapters *"Acts,"* just like in the circus. Each call we go to is its own *Act* if you will, and usually has its own *Side Show*, so it stuck.

I thought carefully about the criteria for my book and how to write it. I chose several factors. The book would be my memories, those of some of my colleagues, and an exposé. It would serve as an insight into what police work is like for those who either don't understand or question everything the way we do it.

Most don't have a point of reference giving them the knowledge and ability to really grasp what police work is, and the reasons and procedures we have for doing almost everything we do.

And a book on police work had to be the unvarnished truth of what really happens on the streets and in the homes of America. I will be straight forward and absolutely will not be politically correct. That's not my style. I will use the common language on the street and in the police culture. Police Work, as in life, is raw and unfiltered and *not appropriate for all audiences.*

Any book on the subject should be the same way. If you are easily offended by strong language, you should probably not watch TV, have a family discussion on any topic, or go outside of your home. Life just isn't that way. It can be harsh and unforgiving, and our job has been as well. So strap yourself in, or don't read any further because it won't be sugarcoated.

And one other thing while we're on this topic, there is a thing called *Cop Humor (CH)*. We have our own way of dealing with the incidents we handle. Whether it is something comical, mundane, or tragic.

You see, we must build up a Wall as we call it, so we can stay somewhat emotionally detached from some of the absolute horrors we deal with. So we will laugh at things that you, the public, might think are terrible and our reaction insensitive.

How could we possibly find any humor in that?

It is a defense mechanism that first responders (police/fire/military/ER doctors & nurses) use as a coping tool. If we didn't do this, we would absolutely lose our fucking minds because of the shit we see! Day in and day out, call after call.

Because of this self-defense tool, our humor can be quite edgy and cut deeply. Not only to you, the public, but sometimes to our families, and most definitely, most brutally, and most frequently, to each other. At the time of this writing, my captain, Mike Cundle, put it the best way I have ever heard; "Warning, Cop Humor Ahead!" We don't mean to hurt anyone by it, but it sometimes has unintended consequences. Don't take it personally..

In describing some people I have encountered, I will sometimes change the names to protect the innocent, the guilty, the stupid, and those who have done me wrong and who I despise.

Yes, we all have those that, for whatever reason, we didn't get along with, didn't like or like us, and for a variety of reasons or none at all, screwed with us because they could. Usually, higher-ranking persons come to mind. But understand this, those I may write about that have done me wrong, or who I don't care for, whose names I have changed to protect myself from a lawsuit, I have said as much to their face. I am plain-spoken, in-your-face at times, and not a hypocrite. A trait that has, on occasion, caused me some self-inflicted wounds. But I will not kiss anyone's ass. More on that later.

I will also use the police codes we use to categorize incidents as some chapter titles (Acts) because they fit perfectly in describing the content. We also use these codes in a *police-slang* among ourselves when talking about incidents, people, women, men, personal matters, and general conversation.

Every business culture has its own language, and police, fire, and the military take it to a *World Class* level. The public also gets a kick from hearing police use our not-so-secret language in television shows and movies. I say they aren't a secret because our codes are public records, and the media and everyone else sometimes use them.

We even gave our police radios to the local media to listen in on our dispatched calls. When they hear about a hot call or something interesting, they can race to the scene and be the first to report for their "Exclusive" and "Seen only here" newscast. Remember what news organizations like to say; "If it bleeds, it leads!"

Another reason I am using our codes is they are unique to police agencies in Miami-Dade County. The general public, HAM Radio operators, truckers, and most agencies around the country, use *10 codes*. These were established in 1937 and later expanded. There are over 100 *10 codes* or *10-Signals*. Ok, so try to remember 100 codes. It gets a little ridiculous having a specific code for everything we do.

Fortunately, some forward-thinking people here decided a long time ago to shorten the number of codes to cover what we do and came up with sixty-one codes that describe everything we do or fit into a general category. We also use the "Q" Code for general transmissions such as "QRU," - "Are you Ok?" Codes limit the radio traffic in dispatching, which can be almost non-stop for busy departments. Can you imagine trying to have regular conversations back and forth during emergencies? It just doesn't work. So, our codes are as follows:

"Q" Codes

"QSL" – Do you receive me?/OK/Affirmative "QTR" – The Time

"QRU" – Are you ok?/Is it safe?/All is clear! "QSM" – Repeat transmission

"QTH" – Give your location/Address "QSK" – Proceed with the transmission

"QRM" – Repeat, I have interference "QRX" – Stand by

"QSY" – Change frequency

General Codes

01 - Call your station/office

02 - Call a number

03 - Radio Shop (going to for service)

04 - Motor Pool (going to for service/gassing up)

05 - Going to your station/office

06 - Transfer (getting off shift)

07 - Cancel (off a call or detail)

08 - On-Call (like a doctor would be)

09 - In Service (available for a call)

10 - Out of Service (not available for a call)

11- Out of Service (personal - we sometimes use this when we have to go to the restroom-urgently)

12 - Meal Break (very important)

13 - Special Information/Assignment (area check/subject check etc.)

14 - Conduct Investigation (general category for those incidents that are not specified)

15 - Back-Up/Meet an Officer (Most important signal for us)

16 - DUI

17 - Traffic Crash (in Florida we call them crashes, not accidents)

18 - Hit & Run Crash (we sometimes use among ourselves to describe meeting women-*CH*)

19 - Traffic Stop (perhaps the most dangerous thing we do)

20 - Traffic Detail (escorts/traffic control/investigation)

21 - Lost or Stolen Vehicle Tag

22 - Stolen Vehicle (Commonly known as *Grand Theft Auto*)

23 - Clearance Check (via radio for tags/licenses)

24 - Complete Check (on persons/vehicle ownership, etc.)

25 - Alarm (burglar/robbery-hold-up/silent/medical/fire)

26 - Burglary (houses get burglarized, not robbed)

26P - Burglary-in-Progress (occurring now)

27 - Larceny or Theft

28 - Vandalism (or when a colleague gets a bad haircut)

29 - Robbery (people get robbed-not houses)

30 - Shooting (happens every day)

31 - Homicide (Murder, Death, Kill – again, happens every day)

32 - Assault or Battery (assault is non-touching/battery is actual touching)

33 - Sex Offense (rape/indecent exposure/etc.-among ourselves-women-*CH*)

34 - Disturbance (commonly used for Domestic Disputes - another very dangerous thing for us)

35 - Intoxicated Person (everywhere-every day-'Instant Asshole' Just add Alcohol)

36 - Missing Person

37 - Suspicious Vehicle

38 - Suspicious Person

39 - Prisoner

40 - Subject Possibly Wanted (for arrest/warrant)

41 - Sick or Injured Person (medical call)

42 - Ambulance (not to be confused with Fire Rescue)

43 - Baker Act (mentally ill person-yes, sometimes used to say "Crazy"- more in another act)

44 - Attempted Suicide (if you succeed, see next code-*CH*)

45 - Dead on Arrival (DOA - As Seen on TV)

46 - Medical Detail (rarely used-Blood/Organ Transport)

47 - Bomb or Explosive Alert (actual threat/device located/gas leak - be heading elsewhere)

48 - Explosion (be elsewhere!-*CH*)

49 - Fire (the guys in the big trucks handle this one) - we direct traffic and drink their coffee

50 - Organized Crime Figure (just like TV and some politicians - ok, maybe most-*CH*)

51 - Narcotics Violator (In Miami? Say it isn't so!-*CH*)

52 - Narcotics Investigation (also used to say drugs - Again, here? Naaa-*CH*)

53 - Abduction (Kidnapping-parental/drug related/serious bad guy)

54 - Fraud (welcome to the fraud capital of America!-*CH*)

55 - Weapons Violation (used to describe guns - "He had a 55 on him" and everyone does!!)

56 - Court (another circus & another act)

57 - Case Filing/Depositions (giving sworn testimony to a States Attorney or defense Lawyer)

58 - Training (your entire career)

59- Off-Duty Assignment (moonlighting-working at a market/stadium/condo/etc. - Read extra money here)

60 - Two-Man Unit (riding with a partner - and no we don't say Two-Person Unit - get over it)

61 - District Desk Assignment (when you have to work the front desk at a station - no one likes it - "Riding the Pine")

Another addition to our codes; when we add the prefix "2" or "3" to some of the codes, such as a *"3-17,"* it means it's an emergency (injury crash in this case) and we would run Lights & Sirens. Someone is injured or could be, and we need to get there fast. The most important 3 signal for us is *"3-15,"* Officers Needs Assistance - NOW!

This one gets your heart pumping more than any other code.

And last, you will read about specific incidents that we have been involved in, handled, or have otherwise been a part of. We call these *War Stories.* Every police officer, firefighter, soldier, emergency department nurse, and doctor has them. These are the stories I've been told countless times; sometimes, you just can't believe what happened. These *War Stories* will be in my and my colleagues' own words. They are the absolute truth, and we like to say that you just can't make this shit up! So enjoy, or not, what you are about to read. It truly is, *The Real Greatest Show on Earth!*

Act ~ 1 A CALLING

"Carry a Badge, Carry a Gun"

There are many careers a young person dreams about when growing up, and there are just as many reasons why someone would choose a particular job or vocation. Many kids think about becoming firemen, policemen, astronauts, doctors, nurses, teachers, sports stars, or perhaps soldiers.

When I was growing up, I wanted to become a professional soccer player. I played from the age of fourteen on during the '70s. I had the privilege of seeing some of the best players in the world play for the North American Soccer League (NASL) New York Cosmos at Giants Stadium. I saw Pele, Giorgio Chinaglia, Clyde Best, Carlos Alberto, and Franz Beckenbauer, my favorite since I played *HIS* position of *Sweeper*.

I say this because Beckenbauer invented the position and was the best at it. My coach Chris Deiner called me the "Keiser" after him. That was a great compliment, and I did my best to live up to that as team captain.

I did pretty well for myself, and in 1979 was voted the best defensive player in New York State. I thought I had a shot. I wanted to go down to Ft. Lauderdale, Fl. and try out for the Strikers, the NASL team and rival to my New York Cosmos.

In a very polite letter from team manager Ray Hudson, I was advised to go to college and that "They" would find me there. That and my father telling me, " No, I'm not flying down to Florida, " was the beginning of the end of my soccer dream. Didn't quite work out the way I wanted. I went to a small college, Western Connecticut State, that didn't have a great anything as far as sports teams. So, like thousands of aspiring young athletes, I didn't go anywhere. It was time to move on.

My first job, at seventeen, was as a lifeguard at the town beach on Tonetta Lake in Brewster, NY where I grew up. I was an exceptional swimmer, and being a lifeguard seemed like a natural job for me. It was ok, but kind of boring because nothing happens on a lake. I'm in no way comparing it to lifeguards on ocean beaches. They are very busy, and it's much more dangerous. But I made a few bucks and got to watch over people. I did this job not knowing watching over people would become my life's work.

1

After graduation, I went to work as a counselor at a day camp for mostly rich kids from well-to-do parents and some celebrities. My buddy Jeff Earl and I got hired together and drove to work, stopping to pick up one of the kids named "Elvis" every day on the way in. We listened to *The Cars* on cassette tape, yes Millennials, *a tape*, and we loved it.

Being a camp counselor taught me even more responsibility than being a lifeguard because you can't take your eyes off a kid for a second. It also kept us very busy. Taking care of a group of small kids is like herding-cats. Ever tried that? They all go their own way. Frustrating at times but a great experience. Especially for an 18-year-old.

I moved to Miami in 1980, a year after my family resettled there due to my father's transfer by General Electric from Manhattan.

They got tired of the cold and snow, but I didn't understand at the time because I was a kid and snow was fun. Not when you work for a living, as I realized later in life.

After a year in college and the move to Miami, I realized it was time to grow up and start earning my own living, I began working as a security guard for a local company, Star Security. I worked construction sites at night. Boring! And condominium complexes at the front gates. Less boring, but I got to meet people and learn the comings and goings of the residents. This is how I met my first wife. She was married. and yes...a very long and sorted story. But I was 18, so give me a break.

I then moved on to work at Eckerd Drugs, a mostly Florida-based retail drug store chain, where I was an assistant manager. Have you ever worked in a retail store that opens daily from 8:00 a.m. until 9:00p.m.? Well, don't. They are long hours, endless product deliveries, cash-counts, stocking shelves, customer complaints, employees bitching about this or that, and district manager inspections. Little did I know that I was in for many of the same issues as a police officer, but I couldn't see that far ahead. As a very close friend, Sergeant Tom Gilligan, would say many years later, "My crystal ball is in the shop." A saying that would become sooo true.

I was admonished continuously for not wearing my tie when the district manager Roger Forky came around. He was a tall man with a command presence and was a former New York State Trooper. My excuse was I was working in the stock room and getting sweaty. Mostly true, but I hated wearing a tie. A prelude of things to come.

My first real exposure to the police came while living at my parent's house. Their neighbor, Sergeant Robert "Bob" Johns of the Metro-Dade Police Department, lived directly behind them. He was a very nice guy, and he and I got to kick a soccer ball around many times between our yards. I first started to see who and what he was, and as a security guard, had several occasions to call the police.

"Metro" as Dade County residents referred to them back then, had a great reputation. "You didn't fuck with Metro!" Bob was my first shining example of being a "Metro-Dade cop," and it got me thinking.

Another significant incident that brought it home for me was at Eckerd Drugs at our Miller Square store. I helped open it when it was new.

In 1981, I was sitting in the breakroom at the back of the store, directly in line with the front doors, having a soda. I heard a loud crash of glass breaking and some "thumping" sounds just outside the breakroom. I ran out and to my shock, I saw a young guy standing by the now shattered front doors, standing but bleeding. The front of the store was all shot to shit. Glass and blood everywhere.

Again, a preview of things to come.

The thumping sounds outside the breakroom were bullets hitting the wall just over my head. Shit! So of course, we called 911, and Metro-Dade-Police responded along with Metro-Dade Fire.

As it turned out, it was a *drive-by* shooting, and a targeted hit by drug dealers on the guy walking in our front doors. It was frightening and cool all at the same time. I got to see Metro cops in their light and dark brown uniforms with leg stripes and their Green & White patrol cars handling this big crime scene, and I was a part of it! "Fucking A!"

The uniforms were unique to Metro-Dade as all other departments wore blue except for the Florida Highway Patrol (FHP). The Green & Whites were striking in their color scheme and easily distinguishable. When Metro was on the scene, you knew it!

3

I moved from Eckerd's to Blazer Financial Services, a small credit and collections company where I worked on small personal loans and then collected on delinquent ones. By then, I was married with no children, making a menial salary. Still, it taught me how important it was to have a good credit rating. I did credit history checks on applicants. I found it astonishing that some folks had the balls to apply for a loan with an absolutely crap credit history record.

They couldn't pay their bills but they wanted a new TV.

The two other "assistant managers," as we were called (I was number three as the newest guy)—in reality, just loan officers—showed me how to pull those credit histories. I remember one of them, so let's call him "Mark." He was teaching me how to do inputs on the credit bureau machine, and I remember him telling me how hard it was to do, and it took him a bunch of tries to get it right.

It was easy!

I followed the format and hit the keys. I just thought wow, you must be an idiot. My gut instinct about him was right on. When I eventually left to attend the police academy, he asked why I wanted to become a police officer because, in his expert opinion, it was a thankless job.

Years later I ran into him and he said the same thing to me. But being a police officer wasn't a thankless job. In his case, the fact that he didn't live up to lawyer Daddy's expectations left him scarred, and everyone else's dreams were for shit. Idiot!

Another thing I began to learn about was professionalism. My then-office manager was Mike Gokel. He ran the place, and I got to see how he treated the staff and the clients. He was very polite and professional in his demeanor. He never got upset and handled everything in a calm manner. I consider him and my father the two most professional people I have ever known. We must have gotten along very well from the start because we have been playing tennis on and off since and are now business partners in my outside endeavor.

During my time at Blazer, I began to think about what I wanted to do because credit and collections weren't it. It dawned on me that being either a Metro-Dade Police Officer or Metro-Dade Firefighter is what I wanted to do.

Early in 1982, I mentioned to my first wife that one of those two jobs was what I wanted to do. She said in no uncertain terms that if I became a police officer, she would divorce me.

So I put it off for a while. But as time passed, I realized that the *pull* to become a police officer was getting stronger. So I decided to apply to both; to be a Metro-Dade Police Officer or a Metro-Dade Firefighter. I told my wife to divorce me. I was going to DO this. Little did I know then I would end up divorcing her. No crystal ball again.

So I applied to both, and I have to say the hiring process for firefighters was much more challenging than for police officers. Once you passed the application and initial background check, the fire department had you attend a physical fitness test held at one of our local parks.

You were required to complete a series of very physically demanding tests, dragging a 120-pound "hose-dummy" a certain distance and lifting a 100-pound hose fifty feet in the air by pulling a rope. Honestly, there were other exercises I can't even remember..

I do remember there was a mile-and-a-half run for time, and the exercise I couldn't wait to do was the swimming test with my pants on. Many failed here as swimming distance or treading water wearing pants is challenging. I am a very strong swimmer so this test was a piece of cake for me. I wish I could have stayed in the water longer. I should have been a Navy SEAL. More on that later.

The police application process was not physically demanding at all. In 1982, you took a Civil Service exam for both police and fire to gauge if you could read and write. If you passed that, you filled out a pretty extensive Confidential Questionnaire that laid out your entire life. If you weren't disqualified for anything outright from your questionnaire, like a felony arrest, suspended driver's license, bad credit history, etc., then you were set up for a 1000-question psychological exam.

This determines whether you had violent tendencies, an uncontrolled temper, or were racist. Did you love your mother, hate your mother, love your father, hate your father. These questions were asked multiple times in different formats. Were you a thief, alcoholic, gambler, or just your run-of-the-mill psychopath.

Every once in a while one slips through the cracks. Nothing is perfect.

During the exam, you are pulled out for a short interview by one of our staff psychologists. I remember being asked if I thought violence was necessary in my job should I become a police officer. At twenty-two years old, and not knowing much, I said it would be given sometimes people can only be subdued with violence, and sometimes people try to hurt police officers. I guess it was the right thing to say. I wasn't crazy since I'm here.

While all this testing is ongoing, you have an assigned background investigator tearing apart your entire life. My investigator was Israel "Izzy" Reyes. I later learned he was an outstanding cop, a very intelligent guy, and he eventually retired and became a County Court judge. They would examine what you said in your questionnaire and compare it to what they found out from criminal history checks, license checks, credit history, talking to your neighbors, family members, and of course your past employers. If you passed all of this, you are then sent for a physical exam by County doctors. Many people fail here for various physical ailments that might disqualify you from the demanding job of being a police officer or a firefighter. My physical covered both my police and fire applications. Fortunately, I was an athlete and perfectly healthy so I moved on.

The hiring process for Metro-Dade can be very long and tedious. Some applicants take two years or more to get hired. There was a large pool to choose from for both jobs, so the departments had their pick and weeded out many. The recruitment poster at the time had the tag line; "*Only 1 in 14 is good enough to wear the Silver Badge.*" I am proud of that and it was true.

Now, not so much. Yes, some young officers may take exception to that comment. They will say the same about the generation that follows them. Get over it.

I was fortunate that my hiring was in the wake of the infamous *1980 Mc Duffy Riots*, the *Mariel Boatlift*, where 120,000 Cubans fled to Miami, the *Cocaine Cowboy Wars* were raging, and I had a Latin surname. Spanish Speaking officers were in high demand and I was hired in seven months. Two years later my brother Pete was hired in six months. Timing is everything, isn't it?

In January of 1983, after I completed both application processes, I was given a final interview at the Metro-Dade Fire Department headquarters. The division chief completed his questioning and told me I was going to be hired and would attend the next fire college class which could be in a month or two.

I was excited I was going to get hired and looked forward to it. As luck would have it, two weeks later my background investigator Izzy Reyes walked into our office at Blazer. I was of course shocked when I saw him thinking something bad was about to happen. He said "Hi," gave me a piece of paper and told to write a paragraph on why I wanted to be a police officer. He then said he wanted to speak with my boss Mike. I was shitting myself!

They went into the back office and emerged about twenty minutes later. When they were done, Izzy took me aside and said I was going to become a Metro-Dade Police Officer, and I was scheduled to start the academy the next month. I was taking a shit again but for the right reason.

Izzy left, and I announced to Mike, Susan, Espy, Jaime, and that asshole Mark, I was getting hired. I was extremely happy because deep down inside I really wanted to be a police officer more than I did a firefighter. Nothing against my brother and sister firefighters. They have been and remain my heroes, but I wanted police more.

I was given a date for the next week to report to the quartermaster and begin the process of picking up my academy uniforms and equipment. I walked in and went to the counter and met "Joe." He was the quartermaster, and that house was HIS! If you didn't need it, you didn't get it. And only Joe decided whether you needed it.

I meekly said I was there to get my uniforms and such. He issued me a number, 3835, which would become MY BADGE NUMBER! The next guy after me in line was Vic Gatel, who would become a life-long friend. He was assigned 3836, and that's how you were issued your badge number which would come to identify you your entire career.

It was so exciting getting my uniforms and a proud moment. You were also issued a belt with a brass buckle, not understanding, of course, that buckle would become a source of great pain and discomfort in the academy. To end my first encounter with Metro-Dade Police entities, we noticed Joe had a sign on the wall that said, "Lack of prior planning on your part does not constitute an emergency on my part!" Welcome to police work!

So I ended my job at Blazer on Friday, February 4, 1983. I had a three-day weekend and began the police academy on Tuesday, February 8, 1983.

And so the adventure begins…

Act ~ 2

"58": Training, Training, & more Training!

Scene 1: The Academy "Class, Drop and Give Me 10!"

Once you make it through the hiring process, you are scheduled to enter the police academy. This is the real first-step to becoming a police officer almost anywhere in the country. I started the academy on February 8, 1983, at 0700 hours. *"BLE 84,"* means Basic Law Enforcement Class. Back then, the police academy and the fire college were held at the Miami-Dade Community College, North Campus here in Miami.

The *police academy* was formally called the Southeast Florida Institute of Criminal Justice. It still is for many smaller departments in the area and hosts a "Self-Certified" academy that a cadet would pay t for on their own.

Miami-Dade and the City of Miami Police Department formed our own academies in the late 90s. Reasons range from cost to the departments to pay for each cadet, and control over the training itself. Less of a "college atmosphere" and more of a boot camp.

Day 1

There were thirty-seven of us starting the academy. We all gathered in a classroom sitting quietly and attentively, awaiting the arrival of our Training Advisers (TAs). These were Metro-Dade Police Department (MDPD) officers for my class which was made up of all but three MDPD cadets. The other cadets were from Homestead PD, Hialeah PD, and Miami Beach PD.

The Miami Beach cadet was Carlos Devarona who would also become a life-long friend and would always call me *Park Ranger* because of our brown uniforms. When he would call me over the years it would be "Hey Boo Boo!" I guess he was Yogi. If the class was made up of mostly Miami PD cadets, then they would have Miami PD TAs. At one time MDPD and MPD classes were combined, but a huge rivalry fight took care of that. Yes, we all don't get along sometimes.

Our TAs arrived, Corporal OJ Anderson and Officer Tony Soto, dressed in the "Brown Gown" as our uniform is called. We of course were thoroughly impressed and since day 1 couldn't wait to wear the uniform. Our TAs are the equivalent of drill instructors in any branch of the military. They would oversee every aspect of our training for the next five months.

Basically they were now our "Daddy." We kinda knew what to expect as far as physical training (abuse) and psychological training (yelling) but most of us being young, didn't have a clue. Much to our surprise, Corporal Anderson and Officer Soto began by introducing themselves and then having each one of us stand, introduce ourselves, and state why we wanted to become police officers. Easy enough.

One by one we went around the room. Most said what I said that we felt we could be able to help and protect the public, arrest bad people, and that we felt becoming a police officer was *"A Calling."* This may sound corny to you but it is absolutely true. How else can you describe why you would want to become a police officer, firefighter, soldier or doctor, nurse or a teacher? You have to be drawn to and *want* to do these jobs.

Each profession comes with its own level of intense training, continuing education, and enormous responsibilities for the welfare of others, and unbelievable amounts of stress. So how else can you describe the reasons why?

After the intros, the TAs said right up front before any training began and I'm paraphrasing; "You better come to terms and understand right now that you can get killed doing this job." Wow! Silence. It may sound pretty heavy for someone outside of police work to hear that, but it is necessary, and they did us a favor. Knowing this can happen before we go through all the training and expense only to find out later on that this job wasn't for you made sense. And that does happen, but fortunately for our class no one walked out.

So when all the touchy-feely stuff was done, our TAs finally laid into us. "Get outside, move your asses, hit the floor!" Let the torture begin! We started doing push-ups. And we didn't stop. Unless you are used to physical training at this pace, no one can handle this. Even for those that were in the military and have not trained for a while, it hurts. We were up, we were down. Up, down, up, down! All fucking day!

I was trim, 170 pounds, an athlete, tennis, soccer, skiing, swimming, running. You name it, I did it. Not push-ups. It is a painful process, similar to the military's way of breaking you down, but not as severe. I never did so many push-ups in my life. Then we started running in between. Not in shorts and sneakers yet, but in full uniform wearing patent-leather shoes.

And don't scuff them up. More Hell to pay if you do.

This also drives home the point that no matter what you think of yourself, you are not in shape! I never did so many push-ups. Did I say that already? Oh, yea I did. I can still feel them. That's how much it hurt. By the end of day 1 you could barely move. We went home and the pain in your arms and chest was excruciating. You just wanted to numb yourself out and go to sleep. You did, not looking forward to waking up the next day.

Day 2

When we arrived at class the next morning—0700 sharp, and don't be late—what did we do first thing? "Move your asses!" More push-ups and running. By now, the lactic acid building up in your arms was just impossible to bear. But we did more. This went on for the first few days. Taking time out of course to take care of classroom and administrative stuff, like you could actually hold a pencil at this point.

Every time the TAs said to "Drop and give me 10!" you almost cried. And the collective "Fuck" or "Shit" you heard at least let you know you weren't the only one that was hurting. And you learned right away that we did everything and I mean everything as a TEAM. There were no individuals in a BLE class.

Once again, the beginning of a life-long concept.

We eventually reached the point where you could not do even one more push-up. You just got into the front-leaning rest position and held it there. "Nope, can't do it." If you tried to do another one, your arms buckled, and you landed on your face. This just added insult to more injury. By this point the TAs knew we couldn't go anymore so they didn't yell at us for not going down and back up.

They just kept making us assume the position and try. "Assholes!" But it was all for a good cause.

Now I will not go day-by-day but you get the gist. The academy is physically tough and demanding. If it was easy then anyone could do it. The tougher they were on us the better prepared we would be for what was to come. Possibly fighting for your life. But for now it was just training.

Module 1

Once we got settled and into a rhythm, we bought t-shirts and shorts with our names on them and a number, I was 18, and we started formal run training. We lined up in columns of two, with the class leader up front as determined by the TAs.

Ours was Mike Duggan. Mike was already a police officer and a sergeant in Salem, Massachusetts. He was an older guy and had years of experience over the rest of us so he was the logical pick. His wife Barbara was also a police officer in Salem and they both picked up stakes and headed south. Winters here are much nicer than in Massachusetts.

Contrary to what you may see on TV, you can't just *transfer* to another police department out of state. Every state has its own standards. They had to repeat another academy, and every officer who worked out of state had to redo the academy when they came here too. Commendable to say the least. I often said if I ever went elsewhere I would never do another academy. No fucking way!

So we started running, and running, and running and running. We also learned to sing cadence just like the military. Fortunately, we had a couple of former Marines, Mike Stevens and Gerry Davenport, and both were squared away guys. Gerry was a former White House Guard under the Carter Administration and he taught us how to do the cadence.

> BLE 84-Tough to the Core!
> C-130 rolling down the strip,
> Metro-Dade gonna take a little trip
> One mile One mile! Easy run Easy run! Two miles Two miles! So good So good! Three miles Three miles! Gonna run Gonna run!
> To the sun To the sun! Four miles Four miles! Gotta be Gotta be!

In the shade In the shade! Five miles Five miles! Gotta run
Gotta run!
Five miles Five miles! Gonna be Gonna be!
Fired up Fired up!
Looking good Looking good! Everybody Everybody!
Looking good Looking good! Gonna run Gonna run!
Fit to fight Fit to fight! Driving on Driving on! Metro-Dade!
Driving on Driving on! Motivated Motivated! Driving on
Driving on! Sound off Sound off! Everybody Everybody!
Gonna run Gonna run! To the sun To the sun! Hey mom Hey
mom! Hey mom Hey mom! Look at me Look at me!

On and on and on...

I am paraphrasing and cut the cadence down from the original
but you get the idea. There are other cadences we sang but so you
understand why this is done, it is so we can keep a steady pace while
running and everyone stays in sync. Singing also makes you breath
better while running. For those of you who run or spin, or use an
elliptical, isn't it easier listening to music? So we made our own.

When we weren't in class or had some downtime because of
an instructor's no-show, we ran. Our class leader Mike loved to jog
for exercise regularly, so it was his decision on how to fill that time,
so we ran. As time went on, we could do five miles as a class like it
was a walk in the park with no one struggling. Ah, to be young like
that again.

Besides the endless push-ups and running, we had to learn to
stand at attention, salute, and march as well. We did this every day.
Why? So we can function as a *team*. You learned to move together
and it built a sense of unity and pride. Once you got the hang of it,
it was pretty cool and you felt proud of yourself. Sound like any
other group of people? It's the same concept for the military that
started the whole ball rolling. We just carried it over to our training.

We had a class formation every morning and mustered outside
of the classroom. Mike would be at the front, then the class was
split into two groups, or "platoons," then each platoon split into
smaller "squads." Each platoon and squad had a leader. Again as

selected by the TAs based on your background. We also had a "Guide-On" in the formation. He carried the staff with the class banner. He stood at the front with Mike. This formation was used for everything. Especially for our favorite, Inspections! Yeah!

From day one you learned our codes. Everyone was given a card, and you had to commit them to memory. After all, you were going to be speaking in this alien tongue for the better part of your life, on and off-duty. Your memory recall of these codes would factor into your personal comfort during these inspections. Another part and most importantly, your uniform would come into play as well.

While we mustered for announcements, instructions and then daily inspections, the TAs would walk up and down the formation, slowly, and stare at you up and down, zeroing in on any imperfection on your uniform, looking to "Gig" you for something.

A "Gig" is a "Gotcha," and meant pain. Your grooming was another gig-point they could get you on, like the length of your hair and the closeness of your shave. You may have thought you cut your hair short enough, and then discovered "Oh no-you-didn't!" Push-ups! "Drop and give me 10 or 20" whatever they felt like. You came back the next day with a Real Haircut!

The ladies in our class had to have their hair tied up so it was in a tight bun. They had to make certain their hair didn't touch their collar, and more importantly when we hit the "Road" as we call it, there wasn't a ready-made grab handle for a subject to grab hold of during a confrontation. Ok, a fight! If you understand fighting dynamics then you know where the head goes the body follows. No untied, long hair.

Now on shaving. It was common practice for the men in class, every class, to shave completely. No mustaches, none. I had a mustache. Damn! Many guys in the 70s and 80s had mustaches. It was a thing at the time. I was prepared to shave it but fortunately for me and some of the other guys in class Corporal Anderson and Officer Soto were both sporting 'staches themselves.

Remember it was a thing. And fortunately for us they weren't hypocrites and didn't make us shave them. Good on them! Though they had every right to say, "Do as I say, not as I do," as they were the bosses and we were lower than whale shit. That showed us integrity and how important that would come into play later on.

Now you still had to have your mustache trimmed to no wider than the edge of your lips, short, but you kept it. The other academy classes were not happy about it and one of them had a female TA and she didn't feel sorry for them. Too bad, we kept ours, Nananana! I had and still have mine and always will, though it is *slightly* longer and grayer than in my academy days.

The daily inspections continued. The TAs would scrutinize everything about you while you stood at attention. They would talk to you and ask you questions about anything and everything to keep you distracted. And don't look them in the eye, oh no! If you did, Push-ups! Then they would ask you what your codes were. Cadet Gonzalez, what's a 15, what's a 25, what's a 34, and so on, rapid fire! You had to recall your codes in a split second and then the next one.

Of course in the beginning of the academy you couldn't remember them that fast and you were nervous to boot. "No that's wrong! Class, drop and give me 10!" Fuck! Remember, we did *EVERYTHING* as a *TEAM!* Every time a class member got gigged on anything, code, uniform, grooming, or the TA just wanted to screw with you just because, the entire class did push-ups. We were thirty-seven, and no one passed inspection early on. Can you multiply thirty-seven times ten children? That adds up to the sum-total of PAIN. It was endless!

We also got gigged for our Bic pens not being properly placed in our uniform shirts. By that I mean that somehow your pen flew out of your shirt pocket and landed somewhere in the formation. How did that happen? Figure it out.

Here was another little trick we didn't know. If our Guide-On carrying the class banner got gigged as well, and went down every time everyone else did, but made the fatal error of laying the staff on the ground when he did his push-ups, oh the horror!

He and we lost the privilege of showing off our class banner. You never put it on the ground just like the American flag. It was embarrassing, but we didn't know, and we had to earn it back. That took about two weeks and you can bet it never happened again. So how did our guide-on do his push-ups while holding a staff? He didn't. Someone else held it while he dropped and gave his 10. Simple, right? Painful lesson.

Do you remember the belt with the brass buckle I mentioned in the last act? If there was a least important thing in your life outside of the academy it would have been your belt buckle. Why do I mention this? You see, your buckle was front & center on your uniform and easy pickings for the TAs. When you thought that your uniform was squared away and you trimmed off all the loose threads, which we did every morning as partners, you never get it all. It looked like two monkeys picking lice off each other. And your hair was tight and you knew your codes, here comes the buckle.

The TAs would say that your buckle was dirty, had fingerprints on it, or was scratched. You knew it was clean because you spent anywhere from 30 to 45 minutes at home the night before polishing it. Yes, that much time again in the morning polishing that stupid, fucking belt buckle! And just when you thought it was good to go, the TA would put his big, fat thumb right on it and poof! "Class, drop and give me 10!"

You couldn't win and you weren't supposed to. It was about trying to piss you off so you didn't flame out when you would eventually be on the *Road*.

While the physical training continued every day, there was the academic side to the academy. Here is where you learn law, patrol procedures, understanding human behavior, first-aid, policy, report writing, crime scene investigation, crash investigation, citation preparation, radio procedures, de-escalation, and pop-quizzes on your codes and spelling. You better have your spelling down because you were going to be writing some type of report for the rest of your career.

Remember, this was 1983 and there were no computers and *Spell-Check*. You carried a pocket dictionary when you hit the *Road* so you can get it right. They placed a great emphasis on a well-written report since it might end up in court and the whole world would know what kind of writer you were. Not so much today. Computers have made most people lazy and therefore stupid! And if you're one of those and this upsets you, get over it.

Learn to properly write a report without artificial help you moron!

Each major block of instruction carried with it an exam. Law being the big one, but you had to pass each, nonetheless. Passing these blocks was stressful, so we formed study-groups and got together after hours in preparation for these tests. You had the main exam and one make-up. If you didn't get the make-up you washed out before the end. No one failed, but a couple came close.

One kid in the class nicknamed "Rock & Roll," was nineteen years old and very immature. We had to push him to study, and he barely made it through the five months, and unfortunately, he washed out after graduation. You had to really want this and to quote a famous American, Gene Kranz, the NASA flight director for the Apollo 13 mission that suffered catastrophic equipment damage and almost lost the crew, "Failure is not an option!" I personally was not going to wash out. I guess Rock & Roll didn't want it badly enough.

As the academy went on we became more comfortable with our new reality and got into a "groove" if you will. You learned what to expect on a daily basis and you gained confidence as each day, each quiz, each test, each run, and as each inspection went by. You felt strong and that transcended everything you did. As each day went by you could see the finish line, though it was still a ways off.

We didn't go through it without stress or controversy. We had an Understanding Human Behavior instructor, a civilian, an academic who didn't seem to care for law enforcement and talked down to us. No one liked him and we made it clear as did every academy class that he instructed. You would think the powers-that-be who knew this, would find someone better meshed with the cadets as did all the other instructors. But I guess he was the only one available.

War Story or Rather, Oops!

So, *Cop Humor* came out early on. One of the guys in our class, Bobby H., was great at impressions and he had this instructor down pat! During one of our breaks Bobby started to do his impression and walked around the room acting like this guy did, talking down to us but had us in stitches. What we didn't know was this instructor was outside the classroom watching. I guess he didn't like it much.

A bit later, he walked into the room to resume class, walked up to the instructor's desk, and abruptly threw all the books onto the floor. He clasped his hands together with his two index fingers pointed up and placed them to his mouth. He walked around in silence for about five minutes. We of course did not know what was going on. Then he quietly began to paint a picture for us why he was upset. There was a collective gulp! Oh, oh, we're going to get it! And we did.

Once our TAs found out we got ripped a new one. We had to write a "Memo." That's the report you write throughout your career explaining your actions for something you screwed up on, and in this case we had to state why making fun of someone is wrong and that it wouldn't happen again. Interesting though, we didn't get PT'd for it. I guess our TAs didn't like him much either.

One course of instruction was swimming. Yes, we had instructions in, believe it or not, learning how to swim. As a former lifeguard and swim team member I looked forward to this, only to be disappointed because the course of instruction was two, four-hour blocks of instruction on two different days.

This was a joke! I could have spent all week in the pool. But there were some officers who couldn't swim. Yes, in Miami, surrounded by an ocean on one side, canals and lakes inland, and a pool in many homes. There were cadets that never learned how to swim. Now don't get upset, but it is prevalent in the Black Culture that kids don't learn how to swim. It may sound like a stereotype but facts are facts. I didn't make this up. Many black kids just aren't taught to swim, and it's not their fault. As is the case with anything with kids, it's up to the parents to teach them. So what happens when they reach adulthood? They just can't do it and are terrified of the water.

Part of the testing is to tread water for fifteen minutes. Not easy if you can't or are a weak swimmer. Another exercise is to swim to the bottom of the pool and retrieve a brick and bring it back up to the surface. You can't do this if you can't even let go of the pool's edge. I helped a couple of our classmates just letting go of the edge and coming out to the open water. There was no pass or fail here. It was just practice and an "exposure" to swimming. Hopefully, the folks who couldn't swim would never be "exposed" to the water during their career. Fortunately in today's academy, the cadets swim for a solid week with a test at the end. Good thing Fire Rescue personnel become certified divers.

Module II

This evolution of the academy took us to firearms training. A very necessary part of being a police officer in the western world. This is where we learned how to fire a weapon and all the responsibility that comes with it. For many of us, like me, it would be the first time we actually handled and fired a gun.

Back then, we carried revolvers; "Six-Shooters" as did law enforcement dating back to the Old West. The gun held six,.38 caliber rounds, and we had another twelve on our gun belts in "speed loaders." Yes, a whole eighteen rounds on us. Seems funny now in the 21st Century as we carry semi-auto pistols with high-capacity magazines. I personally carried a Glock 17, 9 mm, with four extended, twenty-two-round magazines totaling eighty-nine rounds with one in the pipe. Seems archaic now, but that's how it was.

You first learned the parts of the gun and were tested on them. Then you learned how to load it, hold it, draw it, retain it, and ultimately shoot it. The first time you did shoot it was intimidating. It was something completely foreign if you were not in the military or a hunter. I was neither as most weren't.

While you are learning this new skill, add to it *Stress-Inspections*. These differed from our usual daily inspections in that the firearms instructors, wearing red shirts, most shooting fanatics and former military, had pretty much cart blanche to fuck with you to no end. They couldn't touch you, but the yelling and screaming was quite a lot to take. This was designed to push you even further to see if you would lose your cool under pressure. Remember, people out on the *Road* are going to yell at you and worse.

During one of these stress-inspections, three of the instructors zeroed in on Mike Stevens, one of our former Marines I mentioned. Mike had the Marine Corps emblem tattooed on his right arm. These instructors surrounded Mike and started to lay into him and make unflattering remarks about the Marines and his tattoo. They ordered him to sing the Marine Corps hymn, but Mike, having been through this type of training before, said that he will not disrespect the Corps by signing the hymn and making fun of it, "Sirs!" You know, he left them speechless. They didn't know what to say and I think they actually respected him for standing up to them and walked away. Way to go Mike!

That ended it for Mike for the moment, but not the rest of us. We were yelled at, made to do more push-ups, made to run to the front gate of the range about 100 yards away and pick up a rock, run back to the instructor and present the rock only to be told "That's the wrong rock Maggot! Now drop and give me 10!"

My brother Pete went through the academy two years after me when he got out of the Army. He went through Boot Camp and was an MP for four years, so he knew much of the game, and I also gave him a head's-up on what to expect. When a firearms instructor told him to run and find a rock, he did, and when he was told that he had the wrong rock, he opened his other had with another rock. "God Damn It Gonzalez you asshole! Give me 10!" They didn't like that much so he paid a price.

In addition to this, they inspected you on the cleanliness of your newly issued revolver. We shot every day and therefore had to clean them every night at home on our own time. You made sure you polished that gun inside and out. You could spend two hours at this only to be told that your gun was dirty. There was no winning, and you weren't supposed to.

Then there was the shooting itself. For those of us who never fired a gun before it was a stressful time. You were learning a new skill that would impact the rest of your life and had to qualify in order to carry the gun, and quite possibly stay in the academy. We shot at human silhouette targets that were colored black. This type of target was common throughout the industry. You had to score a 110 out of a high of 300, meaning each zone on the target had a numerical designator assigned. The closer to the Center of Mass (torso/chest area), the higher the score.

We started shooting at the fifty Yard Line, then moved closer for each course of fire. The 25-, 15-, 7-, and 3-yard line. The closer you got the easier it was. I can tell you at fifty yards with a revolver, standing or lying prone, you couldn't make out the lines on the target or even see if you hit the damned thing.

Many of us found this difficult, but not Jerry the former Marine White House Guard. Jerry grew up in Montana and shot everything since he was a little boy. He shot a perfect 300 most of the time like he was standing at the 7-yard line. He was the "*Tackleberry*" of our class from *Police Academy* fame. Every class had one. You know the guy who slept with his guns. The rest of, not so much.

The Most Stressful Time

Qualification was on a Friday. You had to pass in order to move on. About seven of us didn't make it and for me it was doubly stressful. What I didn't tell you before is that my father Norberto had been diagnosed with Colon Cancer the year before. The night before I started the academy he suffered a seizure. I flew over there and followed Fire Rescue to the hospital. They then diagnosed him with a brain tumor, and the day we were qualifying he went into surgery to have it removed, but I couldn't be there with my mother Noemi while he was under.

My mind was not on my shooting to say the least and I didn't qualify. It was disappointing and embarrassing. So those that didn't qualify could not rejoin our classmates on Monday at the academy and had to go back to the range to try again. Did I say stressful? Fortunately, my father came through the surgery ok and on Monday, I and all the others qualified.

But this episode had long lasting effects on me. Every time I had to go the range and stood on the line, I went back to that day my father was in surgery and had a difficult time. So much so I went to our Psychological Services Section for some counseling to help me get through this. It took a while, but I was able to overcome this stress.

I never became that guy who could shoot a 300, but I did become a good tactical shooter. I worked on my draw and was super-fast like a Samurai drawing his sword. The first to draw his sword usually won. That became my mentality and I could move and shoot when it counted. I was good in combat mode, but not necessarily pure target shooting.

And about that; the scoring process changed some years later from 110 out of 300 because we learned that under stress, meaning a combat confrontation with an asshole-bad guy, that even the best target shooters can lose up to 80 percent of their accuracy. When its life & death, the equation changes and you may be lucky to hit anything. Because of this, we and most departments went to a Pass/Fail system meaning you had to just hit the target a minimum number of times.

You see, the public, the courts, the lawyers, and the anti-police activists have watched too much TV and movies and think every police officer should be able to shoot the gun out of a bad guy's hand, or just "wound him" in the arm or leg. Let's call bull shit here! It doesn't work that way. Real Stress is a Motherfucker! Unless you've been in a situation confronted by an armed subject in your face you can't understand.

War Story by Sergeant (Ret) Jack Breen, Metro-Dade Police Dept.

Jack Breen was my corporal and then my sergeant during my rookie year (1983-1984) on the midnight shift for about four months.

He was a former Marine, a firearms instructor, and had been on the job for fifteen years at that point. He was a great mentor and also helped me with my shooting. He never talked down to me, and I love and respect him for that. He told us about a confrontation he had not that long ago at the time.

He and his partner Marcia Reeves confronted a subject holding a knife, at night and in the dark. Jack told me when the subject pulled the knife he was about 4-5 feet away. He reacted and withdrew his revolver and fired.

Six times! Point Blank! He missed all six.

Marcia then fired and hit him once. They then grabbed and disarmed him. Imagine Jack's surprise when he didn't hit him at all. Can you say, "Oh Shit?" That is what really happens to police officers under that kind of stress.

So those of you who think you know how to do our job and tell us we should have only "winged" him, just Shut the Fuck up! You have no idea what you are talking about. I suggest you pick up a badge and gun and walk down a dark alley and see how you feel. Not so brave now, are you?

Another little change that took place in the '90s because of race activists was the change in the color of police practice targets from black to blue. Why? Because those activists claimed that because the targets were black, it predisposed police officers to shoot Black people. WTF? Are you kidding me?

We thought that was the most ridiculous thing we ever heard. The target was just that; an inanimate, static paper silhouette that we practiced on. Nothing more. It didn't point a weapon, attack you, or run, nothing. Persons of any color, wearing multicolored clothes, can scare the shit out of us. This notion is stupid and I'll tell you why. For the last twenty-five years give or take, I have been practicing on unarmed, blue targets, and you know, I have never even pointed my gun at let alone shot an unarmed Smurf! Have you?

Now we're back in class and continuing with the rest of our training and over time, the physical training got easier with the exception of Defensive Tactics (DT). We had a gym in the building with a large mat, where we did martial arts-style training with police instructors that were experts is self-defense.

I particularly enjoyed this evolution as I already trained in Jujitsu and boxed as a teenager. We did strikes, throws, joint manipulation, falls; yes you learned how to fall because every fight that you would ever be in during your career *will* end up on the ground, so falling and not getting hurt is important. Many at our age have never been in a fight or trained in self-defense, so this was important as well. As with everything else, there was a final exam for DT. During this test, you had to be the defender and attacker. They paired you off with a partner during the training so it benefited you both to make the other one look good.

A Sun-Soaked Story

On the Sunday immediately before the DT test a group of us with our wives decided to go to Key Largo in the famous Florida Keys for some sailing and jet skiing. We spent the day on jet skis and a Hobie Cat catamaran. I sailed when I was a teenager so I was the helmsman on the Cat. We were out there all day, in the sun, no shirts, drinking beer and having a blast just letting off steam. Something you had to learn to do during your career.

Well, for you folks that don't live in Florida or have never visited, the sun here is extremely strong all year long. What did we all get? Sun Burn! I got it pretty bad. You can't move or touch your skin without a great deal of pain. Most of you probably know this.

The next Tuesday comes and its DT exam day. We were going to be tested on all those things I previously mentioned. Remember throws and falls? You were able to choose your partner for the final, and because I had martial arts experience and could make you look good when you performed a throw, no less than six classmates chose me to be their *Uke* or loosely translated as Training Dummy for their test.

26

I had to perform my test then get thrown by my classmates. Six exams meant at least five throws per cadet. Did I say I had a bad sunburn? You can imagine what it felt like to land on my burned skin thirty times. Ouch!!! I was in so much pain but I had to suck it up so my classmates did well on their tests. I made them look great, but it came at a price. Lesson learned; use sunscreen or wear a damned shirt!

Another evolution in our training was First Aide. Every police officer in America learns how to assess and treat someone's injuries or medical condition, to a point. Very experienced paramedics from Metro-Dade Fire Rescue gave us this instruction. We had book-study, as well as extensive practical exercises. I looked forward to this training as a former lifeguard, and I already had a background in this area. This training was more extensive than I had received as a lifeguard, but I really did well in this class having scored a perfect 100 on the practical exam and a ninety-nine on the written. I finished No. 1 in my class in First Aide. This would come into play later on in my career.

We continued on with our studies, working hard, passing quizzes and exams, more PT and running, and had quite a bit of down time as instructors would cancel or not show up at all. When we didn't fill this time with running, we just hung out in class or the courtyard in our building. Never leave cadets with nothing to do.

An Ill-Advised Gambling Story

During one of these down times on a Friday, a group of the guys were bored and decided to spend the time pitching nickels in the hallway. What is this you ask? You flip nickels at the bottom of the wall, and whoever keeps his closer wins the pot. What they didn't know was this was technically gambling since they were using money.

None of us knew this.

So as luck would have it one of the instructors (that Human Behavior instructor no one liked) caught them and the Shit Hit the Fan! They/we were severely admonished (yelled at) and the five of them were turned into the administrative lieutenant.

My class buddy, Vic, was one of them.

So in addition to being called on the carpet, they each had to write the "Memo" I've told you about explaining their ignorance and actions, and that they didn't know it was illegal and would never do it again. The worse part about it is that they were informed they might be fired for their transgression and spent the entire weekend thinking that they would be come Monday. You work hard and pass all of your exams, and they might drop you because of a moment of unintentional stupidity? Fortunately, they only got yelled at some more and didn't get fired. That was a close one! A valuable lesson for the life ahead.

The Medical Examiner's Office Field Trip

As we were nearing the end, one of the really fun-filled things we did was the trip to the Medical Examiner's (ME's) Office. Children, can you say the word *Autopsy*?

One of the realities of police work, unlike almost any other job in the world, is that you are going to see dead people. Lots of them! We are the ones who pick up the pieces when people—or *Stupid Human Tricks* as I call them—leave mayhem in their wake. This is something you have to get used to or you can't do the job. Period! I'm not saying you have to like it, just learn to deal with it, especially at the time we were entering police work. The time of the *Cocaine Cowboys*.

So we had to take a bus trip to the Broward County Medical Examiner's Office instead of the Dade County Medical Examiner's Office, why? Because the Dade County office was so overwhelmed and kept well supplied with cases, largely in part due to the aforementioned *Cowboys* they could not accept academy field trips at that time, so we went north.

I mentioned cops develop their own sense of humor in order to deal with the worst that life offers. Well, coroners have their own, unique version of it as well. We arrived at the office and were briefed on the two cases we would be viewing this day.

One was an apparent suicide case where a woman drove her car into a tree at an estimated 80 mph. When you crash a car at that speed, it tends to destroy the human body. Not a pretty sight.

The other case was that of a "Floater." That is a common term we use when someone is found floating in the ocean, a lake, or canal for a period of time. Ours was two days old. Do you know what a body smells like after decomposing in water for a couple of days? Hopefully, you do not. It is the worst smell you can imagine. Some of the class got the head's up from previous classes and had perfume packets to hold under their noses, or Vapo-Rub to rub in their nostrils to try and mask the smell. Yeah, good luck with that. It was absolutely horrible. Most were trying not to lose their lunch, me included.

Now, remember I mentioned a coroner's humor? Well, our tour-guide doctor decided that while he was performing the famous "Y-Cut" into the decedent's chest, he would grab a sandwich from his pocket and take a bite. Sick Fuck! Several of our classmates went running to the bathroom and you know what happened next. Welcome to the ME's. office boys and girls!

Graduation Day

We had busted our asses for five months, passed all of our exams, ran and did push-ups until we could do them standing on our heads, recite our codes and criminal statutes, endless training scenarios, and could pretty much handle anything thrown at us. Now we were getting ready for graduation. Ours was on June 17, 1983. A proud day to be sure. We rehearsed for the ceremony, and several of us had parts to play. I was to lead the class, family, and friends in the *Pledge of Allegiance*. I practiced for several days because I didn't want to screw it up. Mike Stevens recited the Code of Ethics, a standard that we would come to be held higher to than most any other segment of society. And we all went and got fitted for our *Brown Gowns*. We couldn't wait for graduation.

Ours was very special in that one of the TAs from another class, Officer Dave Tipps, put on a little skit for the family and friends that had never been done before. He dressed up as Darth Vader, complete with helmet and cape, and while using a microphone walked around the auditorium speaking in that deep, James Earl Jones voice, representing the *Dark Side* of the Force, and telling we young *Jedi Knights* and our families, what were about to confront. It was cool to say the least and drove home a very important point.

We would get into some shit.

The ceremony went on and after all the speeches you receive your *Silver Badge*. The Metro-Dade Police Department Director at the time, Bobby Jones, would hand you your badge for a photo-op, one at a time. But that wasn't the best part. You still had to pin it on your uniform. But you didn't do it, you chose someone special to do it for you.

Some chose their wives, husbands, girlfriends, moms, etc. For me, it was my father Norberto. He initially wanted me to follow him into General Electric, then he wanted me to be a lawyer. He also sat me down in the fall of 1978 in a Chinese restaurant in Danbury, Connecticut, and told me that I should consider an appointment to the United States Naval Academy in Annapolis, Maryland. I had the grades and was an accomplished athlete, so I could have done it. I hated school and wanted out. That ended that.

But now I was graduating the police academy and I think he finally understood this was what *I* wanted to do. He was also very sick as the cancer was now taking hold. We didn't know at the time he only had seven months left. So he pinned my badge on me and he was so proud.

I saw that look on his face one other time. I was in high school and we were playing a soccer match in the rain, and it was one of the very few games my father was able to attend. He was standing on the sideline with several other fathers, when I let go of a screamer from about thirty yards out. I had a very strong leg and this bullet whizzed by the keeper.

Besides everyone cheering about my goal, I happened to look over to the sideline and saw all the other fathers congratulating mine. I could see that smile across the field and he finally got to see how good his son the *Captain* was. That was the look he had while pinning my badge on me. I'll never forget it. I was fortunate to relive that moment in reverse, when years later, my son BJ graduated the academy, and I got to pin his badge on him. Some of the best moments of our lives.

When it was announced we were now Metro-Dade Police Officers, and good enough to "*Wear the Silver Badge*," we realized it was finally over, and the weight on our shoulders was gone. Up until that time, it would be the proudest moment in our lives. Little did we know what we were in for….

Act - 3 Riding Assignments, FTOs

& Potluck!

Scene 1: Field Training Officers : _Our New Daddies, or Mommies_

So now we are proud graduates of the police academy. We are wearing our new _Brown Gowns or Blues_ and have our shiny new _Silver Badges_. Our shit doesn't stink! Or so we thought. The next phase of our training takes us to our first assignment, and into our next evolution which in Florida is formally known as the Field Training & Evaluation Program. We refer to it as _Riding Assignments_ or _FTO Phases_. FTO is short for Field Training Officer. These are the officers who are going to take you out on the _Road_ for the first time and teach you how police work is really done. Almost to a person you will hear; "Forget everything you learned in the academy; this is how it's really done!"

I became an FTO later in my career and never subscribed to that philosophy. The academy gave you the foundation for your job through theory and procedures. Now you're actually applying everything you learned. This doesn't always easily translate to the _Road_. Theory meets Reality.

Phase 1: FTO – Officer William "Scotty" Bryant

You are going to spend the next three and a half months with three different FTOs, one month a piece. You are required to spend each phase (a month) on each one of our shifts, Days, Afternoons, & my least favorite, Midnights. My first shift was on afternoon shift from 2:00 p.m-10:00 p.m., or 1400-2200 hours as we converted to military time in the later 80s.

My three FTOs in order of appearance were Officer Scotty Bryant, Officer Al Goodall, and Officer Larry Kraslow. All were great yet all were different. Each FTO is going to train you on how to actually _BE_ a police officer and evaluate you daily on your performance and progress. As with any training program anywhere, you were expected to pass and continue to the next phase. You can repeat phases if you were seriously deficient but, if you were that bad, you'd wash out of the program. This was rare and in case you didn't know, it is extremely difficult to terminate a government employee. There are quite a few people over the years not cut out for this job but are still here.

When Scotty and I first met, as is done with every first FTO/Rookie meeting, you have *The Talk*. This is where the FTO tells you what he/she wants you do to, how to act, where to sit, what to say, what equipment & supplies you should have with you, and in case the proverbial *Shit Hits the Fan*, what you should do.

After this chat, you finally get to sit in a police car for the first time. Sometime prior to my academy class, there were what we call *Blue Shirt Ride Alongs*. The department used to have 3-day riding assignments while you were in the academy (blue shirts) as an exposure to the *Road* prior to graduation. This was designed to open your eyes as to what you would be getting into and weed out those who made an error in their career choice. We didn't have these ride-a-longs because we were trying to get as many cadets trained and out as soon as possible. These rides were reinstituted years later, so getting in the car was truly my first time in a real police car.

Cool!

Now don't expect to drive right away. You have to learn to walk and chew gum first. The first thing you do is check into service. Your FTO will show you once, and then you're expected to do it from that point forward;

"5313 – New Crew. Badges 2302 & 3835, Two-Man Unit, Cage, 09."

You started with your unit number. "5313" meant we were Station 5 (the 5) Third Shift (3-Afternoons) Area 1 (the First 1) and Third Unit is seniority on the squad (the 3). *Two-Man* meant that there was two of you. If you are offended by the masculine connotation, get over it. It was the '80s, and it's still used today. No disrespect to women.

The *Cage* meant you had a physical steel and Plexiglas barrier between the front and rear seat where the bad guys sit so they can't do any harm to you. We call it a *Cage*. Some of the people we arrest act like animals so there you go. The *"09"* means you're now *In-Service* ready for a call. Each district, each shift, and each squad worked the same way. Many years later the unit numbers were simplified, but this told anyone exactly who you were, where you worked, and where you fell in the pecking order. The lower the unit number the higher your seniority.

So Scotty checked us in and we waited for a call. You have to pay close attention to the dispatcher and listen up for when your unit number is called.

In the beginning you are not tuned into the radio and you miss a lot of transmissions. This is normal. There are non-stop transmissions coming over the radio and it's completely foreign to a rookie. Besides listening, your FTO is talking to you imparting knowledge and wisdom which you can't really understand yet. You're nervous and excited, your head is looking out the window like a dog, and you are overloaded.

Then your call comes in.

I remember my first call, a "*25-Audible*." That's an alarm call to a residence called in by an alarm-monitoring company. I don't remember the exact address, but I remember when we arrived, we found the front door partially open and a German Shepard dog running around.

When we find an open or unlocked door we are required to search the structure to make certain there are no bad guys and no one is in distress. So, on my very first call as a new police officer I had to draw my gun and conduct a building search. Can you say Stress? Fortunately, there were no bad guys and no one in need of help.

The owner didn't respond, which is typical; so we secured the house best we could, left and wrote our report at another location. You always find a safe location to write your report so you are not exposed to ambush since you are preoccupied with writing. Do you have to be aware of your surroundings when doing something as mundane as writing a report? Well, a police officer does. Keep that in mind. "5313, report written, 09." Back in-service for the next call.

This is how it works and with us the next call is usually minutes away if not immediately. As a major metropolitan agency that serves a large population, calls can be endless. "*09-QSK.*" That means proceed with the next call. You can sometimes, many times, go non-stop all shift long without a break. This is what you signed up for so suck it up Cupcake!

As the month went on, Scotty and I became close as you do with most anyone you spend that much time with. We got along great. He was easy-going, calm, smart, knew how to teach, and took great pride in what he was doing.

He had only two years on at the time, but in Miami, two years during that time was the equivalent of ten years in the less populated, less crime and drug infested areas of the country. Those officers who work dense population areas anywhere in the country will agree. Experience comes fast. He showed me how to write a report, how to stop a car and write a citation, how to stand when talking with the people involved on our calls, how to arrest someone, search them, place them in the car, in the holding cell, how to attend court, and how to take a *"12,"* which is a meal break. Very important.

I learned who you have to call for follow-up on different kinds of calls and crimes, such as contacting Homicide for cases involving dead people, either by murder, natural causes, or by accident.

A Sad Story

I am going to fast forward three months to my final riding assignment at the end of my training phases which was the last two weeks with Scotty again, because this story involves learning procedures and what <u>not to do</u>. So on my last two weeks I'm back with Scotty and he is sitting back and letting me handle everything as is customary on Phase 4 and about to be cut loose on my own.

We get a call; "Beeeep, Attention all units, "*3-17,*" child struck!" The call was that of an 11-year-old that was hit by a vehicle. Anything involving children sends chills down your spine. It was on SW 64 Ave just north of Bird Road next to the school at dismissal time. A little girl—her name was "Sunshine"—was walking home on the side of the road. There were no school zones back then. She was struck from the rear and sent airborne. She landed about ten feet in front of the car that hit her.

She was rushed to Miami Children's Hospital by Metro-Fire Rescue but didn't make it. Scotty and I were devastated. Anytime a child dies is tragic, but we have to do our job. We closed off the street per procedure and held the crime scene for the responding Traffic Homicide detective who would conduct the reconstruction of the crash as is done with every fatality or critical injury crash. This is for possible future criminal charges in court, as well as civil litigation. These are highly trained detectives and experts in this field.

We also notified our sergeant, which is required so he could notify up the chain-of-command. We held the scene, and I began writing my report. Detective Frank Polito arrived and as is customary, the handling officer walks the detective through the scene. As I was showing him where she landed and where we thought the vehicle struck her, he asked me about one of her sneakers. He wanted to know where the sneaker originally was and why we had moved it.

We were both puzzled, Scotty and I. What we didn't know was sometimes, when struck with significant force, it can knock a person right out of their shoes, laces and all. The shoe stays in the exact spot of the strike.

You have to be a crash reconstruction expert to understand the dynamics of this which we were not. That spot is where Sunshine was walking when the car hit her. Det. Polito ripped us a new asshole for that. He had to reconstruct the crash, and that was a key piece of evidence.

You can bet that Scotty and I never made that mistake again. More importantly, Sunshine was my first fatality crash of many to come, and I still feel the pain of losing her. Imagine how her parents felt and still feel to this day. You will never forget these tragic events. I hope her parents were able to move on over time. I am so sorry for them.

Back to Phase 1. As the month went on, I gained more confidence and Scotty let me handle more and more on each call. After two weeks I was driving. That was a blast! Especially running *"3s."* If I do say so myself, and I will, I was taking to this like a duck to water. No expert by any means, but it was coming easily. I couldn't believe I was getting paid for this.

Call-to-call, domestics, burglaries, robberies, disputes, you name it we handled it. Everyone did. Reports and listening to the radio were the hardest things to learn. There are so many nuances to reports because they all differ based on the type. How do you get to Carnegie Hall? Practice! It eventually comes.

Listening to the radio and hoping you didn't miss a call was stressful. Besides the young face, generally fit appearance and neat uniform, there is another way to spot a new officer.

Have you ever seen a dog with its head tilted like it's trying to figure out what it's looking at or hearing? Well, a new officer has his or her head tilted toward the handheld radio on the gun belt, with their hand on the volume button turning it up and down, trying not to miss a call. Can you picture that? We all did it.

And when you did miss that call if it wasn't of a priority nature, your FTO would let it go unanswered until the dispatcher repeated it and you finally heard it. Now, pull out you notepad and write it down quickly. Ah shit, I have to ask her to repeat it! Everyone missed calls. Just for grins though, your FTO would ask you "Did you hear that call?" Deer-in-the-headlights look. And then you say sheepishly, "No. What was it?" Your

Sgt. (Ret.) Bert "Maverick" Gonzalez

FTO would say there was no call. Just seeing if you were paying attention. Shit!

Phase 2: FTO – Officer Albert Goodall

So Scotty passed me onto Phase 2, and it was on the Midnight Shift with Officer Al Goodall. Al had been on twelve years by then and had a reputation of screwing with his rookies. Some of the other guys actually felt sorry for me. I looked forward to it.

We met at roll call for the first time and had *The Talk* just like I did with Scotty, and we hit the road. If you have never worked a midnight shift it is a completely different animal than working during the day. You see people you wouldn't normally see, and the activity is very different. There are only a few types of people out at night; people who work late or over night shifts, partygoers, us, and mostly bad guys and degenerates. Unless you are part of the first three groups, you are probably up to no good and we encountered a lot of them.

The one good thing about Mids is the lack of traffic. We get around pretty easily and running *"3s"* is less dangerous because you have less of a chance of getting hit due to heavy traffic. The lack of traffic also makes you think you can drive faster. A hazard of the job.

Al was very experienced and enjoyed doing traffic enforcement, especially DUIs, *Driving Under the Influence*. Remember the partygoers I mentioned? Well, there was no lack of clubs in a party city like Miami, especially at that time which was the *Cocaine Cowboys Era*. Babes, booze, and blow were EVERYWHERE!

The squad I landed on had an informal competition to see who could get their DUI first. Now don't think we were making up arrests for the sake of arrests. Some of you will but you would be wrong. We didn't have to because everyone was DUI!

The squad had a particular club that they liked to watch in their patrol area and it was called Desirae's. It was at SW 97 Avenue and Coral Way, a coke-den like most, and full of stupid partiers that inevitably climbed behind the wheel, so it made it easy.

We would sit down the street in the wee hours and just wait. One by one they would drive out of the parking lot. Within seconds they would be weaving all over the road. We would follow for a bit to make certain we had a real DUI, then we would initiate the *"19"* (Traffic Stop). As soon as you walked up to the window you could smell the odor of the alcoholic beverage, or should I say beverages? We would then ask if they knew why we stopped them and of course they would plead ignorance.

"You're kidding, right?"

Time to get out of the car and do the *Roadside Test*. You know the one where we ask them to close their eyes and touch their nose, walk the line, and stand on one foot. Most of the time they could barely stand or walk, let alone do *Roadsides*. And when we arrested them they of course would say "I'm not drunk, I'm fine!" Idiot! Off for processing we went where a D-O Tech, a Drunk-o-meter Technician, would administer the *Blow-Test*, which is where you blow into the machine to measure the amount of alcohol in your system.

The legal limit in Florida is .08. I have seen people blow.34 and everything in between. If you think you can drive like that you're dumber that you think.

Al really liked doing DUIs, but he showed me how to be safe as well. He had this little thing he did to catch you off-guard. Knowing your location at all times was paramount because in case you got into a *jackpot* as we called it back then, meaning you're in deep shit and need help, a fight, a crash, a gunfight; you needed to know where you were so help can find you.

So Al would drive aimlessly through a neighborhood and the darkest street he could find. He would then slam on the gas and put the car into a skidding spin, and yell at you, "*3-15, 3-15, we're shot, where are we?*" I then had to give our exact location under duress. If it was real, you better be able to tell the dispatcher on the radio without screaming like a little bitch *(CH)* exactly where you were. Al did not catch me not knowing where we were because Scotty warned me about his technique. I got the word about Al.

Yes, I cheated, just like Captain Kirk did during his *Kobayashi Maru* test in the academy where he changed the conditions of the test so he could win. Still, it was good practice as he reinforced at least three times per week. Two things here; yes, I am a *Trekkie*, and winning in police work is everything. Like it was said in the movie *Top Gun; "In combat, there are no points for second place!"* So we cheat all the time. We have to in order to survive.

Al and I continued on our month together and I remember him telling me if he ever got hurt, not to let Metro-Fire Rescue take him to the then named American Hospital. It had a terrible reputation for not saving seriously hurt people, and this was known across the board. Later that year I ended up arresting one of their doctors who was called in for an emergency who was guess, DUI! Like I said, a party town.

We handled a ton of domestic disputes during that month. It is amazing how many people are up in the middle of the night going at it. I guess no one is immune from it and I'm sure as you're reading this you too have been up once or twice with your significant other arguing over some bullshit thing. The difference is when it escalates to the point of calling *911*. We handled plenty, but I'll cover that topic much more later on as it merits its own act.

Al was also a department driving instructor and man could he drive. I watched and learned, but what he didn't know at the time was that driving was a passion of mine as well, and I did a little Auto-Cross competitive driving in my late teens.

A year later I became a driving instructor as well under head instructor Sergeant Bucky Green, and Al was one of his instructors who certified us. There was a driving course at the academy at Miami-Dade Community College North campus, and Al owned the course record. On course record day where everyone tries to take the existing record, Al held the stopwatch. I finally made my run. As I crossed the finish line, Al jerked his head back and said "Naaaaaa!" New course record! Time for the young lion to take over. Another proud day for sure.

We finished out our month together but I can say with full confidence I learned so much from him. He was a great teacher and while others heard some bad things about him and didn't want him as an FTO, I'm really glad I did. They should all have been as fortunate as me.

Phase 3: FTO - Officer Larry Kraslow

I then moved on to Phase 3 of my riding assignments and onto the day shift with Officer Larry Kraslow. Larry was a very smart, reserved, pensive person and liked to slowly analyze each situation.

After the *Talk* again on day one, I was driving full time. It was coming rather easily by now, though there was still a world of things to learn. I just mean I was comfortable and looked forward to every new challenge. Larry lectured and guided me and was working on refining my report writing skills as well as conducting a lot of traffic enforcement.

We stopped a bunch of vehicles, gave out warnings and some citations, but the goal was to safely learn the skill. Traffic Stops are probably the most dangerous single event a police officer handles, walking away from it requires being on your toes and a little luck.

We also handled more domestics, and yes, they never stop coming, and *"25"-Audibles*. Alarms were endless. The alarm systems of the day were in their infancy and they went off *all the* time. They were too sensitive and any vibration or noise, like a pet or a rain shower, could set them off.

We responded to every one in case *that one* was a *Good One!* Meaning, a *"26"-Burglary*. When a storm blew through with hard rains and thunder, it seemed like *every* alarm in Dade County went off. It was common to get 30, 40, 50 or more alarm calls at once. What was our solution to this? One-man units were sent to our Communications Bureau and the officers would pick up what was then called "Blue Cards."

At that time technology wasn't what it is today and *911* call-takers would actually send a blue card via conveyor belt to the dispatcher with calls on them. Not electronically as is done in the modern era. Very "old-school."

So we would pick up said "blue cards" with 30 or 40 alarm calls and as a one-man unit, respond to them in the rain and check them to make certain they were not a burglary or otherwise a priority situation and we did this alone! Today that would be completely against current officer safety practices and our contract. But we did. You could be tied up for three or four hours on this, but it had to get done. The best solution to this was when a lieutenant or senior sergeant with some stones got on the radio and ordered that all the alarms that came in with the storm be *"07'd,"* canceled. Fuck it! My kind of supervisor!

On the day shift you had a lot of *Burglaries-In-Progress* calls because that's when most people are at work and the bad guys know it. Either by alarm or by neighbor, we get the call and race over there. Most of the time we were too late, but every once in a while we would get lucky and catch them inside or running from the scene. That's a rush! Foot chases and sometimes a struggle or an all-out fight to take them into custody. We had our share.

Larry was not aggressive by nature at all, but he was a big man and could take care of business when he had to. He was a 'talker' and communicated well with people. He did gig me on something though.

We would be talking with the person or persons we were involved with on a particular scene. He pointed out to me I tended to stand with my right hand resting on my revolver. Not grabbing it but just on top of the grip. He said it looked "aggressive," when most situations didn't call for that kind of posture.

I did do this but my reasoning was this; in the academy, we were trained that 50 percent of all police officers in America that were shot, were shot with their own weapon.

Now think about that.

That means in these confrontations, the officer had his or her gun taken away by some shithead-bad guy and shot with it. So *Gun Retention Training* became part of each academy and continued on during *In-Service* training. I made myself a promise in the academy no one was ever going to take my gun from me, and I would take the son-of-a-bitch with me if it ever happened. I still stood that way to the end of my career. Not going to happen!

Though I was good at the mechanics of driving as I said earlier, Larry taught me how to navigate day shift traffic. Sounds mundane? Believe it when I say congestion during the day can keep you from getting anywhere quickly, and learning how navigate can speed up arrivals to your calls.

I tended to make left turns while driving to our calls and with congestion we found ourselves waiting in turn lanes an awful lot. Larry said that we should set ourselves up, when possible, on routine driving to only make right turns. You know, he was right.

In high-traffic areas you wait endlessly trying to make a left turn, especially when there is no left-turn-signal let alone an open intersection with a blue-hair in front of you. We have a lot of those in sunny South Florida. UPS trains their drivers the same way in order to make those deliveries as quickly as possible. Makes sense.

Larry and I finished our month together. We had an enjoyable and great learning experience, but less than a year later when I was long on my own, I returned to his day squad as just another member, and we ended up riding together as *Partners*.

This time we were equals, not FTO/Rookie, and shared the work. Though, by that time Larry was attending law school at the University of Miami, and his studies were monumental and difficult. So we made a pact; I would write the police reports and Larry would do his law reading.

It worked out quite well. I was still learning, so I got more practice, and he got valuable study time. Later, Larry left the job and became a real-estate lawyer. I can say that in some small measure I helped him pass the *BAR*.

Phase 4: Back With Scotty

As is customary when you pass your three phases, you enter Phase 4 where you go back to your first FTO for two more weeks. The reason for this is your first training officer can evaluate the progress you made since you were first with them, and hopefully let you *Solo* in a short period of time.

During this final phase, the FTO sits back and lets you operate as a One-Man Unit, meaning you are supposed to do everything by yourself. This is the final preparation for when you are on your own. By no means does this mean you know everything, it just means that you have reached the next *Belt* level and are performing well enough to join a squad as a new member.

Scotty and I picked up where we left off, and he decided after three days of this phase I was ready to go my own. A proud feeling indeed!

Scotty approached our sergeant, let's call him "James Walsh," and told him "Bert's ready to go!" This doesn't usually happen before the rookie finishes out the two weeks. Well, it wasn't going to happen here either.

Sergeant Walsh didn't want to let me go on my own, not because I wasn't ready, but because he just didn't feel like it and somehow if I made a mistake it would come back on him. Coward!

As I came to know more about him over the years that followed, I learned he wasn't a nice guy and a general prick overall. He wasn't liked and the officers didn't want to work for him. No matter, Scotty and I went on for the full two weeks and had a great time. It was during these two weeks however that Scotty and I handled the fatality of little girl, "Sunshine" I told you about before, so it wasn't all fun and games. At the end of the two weeks, Scotty and I parted ways, and I went on to my first squad as a functioning, *One-Man Unit.*

The thing about FTOs like most personnel in any profession is though everyone was trained the same way, personalities come into play and greatly impact the training message, how the lessons are received, and ultimately how successful they will be. I was fortunate to have excellent FTOs and will always appreciate and honor their teachings to me.

Others weren't so lucky. If you got an FTO who was lazy, nasty, didn't talk much to you—which makes for a long month—and generally didn't care, then you weren't going to learn much. There was one FTO I worked with later on as a fellow FTO, who said he was treated badly by his FTOs so that was good enough for his rookies.

Bad philosophy! It's akin to having an alcoholic parent and not breaking the cycle. Unfortunately in cases like these, police officers are flawed human beings just like everyone else. We bring to the job all of our life's experiences and that can affect the way we perform.

To all of my colleagues who share my philosophy and care about their very noble calling, congratulations on a job well done and continued success. To those who somewhere made a wrong turn, either correct it or get out! I can't say it any other way. Being an FTO makes you perhaps the single, most important individual in a young officer's career. You are *Sensei - The Teacher*. What you say and do will impact that young mind forever, so do it right.

Scene 2: On My Own: "Oh Boy Is This Great!"

I reported at 1600 on a Tuesday to my first squad. I was sitting quietly in the roll call room at Station 5 awaiting the arrival of my squad mates and my new sergeant. I didn't know what to expect as they started to arrive. Most were very senior and one or two had just a few months on me.

Sergeant Vicky Pane came in and began addressing us. She read BOLOs (*Be-On-The-Look-Out*) information from the board, told the squad what she expected that day, covered any pending issues from the previous week, and introduced me to the squad.

It went rather easily and I was welcomed. No, I didn't have to sing or dance like some unlucky rookies had to do, so it was good. Sergeant Pane dismissed the squad and had a short meeting with me. She told me what she expected and her squad procedures. The same thing I have done when I either got someone new or took over a new squad. The sergeant is King, or in her case, Queen, and it is *Her Way!* She told me to be safe, let her know if I get stuck on anything, and cut me loose.

I signed out a patrol car. We had pool cars back then that basically ran 24/7, a handheld radio, and I loaded up the car. I checked in on the radio: "5348 new crew, badge 3835, one-man unit, 09." And I was on my own. I remember that feeling of driving north along SW 117 Ave heading to our patrol area, and I was as giddy as a little girl who just got her first *Barbie Doll* for Christmas. Ok, a better analogy; a little boy who got his first GI-Joe.

What a feeling of freedom it was to be alone in my very own police car. I remember it vividly thirty-seven years later. I get my first call and now it's time to step up and take care of business. I don't remember what that call was, but it was routine so no lights and sirens. It didn't take long after that when I got my first "*3*," and it was, you guessed it, a domestic. One of hundreds to come.

What I remember most about that first week was that I handled a child molestation case, had a civilian observer ride with me, an injury crash, and a barricaded subject where a father lost his mind, took his family hostage and threatened to kill everyone. I was holding an inside perimeter point in the back yard along the fence, hiding behind a tree with my revolver pointed at the house in case the father came out shooting with his rifle. Yea, like I had any clue as to what to do. I stayed there a good two hours until I was relieved by an SRT (Special Response Team) member.

That is what we have always called our SWAT team. He took over, and I was sent to the outside perimeter. The good thing was our negotiators talked him out, and no one was hurt. And that was my first week. A prelude of the craziness to come.

Act - 4 Running "3s" Lights &

Sirens - Warp Speed

Scene 1: The Ultimate Driving Machine

When you become a police officer or firefighter, especially a police officer, the most prevalent activity you do is drive a car. Except for the downtown areas of major cities where some foot-posts still exist, an officer gets around in a patrol car.

Whether you are in an urban setting or a very rural area, the patrol car or *Cruiser*, has replaced the horse from the days of the *Old West* and gets us around pretty quickly. By virtue of being a *first responder* means we need to get to the scene of an emergency or priority very quickly; sooner rather than later. Someone's life depended on the time it takes us to get there. *There* could be anywhere, your home, business, scene of a crash, school, mall, or the middle of the street.

A police officer receives an emergency call over the police radio. After either writing it down or clicking a button on the computer these days, he or she then turns on the *emergency equipment* as it's called; the overhead lights (Reds & Blues) and the siren. Now he/she is stepping on the gas and heading to the assigned emergency.

We call this *Running a "3."* Any one of our signals prefaced by a 2 or a 3 is a lights & siren call. Remember, that's for agencies in Miami-Dade County. As I look back, running *"3s"* is probably the single thing I've enjoyed the most about the job. As I told you in previous chapters, driving is a passion, and what better way to indulge that passion than to drive fast, through and around traffic, with your lights & siren wailing away? There isn't any.

When we get that *"3"-Call*, it's like the switch goes on, the heart starts pumping and the adrenaline rush is amazing. While everyone else is driving slowly and stuck at traffic signals, we get to bypass all of that, safely of course, and continue to whatever we are headed to.

The sheer enjoyment of running *"3s"* can only be understood by someone that has a similar activity in their own job or hobby. It puts you in a realm that is both euphoric and dangerous. More on that later. I cannot say how many *"3s"* I have run in my career, but what I can say I have loved running each one of them.

Getting through traffic whether passing it on the left, the right shoulder, on the left side of the median when traffic is jammed and can't move (against policy-but done-many times) occasionally up and over a sidewalk, is an absolute blast! You need us to get there and we need to get there.

Now I'm not saying an officer should just blow through a red light or stop sign. That is illegal and against procedure. We are required to enter the intersection safely, slow, stop if necessary, look, and proceed when clear. We just don't have to wait. Though every once in a while an officer will take an intersection without at least slowing to check for cross traffic and bad things happened.

Running a *"3"* is what police and fire are most noted for. Every TV show or movie emergency depicts police cars and fire trucks running lights and sirens. The so-called *Reality* police shows have the camera inside of the car focused on the officer and the roadway ahead so the audience can get some of the *feel* of driving the car on an emergency.

It's akin to having a camera in a rollercoaster where you get some of the sensation, but it's not like the real thing. You have to have the sights, sounds, smells, and the feel of the car swerving around traffic, which gives you pure enjoyment; at least it did me. Contrary to the catchy BMW commercials, a *Police Car* is absolutely the *Ultimate Driving Machine*! Sorry BMW, but you can't do the things in your car that I can do in mine. At least not legally.

Scene 2: The Chase

You learn how to run *"3s,"* emergency calls and the like. Now, when you try to stop a car for a traffic violation or because you suspect it was involved in a crime, you light them up and they take off - *Fleeing & Eluding* is what the law calls it. We call it a *Chase* or *Pursuit*.

I've told you how much fun a *"3"* is; now a *Chase* is a *"3"* on steroids! This is what everyone wants to see on TV or in a movie. Any cop show worth its salt will have a chase scene, some better than others, like the iconic chase scene in the 1968 Steve McQueen movie *Bullitt*, which is considered the best movie car chase of all time. If you are old enough to remember the movie, then you know what I'm talking about. It was wild and on the edge of out of control. Sometimes out of control.

That is what most chases are like. You are focused on the bad guy ahead of you trying to get away and you're not going to let him. While there are rules governing how fast you can drive or maneuver, it is very difficult to follow them. The adrenaline dump is so strong you have to constantly fight against just blindly following the subject and doing what he does, especially when you are young. Chasing the *Rabbit* is hard to let go of.

So you're in the chase. Lights & sirens blaring, trying to keep up with the asshole that's blowing through intersections, cutting off other drivers, all the while you have the radio mic in your right hand calling out the chase to the dispatcher and the other units that are trying to get to you.

In America, you drive a police car with your left hand. You are using that mic in your right, and under normal circumstances talking and driving can be difficult enough. Now you are flying around chasing the rabbit, trying not to crash, calling it out, and trying to do it *calmly*. Yes, I said calmly. Sometimes it can't be helped and officers are screaming into the radio and no one can understand him or her. The dispatcher has her hands full trying to interpret and relay what the lead unit is saying, using a *Jedi Mind-Trick* to settle down the officer.

Having said that, the chase is absolutely the biggest rush you can get. You are flying around, darting in and out of traffic, around every obstacle you can imagine, wondering what you are going to do when you catch him or not, and trying not to crash your car.

I have been involved in countless chases early in my career as we had a very liberal pursuit policy. Basically, we had virtually no pursuit policy for the reason we we're chasing. You try to stop a car, they flee, we chase! Any reason.

It could be that the driver simply had a suspended license or no license, a warrant, just committed a crime like murder, robbery, or burglary, it's a stolen vehicle, had drugs in the car, or just plain panicked and started running. We couldn't know and it didn't matter. *"5309 Chase!"* And it was ON!

We chased the bad guy until one of several things happened. He stopped and gave up. Rare and damn! I mean, oh good. He stopped, bailed out and ran. Better! Usually what happened was a foot chase ensued then a perimeter was established with K-9 units and a helicopter.

The subject stopped and decided to fight. Sometimes. Crashed and ran. Many times. Fleeing subjects are like cockroaches. You just can't kill them no matter how bad the crash was.

And finally and worst of all, they crash into an innocent person minding their own business. While the courts have ruled the police have no culpability in these cases because we are not the ones fleeing, it does hurt everyone involved when an innocent person gets injured or killed. This prompted changes and very restrictive pursuit policies in recent years. And that's a good thing. Though the newer generation of police officer doesn't get to experience the thrill of countless chases like me and my contemporaries did, more civilians and more officers are not getting hurt or killed.

Having said this, there is nothing like the chase. One of the most thrilling and frightening things in a chase is going through a toll plaza at 100 mph. You read right. A toll plaza. Here in South Florida we have the Florida Turnpike, and while toll plazas now are pretty much a thing of the past, in our past the Pike had them everywhere, and we usually found ourselves chasing the bad guy through them. We go where he takes us.

Now we're doing warp speed on the Turnpike and approaching a toll plaza. While a toll lane looks fairly big when you're going through it at 2 mph, it gets REALLY small when you're doing 100. During most chases we get a *caravan affect*, meaning that all the units in the area join in and it's a sea of red & blue. 10, 20, 30 greyhounds chasing this rabbit and bearing down on the plaza.

The toll attendants see this too and have learned to duck down in their booth which is surrounded by concrete, for good reason, and not watch the chaos. The bad guy goes through the toll, whoosh! Then police car after police car; whoosh, whoosh, whoosh, whoosh, whoosh, whoosh, times thirty!

The most frightening thing is as you're approaching the toll you're saying to yourself, "That looks really fucking small. Am I going to make it?" or something like that. You line up your car the best you can because right now it's not about the asshole but about you making it through. Remember, you're moving at 100 mph!

As you are entering the toll, you are holding the wheel with a death grip, and you close your eyes, and a big Whoosh! I made it! Fuck! Wow! And back to the chase. Nothing like it! Unfortunately, bad guys have crashed into tolls and it isn't pretty. Fortunately in my time no officer ever did.

Two last things about chases and *"3s."* First, after the movie *Top Gun* came out in 1986, and later in 1988 I earned the call-sign *'Maverick'* (more on that later) by a squad I'd recently joined, and I adopted the movie's iconic theme song *Danger Zone* as my *"3"* and chase song. I played it on my radio every time I was running a *"3"* or in a chase.

My squad mates would tell me later that they could hear it on the radio in the background. Just having fun. Second, the bad guy ran and endangered everyone on the road around them, including the police. How selfish and reckless.

However, at the end of the chase there is a toll to be paid by the bad guy for his ill-advised decision to run. Especially if he fights at the end. I'll let you decide what the cost of that toll was.

Scene 3: "3-15s"

As I outlined earlier, any signal with a *"3"* in front of it means it is an emergency. Our signal for a *Back-Up* is a *"15."* A *"3-15"* means that an officer needs a back-up NOW! This is the worst signal that we can get.

When officers are engaged with a subject like a fight, or at worst a shooting, and that call goes out, your heart stops when you hear it. It is so important our new radio system even has a distinct tone for *"3-15s"* that differs greatly from the normal *"3"-Tone* so that it gets your attention.

When you get the call and your running *Balls-To-The-Wall* to get there, you're wondering what you are going to find and what you are going to do once you find it. You fear the worst is happening, and unfortunately, sometimes it does. Your brother or sister has become seriously wounded or even killed.

Getting there is the only important thing in the world for those few minutes, which can be a lifetime for the engaged officer. Have you ever been in a fight by yourself and wondered when and how it was going to end, would you win, would you lose, just survive? That's what it feels like to the officer in the jackpot you are trying to get there to save.

I have been on both ends of this dynamic. Fortunately, only a couple of times as the one in the fight, and the rest as the one trying to get there.

This is as stressful of a signal you can get. You drop everything you're doing which includes leaving your meal, or even when you are tied up in the bathroom, if you can. Someone's safety and possibly their life may depend on it.

We don't take kindly to someone trying to hurt one of our own, and we will do whatever it takes to get there. If you're the one hurting our teammate, when we arrive there is going to be Hell to pay. That's how serious this is for us. If you don't like what I'm saying then don't put yourself and us in this situation.

A Lesson-Learned Story: Waiting for the Cavalry

As a fairly young officer, about twenty-eight years old in 1989, when working the day shift I was dispatched to a *"22,"* call of a stolen vehicle, taken by the reporter's twenty-two-year-old son. How ironic.

I arrived and was met by the subject's sister, who put her mother on the phone, the vehicle's owner. Mom told me her son keeps taking her car without permission, has a suspended license, and spends his time smoking marijuana with no job and has become impossible to handle.

I advised Mom that if I take a "22" report I will have to enter the stolen information in the system and if or when her son gets stopped by police he will be arrested. She said she understood. I can tell you she was desperate at this point.

As I hung up with her, Junior pulls up in front of the townhouse. I met him outside and asked him for his license since I observed him driving. He said he didn't have one. I informed him his mother now wanted him arrested for taking the car. He said it was a mistake and he would straighten it out with her. He was quite belligerent at this point and started to walk away from me. I told him not to or he would be arrested. He walked away, and I realized I just committed myself.

Mistake? Maybe. When we use words like "or else," we are at a point of no return.

He walked into the living room and grabbed the phone. I was committed so I snatched the phone out of his hand, grabbed him by the arm and told him he was under arrest. I spun him around and placed a handcuff on his left wrist. I grabbed his right arm and tried to bring it behind his back. By this time he realized what was happening and resisted.

He pulled his right hand away from me and oh, oh, it was on! I realized that while standing in the middle of the living room I would not have any leverage to get him cuffed, so I slammed him into the wall. I still couldn't get him cuffed so I had no choice. I turned him around to face me and started throwing punches into his abdomen. Then I gave him multiple elbow-strikes to the face to soften him up. I turned him back toward the wall and tried to cuff him again.

I still couldn't get both hands behind his back. I spun him around again and gave him another barrage of elbow-strikes. I mean I pounded this kid but what could I do. Losing was not an option.

Now there was his blood everywhere! I took him to the floor. By the way, which is where EVERY fight we are in ends up. No exceptions. I was heavier than he was and I had wrestled so I locked him up in a hold that he couldn't escape, grabbed the radio and yelled *"3-15!"* I couldn't get him cuffed, I was alone, we were in a fight, and all I could do was hold on and wait.

Fortunately, his sister didn't jump in as she was on my side and was picking up my pen and name tag as they came off my uniform. Lucky for me.

As I held on for close to six or seven minutes, which seemed like an eternity, the cavalry finally busted through the front door.

My squad arrived and just imagine what they saw. Their squad mate on the floor wrapped up with a subject, blood all over him, me, and the tile floor. It looked like I gutted him and fearing the worst had happened to me. They handcuffed him and put him in my car. Fire Rescue came to treat and clean him up. I cleaned myself up and now it was time to take him to the Dade County Jail's medical ward known at that time as *"Ward-D."*

On the trip down, he's yelling and screaming at me, threatening to sue me and all that bull shit we hear. I ignored him. He continued, and I ignored him. By the time we arrived at Ward-D, he was crying and begging me to talk to him. I delivered him inside to the jail-medical staff. They asked him what he did to get his ass kicked. He was still crying.

My sergeant met me there to begin the *Use of Force Report* he was required to prepare since I basically did kick this kid's ass. I told him what happened and he submitted it. Lesson to be learned here about a mistake many of us make. Don't use words like "Or else" if you can avoid it. And if you crossed that line, make sure you have back-up already there when "Or else" fails. Trust me.

The end of this story comes about six weeks later in court. The young lad is now facing Battery on a Law enforcement Officer, Resisting Arrest w/Violence, Grand Theft Auto, and Driving w/Suspended License, and is in court with his father. The judge goes through the calendar and his case was passed for the break so the prosecutor could speak to him and possibly negotiate a plea.

As the court goes into recess, the father asked to speak to me. Here we go. I'm going to get threatened with a lawsuit, complaint to my department for excessive force, you name it.

Much to my surprise, his father thanked me for doing something he couldn't do himself. His son was out of control and going nowhere. He and his wife didn't know how to reach him and were at their wits end. The beating I threw him, because I had to not because I wanted to, and understand the distinction, woke him up and was the incentive he needed to straighten out his life. He had just enlisted in the US Army and was going to turn his life around.

He actually apologized to me for putting ME through that. Wow! Never expected that. I of course didn't oppose the State deferring the charges and later dropping them upon his successful enlistment. I wonder how he's doing. Lessons learned, for both him and me.

Scene 4; Moving Cones

Now back to the dangers of just driving a police car. Since we spend so much time behind the wheel, it is the most continuously dangerous thing we do. Yes, I said the most dangerous thing a police officer does, or for that matter Joe and Jane citizen, is drive a car. You heard me right. Most might think that driving is a mundane activity and it's no big deal. They would be incorrect.

How many crashes do you see on the streets on a daily basis? Just on your way to or from work? Carnage is daily in urban areas. Now, you drive to work, home, and for your leisure activities. A police officer drives all day and night, in and out of traffic, lights & siren or just fast, navigating around all those people in their cars with the windows up, AC or heater on, radio blasting, on their damned phones and not paying attention.

We refer to you as *Moving Cones*.

When a police officer, firefighter, or anyone first learns to drive, we do it on a cone-course. This teaches you the basic skills. Don't hit the cones, pretty simple. Now there's you driving with all of those distractions I mentioned and you're moving in and out of your lanes suddenly changing direction without warning. Hence, *Moving Cones*.

When we are on a *"3,"* YOU are required to yield to the emergency vehicle. What does that mean? Get the Hell out of the way! I can't say it any stronger. When an emergency vehicle is coming up behind you or toward you, you have a duty to clear the lanes you're in. In Florida, the statute reads:

316.126   Operation of vehicles and actions of pedestrians on approach of authorized emergency vehicle. —

(1)(a)   Upon the immediate approach of an authorized emergency vehicle, while enroute to meet an existing emergency, the driver of every other vehicle shall, when such emergency vehicle is giving audible signals by siren, exhaust whistle, or other adequate device, or visible signals by the use of displayed blue or red lights, yield the right-of-way to the emergency vehicle and shall immediately proceed to a position parallel to, and as close as reasonable to the closest edge of the curb of the roadway, clear of any intersection and shall stop and remain in position until the authorized emergency vehicle has passed, unless otherwise directed by any law enforcement officer.

Right out of the book. So please, listen up, get off the phone and pay attention! Your life and mine may depend on it.

I have found it astonishing how some drivers have no idea what to do, and worse, don't care we are trying to get through, unless of course it is *THEIR* emergency we're going to. And when we add speed to that it makes it extremely dangerous. Our lives are in jeopardy every time we get behind the wheel. More police officers are killed in traffic crashes historically than by assault. Sometimes it is through our own fault, but usually because of someone else's.

Let me lend some perspective on crashes for both here in Florida and nationally. According to the 2016 report from the US Department of Transportation, National Highway Traffic Safety Administration, National Statistics, there were:

7,277,000 total crashes reported. Of those, 5,065,000 were involving property damage only. 2,177,000 resulted in injuries, and 34,439 were fatal crashes. Closer to home, in 2016 the Florida Department of Highway Safety and Motor Vehicles, reported that there was 395,785 crashes in Florida: 165,940 involved injuries, and 2,935 involved fatalities. Of those total crashes, 5,223 were confirmed involving alcohol. Yes, drunken idiots that thought "I can drive, I'm not drunk." And the majority of crashes, 115,352, involved drivers between the ages of 18-24. I wonder why? Could it be the damned mobile phone? Mmmm. Maybe.

Still closer to home for my colleagues in Miami-Dade County from all agencies, there were 8,223 crashes here, twice that of the next closest county in Florida. Can you say Bad Drivers?

So folks, pay attention, get off the phone, look and listen for emergency vehicles coming up behind you. Get out of the way so we can get to the people who need us, and everyone goes home. All of our lives may depend on it. But like I said, *The Ultimate Driving Machine!* I'm going to miss it.

War Story

Of the many chases I've been involved in, I want to tell you about the stolen Green & White we chased in 1988. Yes, one of our own police cars. I was an FTO on "Mids" with my rookie Jorge Carreno, who is now a Homicide Lieutenant. Way to go! I was driving. My partner, Officer Dave *Jester* Farris was with his rookie.

It was a quiet night with not much happening. One of the other midnight officers Jorge, was on a *"19"* (traffic stop) on NW 12 Street at about 84 Ave. He arrested the driver for a firearm violation (everyone has a gun) and had him cuffed in the back of his cruiser. Jorge was at the driver's car filling out paperwork.

Unbeknownst to Jorge, the subject was flexible and able to slide his hands from behind his back, down his legs and get them in front. Also unbeknownst to any of us, the police car that Jorge signed out that night did not have the rear door handles disabled as all police cars do so a prisoner cannot open the rear doors.

He did and jumped into the driver's seat of Jorge's car and he's off! Imagine Jorge's surprise as his G&W is driving past him. *"Awe Shit!"*

Jorge got on the radio and called it in. Units responded to locate the Green & White *"22"* (stolen vehicle). David got there first and pursued the suspect southbound on NW 87 Ave. We were northbound on 87 Ave approaching West Flagler Street.

There he is, right ahead of us! He saw us and turned west on Flagler. We came in right behind him and the chase was on! We continued west and then he turned south on SW 92 Ave. I did my driving instructor shit and went wide so I can cut the apex of the turn and get in close. It was night, and I didn't see the gravel on the ground. Our front tires hit the gravel and we slid right into the curb. Bang! What the fuck was that? Tire didn't blow, we're good. Keep going.

Southbound approaching SW 8 Street. The famous *Calle Ocho* you may know from our huge annual Cuban street party every March. It's a large and busy street and he wasn't slowing down. He went through the light at about 80 mph. Noooo! Damned! He made it! That was close. We of course ran into traffic and had to slow. Now he's got a big lead on us.

West on SW 16 Street approaching 107 Ave. Trying to catch up. Oh, did I mention he had the fastest G&W in our station? He did. Now I'm pushing hard to catch up but he was way ahead. Still in sight but ahead.

As we are flying north on 107 Ave, two Florida Highway Patrol Troopers in Mustangs, yes, they had Ford Mustangs then and were known as the *Stang Gang* and boy we're they fast! These two troopers joined in and blew by Jorge and I like a couple of fighter jets buzzing a jetliner.

We did our best to stay with them but it was now their chase. This went on for about twenty more minutes until a *bailout* at Sunset Drive (72 Street) and 137 Ave. The bad guy ran into a wooded area, still handcuffed, but man could he drive!

One of the troopers drew down on him but didn't shoot. The subject had his own gun in the front seat that Jorge had taken off him earlier but didn't do anything with it. Luckily. He got away that night but since we already knew who he was, he got picked up at home the next day. Idiot! That's why it's called *The Long Arm of the Law*.

While we sat on the perimeter trying to find this guy with the helicopter and K-9 units, I remembered the tire. Yup, we/I bent the wheel when we hit the curb at 92 Ave. Shit! Vehicle damage. Have to call our sergeant. But before we did, I had my rookie Jorge write a Florida Crash Report because we would have to anyway when Sarge arrived.

I raised our sergeant Jim Slack, known as *Pappy* to us, and we were the *Black Sheep*, and said, "Sarge, can you meet us on our perimeter point?" We never say we wrecked the car on the main frequency. That surprise is for in person. Though it was minor, Pappy still had to write his administrative crash report which I can tell you as a sergeant now for twenty-two years, we don't like to do. I didn't get gigged for it since it happened in a chase and it was only a rim. But man was it fun! Like I said, I'll miss *The Ultimate Driving Machine.*

Act - 5

Use of Force: Kicking Ass! When We

Have To

Scene 1: The Law is the Law

Much has been made about the use of force by police, especially in the smart phone, You Tube, social media era. Every time police are involved in a physical confrontation it seems, the altercation ends up on some media outlet, and it always, always looks ugly. Fights are ALWAYS ugly, that's just the nature of the beast. What do you think happens when someone doesn't want to go to jail, has hurt or is hurting someone, suffers from mental illness and doesn't want to go to a mental health receiving facility, is drunk or on drugs, or decides he just doesn't like the police and wants to dance? A physical altercation *IS* going to take place and we are going to have to engage.

You see, when we have to make an arrest, the arrestee is not permitted by law to resist and must comply with our orders and submit to that arrest. When they do, the overwhelming majority of the time, he or she gets taken into custody, delivered to the jail, and nothing happens and you never hear about it.

There are hundreds of thousands police/citizen encounters daily where nothing happens and all parties walk away, or are taken to jail, and not a finger was raised in anger. What about those times where the subject doesn't comply with our orders and resists? The law is very clear on this and states that we, the police, have the authority to "use the force necessary to effect the arrest."

What does that mean exactly? It means that the subject is going to jail for the alleged crime committed, no matter how serious or minor it may be, and if they resist, we can use force ranging from simple grabbing and handcuffing to deadly force to take them into custody.

Once the decision is made to arrest and the person resists and that level of resistance rises to the level of lethality against the officer, the officer can use force that can result in great bodily harm or the death of that subject.

How can this be you might say?

We are a country of laws and we are all subject to follow those laws, and when we don't, the police are charged and sanctioned by law to arrest those who violate the law and deliver them to justice. They don't always want to go and the law does not allow for "well, he doesn't want to go so we'll just leave him alone. It's ok, and we leave." Not a chance! It doesn't work that way in law-abiding countries and force may be necessary to arrest those who won't follow them.

Scene 2: No One Likes Watching the Sausage Get Made

Watching the use of physical force is never pretty. Someone or more than someone is going to get hurt. No matter how much we try to hold back depending on the level of resistance and the size and physical strength of the person, they are more than likely going to suffer some kind of injury.

Understand we really don't want to get engaged in a fight or hurt anyone, unless of course they are trying to hurt us. That simply is not permitted by law or by us. I am not religious but I like to say there are two commandments: *Thou shall not lie to the police*, and *Thou shall not touch the police*. If you don't do either of these two things, maybe you don't go to jail, and you won't get hurt. It's that simple.

When those confrontations occur and they are captured by the news, bystanders with phones, or even on police body cams—which are a new phenomenon I will cover more in depth later on—everyone first looks at the altercation and takes a big gasp! "Oh my, look at the police beating up on that poor man!"

Yes, it looks terrible. What you don't see most of the time until police body cams, is what took place to get to that point because the news and private individuals will edit the video so you only see what *they want* you to see to make us look bad. Can you believe some people want to do that? Of course they do. It's sexy and controversial and sells the news, garners sympathy and followers for whatever the social-justice agenda flavor is that month.

So when we have to go hands on with a person, albeit a bad guy or someone with mental illness, the results are the same. The fight ensues and we have to use a variety of force to attain our objective of taking them into custody. We will grab, restrain, twist limbs and joints, use strikes to the body and head with hands, fists, feet, and batons or maybe even a handheld radio or flashlight because it's a weapon of opportunity already in hand.

We will also use what the public calls a *"Chokehold,"* which really isn't. A chokehold means that you are cutting off the air supply to the person by squeezing the front of the throat which we are not doing. We are squeezing the carotid arteries on the sides of the neck which decreases the flow of blood to the brain and when done effectively renders the person temporarily unconscious.

The name of this technique is called the *Applied Carotid Triangular Restraint* or *ACTR* for short. The more accurate description of this would be what we have seen in professional wrestling shows known as a *Sleeper Hold*, because it puts you out like you were falling asleep.

Fear not, we revive you immediately *AFTER* we handcuffed you while you were out by giving you a few back-blows like we were burping a baby, only harder.

Most of the time we don't even have to do that as the person comes back around quickly once we let go of the sides of your neck and normal blood flow is restored.

Does it look bad? You bet. But there are no lasting effects and we call Fire Rescue to get you checked out and take you to the hospital for observation. So relax, we are not killing anyone that way, at least not on purpose. Can a slip and a crushed windpipe occur? Sure it can. But remember it was the subject who decided to fight with the officers, not the other way around. Oh well, *Shit Happens*. Remember again, that failure is not an option for us.

Scene 3: Riding the Lightning

We may also employ the use of the Taser. It is officially called an *Electronic Control Weapon* or *ECW*, that when used effectively, sends electrical impulses through your neuro-muscular system, locking you up like you had one massive cramp that renders you incapable of moving and hurts like you can't fucking believe.

Each *cycle* as it's called lasts for five seconds. One trigger pull, one five second burst, then it's over. No lasting physical effects. None! The more you resist the more cycles we hit you with until you stop being an asshole and submit to the arrest. Don't resist and you won't get zapped! It utilizes 50,000 volts of electricity to deliver the shock through the darts and wires.

That is a bit misleading because that voltage is the power necessary to push the current and will not kill you. Amperage is lethal and the amps in an ECW are so low that they won't kill you. I said no lasting physical effects, but the psychological effect works.

Most people who have been Tased, including cops going through training, will tell you they don't want to go through that again. When I was trained and certified to carry a Taser, we were required to *Ride the Lightning* as we nicknamed it, and it is just that. Did I say it hurts?

We had to feel it so we can articulate, should the need arise in court or through our attorney, what the *Taser* does to you and how it incapacitates you if a bad guy gets your ECW away from you or has one of his own.

Why? If he hits us with it we may be incapable of defending ourselves and they might kill us. So heed the warning; if you are a bad guy who tries this we are going to shoot your ass! We won't wait to see what happens. Don't like that? Don't bring an ECW to a gunfight!

And while we are talking about Tasers, all of you who watch TV and movies and say why didn't the police *TASE* him when he was holding a knife? I go back to the accuracy of shooting under stress in my chapter on training.

The Taser isn't guaranteed to work either.

The two darts that it deploys have to penetrate the body in an adequate spread pattern from each other to complete the electrical circuit in order to properly incapacitate the subject. This is difficult to do under stress once again, and it is not an exact science. It is a battery-operated electrical device and doesn't always work. While deploying it, another officer stands by with a gun drawn just in case something goes wrong and the subject is still able to use deadly force against us. Taser International, now called Axon, developed a great tool for law enforcement, but nothing works 100 percent of the time, so we use back-up. Did you know that Taser name comes from an 1800s patent called the *Thomas A. Smith Electric Rifle?* Bet you didn't know that. Good job Guys at Axon!

Now on the use of the Taser by Hollywood in TV and movies, once again doesn't accurately portray its use. Directors either take too much dramatic license or they have terrible technical advisers. I think the former. Retired cops and military know better.

They depict bad guys hitting someone with an ECW, knocking them out and dragging them off somewhere like in a kidnapping. BULLSHIT! It doesn't knock you out, only temporarily incapacitates you. Lastly, the Taser killed no one. No matter what you heard reported by the news, the police use of the Taser where someone died was because of an underlying medical condition. It doesn't stop your heart or fry your brain.

There are many, many conflicting medical opinions on this where some doctor claimed the person died by the use of the ECW. Taser International has to defend themselves continuously against lawsuits and sometimes settle because that's the way our civil courts system works and it's just cheaper to do so.

Taser doesn't need me to defend them but if its use was sooo lethal as reported, why are most police agencies still using them? Mmmm. The person that died was usually suffering from what's known as *excited delirium*, formally known as cocaine psychosis, which is directly related to drug use, or another underlying drug or medical condition.

We didn't kill them. They killed themselves. We just intervened at some point. We are also trained to hit someone with the ECW as quickly as possible who is combative due to excited delirium because the sooner we can get them under control and get Fire Rescue to treat them, the better chance they have of surviving the psychosis. It's the drugs that fries your brain and stops your heart. Not the ECW and not us.

A 108 Degrees Story

In February 1989, I was working the midnight shift in our Midwest District. I was an FTO but didn't have a rookie that month. It was one of our cooler nights and it was in the '50s. Not cold for the rest of the country but cold for us and I remember I was wearing my jacket.

I received a call to assist a City of Miami officer and a Florida Highway Patrol trooper at the on/off ramp of NW 57 Ave to the SR 836/Dolphin Expressway. I rolled up on the scene and the two officers had a young man, 21, lying on the median of the ramp.

They told me that they found him wandering up and down the ramp and that he appeared to be on some kind of drug. All of a sudden, he sat up, got to his feet, and started running up the ramp. I gave chase, grabbed him and took him down in the grass. I cuffed him and ordered Fire Rescue. I noticed that he was sweating profusely. Remember it was a cold night in the '50s. I was standing over him waiting for Rescue and was joined by some squad mates.

Marcos *"Slider"* Velazquez was with me, and when I looked down at the kid, I asked Slider to look at him as well. I saw he had that dead fish-eye look. Slider said the same thing. Rescue pulled up and I uncuffed the kid. They put an EKG pad on him and I remember the paramedic saying, "He's gone!" Fuck!

So now I have this kid that died with my handcuffs on, SR. # 698322. Still have them. And now the death investigation begins. Homicide, Internal Affairs, statements, questions, and all that comes with it. It was my first *In-Custody* death, and the feeling wasn't pleasant.

I had one of our squad mates, Rosy, who was working the front desk that night, call the PBA, our union, so they could have an attorney respond to represent me during the investigation. Yes, we get to have legal representation just like everyone else.

My partner *"Jester"* responded with his rookie to handle the call. As I was walking toward him and he was walking up the ramp to the *"45,"* he asked me what happened. I said, "You're handling it." He asked again "What happened?" And again I said, "you're handling it." He asked, "is he dead?" And again I said, "You're handling it!" He and I still laugh about it to this day *(CH)*.

My PBA attorney arrived and he told me that I would have to give a statement to Homicide, and monitored by Internal Affairs later that night, but not to worry because it appeared that the kid's death was caused by drugs and this happens quite often. I was still worried because I hadn't experienced this before and I thought I may have done something wrong. I did not.

The kid was from Miami Beach, well off, and partied a little too hard that night. He suffered from Cocaine-Psychosis. Three hours after he died his body temperature was still 108 degrees according to the Medical Examiner, and this happened all the time as cocaine was *everywhere* during the '80s. Having a party? Serving booze and coke. Anywhere you went it was on the menu.

He fried his brain basically, and his death had nothing to do with me and no one was going to save him at the point when police found him. Very sad for his family no doubt. He was wearing a blue jacket and jeans. However, for the *CH* side of it as we always did and for months afterward, every time I handcuffed a subject, Jester, Slider and the other guys I worked with told the *"39"* that the last guy that wore those cuffs died.

Thank guys. Appreciate that. Dicks!

Scene 4: The Night Stick

The other weapon we use is the police baton. Yes, the *Night Stick* as it used to be called. This weapon has probably been depicted on video, either real or in drama, more than any other tool we have other than all those shooting scenes. It was made famous in the movie *The Blue Knight* by the late, great actor George Kennedy when he walked a beat and quite effortlessly twirled it in his hand.

This sent the message that if you get stupid with me you're going to get kissed by my friend here. The baton has come in different forms, shapes and sizes over the decades, and is utilized in both road patrol and crowd control situations.

It is categorized as an intermediate weapon that can cause death but it's not usually used in this manner. When a subject fights the police, the baton is used to strike at the hands, arms, torso and legs in order to subdue the assailant, and to be clear here the person *is assaulting us* and we are defending ourselves and trying to take them into custody. Will it cause injuries? Of course it will, but that is the price you pay for fighting us.

If the subject were to escalate to deadly force by producing a gun or knife or manages to grab an officer's gun, the baton in hand would now be authorized to be used as deadly force, and in that split second decision that officer has to make, either strike with the baton or drop it and go to gun. He may have to use the baton and crack the fuck over the head to prevent him from killing the officer. All bets are off when a bad guy does that. Don't like it? Too bad. Don't try to hurt us.

The most infamous use of the baton caught on camera has to be the Rodney King incident on March 3, 1991, where LAPD officers were filmed striking King multiple times, fifty-six as I recall, in what became one of the most notorious police-involved incidents in recent history.

What you didn't see at the beginning of the incident was when NBC broadcast the video on TV for the first time, was how King beat the female trooper on the hood of her own patrol vehicle which led to the chase and ultimately the *"beating"* as it's known.

The officers chased him down, corralled him, and continuously struck him with their issued side-handled batons, known as PR-24s. Was it ugly? You bet it was. But was it legal? The officers were acquitted in state court because they followed procedure and state law. He was resisting and not complying, to a point, and they continued to strike him.

Would my colleagues and I have continued to strike him like that? I have to say no. What we would have done like we always do is gang-tackle the subject. If the subject doesn't pull a weapon, we are coming after you like you were carrying the football.

It's how almost all officers in the South Florida area handle this. We will overwhelm you with such a show of force and mass of bodies that there is no way you are going to defeat us.

In the process, because you decided you wanted a shot at the title and thought getting a cop-trophy was cool, we are going to kick your ass and you are going to the hospital! Could the King incident have happened here? Sure, but we've learned from our own history; December 17, 1979, when officers in our department which was then known as the Dade County Public Safety Department, were involved in a chase and ended up killing Arthur Mc Duffie in a beating using 5-cell Kel-Lights instead of batons.

Due to what was a very controversial trial and acquittal, which led to the infamous 1980 Miami Riots, the department got rid of those very long flashlights and changed the way we take down subjects. If you don't have a weapon in your hand or on your person, we are taking you down! Again, don't like it? Don't fight us. You will lose!

War Story

In 1990 during the afternoon shift in Midwest, my partner Frank Moreno and I were on patrol when we received a *"2-32"* call, a fight in the middle of the street involving two guys. We ran a *"2"* (lights & siren) and arrived right after another two-man unit arrived and had the warring factions separated.

We discovered the eighteen-year-old male was smacking his girlfriend as they were driving. Behind them was a US Marine who was on leave with his wife and witnessed this. True to form, the Marine pulled up next to them and told the eighteen-year-old to knock it off. Well, the young lad didn't like that and colorful metaphors were exchanged and the two stopped in the middle of the street and began to dance.

We had the lad straddled on the hood of one of the police cars, and after we learned the circumstances surrounding the incident, Frank gave me the hand signal the young man was "going," meaning we were going to arrest him for battery on his girlfriend and the Marine. When we informed him he was under arrest and grabbed his wrists in order to handcuff him, he stiffened up and the *Last Tango in Paris* was on!

A fight ensued and as I've said, we went to ground. We were down and I grabbed his head from the front and pulled him down onto his knees. Frank and the other officers were behind and on the subject's side. This kid was as strong as a bull and just as pissed off.

What we learned later from his girlfriend was that he was on steroids and now suffering from *"Roid Rage."* Great! This was not going to go quickly, and he was not going to enjoy it. I had my Stream Light aluminum flashlight in my hand, remember, weapon of opportunity, and I began to strike him in the chest while telling him to knock it the fuck off! He didn't listen. *"Stupid is as Stupid does."*

Frank had to kick him and after a couple of shots kicked me in the head. "Hey, you kicked me!" "Sorry." And the fight continued. More shots with the flashlight and another kick to my head. "Dammit, Frank!"

In almost every fight that we're in, we end up hitting each other. It can't be avoided. Too many hands and feet flying. The ultimate goal and only goal is to win. Period! Some lumps are part of the deal.

High-5s all around because of our successful *Eight Second Ride* of this bull *(CH)*, and we finally got this kid into custody, with hands cuffed and legs restrained so he couldn't kick us or kick out our car's windows. That happens all the time as well.

We transported him to Jackson Memorial Hospital's "Ward-D." When we arrived we had two corrections officers and a nurse meet us outside with the requested wheelchair as we had tied his legs and he couldn't walk. We sat him in the chair and you could see twelve, round, red welts on his chest and abdomen where I was reaching out and touching him with the back of my flashlight.

Yes, it took that many along with assorted other shots to subdue this kid but never a head shot which was not our intent. Have you ever been in a fight with someone who was on steroids and was three times stronger than he should have been and stronger than you? Don't. It's hazardous to your health!

As the young lad sat in the wheelchair broken, bleeding and sobbing, the nurse asked him "What were you doing this evening young man?" Young squire answered and I quote, "I was being an asshole!" Lesson learned. We win, you lose, and don't fight the police!

This was just one of many fights I have been involved it. And know this; in each and every physical altercation police are in, there is always at least one gun involved; ours. That means the subject has a gun available to them should they try to go for it, and sometimes they do and officers die by their own weapon. Fighting an officer is considered deadly force against him or her, and we will respond accordingly.

So to be clear, you are not allowed to fight the police. We decide based on facts on the scene if you are under arrest for an alleged crime you may have committed, or we are taking you into protective custody because you have a mental illness or you got yourself screwed up on drugs and/or alcohol. You have to comply with our orders and are not allowed to resist. That's the law and the law is clear. We can use the force necessary to take you into custody. You'll have your day in court if it

Sgt. (Ret.) Bert "Maverick" Gonzalez

makes it that far, guaranteed. Come peaceably or kicking & screaming. Your choice, but you are coming.

Act ~ 6

"34s": The Domestic

Scene 1: What is a Domestic?

There is no more complicated call police officers respond to than the *domestic dispute*. Not a single day goes by that police in *Any Big-Town USA* aren't handling thousands of domestics. The *"34"* signal we use means a "dispute" of any kind, but we normally refer to the domestic when we use this signal because it is so common.

The domestic dispute occurs at all hours of the day or night, weekdays and weekends, holidays, essentially at any time. They are more prevalent in the evening and on weekends when more people are off from work around one another, and getting on each other's nerves.

Most marital issues surround financial concerns. Tell me if you have never had an argument with your significant other about money? You would be lying if you said no. This issue brings out the worst in people, especially when it's at home with nowhere to go and you have nothing else to do but argue about it. Even the wealthy argue about this, albeit less frequently and for different reasons, but money is—more often than not— the root of all evil.

Another common reason couples get into a loud or violent dispute is infidelity. Someone got caught screwing around and now there's hell to pay. It is easy to understand why this leads to a fight because a trust has been broken and deep feelings have been hurt. The injured party wants to know why this was done to them and sometimes wants to exact revenge.

This also leads to physical altercations which can get completely out of control. People get hurt and someone or more than someone ends up going to jail. A huge reason why people get into arguments and then it turns ugly is alcohol. Yes, when some people are sitting around and they start drinking, and drinking, drink some more, and still more, the fuse gets lit.

Anything will set them off and these are some of the most violent calls we respond to. I once saw a t-shirt in Key West that said, *"Instant Asshole; Just Add Alcohol!"* There isn't a truer statement.

I can't say how many domestic disputes I've responded to, but it's in the high hundreds to a thousand range. Over the course of a career that may not sound like a lot compared to the thousands of other calls an officer may respond to but consider that number multiplied by thousands of officers. There are a lot of "*34s*!" Too many!

Someone or some family is always fighting about something. The TV is too loud, the garbage wasn't taken out, your brother is an asshole, your mother should mind her own business, your sister is a bitch, and it goes on and on.

Here's one most couples might identify with; "You watch too many sports!" Especially football.

The "*Football Widow*" was born a long time ago, and this happens all the time during the season. I watched too much football when I was younger and got into the occasional argument with my then wives.

But I changed. I've watched a lot less football for two reasons; I boycotted the 2017 season because of the idiot, selfish, millionaire players who chose to kneel down and protest me (police), more on that later, and sadly my Miami Dolphins just plain suck now.

My wife Rosy does watch the games with me but what's the point? I get disappointed and pissed off. We saved a lot of time during the 2017 & 2018 seasons and got more things done on Sundays. But you can see why, albeit stupidly, how this can lead to arguments and many times the police get called to intervene and throw the flag!

Scene 2: 'Tis the Season

The Holidays. Ah yes. Cheer and good tidings, joy and peace to all. Everyone is gathering around the fireplace, Christmas tree, the patio, Domino table, la *Caja China*, and the family table enjoying the season and looking forward to the New Year.

These are the holidays we all wish we had. I'm not being sarcastic. This truly is what we all were brought up to hope and expect. But the truth is in the modern era the holidays, Christmas, is a highly commercialized retail season with the expectations of buying gifts for our loved ones. This aside from the family gatherings, causes the most amount of stress for the average family.

Parents have to figure out what to get their kids, Santa believing age or not, and gifts for each other. What does this boil down to? Money. Of course. Gifts require money, and many times there just isn't enough to get the job done. What does this lead to on Christmas Eve or Day? Arguments and fights. I have worked many a Christmas Day, and we dreaded going to a *"34"* on this day of all days because it is not going to be pretty.

Someone didn't get what they wanted; petty but true. Too much money was spent; always. The family couldn't buy gifts for the little ones or get a tree, many times. The expectations are so high for this day that the reality is a disappointment; usually.

These things lead to fights and we have to go and try to calm everyone down and convince them "it isn't that bad." It is because it is *their* reality and no matter what we say it is not going to change things in the short time we are there. We are only trying to keep the peace and keep people from hurting or literally killing each other. Add alcohol once again and you have a recipe for disaster. Unfortunately, sometimes that does happen.

More times than not, it's violent and loud and we have to make an arrest on Christmas. Trust me when I tell you that is the last thing we want to do. No matter what the age of the kids, when mom or dad goes to jail it is one of the worst things that can happen to a family.

You hit your spouse or significant other, you leave us no choice. You're going to jail. Christmas or not. Instead of a nice holiday meal, its bologna sandwiches at the *Graybar Hotel* with the rest of the drunks, degenerates, robbers, burglars, and assorted other *"39s."* Merry Fuck'n Christmas!

Scene 3: You've Lost That Loving Feeling

Another huge reason we get called is custody and visitation issues involving divorced or unmarried parents, Baby-Mamas and Baby Daddies *(CH)*. Don't hate the player, hate the game. If you have never been divorced or had children with someone else in this respect, you're lucky. Even though you were in love at one time, we sometimes lose that loving feeling and the divorce eventually happens.

If both of you can go your own way, great. But if you have kids, not so much. There is no stronger instinct than protecting your children, and *EVERYTHING* centers around them in a divorce.

As a parent, you should want to have custody of your kids. The mother though, is usually the *primary residential parent* meaning, the kids live with her the majority of the time. Florida is a *joint-custody* state; therefore the parents share custody and have an equal say in the raising of the children.

The kids live with mom but she has to ask dad about school, church, sports activities, etc. When junior or missy goes to the doctor or ER, mom has to let dad know so he can consent to treatment and/or meet them there. That's the way it's supposed to work. No one parent has sole-custody of the children unless a court order states that, and even then it is a rare situation where either parent, let alone the father gets sole-custody.

I am one of those fathers. Without getting into the *why* because it was very personal and difficult and was a very contentious first divorce for me because of the situation. Yes, first and after much effort by my attorney, the court granted me sole-custody of my daughter with no visitation allowed by her mother. Long story and like I said, very personal so I will leave it at that.

This is however the exception and not the rule. The courts are automatically biased for the mother and the father is the one who gets the visitation and pays, most of the time, outrageous amounts of child support.

So most divorces are contentious and get very nasty, my first like most was no exception. Feelings are hurt, money, property, and the marital home are involved, and hatred and revenge rule the day. Oh you bet revenge is in there. Especially when one spouse found that loving feeling elsewhere.

All that the scorned spouse, usually the wife, thinks about is how to get back at that "son-of-a-bitch!" Did I strike a nerve? Tell me I'm wrong. It's human nature to feel that way. Feelings get hurt and the person wants to lash out.

So during the separation and after the divorce there is the temporary, primary residential issue, visitation and child support until decreed by a judge. Most visits are set up for every other weekend and once during the week depending on the couple's circumstances.

This is where we come in.

The father goes to pick up the kids for his scheduled time with them and the wife doesn't let him have the kids. Call the police. The father shows up unannounced to get the kids. Call the police. The father doesn't return the kids on time at the end of his visitation. Call the police. Child support wasn't paid on time. Call the police. Get the picture? Call the police. We get called for each and every dispute or violation of a custodial or visitation order all the time.

So what do we do? Nothing! We can't. It's a civil matter between the parents, and a divorce decree is a *civil* order not a criminal one, and we have no jurisdiction over the situation. The court order has to state, which is rare, the police have the authority to take custody of the children and deliver them to the parent with the current rights. Otherwise, all we can do is refer the parents back to the courts or their attorneys to seek a remedy to the violation of the divorce agreement.

We make sure the situation is calmed before we leave and we write a useless report about the dispute. Yes, useless. We cover our and the department's collective asses, by documenting what happened in case one spouse goes back and kills the other.

Everyone seems to think, including and especially the attorneys, call and get a police report; that will fix things. Society seems to believe a police report cures everything. It doesn't, but they call, so we go and write a report only to document the incident. No action is usually taken; we pick up the flags and replay the down. That's it in a nutshell. Civil matter.

But sometimes the relationship is so deteriorated and volatile, the parents can't even go to each other's homes without getting into it, and the court orders the child-exchange on visitation days and times take place where? At the police station. Yes, the parking lot of many a station house has been the drop-off/pickup site in our presence (read referee) so the parents won't go at it, we hope. Doesn't always work, but it helps.

Scene 4: By the Power Vested in Me...

Domestics are highly volatile situations and people get hurt and sometimes killed. We the police have to become psychologists, counselors, and magicians in order to diffuse many of these disputes. So we have to have the gift-of-gab (*Tony Lip*-bull shit) and a golden tongue (sometimes lie) to calm the parties down. Whatever it takes.

This sometimes makes us come up with shall we say *creative* ways in order to accomplish this. We sometimes try the power of suggestion to get one of the parties to leave the home for a while, usually the man, so things can settle.

Contrary to popular belief, without a court order we can't *make* anyone leave their home. We don't have that authority and we aren't a third world or totalitarian country. Imagine if you were made to leave your house with no real place to go. The suggestion to leave is simply to avoid continued hostilities and the possibility of someone getting hurt and an arrest being made. Most of the time one of them will leave for a while. A temporary solution at best.

We will offer some counseling and a few words of advice and hope that someone listens. Most people are so upset that very little of what we say sticks. We hand out brochures for some resources but this is more of a CYA for departments to be able to say that the people were provided with *something* that they can access. Works once in a while.

But one of the things I did occasionally back in my early years, and this only works with folks that aren't very educated or sophisticated. Now don't start Tweeting and holding protests against me, this is the way it was, and we were just trying to diffuse a very volatile situation.

I would conduct a *Badge Divorce*. Yes, that's what I said. I used this technique when the couple absolutely insisted they wanted a divorce *Right Now* and there was no way they were going to stay together. I would tell the dueling couple I would give them a temporary *Badge Divorce* that would only last for thirty days. They would have to file papers for the permanent one.

What is it? I would tell them to each place one hand on my badge, and I would say; "By the power vested in me by the State of Florida, Dade County, and the Metro-Dade Police Department, I now pronounce you temporarily divorced."

Yes, I was taking advantage of some people, but I kept them from taking to killing each other again, and at least for the time being the situation was diffused. It worked and off to the next one. That is what was sometimes needed to do to get the job done.

Scene 5: Cuban Divorce

So it is no secret the Miami populous is predominantly Cuban, and as such this is the dominant culture that has the strongest roots and the most influence and personality here. With all the good things the Cuban culture brings as with any dominant peoples, there are some bad things it brings as well.

In the early 80s we had both Cuban and Columbian drug dealers (Scarface). Currently, we have a great deal of fraud (more recent arrivals). But as it relates to matrimonial bliss, we have the *Cuban Divorce*. In other cultures it may be called something else but here that's what we call it.

Separation, divorce, and other family tragedies are rough on anyone and it can cause anxiety, depression, stress of course, and desperate acts resulting in further tragedy. During the same 80s period in the Cuban culture, Cuban men, instead of getting a divorce through the courts would be so distraught they would literally hunt down their wives wherever they were and shoot them where they stood. I am not exaggerating when I say this. It became so prevalent that the term was coined.

The most infamous incident that encapsulates this phenomenon is an on-air shooting captured by a *Telemundo* TV program called *Ocurrio Asi* (It Happened That Way).

A reporter was at the grave site of a teenage girl with a mother who had lost her daughter to suicide and was conducting an interview. The father and husband blamed the mother for their daughter's death and arrived at the cemetery. While they were taping, the husband walked up to his wife and shot her in the head. The husband was so out of his mind with grief and rage he lost all control.

Aside from the tragedy that took place, the reporter screamed at her cameraman to make sure he kept filming. Disgusting. Shame on you. But this was the way these disputes sometimes escalated and to this date occasionally continues to happen.

One absolutely terrible incident related to this phenomenon was one I was involved with in the early 90s when I worked the Midwest District.

It was a dayshift, and we had received a BOLO on a vehicle driven by a father who abducted his very young son and was on the run. We found them. On NW 117 Ave just north of 25th Street, the car was found completely burned, just a shell left, with the father in the front seat, and the child curled up behind the passenger seat as if he was hiding from the fire.

If this makes you cringe, it should. It did me and my squad mates and does to this day. Not only was it absolutely unthinkable, but extremely selfish by the father. How can someone do this to their own child? They can and it happens all the time. No wonder we drink!

A Domestic War Story

In the fall of 1984, I was working on the Crime Suppression Team (CST) in our Southwest District. We were in uniform at that time before transitioning to plain clothes and taking back-up signals with the uniform platoon.

It was afternoon shift and early evening when the call of a *"2-34"* *Domestic* went out. About six of us responded to find an asshole-drunk of a husband beating his wife. We were at the kitchen sliding glass door, which was locked with him on the inside, grabbing his wife's hair with his left hand, and I shit you not, a beer in his right. She was crying and screaming.

We were yelling at him to open the door, and he was yelling back at us; "Fuck you! Fuck you! You can't come in. Fuck you!" All the while tossing his wife around and never letting go of her hair. It was intense, and we were seething.

As you can imagine, we were desperate to get into the house, but we were afraid to break the sliding glass door. Ever see one when it shatters? Razor blades everywhere.

This went on for about two minutes and much to the credit of the wife while being held by her hair, she reached under her husband and unlocked the door. We flung that door open and Surprise motherfucker! We piled on that prick like the player carrying the ball in a rugby match and we all went to the floor. Bam!

Unfortunately, the wife went with us. He never let go. So now we're trying to make him let go of his wife's hair and he won't. We are pounding this guy and I mean throwing him a beating. Nothing. He was so plastered that no matter what we did he wouldn't let go.

We had him on his belly, face down with the scrum on top of him. All of a sudden, the only female officer with us Billie O'Brien, good police and not afraid to do anything, reaches in, grabs and squeezes him by the balls! If you could have heard the scream he let out.

The hand opened up, the wife freed, and Mr. Drunk Asshole was cuffed and finally went to jail via Jackson Memorial Hospital's Ward-D. Billie did what no male officer would do. It hurts just thinking about it. We are too macho and respectful of the *Jewels* to do that. But Billie did and it worked. Good for her, bad for the husband. Case closed!

Scene 6: A or B? The OJ Effect

By now in America, everyone knows who OJ Simpson is and what he was accused of and tried for. If you don't, you've been living in a cave somewhere. Before I give you my opinion on his trial, I will tell you that as a football fan, like most everyone else in America, I was a big OJ fan, both in football and the movies, and enjoyed watching him play. He could run like few before or since.

As a matter of fact, I was watching the Bills game against the Jets when he broke the 2000-yard mark. Phenomenal!

Fast forward to the *Incident*. Given all the evidence, the DNA, the *Chase*, and what most of us in law enforcement call his *Suicide Note*, he killed Nicole and Ron. No question in my mind. What he did have was an absolutely brilliant attorney in Johnnie Cochran, an inept judge who had no control of the trial (hope he enjoyed all the hourglasses), a district attorney's office that can't seem to convict a ham sandwich when it comes to celebrities, and a jury that would not convict OJ in a million years. The racial divide caused by the trial aside; his case had a lasting effect. It changed the way the police handle domestic cases. Hence, what I call *The OJ Effect*.

Before this case and throughout the previous decades, domestic cases where police were called, including calls where one spouse was battered or assaulted with minor injuries, were handled as a *private matter*. We didn't usually get deeply involved nor make an arrest, especially when the victim spouse (usually the wife) didn't want us to. Boy how things have change! And for the better. As society evolved, the law evolved with it and so did we. Slowly, but we did.

Now we have specific laws defining *domestic battery* and arrests are frequently made and detective bureaus specializing in domestic crimes have been created. But how did we evolve?

In the wake of the OJ Circus, the Metro-Dade Police Department began a field-study on domestic battery calls where we encountered minor injuries on one of the parties, again usually the wife. If there were serious injuries or a weapon was used it was a felony and an arrest was made and the call didn't qualify for the study.

The study focused on escalation and recidivism. If nothing was done and no arrest made, then how often did the battery reoccur? If action was taken, an arrest made, then how less frequently did it happen again or with less severity? What the OJ Case did expose was the increasing frequency of the incidents and escalating severity of the assault. It is said in homicide investigations where a married or otherwise attached person is killed, first look at the spouse, not the butler!

A or B - A Spin of the Roulette Wheel

The parameters required us to inform our dispatcher we had an eligible case for the study, a conclusive, misdemeanor battery with minor injuries where we were certain one spouse or the other committed it. The dispatcher would then hit a button on her or his console, and the computer (roulette wheel) - "come on Red"-just kidding (*CH),* would spit out an *A* or *B.* An **"A"** would signify an arrest is to be made. A **"B"** would mean not to make the arrest. So we would follow the computer's prompts and make or not make the arrest. Cops being cops, we would of course say out loud, "Ooh, an **"A,"** not your lucky day pal" or something like that (*CH).*

After six months of this, the numbers were compiled by the academics administering the study, and they revealed the more arrests we made, the more incidents of domestic battery and assaults were reduced or eliminated, and in turn, reduced the amount of times we returned to that particular couple.

Not perfect but it worked. Thank goodness it did. So if you're going to get into it with your significant other, think twice before raising a hand. Someone will get hurt, we will come visit you, we will throw the flag or Red Card at you and you'll be ejected from the game.

Scene 7: The Most Dangerous Call

Because of all the factors I have outlined revolving around the *domestic "34,"* please understand this is the single, most dangerous call we handle. I'm not talking about an active shooter or a street shooting taking place. Those are actually rare and we usually arrive after it's over. But the *domestic* happens every day everywhere, and because it's so emotionally charged it poses the greatest threat to us.

First, we are responding on a *"3"* signal, navigating traffic which is dangerous at speed and under stress. We are pulling up to the house, and good training will dictate that we stop a door or two down so we aren't directly in front of the house if avoidable.

Parking and walking up to the door are the most vulnerable positions for us because we are completely exposed with nowhere to hide. That walk up to the door is *No-man's-land.* And when we arrive, we DO NOT STAND IN FRONT OF THE DOOR! I love TV and movies, but when I see police standing right in front of the door and knocking on it, it drives me nuts.

I start cursing at the TV and say, "Where the hell are the technical advisers?" Ok Bert, calm down. The directors take liberties and get it all wrong.

My colleagues hired to advise on these shows know better. But understand my point. In front of the door is a big no-no. It can be a *"Kill-Zone"* and has. We do our best to stand to the side. Why? Because that's where the gunshot is going to come from.

Drunk, drugged, mean, criminal, or just plain evil assholes don't want the police at their home for many reasons. We might find the drugs or other criminal activity or arrest them for a battery. So they ambush us as we are walking up to or standing in front of the door. This is all *before* we even get inside.

There have been many occasions where officers were walking up to the door and were shot in front of the house. It's easy pickings for the asshole inside. This still happens to this day and during the course of writing this book it's happened at least five more times in America that I'm aware of, not just during my thirty-seven years on the job.

Once inside, we have to separate the parties. Two, three, five people, whatever it may be. The whole family is involved including the kids. We have to watch everyone and keep them under wraps, meaning no one gets to walk around freely because there are weapons everywhere potentially.

It's their house and they could be hiding a gun almost anywhere. A seat cushion, a drawer, closet, or on them. We also scan for potential weapons such as knives in the kitchen, scissors, a letter opener, even a screwdriver. Multi-tasking to the Nth degree.

Now that we have everyone separated and gathering their versions of what happened, any little word or phrase can set them off again and they go after each other in front of us. If a battery was committed, we'll make the arrest.

Even when no actual crime was committed, they will do something to get arrested or talk their way into jail. And many times when we make the decision to arrest, Joe or Jane decide they are *not* going to jail today and it's on! Assholes & Elbows and we are in a knockdown, drag-out fight.

"*3-15s*" are going out over the radio and the world is responding. This happens every day. Don't think so? Ride along with us. You'll see. Stand closer to them, and you'll see even more clearly.

Nothing astonishes the young, inexperienced, not-yet-tainted, officer more—when we make an arrest for serious injuries against the wife/girlfriend/baby-mama, bleeding profusely, eyes blackened, lips split and worse—than when we take the guy into custody, and she starts with "Don't arrest him," "I need him" "I love him."

As we are cuffing the subject, she jumps on our backs and tries to stop us from arresting the love of her paycheck; I mean her life (*CH*).

Now we are not only fighting with him, but we are also fighting with her. Throw the flag, "Personal Foul"-everyone goes to jail.

We have actually taken the whole family once. Eight people. All arrested. And that's just my personal experience, and I'm not alone in this. Ask most veteran officers. Same call. Same result. We get the call to stop the violence, and we become the enemy when we act. Tell me how this isn't potentially the most dangerous call we go to. I'm afraid this type of situation will never stop occurring. Once you've lost that loving feeling, lovers will become fighters and it will get ugly for all involved. Good times.

Act ~ 7

"43s" ~ The Baker Act

What Bat-Shit Crazy Is Really Like

Scene 1: Mental Illness - Society's Problem

It is well known there are a great many people in our society who suffer from some form of mental illness. From the mild to the severe, they have difficulties navigating their daily lives. Many are touched by this either by having a mental illness or knowing someone who does, not unlike most people are touched by cancer. Same reasons and almost as bad.

I am going to describe what it's like to interact with these folks and please don't misunderstand, it is a very serious societal condition and I am not making fun of any one individual. I am however going to inject the same *Cop Humor (CH)* I have been infusing throughout this book because even though most of the time these folks are not necessarily in control of their behavior, some of their behavior is downright funny, and cops being cops, we tend to see the humorous side of things so we don't become *Bat-Shit Crazy ourselves*. So once again, please don't email me or go on a Tweeting rant or hold street demonstrations in protest of my taking a comical slant on some things. It isn't necessary and I don't care.

People suffer from many forms of mental illness and fall into a state of irrationality which many times manifests itself into violent or hurtful behavior requiring intervention. Who do you suppose are the folks called to intervene in that behavior? You guessed it, the police.

When someone is in *Crisis*, as it's called, they are experiencing a psychotic break where all normal behavior as we understand it is no longer the reality and they behave irrationally. All attempts by either themselves or family and friends fails to bring them back. The police get the *911* call to respond and take control of an out-of-control situation.

Once there, we have to figure out what the specific issue is with the individual. We conduct an *assessment* of their behavior and

92

mental state and we try to figure out, if we can, what their particular condition or co-occurring conditions are.

Do they suffer from Bi-Polar Disorder, Schizophrenia (seemingly the most prevalent disorder), Panic & Anxiety disorder, Antisocial and Borderline Personality Disorders, or have a drug and/or alcohol induced condition making them act out in an abnormal way among many others.

Sometimes they experience delusions, hallucinations, and disorganized speech. Hallucinations can be very dangerous to us because if they see us as the enemy and many times they do, those hallucinations may lead to an attack on officers. Then we find ourselves in a *Use of Force* situation where we and/or the person with mental illness can get injured or even killed in response to the attack on us.

Understand we assess the totality of their behavior and information given by other persons on scene. We do not perform a diagnosis. A diagnosis is performed by a clinician, who is a healthcare professional with many years of training and education in the field, which we are not.

A healthcare professional has hours, even days, to render a diagnosis in a safe and controlled environment. We have to do our assessment in minutes or even seconds depending on the severity of their behavior.

Once we make a determination the person is suffering from a *possible* mental health disorder—based on their behavior and the circumstances—and that without intervention is in danger of becoming harmful to themselves, harmful to others, or is self-neglectful, we can then take them into protective custody. We then transport them to a *CSU*-a Crisis Stabilization Unit, which can be a hospital with a crisis receiving unit, or a stand-alone facility specializing in this field.

The authorization empowering us to do this in Florida is the law known as the Florida Mental Health Act of 1971. Better known as *The Baker Act*. Florida Statute 394.451, which was sponsored by Florida State Representative Maxine Baker from Miami, who served from 1963-1972. This gives us the authority to essentially *arrest* someone from their present location and condition and deliver them to a CSU.

Don't misunderstand the use of the term arrest, it simply means to seize someone by legal authority and take them into custody whatever the reason, they are not free to go. Hence, an a*rrest*.

Representative Baker saw a great need for a law rendering assistance to those who couldn't determine for themselves they in fact needed help and that immediate intervention was necessary. Who are the most immediate interveners out there? You guessed it again, the police.

The *Baker Act* allows us to take someone involuntarily for an examination to a CSU and once there, they can be held up to seventy-two hours for a more thorough evaluation, and clinical diagnosis and treatment by medical staff. The use of the term *Baker Act* has become synonymous for us when referring to someone who we might say is crazy. Again, a generic term we use in passing and no disrespect intended, so no need for another protest.

Scene 2: Oh Boy, Here We Go

So now that we've covered why we get called to take someone into custody for being in a mental health crisis and the responsibility and power vested in us to do so, let's cover how we do it and how sometimes it doesn't go according to plan.

A person suffering from a psychotic break is as unpredictable as a shark in the water. You have no idea how they are going to behave and react to your presence. Dealing with a bad guy is actually easier because you know he is, well, a bad guy, and he is a threat to you so your guard is up.

Someone who may be a *Baker Act* can act in any way possible so you had better be prepared for anything. They can be very submissive and meek and try to hide from reality and therefore might be very compliant with you when you take them into custody. These folks aren't the problem. The call that is the problem is the one where the person is tearing up the joint, throwing and breaking everything in sight, and wants to fight everyone.

Now, go and stop him from doing that, take him into custody (handcuffed-everyone goes this way for their safety and ours) and deliver them to a CSU. How many officers does it take to do that? A minimum of two, since we have a two-man call policy in such situations. Better and smarter would be five or six, and when a call like that goes out we respond in mass. Ever get into a struggle with someone with mental illness or a drug and alcohol induced psychosis? Don't! Again, it's hazardous to your health. They are as strong as a bull and feel virtually no pain.

Any officer in a busy jurisdiction or even in quieter ones has encountered someone in this condition. The resulting physical altercation can be one for the books. Where the bad guy eventually surrenders to the beating you give him because it's *real* to him and it hurts, the mentally ill person is disconnected from reality and almost no matter what you do has little to no effect. All you can do is get them handcuffed, legs tied, and transport them in that condition.

Now you arrive at the CSU and it's time to take them out of the patrol car that five of you struggled to shoehorn them in at the beginning of this dance. We then have to carry them into the Unit because most CSU staff won't bring a gurney out to you to lay them on. Thanks a lot, appreciate it!

Once inside, we have to place them in a secure section of the Unit, if they have one. Many CSUs are general hospitals designated as receiving facilities where their intake is the Emergency Department. They may only have a room with a curtain (great) where the person is "secured."

Truth is, They're Not!

Fortunately, most have a designated room or two with locking doors. Two things happen at this point; they either eventually calm down on their own, not likely, or you inform the staff the person needs to be strapped down and physical restraints applied. Here in lies another problem; on quite a few occasions the staff, meaning the attending physician, is reluctant to use physical restraints because it can be detrimental to the psyche and wellbeing of the patient and some even cite that it's inhumane.

Understood, to a point. But what will be more harmful to the patient when we take the handcuffs off and they didn't get with program here, is the reintroduction of the beat down we will have to again administer because the staff refused to strap him or her down. Is that inhumane enough for you?

There is another option *WE* like when the staff employs it; it's what's referred to as the *Cocktail*. This is an injection of one or several drugs known as *Chemical Restraints* that are wondrously effective and the best part is no one gets hurt.

Unfortunately, some doctors are reluctant to use these as well, but along comes a nurse to save the day and says screw it! *"Holy Needle-Stick*

Batman!" Bam! Injection delivered and you watch the fight go right out them. It's beautiful and everyone goes home in one piece, except the patient of course. They have an appointment with the Shrink.

This scenario played out many a time. Though we give fair warning to the staff that once the cuffs come off *Mr. Hyde* is making a reappearance, they insist we "just leave them there, they'll be fine."

Sure! Officers have "just left them there" and walked away and guess what happens then? "Oh, we need the officers back!" Nope. You took custody of them. Now they're your problem. Once we turn over custody we are done.

The fight is now the responsibility of the CSU. You didn't want to listen to the dumb cops so there you go. How's that working for ya? Here's a suggestion for any doctor or CSU staff that wants to go against our advice when we bring in a violent *Baker Act*; come out to the original scene where *we first* find them, pick your partner and Do-Si-Do! Your lab coat is going to get a little dirty and it'll be a dance you'll never forget. Maybe then you'll listen to us.

There have been many knockdown, drag-out fights with someone we have taken in on a *Baker Act*. The same rules apply to a criminal arrest where the use of force is directly proportional to the level of resistance in order to take them into custody and to protect ourselves.

We don't want to hurt them but they don't know that they're mentally ill! You can't reason with people in crisis because they can't understand. Just like arguing with an idiot. Except the person with mental illness has no control.

The idiot is well, an idiot, and that's the problem. If they were in control of their faculties then force wouldn't be necessary. A popular tool for this is again, the Taser.

Baker Acts and drug & alcohol induced psychosis patients are the primary reasons we went to the Taser to begin with. It is a more humane way of taking someone suffering from these conditions into custody. If you agree that lighting them up and making them do the *chicken* is humane, at least there is a less likelihood of severe injury.

Scene 3: Now Go Grab Him

One of the worst kinds of people to deal with under some form of psychosis is the *Naked Guy*. You've seen the 10 O'clock News where the police are seen chasing a naked dude down the street because he ingested (voluntarily used) some drug and it went sideways in the worst way. Once again, call the police!

These folks are going at a hundred miles an hour, heart rate is in the hundreds, body-temp is peaking at Death Valley hot, they're completely covered in sweat, seeing spiders crawl up their bodies, swinging like a Great Dane in the park, and feeling no pain whatsoever! Now go get him Spanky! The ensuing physical altercation is nothing short of disgusting.

Even though we may have time to put on gloves, those only protect our hands. You are going to get slimy, filthy, sweat and perhaps other bodily fluids on you when you take him down. There's no getting around it. You have to grab body parts and you may not like what you grab or slaps you.

It's just as bad taking a naked woman into custody. You try and avoid the boobs but, no dice. This is one of those times we don't like seeing a woman naked. Nope. And all the while Fire Rescue is sitting back with a bag of popcorn enjoying the show until we deliver the person to them.

In all fairness to them, their policies preclude them from getting involved, but some will jump in and help as long as there are no weapons involved. End result? *Baker Act* transported and a shower and change of clothes required. Yuck!

Scene 4: Goodbye Cruel World!

The most often cited statement police hear when encountering a person with mental illness causing us to take them into protective custody is they want to kill themselves, or they just don't want to live anymore.

The reasons are many. They are hearing voices telling them to kill themselves, their girlfriend or boyfriend broke up with them, yes, some say that even though you might say there are plenty of fish, etc. They've lost a loved one like a spouse of many, many years, or the loss of a child. The worst. They are not taking their meds and it's making them psychotic. They can have such a severe condition and can't cope that the only way out is the thought of suicide.

Whatever the reason we get called to intervene. We conduct our assessment and then we hear those magic words; "I want to kill myself." At that point it's a done deal. "You're going!" We don't have a choice whether we believe them or not, and we often don't believe them but it's not our call.

We are not clinicians and can only go by what someone tells us and what we see and hear. There are many times after we transport them the doctors don't agree with our assessment, but then again the patient is now in a clinical setting and stabilizing so the dynamics have changed from when and where we found them.

Imagine if we decided that this person is full of shit and didn't take them in and then they do kill or attempt to kill themselves? What we would hear is "what does that cop think he is, a doctor?' Exactly. Once you tell us you want to harm yourself in any way, you're a *Baker Act*. Period.

Baker Act Stories: Vignettes - If You Will

I have personally Baker Acted and been on scenes with my officers for so many people taken into protective custody during the course of my career, I can't even begin to count. Here are some short **Stories** involving the *Baker Act* and the reasons I took them into protective custody. These are just some of my stories in the naked city. We all have them.

In GOD We Trust

My partner Eddie Pena and I responded to a home off SW 122 Ave in the evening back in 1983, in regards to a young guy who wouldn't eat, respond to his family, get dressed, or act normally as far as the family was concerned.

Eddie and I found him kneeling on the floor of their living room, hands clasped, praying, and repeating **John: 316**, over and over and over again. We tried talking to him but he was incoherent and not responsive. When I say over and over again I mean he didn't stop. His family said that he had been diagnosed with schizophrenia so a decision was made to *Baker Act* him.

Eddie and I got in behind him and each took hold of a hand and placed them behind his back and handcuffed him. Easy enough and all the while he continued; **"John: 316, John: 316.**" We walked out to our patrol car and when we opened the rear door and leaned him toward the car, handcuffed, he jumped up and put his feet on either side of the door and blocked us from putting him inside. He pushed back, and we all landed on our asses.

Remember I said unpredictable? It was a struggle with him but we finally restrained his legs and with a few minor bumps and bruises for all, we stuffed him in the backseat and off we went. **GOD** was nowhere to be found.

A Good Cleansing

We responded to a residence and I remember I was about twenty-six and the woman in question was thirty-one. She was very pretty and calm as can be sitting at the kitchen bar. As we were interviewing her family, I noticed that she had a Martini glass in front of her but didn't make anything of it. Her family told us that she had a diagnosed mental illness and she thought that she had the Bubonic Plague.

Mmmm. Ok. Pretty concerning but go on.

I interviewed her to confirm the family's account, and she told me she had the Bubonic Plague and that the only way to get rid of the Plague was to drink Clorox. You read right. Bleach. She said it with a straight face with no expression.

Ok, getting better. And that Clorox, name brand top shelf only please, was in that Martini glass sitting in front of her. What? And as we looked at her she picked up the glass and took a swig of the bleach. Shit! I took the glass from her and took a whiff. Sure as shit, Clorox! I turned to my partner and said, "Time to go!" And she did. Now that's *Bat-Shit Crazy!*

Damn Kids

My partner Charlie Ferrante and I were working our Hammocks District, afternoon shift, and responded to the home of a doctor who worked at the Dade County Jail.

A friend and colleague of his called *911* from another location, a doctor herself, who I spoke with on the phone. She advised that her friend who is a Cuban immigrant and very religious, was having a very difficult time with the fact his daughter, who was an adult, was unmarried and pregnant.

He felt it went against all of *His* beliefs and she had brought dishonor to him as her father. He was sitting in his chair with a beer in hand, one of several he had had. He told his colleague he wanted to kill himself and she was very concerned "he might hurt himself." "Hurting oneself" is a widely and wrongly used euphemism for suicide.

He never told us he wanted to kill himself as he knew full well as a doctor if he made any comments to the affirmative (the Magic Words) we would *Baker Act* him. But there was enough supporting information provided by the reporter, coupled with his inebriated state and his daughter's perceived dishonor of him, we felt we needed to take him.

He didn't like it and his depressed state now turned to anger with us. Now we were the enemy, he was a doctor, and we were just cops and he was going to sue us.

Get in line.

Moral of the story; don't tell your friends or family you want to kill yourself. We are going to get that call. Hard core religious beliefs can be a MF!

Wow, Just Wow!

My partner and one of my best friends, Bill Duclo, and I responded to a townhouse in the Sable Chase development of our Southwest District. A woman was having a "breakdown" and neighbors called the police. We entered this woman's townhouse, and she was wearing a shirt.

That's it. The basement was bare.

Apparently, she had been yelling at who knows what and the neighbors, both fearing for her safety and having had enough, called us. She came onto us right away. She made glaring and explicit sexual advances toward us and tried groping us.

Now, it was of course understandable since we were both handsome, in shape, and cut quite the image in a uniform. Come on! *(CH)* Seriously now, she was out of her mind. I mean she just met us. No drinks, dinner, nothing. Just right to it!

Ok, "Houston, we have a problem."

We decided to *Baker Act* her and given her somewhat disrobed condition, we also decided to have an ambulance transport her for us on a gurney so we wouldn't have to touch her. The ambulance arrived and the medics placed her on the gurney.

Now, I'm going to state exactly what happened so you can get the *Full Monty* here and visualize the scene. Remember, unfiltered. The medics tried to place a blanket over her lady parts. Didn't work.

As they were wheeling her out of the house, and with a good 10-15 neighbors in attendance and two completely stunned cops and here's why; she flung the blanket off herself, spread her legs and began quickly and roughly pleasuring herself.

Gets better.

While doing this, she's yelling at the both of us "Fuck me! Fuck me! Fuck me! You guys, I want to fuck you both! Come on, fuck me! Eat my pussy! Eat my pussy!" And it went on and on. I kid you not. After the initial shock, Bill and I busted out laughing. We were tearing we were laughing so hard. There was no way to contain ourselves. Off to the *CSU*. Talk about a *Box of Chocolates!*

What CIT Officers Do

By Officer Chris Rodriquez

The year was 2015. My partner and I, Officer Sergio Pagliery, worked the midnight patrol shift in the Intracoastal District. We rode together raising hell, in a good way, every night.

The time was about 0100 hours, and we were dispatched in emergency mode, lights and sirens, to a house in the western part of the district, an area prone to shootings and robberies. Being familiar with the area, Sergio and I mentally prepared ourselves and started talking about a game plan.

The call for service involved unknown people driving by the complainant's residence and threatening her. We arrived at the residence, no vehicles, no people, no one was outside.

We were greeted by an elderly woman so let's call her Agatha. Agatha talked to us briefly and at some point, we realized Agatha was not mentally well. She told us people were hacking her computer and coming into her house through the computer screen.

Ok, it's certainly possible someone could breach a home computer, that's not so unbelievable. The moment we realized Agatha wasn't all there was when she said the hackers were doing voodoo and throwing blood at her, inside her house, in her bedroom, and blood was everywhere. Clearly, Agatha was hallucinating.

Officers in Miami-Dade County receive top notch training in mental health related calls for service. The training specifically teaches officers how to identify people in mental crisis and how to best help them navigate said crisis, referred to as Crisis Intervention Team training, or *CIT*.

Agatha was convinced people were inside her house as we spoke to her. We were taught in training never to acknowledge hallucinations or delusions, but I decided to try a different approach. While we weren't confirming Agatha's delusions I wanted to put her mind at ease, so Sergio and I "cleared" the house, announcing our presence and searching each room with our guns out. As expected, no one was in the house.

We didn't outright ask Agatha about being diagnosed with mental illness, but we danced around the question in a sugarcoated way so as not to offend or upset her. Agatha insisted that she was mentally coherent, and that she did not suffer from any form of mental illness.

Would it have been easy to just throw the handcuffs on Agatha for her own safety and transport her to the nearest hospital under Florida's Baker Act Statute? Sure. Would it have been just as easy to say, "have a good night Agatha!" and leave her alone in her house? Absolutely. Another officer told me once, "get this mentality of not being able to do anything for people out of your head rookie, we are police officers, there is always something we can do for people."

We decided to talk to Agatha for about forty-five minutes, when finally, she agreed to go to a hospital for an evaluation. We achieved our objective. We helped an elderly woman get the help she so desperately needed and did it in the nicest way possible. We dropped Agatha off at a nearby hospital and left, not thinking much more of it because this was our job, this is what we did, we helped people, and it was just another mental health call for service.

A few nights later, the desk officer called us saying a package with our names on it arrived at the station. Sergio and I looked at each other, what the hell? A package? Why the hell did we receive a package? Who did we piss off this time?

We walked in and, to our surprise, it was a thank you gift from Agatha! She sent us cider, mixed nuts and mixed flavor cookies with a card. I remember reading the card. Agatha thanked us for our genuine care and attention to her incident.

She stated she still did not believe she was mentally ill, but only went to the hospital because of how nice and personable Sergio and I were to her. Agatha wrote that she planned to have cameras installed to prove "she wasn't crazy," not that we ever called her crazy. We never heard from Agatha again. We hoped she would find the help she so desperately needed.

Author's Note:

This story from then Officer Chris Rodriguez, perfectly illustrates what a properly trained officer in the area of Crisis Intervention does in seeking a resolution to someone's crisis, albeit a temporary one. He followed his training and was able to help someone, because that's what we try to do with the folks we get called to assist. It doesn't always work, but we try, nonetheless. Good job Chris & Sergio!

This next excerpt is provided by my good friend and mentor in the Crisis Intervention Team program, Habsi W. Kaba, MS MFT CMS. She is the director of the CIT Miami-Dade and Police Mental Health Collaboration - 11th Judicial Circuit - Criminal Mental Health Project.

Habsi has trained 8,000 police officers from every agency in Miami-Dade County over the last seventeen years and has taught all of us how to better interact and help our folks who suffer from mental illness. I functioned as her "Lead Police Coordinator" as she called me for all of Miami-Dade County and she personally taught me a thing or two I didn't know, even after twenty-seven years of police work when I attended her class in 2010.

She has both a national and international reputation and is sought out by agencies all over the country for consultation, training, and guidance. Habsi will provide the more serious side of the mental illness crisis we have in the US.

A Greatly Misunderstood Challenge

I'd like to speak about *Florida's Mental Health Act*, known as the *Baker Act* to most— and misunderstood by many—and my experiences in this realm and my relationship with law enforcement.

In 2003, I was an eager mental health professional with a Master's Degree in marriage and family therapy, ready to start the next chapter of my career.

After ten years working at a psycho-social rehabilitation center with an average of 300 individuals living with schizophrenia, mood disorders and depression, I was offered a position with the *Eleventh Judicial Circuit - Criminal Mental Health Project*. I would become the first *Crisis Intervention TEAM (CIT) Coordinator* for Miami-Dade County (MDC), a role that was new, unfamiliar to most, and as it turned out, much needed.

My sole job, so I thought, was to provide police officers with a 40-hour training course & certification called the *CIT Memphis Model*. Memphis is where it all began. CIT training is a specialized course preparing police officers to better understand mental illness, identify signs and symptoms, de-escalate persons in crisis, navigate through the mental health system, and divert to treatment instead of to jail, when appropriate.

With some reservations, and thanks to my father's wisdom and a judge with a vision, I accepted the position and entered the world of law enforcement with a front row seat to a broken mental health system. Yes, broken, mishandled, mismanaged, abandoned, and by default, a system that landed on the shoulders of law enforcement.

If you can't handle it, don't worry, the police will take care of it, but not without societal judgment and punishment. What could go wrong? But what can we expect from law enforcement when society fails to give them the tools, knowledge, and resources to succeed? The real question here is should police be the first responders to *all* mental health calls in the first place? We've come to rely on police for almost everything and it's become too easy to call *911*.

My best schooling since I began teaching law enforcement in 2003, has been working side by side with police officers, witnessing mental health calls for service, and pioneering a co-response approach to crisis calls. Not only did it give me a first-hand look at the problem, which included barriers for law enforcement and persons in need, but it also gave me an opportunity to personally stress the system.

I quickly learned there was a pattern with most calls. I learned from families or individuals themselves in crisis who lacked an insight into their own mental illness (known as Anosognosia).

They desperately needed psychoeducation on mental illness, treatment and rehabilitation, had addictions coupled with mental illness (known as co-occurring disorders), were unaware of how to access the system and largely lacked coping skills, and had little to no support.

Culture, low socioeconomic status, homelessness, and stigma also play important roles that must not go unsaid. This revolving door is all too familiar to police officers who by Florida Statute; "S*hall* initiate involuntary examination when meeting the *Baker Act Criteria* and are responsible for the transportation of an *involuntary* person to the most appropriate or nearest receiving facility."

The *Baker Act*, in the eyes of the community and law enforcement was perceived and still is to many, as a *catch-all solution* until the person is discharged from treatment, commonly within seventy-two hours.

This is where the misunderstanding occurs. Daily, I find myself educating families and law enforcement on the following: the *Baker Act* provides a person with emergency services and temporary detention for evaluation and treatment, on a voluntary or involuntary basis. If deemed necessary, a petition can be filed in court for involuntary placement to a facility. Otherwise, once a person is discharged, it is up to that person to follow through with treatment and services. Thanks to former Florida State Representative Maxine Baker, we have these rights.

When the challenges experienced by a person with mental illness become too great and they begin to use the system often, they become known to law enforcement as *Frequent Fliers,* and *High Utilizers* to mental health providers.

They become conditioned to call police when in crisis (or perceived crisis). Why police? Because police will always respond and deliver them/you to a nearby facility for evaluation and treatment, simple as that! And if you're thinking "or to jail," thanks to *CIT Training* and the outstanding work done by CIT trained officers daily, the number of diversions to treatment in Miami-Dade County are outstanding, and we have the numbers to show it.

In 2019, 1 out of thirty-five police departments reported 7447 CIT calls and only three arrests! That's right, only three. Those numbers may seem high to you but it's no wonder since Miami-Dade County has one of the highest percentages of people with mental illness in the US. The national average of the rate of mental illness is about 3 percent. In Miami-Dade County it's a whopping 9 percent! So police and mental healthcare providers here are busier than anywhere else.

Another reason and most importantly why a person may call police when in crisis, is because we have failed to provide them with the knowledge to understand mental illness, reduce its stigma, and give them the resources needed to access and navigate through the system. We don't make it easy for the average person, much less someone with a mental and/or cognitive challenge and worse, in crisis.

There are many myths about mental illness I would like to clarify. The first and most important is most people with mental illness are NOT dangerous. In fact, they are most often victims of violence and are taken advantage of due to their vulnerability.

Second: Recovery is real and people with mental illness can not only survive but thrive and they do! There are physicians, attorneys, judges, police officers, teachers, celebrities, and many other successful individuals living (not suffering) with mental illness.

Third: Medication, although important and necessary for some individuals with mental illness; in my professional opinion is not the secret to recovery.

In my 27 years of experience, I find the most essential element to recovery and wellbeing is a support system…we all need connections.

Last, every one of us is living with a symptom or two from time to time or perhaps all the time; on some days we could be just a diagnosis away from a mental health disorder. Yes… it's true. Think back on your own life and remember those times where you struggled with just day-to-day issues.

What about the Blue?

This brings me to the most rewarding part of my job and my purpose. As a Marriage and Family Therapist and a Mental Health Professional, I am frequently reminded that many of those who serve and protect others are guilty of self-neglect.

Whether it's stigma, pride, culture, or the overwhelming feeling of "I don't have time," they abandon their own needs. I love the scene in one of the Superman movies where Superman sweeps Lois Lane into his herculean arms and ascends into the sky.

Noticing Lois's fear and hesitation, Superman says; "Don't worry, I've got you!" Lois then responds, "But who's got you?" How great is that! I play this scene at the beginning of each *CIT Officer Wellness* segment and can't help but wonder… who's got you my dear Officer? You should see the look of wonder in their faces. It's a powerful and enlightening moment. We have to take care of those who take care of us, don't we?

After many years facilitating CIT training, I am very grateful to have developed trust and great friendships with officers and their families throughout that time. Anyone who is familiar with the police culture knows this doesn't come easily or often, but is most gratifying and a great privilege should you be let in.

Through trust, credibility and acceptance, officers have shared their own personal pain and sorrow. First, for those of you unfamiliar with the world of law enforcement, you should know that when you befriend a person who is a police officer, you have a protector and friend for life. Someone you can call if you're in need at any time and who has your back and will always make sure you get home safely. Most love animals, will watch your bag even if you're sitting right next to it, make sure your taillights are working and will always, always, sit with their back to a wall. Count on it!

You should also know behind that badge is a beating heart with emotions. Yes, it's true, they feel, they are human... And as they feel inside, deep inside, they're reacting to their environment. Thankfully, their cortisol level protects them by keeping them alert and performing at their best where their training and experience converge; where their reaction to threats and danger results in catching the bad guy, or saving a child, and watching their back and that of their partner.

But after that adrenaline high is over...it often results in a crash. And sometimes, brings a flashback or sleepless nights with recurring thoughts of something they saw, heard, or felt; things no human should ever see or experience. A police officer will see more in one day than most of us will see in a lifetime.

I will never forget that day I rode with an officer and we responded to a signal *"45,"* the scene of a deceased person. This was a 40-something year old man who appeared to have been dead for at least twelve hours. His skin appeared very white with a tint of blue and the smell, well... indescribable and unforgettable.

I had a hard time going to sleep that night and that was about thirteen years ago... Imagine, that was only one experience! It is said that we are a products of our environment. Trauma is real and this can result in officers more likely to die by suicide than in the line of duty.

Numbers released by *Blue HELP* in January of 2020, show that in 2019, 228 American police officers died by suicide.

So who is protecting our protectors? Who is making sure police officers and all first responders are receiving awareness and the treatment needed? Where is the legislation, policies and benefits addressing first responder mental health needs? How can we expect police officers to take care of others and make split decisions when some or many are dealing with their own mental health issues linked to stigma, fear, pride, lack of a support system or access to services, sound familiar?

I often say my greatest teachers have been police officers and individuals living with mental illness. In delivering the gold standard of mental health training in Miami-Dade County to nearly 8000 officers to date, I've learned many things. My most valuable lessons have been that we are more alike than we are different, that listening to each other instills understanding leading to compassion, and in the end we all just want the same thing; to be safe.

No matter where we come from or how differently we think we can find common ground, we can create a safer and healthier community for our children, and maybe, just maybe, even the world.

Act - 8 "3-30s" & "31s"

Murder, Death, Kill

Scene 1: Eye Opener

Inherent and inevitable parts of police work are the death investigations a police officer in Metropolis will handle many times over the course of their career. *"30s"- Shootings*, and *"31s"- Homicides*, are par-for-the-course in police work.

Depending on the type of area you work, you will have a great number of 30s, such as in economically depressed areas or *ghettos* as we have commonly referred to them.

These are high-crime areas with a great deal of drug activity, such as our Northside District and the City of Miami's Over Town District. These areas are also infamous because this is where the *1980 Miami Riots* took place. Every Gotham City and the not so large ones have them, and the bulk of hard-core police work takes place in these districts, precincts, and sectors. Shootings are commonplace, and we are all affected by them.

When I was promoted to sergeant in 1998 I was assigned to the Northside District. I was used to a busy pace of work in general, but in Northside much of the work was handling shootings.

We would have a shooting every few days, mostly on the afternoon and midnight shifts. These hours had the most criminal activity and when things went sideways, Bang! A shooting. But shootings happen anywhere and everywhere and for any reason. Drug deals gone bad, gang related and retaliatory hits, domestics, road-rage, and just getting pissed off at someone because some guy looked at someone the wrong way or "he disrespected me" or "my woman." Valid reasons for sure.

These shootings *are* going to happen and every officer has to prepare themselves for the carnage they are going to see. Cadets are shown pictures in the academy of homicide scenes but it doesn't really give you the full affect until you see it up close and personal.

Everyone is at first shocked and disgusted at what they see. The wounds left by gunshots and stabbings catch you off-guard for a bit, and you can't believe you're seeing someone who is dead and the manner in which they were killed or died.

But after a while of handling death investigations as in any other aspect of life, you get used to it. "How can you get used to seeing dead people?" you might ask. You have to build that *wall* I've talked about. It protects you from the emotional strain witnessing death on a regular basis causes you.

Unfortunately, it becomes routine to see death and that is a sad statement to make, but death is a part of life, whether natural, accidental, or inflicted, and someone has to handle these incidents and that's what we do. Death cases are so common that every medium to large sized agency has long established Homicide Squads and Bureaus to handle these investigations.

These detectives are notified every time a uniform officer responds to call involving a death. When the death is caused by the hand of another, a *Homicide*, or is otherwise suspicious in nature these detectives have to conduct a thorough investigation and levy charges against a perpetrator if warranted or determine the cause of death.

It is a specialized field and these units get the most resources as they should because it is the highest crime against humanity that there is.

When a homicide squad responds to a scene, these detectives understand that they may not be going home for a period of 24 to 48 hours as this is the most crucial period in the investigation if you don't already have the subject in custody. Many homicide detectives have a change of clothes and a razor at the office for this purpose. Yes, *most* homicide detectives are men, so if the squad has any female detectives you can disregard the razor.

Scene 2: "Attention All Units, "3-30!"

Invariably, every officer is going to get the call of a shooting. In our case we will get it as a *"3-30,"* our code for a shooting. When you get your first one, you get so amped up by the beep-tone and the possibility of arriving in the middle of a shooting you're scared out of your mind.

Excited but scared.

Your heart is racing, compounded by the sound of the siren and navigating the traffic around you, enroute to the scene. You're wondering what you'll find and what you are going to do when you find it.

As young officers we all go through this. You're also hoping Fire Rescue gets there before you do so you don't have to touch anyone. But we're all trained in First Aide, right? Yes we are, but no one wants to touch someone that's bleeding out or is missing body parts. But we may have to as we are usually first on scene.

Another thing you learn about shooting calls as you become more seasoned—especially if you work areas with frequent shootings like our Northside, Intracoastal, and South Districts, Miami's Over Town and the City of Miami Gardens* in the northern part of our county—is to wait for the dispatcher to advise that the Complaint Desk (*911 call center*) had received several calls on the shooting, not just one.

Many times they are false calls just to make the police respond. Nowadays it's called *SWATTING*, but it's been around forever. So before we start going balls-to-the-wall on a shooting, we wait. More than one call and it's usually a good one.

When you arrive, the first thing you do is make sure the shooting is *OVER* before you do anything else. The bad guys may still be in the area, or with a domestic related shooting the significant other that did the shooting or stabbing may still be in the house or apartment and take exception to your presence. Therefore, we have to secure everything and everyone before we can render aide or begin locking down the scene. If the subject or subjects just fled or are at-large in the area, we have to quickly gather a description and issue a *BOLO: Be-On-the-Look-Out* for the bad guy, which is broadcasted to other responding units. This is all accomplished within the first few seconds or minutes of arrival. Once we make certain no one else is shooting or otherwise a danger to us, then we begin aiding those that are injured. Sorry folks but we come first.

*(Author's note: Miami Gardens is nicknamed *Murder Gardens* for good reason. Before some of you folks get upset with me I didn't name it, the residents did.)

Scene 3: The Bad Guy Is In There, Now Go Get Him

Once you've arrived and all appears to have calmed down, for the moment anyway, securing the scene usually comes next. But what if you discover the subject has fled to a specific location, like a house, an apartment, a warehouse, or some other structure and is hold-up inside? Well, now you have to go and get him. What? You heard me right. Now it's time to capture the guy who committed the murder-death-kill.

It's our job to investigate the scene, but it is also our job to apprehend the bad guy. Many times it's during what we call, like *Sheriff Buford T. Justice* would say, *"In Hot Pursuit."*

In legal terms it's referred to as *Fresh Pursuit*. Meaning the crime is fresh with little or almost no time between the act and your pursuit of the subject. In hot pursuit it is better to apprehend them sooner rather than later, so now we are likely to face a confrontation with the subject in order to accomplish that.

This means it's time to put on our big-boy and big-girl pants and make entry into the structure, and *THAT* can be quite hairy, in a word. You are making entry through some kind of doorway or opening, into an unknown and unfamiliar area, perhaps in the dark, with an unknown bad guy with an unknown type of gun or weapon, and an unknown intent. Ready? Move!

It's our job to do this all the while not knowing what the outcome might be. I have done this many times with fellow officers or my own team where we've worked together for a while and know each other's moves.

Even so, going through a door after the bad guys is both frightening and exhilarating and it gets easier the more times you do it. Special Response Teams (SRT) like ours and SWAT teams in general train endlessly on entries and always work as a team.

But most of their entries are done with the element of surprise while serving warrants and catching the subjects asleep. The most dangerous time for SRT is making entry on a barricaded subject who is armed, may have hostages, and knows they're coming. That's the same as a hot pursuit.

Everyone knows where everyone is and a lot of loud shit is about to happen. These operators are exceptional at this and I'm proud to say that the Miami-Dade Special Response Team is among the best historically.

But for the rest of us mere mortals, we have to make entry without all of their training, weapons and equipment, and without an entire team. Remember chasing after a bad guy through any doorway is a crap-shoot at best if most things go your way. So when you see officers, young and old alike, in hot pursuit of *The Bandit,* stay out of the way and thank them for going into harm's way for all of us.

War Story

On Monday afternoon, December 21, 1998, during my first year as a sergeant, my squad and I were working the Northside District and things were non-stop busy as usual. Handling domestic after domestic, robbery after burglary, argument after whatever pissed someone off, when we heard; BEEEP, "Attention all units, "*3-30,*" 2700 Block of NW 62 Street. Multiple people shot."

We of course responded in mass on a "*3*" to the area to find the location was a little, free-standing grocery store about the same size as a two-car garage, with two people shot in the doorway bleeding profusely, blood and flesh spattered everywhere.

The two "victims," asshole-subjects themselves, were targeted by other asshole-subjects and shot in a drive-by as they were exiting this grocery store. Yes, gang related.

The shooting was done with Ak-47s and the spent shell casings were all over the street. The front of the store was riddled with bullets, and the two "victims" suffered massive trauma all over their bodies, one of them later died at the Ryder Trauma Center. We tried to obtain witness accounts so we could issue a BOLO for the subjects, but of course no one saw anything. This was typical.

So we had *another* shooting scene to secure as the district was a hotbed for them, and we shut down NW 62 Street, running the yellow crime scene tape, canvassing the area for other witnesses and evidence, and making notifications up the chain-of-command, and to our Homicide Bureau.

Time to sit back and wait for the investigation to take place. Now, when I said the location was a grocery store, technically it was by its name and the fact it had shelves for food items, but the shelves were almost completely empty. How can this be a grocery store with no food? It wasn't. It was a front for street-level drug dealing and everyone knew it.

It would get shut down by the police and get reopened under another name. Same old story as is in many other cities around the country, and this is just a minor footnote in these types of shooting incidents.

Throughout the major cities these incidents occur daily. New York, Los Angeles, Washington DC, Atlanta, and as of late and perhaps with the worst frequency of shootings in modern times, Chicago. This type of crime overwhelmed our colleagues there, and they can't keep up with it or address it properly. Best of luck to them.

Now why do I remember this one specifically among all the shooting scenes I have been on either in Northside or the several other districts I've worked? Well, it was a Monday night, the Denver Broncos were in town to play our Miami Dolphins, when they were still good, and it was Marino vs. Elway. Can't get better than that. We were all Dolphin fans and cops being cops, we figured out a way to watch the game even though we were working.

You see, we had a Channel 10 News van on scene for the live shots for the news breaks and telecast after the game. The camera man had the game live on the monitor inside the van, so my squad and I took turns watching the game while we rotated security on the scene. There wasn't much else to do since we couldn't leave until Homicide and Crime Scene finished their on-scene investigation, so we watched the game.

Much to our delight, *"Danny Boy"* as my mother called him, out-slung Elway for a 31-21 victory. A rare occasion these days, but we made the best of a very tragic and sad incident. Remember the *CH here*.

My point to this is a serious one though. These incidents are so frequent in Metropolis that we as a society have become numb to them, and as police we have to be a little more numb in order to process what we see and handle.

We were handling a murder yet we watched a football game during the aftermath. The most stunning irony for me of this entire incident is it took place on a street named after a man who stood for peace in the face of violence at every turn, and in the end it cost him his life. NW 62 Street is also named after Dr. Martin Luther King Jr. How tragically ironic is that?

Scene 4: The Crime Scene

As seen on TV cop shows and movies, every shooting or homicide carries with it the famous *Crime Scene markers*. The area cordoned off with the ubiquitous yellow tape that reads; "POLICE LINE DO NOT CROSS."

They partitioned this zone off so that the detectives and crime scene officers and technicians could conduct their investigations in relative security without interference.

Crime Scenes contain the bodies with homicides, natural or accidental deaths, spent shell casings from automatic weapons which are commonly used, the blood and blood trails which lead in and out of the scene, knives if used, DNA and fingerprints, the discarded clothing left by Fire Rescue as they treat the victims, and any other objects, items, or equipment that may or may not be part of the scene.

They could be clubs and baseball bats, tire irons, machetes (common in South Florida) even vehicles used as weapons. We designed this secured area to keep out the public, the media, and anyone else that doesn't have business being there, which includes other officers and command staff. All cops want to see what the scene looks like, and many command staff members show up and walk through the scene just because they can. They have no real purpose there other than to show their face and want in. They can stand outside the tape and get their updates from the lead detective or investigating supervisor just like everyone else.

Why are all people other than the investigators kept out of the scene? Because they can compromise the investigation by walking over or disturbing a crucial piece of evidence. Simply by touching something we don't yet know is part of the crime can compromise the case.

Shell casings get kicked around, blood evidence is stepped on and then we have footprints we didn't have before, and never recover anything. Now your prints are part of the crime scene and have to be eliminated knucklehead! Scene security is something preached starting in the academy, and continuously throughout our careers. Yet, we seem to screw it up repeatedly.

Recently, we had a shooting at a strip-club in our district. Do tell, a shooting at a strip-club? Anyway, the scene had shell casings everywhere and some gold badges kicked them around. Not good.

This pissed off Homicide of course and prompted a visit to our district's *in-house training* as we call it at the Airport, by crime scene officers to explain once again, the importance of scene security. You'd think that we would have learned this over the many years that some of us on scene that morning would know.

Here is a piece of advice for all my colleagues throughout the law enforcement community on behalf of all of those investigators; stay the fuck out of the scene! Unless you're actively involved in the investigation, take a perimeter point, drink your coffee, and keep everyone else out. You'll be thanked by the investigators and perhaps one day when you become one yourself you will appreciate this more.

Act 9 Taps

Scene 1: It's Not If, but When

In police work, as in life, there are certain inevitabilities one cannot change or avoid. The sun will rise and set. Day turns into night and back into day. This we know.

In life, death will eventually come to us all and hopefully it is far down the road for everyone. In our line of work, it is an inevitability an officer will die at some point during our careers, and not just once but many times over. Learning to cope with these losses comes with the job, but it isn't easy and can be very difficult if that loss is of a colleague that you worked with.

The academy does its best to prepare you for this part of our profession, but all the lectures, statistics, and advice can't really get you ready for the shock you will feel when it does come. Like us, firefighters and the military know this all too well, and you may say to yourself you'll be ready when the time comes, but you won't.

As a new officer, you're kind of oblivious to this aspect of our profession as you try to get through your training phases and prove you belong here. Going from call-to-call and essentially having a grand old time doing it. If we're lucky, it doesn't come for a long time, and as in the case of many rural areas like *Smallville*, never at all.

Once again, busy jurisdictions suffer the most and Miami-Dade County is not immune to it. We, like other large cities and counties, handle into the high hundreds of thousands of calls each year, and when you add all the municipalities within our county, especially the City of Miami, you're past the one million mark of calls handled. This doesn't include the number of traffic stops or the additional tens of thousands of citizen contacts. As you go about your business, things seem routine and it's an ordinary day. And then one day reality strikes.

Scene 2: My First Loss - No Easy Day

One of those "routine" days was December 24, 1983, Christmas Eve. I had been on my own for a couple of months after finishing my riding assignments with an FTO and was now partnered up with Officer Ed Pena. Like me, he was a rookie out on his own for a couple of months more than I was.

We were working our first assignment which was the Southwest District, or Station 5, and were on the 4:00 P.M. to midnight shift. It was an extraordinarily busy shift, but that day was a little quieter. At around 5 o'clock or so, we were at Ed's house having Christmas Eve dinner with his wife and mother-in-law, since we were on duty and his house was in our patrol zone so it was convenient.

We were enjoying a Cuban dish of Arroz y Bistek (rice and steak) Cuban style, when we heard over the radio; Beeeeeep, "Attention all units, *3-30*, officer down!" It gives me chills as I write this and remembering everything that came after that. We literally dropped our utensils and ran out the door to our Green & White without even saying a thing to Ed's wife and her mother.

The location of the shooting was the Park & Ride on SW 72 Avenue behind the Dadeland Mall at the east end of our district. We were coming from the west end, a long distance for sure. I was driving and I remember we were flying eastbound on SW 40 Street doing 100 mph. I was doing everything I could to get us there, but the car seemed like it wouldn't go any faster. It could but it was our emotions playing games with us. As we were trying to get to the Park & Ride, we were glued to the radio listening for any info on the officer's condition, and we still didn't know who it was at this point, hoping that he would be ok and find who did this.

Eddie and I never made it to the Park & Ride. We, along with everyone else that hadn't already arrived were diverted to the area of South Miami, a small municipality whose borders were inside of our district boundaries. Someone on the scene put out a BOLO of a young, black male as the subject, and I can't recall the clothing description but it didn't matter.

Every young black male wandering the streets that night in South Miami was stopped and identified, some multiple times even though they were told why and to go home, yet some continued to hang out on the street. We were going to find who did this, no one was going to get in our way, and no one was safe from a takedown.

It wasn't until thirty minutes to an hour after the shooting that we found out the officer was Robert "Bobby" Zore. Bobby was assigned to the CPU squad, Crime Prevention Unit, and I knew him in passing as I was an FNG and Bobby was assigned to a specialized unit, so we ran into each other here and there.

CPU worked both uniform and plain clothes and that afternoon were investigating a robbery at the Dadeland Mall. Bobby was canvassing the area around the mall when he spotted a B/M fitting the description at the Park & Ride by a pay phone.

I have the name of the subject but I won't give him or his family the satisfaction of having it here in print forever. Let me say this if we could have killed him we would have. Bobby approached the suspect by himself and got into a struggle. The asshole-bad guy managed to get Bobby's gun and shoot him. He then got into Bobby's unmarked car and drove away.

Or so we thought.

Bobby, shot and bleeding out, managed to call *911* from that pay phone. While advising the complaint officer of what just happened, his condition and location, the asshole-bad guy came back and shot Bobby again.

We later heard this on the *911* recording of that call. As I said, if we could have we would have. Bobby was transported by Metro-Fire Rescue to South Miami Hospital. Ironically, the hospital was located in the same area as the asshole-bad guy.

Ed and I along with the rest of the district continued working and handling calls. We were supposed to get off at midnight but that didn't happen. It was a quiet Christmas Eve until the shooting and then all Hell broke loose. We all were running from call-to-call now and it didn't let up until well after midnight. Ed and I even handled a shooting at the Organ Grinder Strip-Club on SW 87 Avenue. No one was seriously hurt and it was just a couple of knuckleheads that got into it.

We call that a "misdemeanor shooting." *(CH)*

In all we handled somewhere between 20 and 25 calls that evening and didn't go home until 6 A.M. the next morning.

But what I remember so vividly was this; at about 1:30 A.M. or so, Ed and I were parked at the corner of SW 80 Street & 157 Avenue in the parking lot of a new townhouse development that was going up. Unbeknownst to me I would move into that development a few years later and Ed would get remarried in my house. Ironic.

We were catching up the numerous reports we were behind on because of the busyness of the night, when at 2:10 A.M., Sergeant Trenary came on the radio and said to the dispatcher, "Advise 5000, (lieutenant) the officer's a *45*," (deceased).

There was a stunned and deafening silence in that car and on the radio. We couldn't speak and all Ed could say as he turned his head toward his window was a soft "Oh!"

We sat there for what seemed an eternity without speaking. This is so clear in my memory and I will never forget it. The dispatcher, bless her and I can't remember who she was, tried to advise Lieutenant Linnett, Unit 5000, of Sergeant Trenary's transmission. She was crying uncontrollably and could barely it get out. Mercifully, Lt. Linnett replied, "I read."

Bobby was twenty-five. He was married to Maritza and had a daughter named Rosemary, now my wife's name. He had been on the job since 1981 after one year at Metro-Dade Corrections. Bobby was born in Manhattan, NYC, on June 18, 1958.

Officer Robert L. "Bobby" Zore
Badge 2244
Metro-Dade Police Department
EOW
December 25, 1983
May you rest in peace our Brother
My First Loss

Scene 3: What Comes Next

The aftermath of the death of a colleague, whether police, fire, or military, brings a great deal of pain as well as glory and honor with it. The pain involved is forever endured by the family of our fallen. But the rest of us carry it with us as well. Yes, it subsides over time as all things do, but it's always there, ever-present but back *there* somewhere, only to show itself when it happens again.

In the week following the death of any officer, preparations are made for what is tantamount to a state funeral. The family chooses where the service and interment will take place, and the department makes the arrangements for the formal honoring of its fallen hero. Hundreds of officers from agencies far and wide will be in attendance with honor guard units from all over.

The fallen officer is guarded by our department's Honor Guard while he or she lies in repose at the church, never being left alone. Ever. The family and friends give their eulogies and you get to hear beautiful stories about Bobby and the others that you may not have known. It is beautiful and painful at the same time, but quite necessary. We sit in attendance unable to do anything for the family. This is perhaps what hurts the most. We're still here and they will never have him back.

After the service at the church, the motorcade itself is an incredibly awesome and at the same time sad sight to see. Hundreds of police vehicles with overhead lights turned on, led by police motorcycles will make their way to the burial site for the interment.

I have taken part in more police funerals than I can count or would like to remember. When the motorcade takes place, our citizens pull over to the side of the road and stop, and many will get out of their cars and pay tribute to our colleague and us.

Thank you for that.

Once we arrive at the cemetery, and it takes quite a while to gather everyone grave side, then the grave side service takes place. It includes some final words from the priest or officiant and then the playing of the Scottish Bagpipes of *Amazing Grace and Going Home*. Then comes the *21-Gun Salute* by the Honor Guard's Rifle Team, and finally, the playing of *Taps* by an officer playing the bugle.

This is where I lost it. I was crying almost uncontrollably, and the pain was deep. I get emotional every time I hear *Taps*, and unfortunately it's been too often. This may sound strange, but I have it on my phone's play list, and when the song cycles around I let it play, as a reminder of those we've lost. We all need to be reminded now and then.

Many of us were young and had never experienced a death like this and there was nothing to do but to get through it. We all felt it. The last gesture made is the presenting of the folded American Flag to the spouse or parent of our fallen. A token gesture perhaps as there is little comfort in receiving it, but important just the same.

A little political aside here if you'll indulge me; I have on my truck's rear window a sticker that reads; *Those who disrespect our flag, have never been handed a folded one.*

Moving on. The service is closed with a flyover by our helicopters and a few years later we added the fire department's rescue helicopter to the formation. The final words spoken are that of a dispatcher where the officer's name, badge number, and *End of Watch* date is announced, with a final *"09/06."* (Transfer). This service may be finished, but it's never really over and it will happen again.

Scene 4: The Numbers

Many folks around the country hear on TV an officer was killed in the line of duty and may not think too much about it. If it didn't happen in their town or they didn't know the officer it wouldn't hit close to home.

That's human nature.

But as I began writing this chapter I wanted to include the numbers of my colleagues that have fallen just since I came on in 1983. What I found was staggering.

My research led me to the *Officer Down Memorial Page* (www.odmp.org) where they do an extraordinary job of tracking everything related to officers assaulted and killed in the line of duty.

The number of officers that have died in the line since that time is 6,302. These include assaults of police by gunshot, stabbing, and physical altercation. As well as traffic crashes which are currently the leading cause of officer deaths, training accidents, heart attacks and several other causes including terrorism.

The average since 1983 is about 175 per year, with the highest being 243 in 2001. This number spiked because of the attacks on 9/11 in New York where the NYPD lost 72, right alongside the 343 firefighters the FDNY lost when the *Towers* came down. All of them heroes.

The estimated total number of police officers killed from all agencies since statistics have been kept in the US is 20,789. That's the capacity of Arthur Ashe Stadium in Flushing Meadows, NY, site of tennis's US Open. That's an awful lot of comrades-in-arms who made the ultimate sacrifice. So please say a thank you to all the officers and firefighters you meet right along with our soldiers. They will appreciate it and remember that they gladly do their jobs for you.

Scene 5: A Final Goodbye

I cannot end this chapter without talking about two very close friends that I have lost in recent years. One a partner, the other a civilian coworker. Their deaths occurred while I was much older, more seasoned, experienced, and hardened, but they hurt non-the-less and I sorely miss them.

Officer Henry Malcom "Mal" McAleenan "A Cop's Cop"

Mal and I first met in 1994 when we were both assigned to the Hammocks District. Ironically, we met during the aftermath of the drowning of a little boy in a lake behind his apartment. That was a tough day.

Soon after, we ended up on the same squad and said to each other "Let's ride!" So we partnered up and became inseparable. We got involved in so much together and had a great time doing it.

The highlight of our time together came on April 15, 1995, when we responded to the drowning of another little boy, 3-year-old Christopher Hicks.

He fell into a pool at a house in the adjoining district but we were the closest unit. We arrived, performed CPR together, and the boy was transported to the hospital. He made it! All of us on scene were ecstatic and relieved. Mal and I were awarded lifesaving medals and officers of the year for that. A great honor but what mattered is that Christopher made it.

In 1998 I was promoted and left the district to report to my new assignment. Though we weren't partners any longer we remained close friends. So much so that in 2001 I lived with him during one of my several separations. That's another chapter.

Rewind to Monday, August 21, 2000, I was now assigned to our Police Operations Bureau (POB) and was working overtime on

126

my day off. One of the facilities that was part of POB was Jackson Memorial Hospital, the County hospital, and perhaps the most critical section was the Ryder Trauma Center. One of the best in the country. While working my shift, *"that call"* came over the radio again.

Beeeeep, "Attention all units, *"3-30,"* officer down!" It happened in the Hammocks District but I didn't yet know to whom, how, or why. I only knew that Fire Rescue would fly the officer to Ryder and the chaos that would follow, so I responded there to wait.

I called Hammocks to see if I could find out who it was. Brenda, the civilian on the front desk answered the phone and said "Bert, its Mal." My knees literally buckled.

Now I was scared.

A thousand things ran through my mind as I waited at the bottom of the elevator that takes you to the helipad on the roof. Fire Rescue finally landed and rushed Mal into one of the trauma bays. The team worked frantically as Mal had lost a lot of blood and I mean a lot.

He was a big man, standing at 6' 4" tall and came in at about 265. He was in agony and all I could do was watch. After about twenty minutes they took him to surgery. While Dr. Ginzberg, who was the leading thoracic surgeon, and his team operated, Mal coded four times.

The skill of the team and perhaps a little *Luck of the Irish* brought him back. Mal had had his right femoral artery shot out but I, we at the hospital, still didn't know why. Dr. Ginzberg grafted in an artificial silicone artery and for now Mal was critical but stable. He made it! What we found out next pissed me off and all the others who are good police officers.

Mal was answering an alarm call, one of hundreds during his career. It was an audible (burglar) alarm, hold-up (robbery) and medical alarm combined. The monitoring company called it that way. Mal was the first to arrive and checked the front, and then went around back as we always do. He found nothing out of the ordinary and came back out front.

But his police intuition (I call it *Spidey Sense*) said to go back and check again since it was also a medical alarm and maybe grandma is on the floor and can't respond, so back he went. His back-up officer arrived and Mal told her to stay at the fence line and not to come into the back yard.

This officer was notorious for having poor officer safety practices and he didn't want her anywhere around him. Most of the district felt the same, but marginal and downright incompetent officers are in all agencies.

As Mal went out back again, the two-family Rottweilers were running around barking at him. Most of us wouldn't go back there with dogs that size on the loose. But Mal was an experienced dog-handler from his early years at Homestead PD in southern Dade County, so he knew how to read dogs and felt they wouldn't attack.

As Mal walked around back checking again, for reasons still unknown to this day, that officer panicked thinking the dogs would attack, and from the fence line fired a shot at the dogs at 20–30-foot distance, and instead of hitting one of the dogs she shot Mal in the groin. WTF!

Mal staggered and went down. She dropped her gun and ran off crying. Great. Now here is where I believe the *Luck of the Irish* came into play.

First, the alarm call included a medical alert so three Miami-Dade Fire Rescue paramedics were parked out front waiting. They heard the shot and came running and saw Mal down trying to crawl to them as they tried to get to him but the dogs were very aggressive. One of the firefighters charged at the dogs and created some space while the other two dragged Mal out. They got him in the truck and worked him feverishly.

Two, Air Rescue was already airborne returning from another mission so there was no delay in taking off from their base. Fire Rescue picked a landing zone and while the three worked on Mal, one of our officers drove the Rescue truck to the LZ. They were airborne in no time.

Three, Dr. Ginzberg and his team were still on duty at Ryder and hadn't gone home yet. All three pieces of this puzzle were still in place when Mal got shot. Damn! I am neither religious nor superstitious but when you remove everything else, *Luck of the Irish!* That's all I can say.

It was a long and painful recovery but Mal eventually went back to work. Mal worked the midnight shift and was getting on ok, but by the middle of 2015 he began experiencing some neurological problems with one of his feet landing him in the hospital.

From then on it got worse. Mal suffered from what the doctors described as being like ALS, Amyotrophic Lateral Sclerosis. Better known as *"Lou Gehrig's Disease,"* and he deteriorated quickly.

I was in the room with Mal and the rest of his inner circle. This included Mal's FTO from his Homestead days and lifelong friend Kerry Bathe, now retired to Michigan but of course made the trip upon notification of Mal's condition. We stood by as the doctors told Mal that there was nothing they could do for him and that *he was* going to die. No hopeful day once again, for Mal or us. Helpless, again is what we all felt.

The end finally came on March 6, 2016. A great friend, mentor, and *Top Cop* was gone. Now came the arrangements again, and at his request we had him buried next to his parents. We held a small ceremony at the cemetery chapel where I gave my eulogy. Because Mal's death had not been ruled as In the Line, there was no large motorcade and flyover. But we had our Motor Unit provide an escort and that was fine.

After his death, Mal's inner circle went to work. Led by Sergeant Melinda Matt, she persuaded the Miami-Dade Medical Examiner's Office to take another look at Mal's death and his medical history. They determined his neurological disorder was because of the gunshot wound he suffered in 2000. Therefore, his death was now ruled as *In the Line*, and that not only kicked in benefits for his surviving daughter Melissa but has now immortalized him in our *Roll of Honor* and his name was added to the Miami-Dade County Law Enforcement Memorial at Tropical Park.

Given my known relationship with Mal, I was contacted by our department's Police Officer Assistance Trust that maintains and sponsors our memorial and asked to speak on Mal's behalf at the May 4, 2017, annual police memorial ceremony. I did, and it was a great honor to do it. But I can say that it was an honor I would have gladly done without.

Officer Henry McAleenan
Badge 3892
Metro-Dade Police Department
EOW
March 6, 2016
I miss you old friend!

Buffalo Tom

In March 2007, I found my career "developed" and they transferred me from the Port of Miami to our Crime Scene Investigations Bureau where I sat in *"Time Out"* as I call it, for about three plus years away from the road.

I had a desk job, great fun, but it was easy enough and had some great civilian employees I supervised. One of them came to me and asked if I wanted to play racket ball with them as they needed a fourth. I'm a tennis player but I thought it would be fun.

They partnered me up with Tom Porteus Jr., a civilian employee who worked in our fingerprint section next door as a Latent Examiner. Tom and I met for the first time and now were teammates against some racket-ballers who thought they had a couple of patsies. The bad news for them, we beat them! Haha. The good news for us is that we became friends.

Tom grew up outside of Buffalo NY in Lock Port. He was a die-hard Bills fan and I am a Dolphin fan. Neither one of us is happy with our teams though. But we got along great, had breakfast every morning together, and even played some tennis. He wasn't very good but was an exceptional athlete so he made up for it.

He was also a died-in-the-wool hockey player and loved the Buffalo Sabres. Hence the name on both accounts *"Buffalo Tom."* I used to kid him he lived so far north he sometimes spoke like a Canadian, Aye!

During our friendship I learned Tommy was diabetic since he was seven years old and was dependent on insulin. Tom was living with a roommate and coworker Igor, and eventually moved out into his own place in Pembroke Pines, a town just north of us in Broward County and about thirty minutes from me if traffic moved. Being on his own again, Tommy had an arrangement with his parents, Charlene and Tom Sr. who lived in Lock Port, to call every morning when he woke up to let them know he was ok. Tommy tended to let his blood sugar drop and pass out. If you are familiar with diabetes you know this is not good.

One Sunday afternoon during the fall of 2012 as I was getting ready to watch my Dolphins play, Tom Sr. called me and said that he couldn't get in touch with Tommy and was very concerned about his condition. He asked if I could go and check on him. I jumped into my patrol car and ran a *"3"* to the Pines.

I called Pines Police & Fire on my way and told them to break the door down if necessary if they arrived before I did. They arrived and banged on the door and Tommy finally answered. He was in diabetic shock but they got to him in time. He was treated and I took him shopping to get some food as his fridge didn't have what it should have, especially given his condition. He recovered but from then on I had a key to his house.

It happened once again and again he was ok. But on September 28, 2014, at around 1:00 p.m. while I was getting ready to watch another Dolphin game, I got another call from Tom Sr. He said that Tommy had been sick with a bad flu and he hadn't spoken with him since the morning. He told me a hockey teammate of his *"Buffalo Dan,"* another Buffalo area transplant, was outside of the house but had no key and couldn't get a response from Tommy.

I got into my patrol car and did Warp-9 to his house. I found Dan banging on the door calling for him. I introduced myself, opened the door, and flew up the stairs to Tommy's bedroom. "He's not in bed, shit!" I checked the other rooms, nothing. I ran back downstairs and found him lying on the sofa wearing shorts and curled up in the fetal position.

I looked into his eyes and touched him; oh shit! I told Dan to get him to the floor. I ran to my car, called Pines *911* and told them who I was and what I had. I advised to "start police and rescue I'm doing CPR." I grabbed my defibrillator and ambu bag and ran back inside.

Danny was in shock seeing Tommy like that. He was an air traffic controller and had never done CPR so I gave him a crash-course in rescue-breathing with the bag and coached him through it.

I started compressions and was hitting it hard while I was cursing out Tommy for not being more careful. I saw his eyes and wasn't hopeful as I've seen this look before. Pines police and fire arrived, and the paramedics took over. After about fifteen minutes they transported him to Memorial West, the closest hospital but it was a good one.

After a while, the ER doctor came out and told us that he gave Tommy insulin and because of the chest compressions I did he was able to get his heart started, but he didn't know how long he had been down. I knew. I saw his eyes. Another short time had passed and the doc gave us the bad news. Tommy didn't make it. He was 39.

I now had to make the toughest phone call of my life and tell Tom Sr. his son was dead. I didn't know what to say but to just say it. Sr., as we call him, took it like a trooper. He knew as did I.

Sr. is a Vietnam Vet and no stranger to this but this was *his* Boy. We got through that call and now I had to call Tommy's ex-wife. She was in Orlando with their son Dillon at Disney World celebrating his 9th birthday, which was the next day. I had to speak with a woman I had never met and tell her her son's father had just died. She of course was quite upset and now had to drive four hours back home to the hospital with her son who would be asking what happened. No easy day for any of us. And I say it that way because the people left behind are the ones that suffer.

I made the notifications to our department and Tommy's coworkers and supervisors began showing up. For the rest of the afternoon and evening I had to keep telling everyone what happened. They all thanked me for what I did but it wasn't what I wanted to hear. I went home at about 9:00 p.m. that night and after having held it together all day I finally broke down in my wife Rosy's arms. It hurt. I later ran into the director of our Psychological Services Bureau, Dr. Scott Allen, who told me that everyone is going to have a need to thank me for what I did but it's not what I would want to hear, and he was right. But they all did.

We had a service at work for Tommy and later that week Rosy and I, Igor, Buffalo Dan, and several of Tommy's coworkers flew to Buffalo and drove to Lock Port for the formal services. I was in uniform so I joined the honor guard officer from the Niagara Sheriff's Department who accompanied us to stand watch over Tommy.

At the grave site I presented Tommy's mother Charlene with a folded American Flag and said those words that are always said;

"On behalf of the Miami-Dade Police Department and a grateful nation…" The Forensic Services Bureau later named the fingerprint lab in Tommy's name which was very nice. He was loved and respected by everyone who knew him. I'm not just saying that. It's true.

Losing a close friend and especially someone so young has been difficult. We all miss Tommy very much. The only silver lining in this if you can say there is one, is that Rosy and I have become very close to Tom Sr. and Charlene and think of them as another set of parents, and they too think of us as their kids. Sr. and I talk frequently about politics, work, and he is a reserve officer for the Niagara Sheriff's Department and maintains their boats and helicopters and is a Dolphin fan as well. Though not so much these days. Tommy's gift and legacy to Rosy and me.

Thomas Charles Porteus Jr.
"Buffalo Tom"
Badge 6744
Miami-Dade Police Department
EOW
September 28, 2014
Go Bills!

Act -10 Shift - Work

Scene 1: We'll Leave the Light On for Ya!

There are some jobs in society that are not a *9 to 5* like most and by their very nature require their personnel and resources to work 24/7 - 365. Some that come to mind are hospitals of course, illness and injury never take a break. Fire Rescue - see that last reason among many others.

Our deployed military and base security personnel, your state, county, and city public works and utilities because the lights have to be kept on, and of course the police. Crime and mayhem never take a break as well.

When we come into police work we are told by those who hired and trained us prior to and during the academy we will be required to work multiple shifts during the course of our careers which include afternoon and midnight shifts, weekends and holidays. While we were in the academy we trained on dayshift with weekends off. Not bad, but we were told to enjoy it as it wasn't going to last.

Once we graduated we started our *FTO Phases* with a training officer as I had outlined earlier. My first shift was afternoons from 1400 to 2200 hours. This was particularly good for me because I always hated waking up before the roosters did and wasn't a morning person at all.

Afternoon shift was always my favorite, and I enjoyed the transition from day into evening and still do to this day. Afternoons are the busiest shift because you have rush-hour, people being home and getting on one another's nerves, and partygoers that take us into the night.

Robberies are prevalent during the evening as well as burglaries-in-progress, even though most people are home. Go figure. And another thing that happens often in the evening depending on where you work is the shootings. It seems that asshole-bad guys like to do a lot of their work in the evening as well, probably under the cloak of darkness. This keeps us pretty busy and I can honestly say many, many times working the evening shift I didn't want to go home. I was having so much fun and couldn't believe I was getting paid for this.

One of the great things we used to have in the early days before take-home cars, (a personally assigned patrol vehicle that you were authorized to drive home) was *"Choir Practice."* When many people get off their *9 to 5*, they go to their local watering hole for *"Happy Hour."*

Well, we would do the same at the end of the evening but with our own twist.

Our afternoon shifts would end at 2200, 2300, and 2400 hours for each squad on the platoon, respectively. We would meet behind our stations as we got off for our own beers, pizza, and what not.

At the Southwest District, we had a small, wooded area behind the station that we called *"Russell Park,"* named for our district commander of the time Major Kermit Russell.

We used this time to talk about this call or that one, how we got into a chase or a fight, that crazy domestic we had, or just generally shoot-the-shit. And of course drink! Each squad would report for *Choir Practice* as they got off, and the unwritten rule was that the rookies, on a rotating basis, were responsible for buying the beer and pizza for their respective squads.

Now since unlike some other departments up north that were required to report to work in "civvies," street clothes, and change into uniform at the station, we were allowed to dress at home and then report for duty in our uniform and gear.

And unlike other agencies when we got off work we were still in uniform. So how to buy beer without changing clothes? Mmmm.

As I've mentioned before, we have a distinctly colored uniform, the *Brown Gown*, and the pants have a tan stripe down the legs which is a dead giveaway. Officers from other departments wear blue; their dark blue pants look like well, dark blue pants. Ours look like a uniform and there's no getting away from it. No one wears a stripe down their leg. So why do I mention this? The rookies had to buy the beer but were in uniform.

Our great, stealthy solution to this was to take off our shirts and gear and with our white t-shirts and striped pants, go buy the beer. No one will *ever* be able to tell we were Metro-Dade Police Officers buying beer. Naaaa! But we did and it was allowed, at least no one ever made a deal out of it.

By the time midnight rolled around just about the entire afternoon platoon was in attendance having a good time. I can't tell you how precious this time was for us as it allowed us to blow off steam and bond like few can.

Friday & Saturday nights were *Choir Practice* nights, and you were expected to participate when you could. This of course would occasionally piss off the wife or girlfriend, but at least we weren't at a bar getting into trouble. The advent of take-home cars killed off *Choir Practice* because you can't drive a County vehicle with alcohol in your system.

Not just because you might be a little DUI (Driving Under the Influence). Is that like being a little bit pregnant? But just having any amount of alcohol in your system was verboten while in a patrol car so our beloved *Choir Practices* went by the way of the *Raphus Cucullatus*, the Dodo Bird. It was probably a good thing they did, but we had fun!

The worst shift for me as was for most people was *Mids*, the *Midnight* or *Graveyard* shift as it's called. These would start at 2200, 2300, and 2400 generally, and end at 0600, 0700, and 0800 hours.

The 0800 ending was the worst because you would be getting off when the sun was up and would be squinting like a vampire, so make sure you had your sunglasses with you. Mids was busy at the beginning of the night, which was the end of the afternoon carry over, and would slow down about 0100 to 0200 or so.

After that it could be dead-slow with almost nothing to do except stop cars and conduct some neighborhood or hot-spot patrols. There would still be calls coming in but not at the volume of the other shifts, so you had to keep yourself busy.

The only upside to mids was the lack of traffic. In Miami, like other large cities and counties, it is impossible to navigate during days and afternoons, but at night its clear sailing. Getting around was quick and easy because you can drive faster without traffic.

But beware of the DUI that isn't going to stop at the intersection when you're going through it. Many officers have been involved in crashes with DUIs on mids, either while driving through the aforementioned intersections, or when on a *"19," Traffic Stop,* and the idiot plows right into the rear of the patrol car. The red and blue lights deter most motorists and they avoid the cruiser. Not the DUI, oh no, this guy or gal is *attracted* to the lights and makes a beeline right for them. Pow! Some officers have been killed by DUIs like this and most get minor to serious injuries. Either way it's a bad ending.

<u>Scene 2: Copping Some "Zs"</u>

Now anyone who ever worked a midnight shift, albeit nurses, doctors, bus drivers, the guy tending the draw bridge, anyone, at some point is going to need to close their eyes, cops are no different.

Fire Fighters are the exception to this because they work a 24-hour shift, 24-On/48-Off as they call it, and when not running a call get to sleep in their bunks at the station house. Some stations are quieter than others, but busy stations and especially the paramedic squad, *Rescue*, are getting called out all night. That can be very hard on them but they do get to sleep now and then, we can't.

I had a tough time during my night tours and at times experienced some trouble even functioning. If anyone tells you they've never slept during the night shift, except for that odd-ball vampire who could live at night, they're lying.

You spend your entire life prior to your career being up during the day and sleeping at night. Now you have to change your entire way of living to accommodate working nights. Your sleeping and eating schedules are completely screwed up. Try sleeping during the day with family at home, loud neighbor's kids playing, grass cutting going on, deliveries at the door, and the phone going off.

Just sleeping during the day light hours is tough for a lot of folks. In order to get some sleep when I lived in my townhouse, I actually put a sign on the front door that stated, *Sleeping Policeman-Knock at Your Own Risk."* The interruptions were endless!

I could not function and every once in a while I would meet up with a squad mate, most of us did this, and we would find a secluded spot away from everyone and everything, and park *Adam-69*. Harkening back to the days of the TV show *Adam-12* for the name, we'd park driver's door to driver's door, hence the *"69,"* and one of us would sleep for an hour while the other one sat watch and listened for the radio call. The bosses knew this was happening and it had their tacit approval because some of us needed it and many of them did it during their time as officers as well. But sometimes you would wake up and find your buddy who was supposed to be standing watch catching flies instead. Nice going!

What added to the misery of midnights was having to go to court the next morning. You're already dead-tired and now you have to make a court appearance in either Traffic Court where the violator didn't show up, or a criminal case where you knew it wasn't going to go to trial yet you were required to be there.

And if the case did go, forget getting any sleep that day because by the time you make it home it might be time to eat, shower, and go back to work. Now tell me again how you would never catch some Zs on-duty. Liar!

Scene 3: Seniority - You Either Have It or You Don't

What comes with shift work for any of the professions I mentioned, but especially ours, is having to work weekends, holidays, and special occasions. The way most departments schedule their shifts is on a semi-permanent, but rotating basis.

Our shifts—what we call a "Shift"—is a four-month period of time beginning in early January and goes for three months until the next one. These coincide with the class semester schedule of Miami-Dade College so if you want to continue your education you can work your shifts around the semesters. Pretty smart!

During that time you are on the same squad with the same sergeant and squad mates and have the same days off. Very few uniform squads have weekends off, so each squad has a different piece of the week off because of the necessity to cover the 24/7 requirement of the job. Not everyone can have weekends or even a piece of the weekend. One squad would have Friday/Saturday or Sunday/Monday off. These were the *senior squads*. Others would have Tuesday/Wednesday off and these were the *junior* squads.

What do I mean by *senior* and *junior*? Most departments, by contract, have their shifts set up based on seniority. That means every four months you get to *bid* for the squad you want to be on. You may want to have good days off, be with a buddy, or you like a particular sergeant, so you would bid based on your seniority.

We work, for the most part, an eight-hour shift as do many agencies. Some work "*4/3s,*" meaning four ten-hour shifts with three days off.

And some work *"12s"* which are two, twelve-hour shifts on, and then two off, constantly rotating your days off. Some cops like it, most don't.

The bidding process starts with the most senior officer in the district. He or she bids No. 1 and they get what they want because they are at the top of the food chain. The No. 2 then bids and so on. The same works for sergeants and lieutenants.

This process continues until everyone has bid and every squad position has been filled. When you come out of the academy and eventually get cut loose on your own, you are at the bottom of the totem pole and are lower than whale shit, so no seniority.

As time goes on your seniority increases as long as there are other rookies coming out behind you and they're now the whale shit while you moved up in the intestinal tract *(CH)*. By virtue of being very low in seniority you get the leftovers and could be relegated to mids or afternoons for some time.

Seniority is everything to us so as you move up your shift prospects improve unless you like midnights with Wednesday and Thursday off so you keep bidding for that. Most prefer days or afternoons with at least a piece of the weekend.

I myself have had Sunday & Monday off for a good portion of my career and I liked it. But in the beginning as a young officer and later as a rookie sergeant, I had lousy days off. Yes, when you go up in rank you go back to the bottom of the seniority ladder and start over.

When I was just out of my rookie year and bidding for the fall shift of 1984 beginning at the end of August, I looked at my prospects and chose to work the front desk at Station 5 because I was staring at mids again and didn't care to do that.

The front desk or Desk Operations Center (DOC) sounds important doesn't it, had the 1500-2300, schedule available with Sunday & Monday off. And what comes every fall? Football Season! So I jumped at the chance and didn't have to work mids again.

I didn't do any police work while *"Riding the Pine"* as we call it, but at least I slept at night and had a great DOC sergeant, Linda

O'Brien. Having a good sergeant made your time much better. More to come on that.

Unfortunately, shift work does interfere with your personal life and no matter what anyone says, when you're in one of these professions critical to the safety of the public, the job comes first and duty calls.

This does make you miss a lot of things especially early in your career, like weekends with the family, birthdays, holidays, your kid's sports activities and the like. It's a cost that comes with the job so be prepared for it. If you can't handle this and I am speaking to the reader that is considering police work, or the rookie that just got in, choose another career.

This is how it is and there's no getting around it except for *time*. I have missed many things with my kids over the years but I accepted it and so did they. Two of them went to the academy so I guess they understood because they chose the same lifestyle. The schedule also gave me an excuse sometimes to get out of some of those parties and gatherings I didn't want to go to. "Sorry, I have to work!" That will be our little secret, ok?

Scene 4: Alpha/Bravo

In the *first responder* world, but especially for police, in times of extraordinary circumstances such as a natural disaster (read hurricanes here for South Florida), civil unrest (demonstrations and riots), or a *once in a lifetime* incident (we hope) like *9/11*, we have to mobilize our personnel to have the maximum number of officers and resources working to handle these events.

We call that working *Alpha/Bravo*, which means we will be working at least 12-hour shifts with days off canceled for the event. Somebody's got to mind the store, right?

The term comes from the designation and differentiation of the two shifts: Alpha, the dayshift, begins at either 0600 or 0700 hours and ends twelve hours later if we're lucky. Bravo, Nightshift begins at 1800 or 1900 and goes till morning. This allows us to put the most officers on the street during these critical times with plenty of assets and more importantly, back-up. When the proverbial shit is hitting the fan, the more cops you have out there the easier it is to handle things and everyone goes home.

During these times and especially during the onset of the event, you're required to bring food, snacks, and hydration with you because you may not have time early on to get food. During a natural disaster, there might not be any restaurants or stores open.

Being self-sufficient is important when we're mobilized into what we call *Mobile Field Force* down here. These are platoons of officers who respond to areas around the County for civil disturbances and handle crowd control and looting incidents.

In this configuration what you bring with you may be all you have to eat until the next day. When we mobilize for a protracted event, days and sometimes into weeks, the departments eventually stand-up units for food and supplies and have them delivered to where you're deployed. But do you want to wait 8, 10, and twelve hours or more to eat? I think not, so it's important that you prepare a kit to take with you.

I have been mobilized many times during my career. My first was in 1984 in what we called the *"Alvarez Olympics,"* where a City of Miami Officer, Luis Alvarez was acquitted of shooting a black teenager.

His acquittal sparked a civil disturbance (riot) mobilizing us for several days. No disrespect to Luis but cops name disturbances after the officer that was involved, once again *CH.*

We did the same for the *"Lozano Olympics,"* for Miami officer William Lozano who was also involved in a racially charged shooting. He was convicted at his trial and later acquitted at his appeal. Two "Olympics!" My department had its own inauspicious moment, and it was a whopper!

It sparked what became known in 1980 as the *"McDuffie Riots"* but they were named after the man we killed when we were the Dade County Public Safety Department, Arthur McDuffie. There were four officers acquitted in that case so the media named it after McDuffie. That was a bad one!

I've been deployed countless times during events both in Mobile Field Force mode and as part of my district to cover the hours and work we had. I worked the Eastern Airlines Strike in 1989 when pilots and flight attendants picketed in front of the then called

Doral Country Club, now the Trump National. Eastern later went under.

The Summit of the Americas in 1994 was held at the Vizcaya Museum and Gardens. Leaders of the western hemisphere came together to hammer out trade deals. This led to the summit called the Free Trade Area of the Americas held in 2003. The event was huge and this time I was part of the Mobile Field Force Training Committee as an adviser to the Task Force II commander, Captain Ruben Galindo. I was there like all of my fellow committee instructors to advise on tactics that may be deployed as needed for the crowds.

The committee trained over 1200 officers during the four months preceding the summit, and because of its controversial policies according to anti-free trade activists, we prepared well for what might come.

We were out there for almost a week and had some fireworks where many arrests were made and tear gas was deployed. It was enjoyed by all. Some of these anarchists who came here just to cause problems thought they could destroy our downtown Miami area like they did Seattle in 1999, known as the *"Battle in Seattle."* The place was trashed! Things went so badly that the police chief resigned.

We were prepared and would not let that happen here. Along with the City of Miami, Hialeah, Dade County Schools Police, Broward Sheriff's Office and quite few other agencies from here and around the state totaling 6000 cops, we handed these anarchists an ass-whooping they never saw coming and won't soon forget. We lost a grand total of *ONE* window! Welcome to Miami assholes!

Hurricane Andrew - The Mother of all Alpha/Bravos

The most frequent reason we mobilize is for a natural disaster and in South Florida that means hurricanes. Other regions around the US have forest fires, earthquakes, mudslides, and perhaps the worst, tornadoes. Of these, perhaps fires last the longest and depending how close to a city they get, might mobilize the police for a few days or so.

But in Miami, we get to see the storm coming and have procedures in place to mobilize and handle what is about to hit us. As is with any department's procedures, they come from *Lessons Learned*, and our hurricane response plan was a very painful and hard taught one borne from *Hurricane Andrew* which hit us on August 24, 1992.

The Metro-Dade Police Department at the time didn't really have a plan in place for handling a hurricane response as we do now. The plan was to hope the storm would turn and hit somewhere else. We still do that today as does everyone else, but now we prepare.

When *Hurricane Andrew* was coming across the Atlantic, we didn't really pay much attention to it as the forecast models of the time had it veering away from us to the north. The public and police agencies were not too concerned and went on about our business as usual.

Big Mistake!

Andrew suddenly made a hard left two days out, headed right for us, and kicked into overdrive. What? So now the National Hurricane Center, which is located here in Miami, told us we better get prepared,. Even worse, *Andrew* was a Cat-5 storm. Category 5 is the highest rating given to hurricanes whose wind speeds are over 157 mph.

Andrew ended up hitting us with sustained winds of over 175, and gusts of over 200. "Holy Catastrophe Batman!" And it was. The department was now scrambling to get us prepared and mobilized.

On the day before, Sunday, August 23rd, my wife at the time and I were hosting a christening and luncheon for our three children. But during the lunch, everyone was getting more concerned (read scared shitless) and we had to cut it short so folks could prepare their homes.

I was going to be mobilized that night so time was extra short. We all went home and tried to "secure" our homes. Have you ever seen masking tape on windows in an X pattern? We all did this believing that would somehow prevent the widows from shattering. Man did everyone find out different! I did what I could and by 2200 was at work.

By this time, my assignment was the Hammocks District as an officer and closer to home. We were paired up and sent to the *Don Carter Bowling Lanes* to use as our shelter when the order was issued.

No more patrols after 30-40 mph sustained winds. Gary Schmiddenger (RIP) and I partnered up. We did some patrol for a little while and when we got the word reported to the bowling alley. Almost the entire Bravo Shift was sheltered there.

We had a brand new, concrete station but were sent to Don Carter's? It was well after midnight and we were all glued to the TVs, watching the reports as the storm neared.

Dwight Lauderdale was on WPLG-Channel 10, whom I later played tennis with, nice gentleman, and Brian Norcross was on WTVJ-Channel 6, who became very well known for his coverage of Hurricane Andrew, were calling the play-by-play, and we watched intensely.

The wind was howling like no one's business. When tornado survivors say it sounds like a train, believe them. A hurricane of this magnitude is a giant-sized tornado and stretches for miles across, and as with *Andrew*, spawned hundreds of tornadoes inside of it. Talk about trains! We stepped outside to see it for ourselves at what we were told was more or less the height of the storm, and we saw a Florida Highway Patrol trooper driving down Kendall Drive. How stupid was that?

Back inside we were all just waiting around, taking turns on the pay phones by the front doors calling home to check on our families. Gary lost contact with his wife and the last thing she told him was that they lost a window. Gary panicked, jumped into a cruiser and tried to make it out of the parking lot when one of the aluminum light poles came down in front of him. He quickly turned around and parked the car. This is getting fucking real now!

All we could do was sit tight and hope. I don't recall exactly what time it was but first, we could hear the air conditioning units rolling across the roof. Yes, torn from their mounts and gone! Then the skylights blew out. Pow! Then as several officers were on the phones by the front glass doors, we heard a Wooosh! Wooosh! And then a loud crash of glass, BANG!!!

When this happened all the officers on the phones were running and diving for cover. The rest of us were diving under tables. We thought the whole place was coming down around us. Big tough cops hiding under tables like scared little girls. Well, we were and there's no denying it. We'd never been through this before and didn't know what was happening. A strong gust of wind sucked the full, double set of glass doors, frame and all, out of the building and threw them over the police cars parked nearby.

If you've ever doubted the strength of a hurricane, this would have made a believer out of you. The TV signals were lost as well so now we're in a news black-out. When we realized we weren't going to die, we just hung on for the rest of the night.

Daybreak came and we had lost all communications with our dispatcher and station. We thought we were in the storm's eye, so the supervisors sent out a search party to try to make it back to the station. We didn't know how they were and they didn't know how we were. Keep in mind this same scenario is playing out all over southern Dade County at each of our other stations.

Gary and I were "volun-picked" to go. We mounted up and made our way west on Kendall Drive. When I tell you it looked like a bomb had gone off I am not exaggerating. It destroyed all of the businesses and debris was all over the road. It looked like a post-apocalyptic movie scene and we were just awestruck.

We made it back to the station to find that everyone there was all right, but there were three inches of water on the floor. New station, remember? County contractors, go figure. The bosses had us go back and tell everyone to come to the station so the Alpha Shift could go out, and we were to go home, get some rest and report back at 1200. I dropped Gary off at home, his family was ok, and I went home myself.

When I pulled into my townhome complex's parking lot, I drove into eight inches of water. Then I saw my house. I was without words. The wind stripped the shingles, paper and everything else from my roof leaving only plywood. I remember thinking "what am I going to do?" My family was ok but all sixty-seven townhomes suffered serious damage, and later were all gutted and rebuilt inside.

What was amazing was the bowling alley, police station, and my house were three miles north of the storm's eyewall, and this much damage occurred. What we later found down south was unimaginable!

When we all went back to work that afternoon, we were assigned to patrol all the neighborhoods and do rescues if we could. People were out in the streets and asking us "What do we do?" We said, "We don't know!" We were all completely lost.

We made rescue calls and went looking for our own personnel who hadn't reported in. Many lived in the worst hit areas, their homes completely destroyed.

What *Andrew* did to us was,

1: Kick our ass as a society. The destruction in southern Dade County and the Cities of Homestead and Florida City was beyond belief. It looked like a buzz saw went over the top of the County.

2: It made us come together and learn to take care of one another.

3: Teach us how to prepare for a hurricane. We completely revamped our policies and procedures because of Andrew and we are much better for it. It's been said you learn more from your defeats and failures more than you do from your victories and successes. You sure do.

Alpha/Bravo for us lasted four, count'em, four months. The longest in our history. No mobilization before or since comes close. We were finally able to stand down on December 7, 1992. There are so many more aspects to the aftermath and countless stories from all of us, but I will end it here to say this about police work, both on regular duty and in times of crisis and catastrophe:

"In police work, you always know when your shift starts; you never know when it's going to end."

There's no truer statement about being a cop!

Act ~ 11 Relationships

Scene 1: "33s" - Girls, Girls, Girls

Cops are just like everyone else. We have relationships throughout our lives and careers like any other segment of society. Most of us go into police work in our early 20s, and as such are beginners in the relationship world; in that we may have had girlfriends and boyfriends along the way, but very few are married at such a young age. I am one of those who was married when I signed up and can say there were times back then I wish I wasn't.

My decision to become a police officer was very contentious with my wife was concerned and she threatened divorce. We were young and didn't really know what we were doing or even ready for it. I think there were a few factors involved and perhaps the danger of being a cop was one. The other, I have to believe to be true, was the women I would be meeting during my travels.

I like to think, and have been told, I am a good-looking guy. At least I was in my now long-lost youth, probably still had a few wild oats to sow and perhaps getting married at twenty wasn't the wisest move on my part.

Now don't get mad at me, I have a beautiful daughter from that marriage and now grand kids, but it's not about that. It's about the fact most men and women shouldn't get married at that young age. Some of us— men especially—aren't mature enough to sustain healthy relationships and are naturally going to be drawn to other women. This is human nature. Hunt, conquer, and do it again.

It's engrained in us. We are out in the world, wearing a uniform, are fit, most of us, and have that innate instinct in a "target-rich" environment. What do you think is going to happen? This is no different for soldiers, firefighters, and athletes, because in these professions we tend to be of a more aggressive nature because winning, either on the playing field or the battlefield comes first. That aggressiveness to win will carry over to our relationships with women.

How about musicians? Talk about hitting everything that moves! But for them it's "expected" and therefore condoned, isn't it? When did a musician ever go through a door after an armed bad guy or into a burning building or save a life? Mmmm. "Money for noth'n and chicks for free" right? How about politicians? Need I say more?

Moving on. I know I'm probably pissing off some feminist here but let's not get any holier than thou. It is what it is. But also let's not forget many young women can be as aggressive. Plenty of young female officers think and act just like the men, but we are the more aggressive of the species no doubt. The only difference between us? Women just have to say "yes," and it's a home run. Men have to work for it.

So now we're out on patrol going from call-to-call meeting an enormous variety of people which includes women of all ages. Do you not think women find a young man in uniform to be attractive? Of course they do. It's always been said that women like a man in uniform, and what more prevalent uniform is there in our society that is seen on a daily basis? You guessed it, cops!

What comes with that is temptation. Do you like chocolate and have trouble stopping once you've started? Well, it can be the same. If you're single, have at it. If you're married or otherwise in a relationship, you better have willpower or call your sponsor because it's hard not to indulge.

As you've come to see, I like to highlight the radio codes we use where they fit into telling a story. The code *"33,"* is used for a sex-crime incident, but we use it to describe, among ourselves only, the women we may meet and have a little *"something, something"* with. Another code we like to use and it isn't just specific to cops in Miami-Dade County, cops all overuse their own codes in the same fashion, is the code for a *Hit & Run*, a *"3-18!"*

Yes, it says it like it is.

"You should have seen that babe I *'18nd'* last night!"

"Report written, 09!"

What, you don't think that most men think this way? C'mon Man! We're mostly all the same. Cops just have their own unique way of expressing it. And while I'm on the topic of how men talk about women, I want to call out some of you, athletes in particular, and some of you in other professions who feigned outrage when then candidate Donald Trump had that video leaked where he was heard saying "Grab'em by the pussy," and when questioned about his comment on women said it was just "locker room talk."

Some of you athletes publicly said that you have never, ever, spoken that way in a locker room. Bull Shit!!! And you're full of shit if you think anyone believes that.

What more testosterone fueled, trash talking, women objectifying, place is there than a sports locker room? Most of us talk this way to each other and let me say many of you women out there are just as bad and sometimes worse when you talk to each other about men. It goes both ways and the rules apply to men and women alike, so cut the phony altruism.

We are young, mostly, some never grow up, and we're going to have fun. It's the same for men all over the world. A *"33"* here, an *"18"* there, it's all the same. I have had my share of both young girls and older women alike hit on me, and it's flattering, no question. Sometimes you look at them and think, mmm, maybe? Others you say not a fucking chance! Some are sincere in their coming on to you and with others fueled by alcohol or drugs.

Some male-dominated cultures, and I've outlined the most prevalent ones with ours at or near the top, have their own set of *Groupies* that tag along with them.

Musicians have to be No. 1 for this. *Sex, Drugs & Rock'n Roll* for sure. Who doesn't want to be a rock star? Professional athletes come next, money, fame, and physical prowess, of course. Then there are cops and firefighters.

Each job has its own followers and for cops and firefighters we call them *Badge Bunnies.* There are many names for them such as *Shield Shelias, Lightbar Lickers, Copper Hoppers, Holster Sniffers, Donut Dollies,* and just plain old *Cop Groupies.* Not very flattering to say the least, but *Badge Bunnies* is the most infamous. Goes along with *Playboy Bunnies* I suppose.

Don't launch another feminist demonstration here, I didn't make up the names, but they do fit so there you go. These women like to date cops or firefighters and are attracted to the uniform and the authority that comes with it.

Many of us work hard and play even harder. We don't have the money that rock stars and athletes have, but we have steady careers with benefits and a good retirement, plus the others don't have the authority and legal ability to kick someone's ass either.

Cops, firefighters and soldiers have their own watering holes they hang out at and these are fertile hunting grounds for these groupies, and they only date men, and some men like female cops too, that are in these professions and will latch on to them when and if they could.

Now some may turn out to be all right, but I've seen too many where they roped in a cop, and it ended in disaster. Many of these become *"Fatals"* for short, as made famous by the movie *"Fatal Attraction."*

When the relationship goes sideways and it usually does, this type of personality is very difficult to separate from. They will do almost anything to cling to the relationship. It can't be for our money, right? We don't fly at those altitudes. It must be our manhood, aggressiveness, who knows? But it does happen.

A close friend of mine had a girl who wanted to get married and he wouldn't do it. He was a confirmed bachelor and wouldn't give in. She absolutely ruined his life by making up a crime he committed and then going to Internal Affairs about it.

Yes, that's a great way to make our lives miserable. More later. But she did, and it happens more than you know.

One other one that comes to mind back in the day as they say, was where one of our guys who will remain nameless, stopped a young girl for a traffic violation. He ran a records check on her and out popped a bench warrant. At that time, we had to telephone our criminal records section for confirmation on the warrant, so we had to find a phone because we didn't have mobile phones in the stone-age. He told her to follow him to a gas station, but she instead offered her own apartment which was close by. "Don't do it!" But he did and while on the phone, she got on her knees and *sniffed his holster* if you will. Needless to say she didn't go to jail on the warrant that day and they began dating.

After a while—these relationships almost always head south—he couldn't put up with her anymore and tried to break up. This proved difficult, insert "fatal" here, because every time he tried, the waterworks and "please don't leave me" and all that nonsense ensued. Then his gorgeous, blue/black, Chevy Monte Carlo SS was vandalized, but he didn't make a connection.

He came to us on the Crime Suppression Team, told us of what was happening, and asked for our help. We specialized in surveillances so we set up on his Monte Carlo for several nights.

My partner and I were on the roof five stories up of the apartment building at the Promenade Condos, with a clear eyeball of the parking lot and his car. We had our squad staked out in unmarked cars in the parking lot for a potential take down.

I remember it was cold and windy and of course, boring but it was part of the job. About the third night in we get contact. Here comes what turned out to be his girlfriend *"Alex Forrest" (Fatal Attraction)* and keys his car. We gave the signal and the guys moved in. Gotcha! She confessed to vandalizing his car whenever he tried to break up with her.

It was heartbreaking for us when we told him, but this is the type of personality we sometimes get ourselves involved with because the little head is outthinking the big head. Lesson learned, hopefully!

War Stories - Sort of

There are two particular occasions that come to mind when I think back to my younger days and women hitting on me. I was working off-duty Friday & Saturday nights in 1987, at a shopping center on Sunset Drive that had a night club called the *Banana Boat Lounge*.

It had nothing but problems, hence the hiring of police by the shopping center's management. At that time cocaine was everywhere and it fueled, let's say, some incredibly wild and uninhibited behavior on some of the female population of the time.

I was familiar with many of the patrons because I worked it often. There was this one young girl, early 20s, pretty, that I watched come and go every weekend, and she took an interest in me. Remember the young, handsome officer? Anyway, she would flirt with me all the time.

A couple of things kept me from *"18-ing"* that; I was married, so no. I was working there and if I did hit that and it went sideways it could cause problems for me and the department, and the topper was I always saw her coked out of her head and leaving with a different guy every night.

Problems? You bet. I would never bite and she flat-out asked me one night, "Why won't you do me?" I replied, "because you are the way you are!" That ended that.

Another one that comes to mind, a near-miss for certain, was as I call this, *The Case of The Overhead Mirror.* Around 1986 I was working on the Crime Suppression Team. We discovered an apartment behind the Dadeland Mall that was being used for quite a bit of drug activity and arrested the occupants.

While on scene, I had to make several phone calls and I couldn't use the apartment phone around the subjects, so I knocked on a neighbor's door. I was greeted by a 44-year-old National Airlines flight attendant who was smoking hot! No lie. I asked to use the phone and told her why. She invited me in.

She took me to the bedroom, not the kitchen where everyone has a phone, and she sat on the bed while I used the phone. I was young, trim, and wearing form-fitting jeans and boots, and she liked it! She made quite a few provocative remarks to me but what she wanted me to see was the mirror on the ceiling above her bed.

Need I say more?

To say that I was both flattered and a little intimidated would be accurate. I hadn't yet heard the term *"Cougar"* but man was she!

Now I bet you're wondering did he or didn't he? This is not a steamy, fictional novel with all the graphic details, but I didn't. I was married, and again perhaps too young, and did not succumb to temptation, but I was tempted and later on kicked myself in the ass for not *"Flying the Friendly Skies."* No, that's United not National, but you get the idea. No crash & burn that time.

I'm not saying I was a perfect angel because I'm not. I, like many other men and women. have had an indiscretion or two, but for most of us it has to do with age and a lack of maturity. Some of you might say "he's just like the rest of them!" Yes, I am! Most of us are. No great secret there. It's just part of growing up and learning from it.

Don't hold a march on the National Mall wearing female anatomy costumes in protest of me and men everywhere. We are who we are, we did what we did, and there's no going back and changing it. And young cops and most everyone else will be who they are; young and horny! Get over it.

Scene 2: Marriage, Divorce, Marriage Again and Again

Much has been made on TV and movies about cops getting married, having kids, and getting divorced. Most movies usually depict us as the separated or divorced officer on the trail of a murder subject, drug cartel, or robbery crew, working day and night to solve the case, drinking hard, no sleep, and endlessly pursuing the asshole-bad guys, with a spackling of visitation with the kids, back-due child support and the constant arguments with the ex.

Not all true but some of it is. We are just like everyone else when it comes to day-to-day life issues like marriage and all of its complexities. We get married, have kids, get a house, cars, mow the lawn, drop the kids at day care, all that. But we do spend a lot of time away from home working and that has detrimental effects on our marriages.

Not only do we work quite a bit, between overtime, off-duty jobs, going to court on our time off, our own personal activities like working out and sports, but add in the danger factor to the job as well.

The biggest and most striking difference between our professions, more than any other because we are constantly in harm's way like a soldier on patrol in-country, is this one fact. We may not come back home that day.

This one aspect can be the worst part of being married to a police officer if the spouse is not on the job themselves. Spouses, mostly wives and girlfriends here, have to learn to adapt to the lifestyle and accept this condition of their relationship.

Most do well in dealing with the day-to-day fear and lock it down somewhere deep. But others can't do that, it eats away at their emotions and causes more stress than they can handle.

If the spouse that's on the job comes home and tells his or her wife/husband about their day and what they did, some of those things we take for granted and accept as *just part of the job*, would absolutely scare the crap out of someone who is not a police officer.

I have come home with cuts and bruises too many times to count, and to me the source of those injuries was probably fun. Yes, I said fun. We just take them in stride and look at them as hazards of the job, and most injuries of a minor nature such as earning them in a foot chase or perhaps a fight, are expected as it's the bad guy's job to inflict them in their attempt to flee and not get caught.

Adding to the problem caused by what we see on a daily basis is how we ourselves internalize our own stress. Not just from dealing with the public but dealing with the administration and other headaches I'll cover more later. We harbor an anger that manifests itself in our behavior toward our own family and friends.

Dealing with the worst society has to offer every day can leave scars, not just physically but mentally and emotionally as well, and it can make us very difficult to live with. We begin to see the worst in people instead of the good and get quite pissed off at everything and that seeps its way into our personal lives.

Coming home after a particularly tough day and then hearing what the kids did or didn't do, the wife complaining about this or that and wants to talk about her day, the washer broke, the dog needs to go to the vet, the grass needs cutting, and on and on and you don't want to hear any of it.

"I just chased this asshole for twenty minutes from one end of the County to the other, he bailed out and then we had a foot chase, he then decided to fight, I screwed up my shoulder, my uniform is torn, I did four hours of paperwork, then I had to transport this ass-wipe to the jail where the intake nurse rejected him for a cut on his hand, now I had to take him to the hospital for a medical clearance, back to jail, and then back to the station to drop off the car."

And do you think that I want to hear about a fucking washing machine? Can you feel the stress? I need a beer. Or two, or three, etc. This is what can happen to us and it can ruin a marriage. Police officers have so many other factors going on in their lives that impact who they are and their loved ones as well. We don't mean for it to happen but of course it does.

I'm just pointing this out because it is the baggage that comes with us, but it's not all bad. These are generalities and not everyone goes through this, thankfully.

At some point most of us get a handle on the strain and learn to better manage and shield our families from it. Some were better at it than others from the start.

I lost my father to cancer during my first year on the job. When I began feeling the strain and acting out, I didn't have him around to lean on like my son BJ does now should he need it.

BJ is a lot nicer than I am and I suspect that he won't go through some of the things I did and he's learned from *my* mistakes. But when I needed my father he wasn't there, and I was angry for a while. I felt cheated he was taken from us so young, at fifty-six. The best years of our relationship began when we no longer lived together because we were too much alike.

My first marriage ended because as is the term goes, "irreconcilable differences." So I got divorced and then not too long after got remarried. That continued to have its ups and downs for a while with good times and some not so good.

It was a rollercoaster at best, which was mostly my fault. The anger made me an asshole at times and that isn't good for a healthy marriage, add in all the other factors and divorce is imminent. By the time I finally sought counseling for my own demons, I was separated again, and my second wife had developed her own issues as well and it was a bridge too far to recover.

I had become another statistic. I was always exceptional at my job, but personally I wasn't what I should be. No alcohol or drugs were involved thankfully. I like to drink but never had the desire to drink to that extent. I was just angry and impatient and I was difficult to get along with too much of the time.

Now I am on my third marriage, and too many of us tend to have this track record, but I met my wife Rosy at the tail end of the turmoil and I was a much better person. She was also married a couple of times and we came to each other with what I call *"Battle Damage,"* and both of us had been through the wars.

We had a mutual point of reference and I guess as they say, *"Third time is a charm!"* She also makes me a better person because she is just as strong willed as I am and doesn't let me get away with shit. I still have my moments as most of us do, but I am a much better person for having gone through the turmoil, and now having met Rosy.

We have an excellent relationship and enjoy each other's company. She always had the travel bug and got me to enjoy it as well. We've been all over the US, have visited Canada, Europe, and to Buenos Aires where my last surviving aunt Fanny still lives.

Rosy has unofficially adopted my kids Crissy, BJ, and Lauren, and now we have grandkids she adores. Mine is not a unique story and over the decades much of America has caught up to us (police) in terms of failed marriages, but we were the gold medal winners for a long time.

To my younger Jedi Knights please learn from us, talk to each other, get help early if the signs begin to appear, and treat each other well. It will save you much heartache in the long run. And life is a marathon. Pace yourself and make it to the finish line.

Scene 3: Partners - The Other Marriage

If there is another relationship as strong as a good marriage, or is a bond as unbreakable as an oak, it is cops and their partners. So much has been made through news reports, TV cop shows and movies about having a partner on patrol and the relationship that develops between the two.

When you partner up with someone else, you are in the patrol car for 8, 10, 12 hours per shift, going from call-to-call, crisis to crisis, eating together, fighting and getting hurt together, telling each other lies and stories and things you probably wouldn't tell you wife, husband, girlfriend or boyfriend.

Your world is inside that cruiser and your partner is the one you share everything with. You see, hear, smell, and feel everything together during your tour of duty. After a while of doing that you can anticipate how the other thinks and how they will react to something, just like a marriage.

Ask a soldier how he or she feels about the squad mates they had while on patrol in a combat zone, kicking in doors and getting into firefights, and they will tell you how close they had become during their deployments. While we don't get into firefights every day, thankfully, we are together handling anything and everything day in and day out for months on end, and if you're lucky, for years. I say lucky because not everyone can partner up.

We have such varied personalities, egos, and work ethics that not everyone meshes and sometimes you can't wait for the shift to end so you don't have to ride with this person again.

Fortunately, that hasn't happened to me too often, but I had those I would never ride with unless the sergeant ordered us to. I always liked to work and stay busy, clearing for calls, stopping cars, patrolling neighborhoods, and getting my coffee. When I would ride with someone that didn't share those things, it led to conflict. I had one guy that all he wanted to do was stop girls for a bullshit infraction, give them a verbal warning and then hit on them if they were hot. Not my thing so that ride lasted one shift. Idiot!

I have been fortunate over the years, both as an officer and as a sergeant, to partner up with officers I absolutely would go through any door with and had a fantastic time riding with.

Sergeants don't usually ride with anyone in our department as we aren't set up that way and don't have a *two-man* rule like NYPD or LAPD for example, where everyone has a partner. But from early on I enjoyed having a partner so much that even later as a sergeant I would ride with another sergeant whom I got along with really well, and we would go out on patrol, back-up our squads and get into shit while doing it.

Having a close friend to talk to during the day makes the shift go by more quickly and you share the workload. "You write this one and I'll get the next." Or one likes to drive, like me, and the other would rather ride shotgun.

One of my closest friends to this day, which stemmed from being partners, Officer Bill Duclo, never liked to drive and he knew I did, so I drove while he wrote the reports. Some others did like to drive now and again so we switched, but I drove most of the time.

Having a partner and going through what you do in police work bonds you together so strongly that now your partner becomes part of your family and you part of his or hers. Not only are you together every day at work, but you're also now spending time off-duty at each other's home for BBQs and parties and the like. You become the best man or maid of honor at your partner's wedding, or godfather and godmother to their child.

It sounds like a cliché and perhaps it is but tell me in what other job people don't become close and then socialize together. We just take it to a higher level.

Police, fire, and military go into harm's way daily, and that creates a closeness incomparable and incomprehensible to any other profession.

Perhaps you may put a band aid on a coworker, but have you ever had to put a tourniquet on someone you worked with, pull them out of crashed car, done CPR on them, been in a knockdown drag-out fight, run into a burning building (no I'm not a firefighter but have done that), gone through countless doors with an armed bad guy inside, driven them to the hospital because of a critical injury because you couldn't wait for Fire Rescue, stayed at the hospital with them, drank with, shared with, may have lived with (I have) cried with, attended a colleagues funeral with, and may have even seen killed?

Cops, firefighters and soldiers do all these things together with their partners and squad mates, so becoming close comes with the job. And I wouldn't trade that for anything else. It is *always* about the guy or gal next to you. Who understands what you're going through better than your partner?

I have been fortunate to work with some outstanding officers and sergeants during my career, and they helped make me into the cop that I have become, and I hope I have in turn, given them my work ethic and dedication to duty and service and made them better as well. So I wish to dedicate this part of my book to those *partners & friends* I have had over the many years we served. Here they are, to the best of my recollection, it has been a long road, and in order of appearance:

Southwest District
Officer Ed Pena (My first)

Detective Ed Campbell (Mentor)
Detective Barry *"The Rabbi"* Savage (Mentor)
Detective Les Craven (One great cop!)
Officer Bobby Rodriguez (Dadeland will never be the same)

Officer Mark Silvia (Teacher)

Detective JJ O'Donnell (A roommate when I needed it)

Officer Gary Birkholder (BJ's godfather & what about that home invasion?)

Officer Bill "Duke" Duclo (We kicked ass!)

Midwest District

Officer Dave "Jester" Fariss (Always kept me laughing)

Officer Jorge Carreno (My First Rookie - "Hey Holmes, get back in the car")

Officer Gil Morales (Sheriff Buford T. Justice)

Officer Frank Moreno (Kicked ass & Flan!)

Hammocks District

Officer Gary Schimminger (Andrew was a Mother!-RIP)

Officer Bobby Longworth (What a character!)

Officer Charlie Ferrante ("Hostile, doggy style, any style!")

Officer Omar Moreno (Little Bigger-Brother to Frank-We saved that lady in the garage!)

Officer Henry "Mal" McAleenen (Top Cop-RIP)

Officer Eugenio "Gene" Fernandez (My last Rookie On board the *Enterprise*)

Northside District

Sergeant Jose Delgado (Northside Mulching Unit)

Sergeant Jeff Schmiddenger (Tennis anyone?)

Sergeant Steve Natale (Now take it easy Steve)

Police Operations Bureau/Port of Miami

Officer Sergio Ruesga (We are way out of our area!)

Sergeant Mike Fisten (the Fistenator)

Sergeant Mike Santos (Those cigars were good!)

Sergeant Charlie Daye (My Coach-Goldwings Forever!)

Sergeant Allen Cockfield (My Big Bro!)

Lieutenant Devon Brennon, US Coast Guard (My Little Brother)

Officer Glenn "Digerati" Fonteciella (My Right Hand)

Intracoastal District

Sgt. (Ret.) Bert "Maverick" Gonzalez

Sergeant Tom Gilligan (My Brother from another mother & NBC!)

Sergeant Dave "Jester" Fariss - again (Meet you at DDs)

Airport District

Sergeant Anthony "Tony" Corbin ("Where's one, there's the other" Thank you my friend)

As you can see I have been fortunate to have worked with these great cops, both as partners and squad mates. I will forever cherish the time we spent together. Stay safe my friends!

Act ~ 12 Internal Affairs: Truths &

Myths

Scene 1: What IA is and Why

Every organization of a certain size, by necessity, has an internal office overseeing the conduct of its employees. In the civilian world these entities are usually called *Human Resources (HR)*. In police work it's called *Internal Affairs (IA)* or some variant of that. Whichever way you call it, it sends chills through most employees when they get called to the office due to a work-related discrepancy or concern.

Though no one likes to go there or have anything to do with them, they are a necessary evil if you will, and are the police of the police. *IA* is an independent and neutral (mostly) entity that accepts, investigates, and renders findings on personnel complaints (always in abundance in police work) procedural discrepancies, high-profile *Use of Force* incidents, police-involved shootings, In-Custody Deaths, hostile work environment complaints, police misconduct, other personnel issues not handled by immediate supervisors, and corruption.

Police *IAs* are no different from the *HR* at other organizations other than the fact that they investigate armed individuals with the authority to take life & liberty, that's all.

No one enjoys going to *IA* when given a notice to appear because it automatically signals you may have, and I say *may have*, done something wrong for which a complaint was lodged or questions raised about one's conduct.

Usually made by a citizen and this is the most common reason why one would get called to appear. Most often because the police/citizen contact didn't go the way the civilian thought it should have. In other words, the officer or officers didn't do what was expected, fix the problem, or arrest someone the citizen wanted arrested or they were themselves arrested.

A common reason complaints are lodged is because a person received a traffic citation and thought it was unfair or wrong, and then calls *IA*. Let me say this to the would-be traffic violator; just because you didn't think you committed the traffic violation or should have been given a "warning" instead, is not a valid reason to file a complaint either with *IA* or the officer's command.

If you thought it was unfair, go to court and a judge will decide. That's the system. If the officer wasn't discourteous, then suck it up cupcake! You have no standing because the officer did his or her job and caught you!

The most common reason complaints are filed is for discourtesy. Now don't get me wrong, we sometimes say stuff we shouldn't and it triggers a complaint, rightly so. It's human nature to lose one's cool with someone and say something you shouldn't, like curse at them.

Dealing with the crap that we do and the people who give us a hard time, one can say something less than polite and then a complaint is filed which has to be investigated. Fine. It's happened to me where I probably shouldn't have said what I said but believe me when I tell you the person had it coming.

I apologize if I did yell at someone but it was in the interest of public safety, not personal. There are so many more times that discourtesy complaints are filed just because the person knows it's a way to get back at the officer. Do you like being called on the carpet for anything? No, no one does. But we have to keep ourselves in line and do our best to stay above the fray. We make mistakes like everyone else.

Complaint Story

It was about 1995 when I was working the Hammocks District on the day shift. We just broke roll call at 0730. I headed south to my squad's patrol area to meet up for coffee. I took SW 142 Ave and, just south of 120th Street, a car came out of the side street running the Stop Sign and cut me off.

I "*19'd*" the vehicle and found a mother and daughter on their way to school. When I walked up to the car the first thing mom said to her daughter, and it was meant for me to hear, was; "Looks like you're going to be late now," with the obligatory attitude of course.

So I knew right off this wasn't going to go well. I asked for the "license & registration please." What I got was the "Why did you stop me" question. I followed up with "Don't you know?" Of course she said no. When I told her she denied it and hesitated on handing me her information. When I finally received it I went back to my car to fill out the *diploma* as I call it, because she just graduated from warning to citation, and I asked for a back-up reference "an attitude." Lessons learned from the past. Always have a back-up witness for when things go south. No cameras in those days to show what an asshole the violator was.

The dispatcher sent me my *"15"* and informed me that the vehicle's tag was expired several days now, citation No. 2! When my back-up officer Zeta Cabado and I returned to the car to issue the citations, Mother-of-the-Year was refusing to sign the tickets, which at that time was a criminal violation that could result in an arrest and the suspension of the driver's license.

That was the last thing I wanted to do. It took me almost 10 minutes to convince her that she didn't want to suffer the consequences for refusal to sign and finally, after snatching the ticket book out of my hand, signed the diplomas, I mean citations. Zeta was livid and wanted to *"39"* her. This woman was entitled and nasty. Oh well, on to coffee and work. But wait, there's more…

A couple of hours later I received a message from the dispatcher to call an officer from headquarters. I'll call him *Rob Shrub*. I knew the name but didn't know *him*. He asked me if it was me who had stopped a woman that morning by the name of my violator, and I said I did.

He said he knew her and she did outside work for our department. I said that's all well and good and went on to tell him how she treated me and Zeta. He didn't come right out and ask, but he was looking for me to "take care" of the tickets. Yes, we do that for each other whether it's family or close friends and if, and this is a big *IF,* the violations were minor, and we didn't get an attitude and hard time from them. If they made it difficult all bets are off and most officers understand that. So *Officer Shrub* didn't ask and I didn't offer. Case closed, or so I thought.

Several weeks later I got a notice to appear at *Internal Affairs* as a "subject officer," meaning I'm the target of said complaint. I had to give a statement because I was allegedly discourteous. WTF! So I contacted my union, the Police Benevolent Association (PBA), and request legal representation. We are entitled to legal counsel just like everyone else, even for a non-criminal matter.

My PBA attorney and I met at the *IA* office for my statement. The *IA* sergeant and court reporter swear me in, and the questioning began.

This woman alleged I was discourteous to her, cursed at her, and treated her like a criminal. I answered as to what I did and didn't do and explained how it was just the opposite and the treatment of me and Officer Cabado.

When I mentioned Zeta's name, the sergeant didn't even know there was another officer involved and now had to bring her in as a "witness officer" for her statement. Poor homework on his part. The dispatch records show that Zeta was my *"15."*

At the end of the questioning, the sergeant asked me if I had left anything out or if there was anything I wanted to add. "Now that you ask…" There was, and I proceeded to tell the sergeant that *Officer Rob Shrub* had reached out to me about the traffic stop and inquired as to the circumstances surrounding it, and that the violator did some work for our department.

Now if I had a camera so you could see the look on both the sergeant and my attorney's faces. Why? Because they both thought I was about to throw *Officer Shrub* under the bus by stating that he had asked me to *"take care"* of the tickets. You could hear a pin drop in that interview room. If I said he did, that would have made him a "subject officer" because it's against department policy to take care of tickets, of course, and he would be brought in for that alleged violation which I wouldn't do.

After a pause for dramatic effect because I was quite pissed I was there, I stated *Shrub* did not ask me to take care of the tickets, which he didn't (though he was probing and wanted to). The sigh of relief the sergeant and my attorney let out was priceless.

But by mentioning *Officer Shrub's* name in my statement the sergeant now had to bring him in for a statement about *his* involvement. He knew full well he should have talked her out of the complaint after I explained her behavior to him, or he encouraged her to file one.

Either way he involved himself and didn't protect a fellow officer against a bullshit complaint. Once again, *Ms. Entitled* didn't like that I gave her the diplomas, thought she had a hook and wanted to get her way. Well, screw her and *Officer Shrub* who now had to appear in *IA* and explain himself.

The sergeant called in Zeta and after her statement *IA* cleared me of the discourtesy charge. Now case closed! That's the way the vast majority of these complaints go. So take your diploma, I mean citation to court, and don't waste everyone's time with this bullshit. We all have better things to do.

Scene 2: Corruption & Abuse - Tarnishing the Badge

Another and very important reason Internal Affairs exists is, unfortunately, human nature being what it is, every department at one time or another will have some of its personnel turn bad. They get involved in crimes, take payoffs or rip off criminals, physically abuse people for no good reason, even demand sexual favors for not making an arrest.

These *"Bad Apples"* make us all look bad and have to be rooted out of our ranks. This is where Internal Affairs is absolutely necessary and have a very important job to do.

Some of the public believes all cops are like this but of course nothing could be further from the truth. We aren't and we don't like these rogue cops any more than the public does. There has been corruption in police work as far back as the beginnings of the profession. Again, human nature, and it continues today, especially in countries where the police are not considered important and paid very poorly, like in most countries of the world. Sometimes they have no choice but to take payoffs just to make a living. That's the reality in the Third World.

For us though, police make varying degrees of salary depending on which part of the country they work, how large or small the locale is, so taking payoffs or getting involved with criminals is absolutely despised by good cops.

Most don't even like to joke about it but it does happen and needs to be investigated. Most *IAs* have an entity within or at least specialized investigators that are assigned to go after these rogue officers. They will investigate them just like the police investigate anyone else by pulling their financials, phone records, patrol logs to see where they have been if any crime was committed on-duty and conduct surveillances on them. If the officer is bad, then so be it, investigate, arrest if necessary, at the very least get dismissed from service. We don't need them!

There are umpteen stories over the decades about police corruption which have been exposed and perhaps even glorified in TV and movie fame. The most infamous stems from the 1973 Al Pacino movie *Serpico* where the officer he is portraying is working undercover to expose long-standing police corruption in the NYPD.

We have had our own here over the years and no one is immune to it. I personally know officers I worked with on the same squad who became involved with drug dealers, in Miami during the 80s. I have played tennis many times with cops who were guarding drug shipments.

And when I say I worked or played with them, understand I had no idea about what they were doing, none of us did.

In 1985 Miami Police had the notorious *Miami River Cops* where several of their officers, who had criminal backgrounds themselves that were ignored because of the need to hire in mass after the *Mariel Boatlift and 1980 Riots*, where ripping off drug dealers on the river and killing them. No better than the drug dealers themselves.

Unfortunately for the rest of us, it made all the police out in South Florida look dirty. I can assure you none of us cared for it. The badge is sacred to most of us. Greed and corruption can be found anywhere and you wouldn't know it. That's why it's necessary to sometimes investigate our own.

I have several friends whom during their careers have worked *LA* for a stint, and though sometimes labeled with unflattering descriptions, they did a good job in not only rooting out these bad cops, but also getting bullshit complaints tossed as well.

Scene 3: The Headhunter

As in any entity, you'll have the guy who sees bad guys everywhere and thinks everyone is dirty. The numbers alone dismiss this notion as everybody can't be corrupt or otherwise a bad seed. But there are those

IA investigators that truly believe if a complaint is lodged or suspicions are raised, then the guy must be guilty.

It's not true for the public and it isn't true for the police. The *Headhunter*, as we use the term in this context, is that guy or gal who goes out of their way to find a "crime" or some culpability on the part of the officer.

A byproduct of police work is distrust of most people and we tend to see the bad instead of the good. The *Headhunter* does this with us, and during their investigations will *lead* a witness into saying what the investigator wants to hear instead of what actually happened. This has happened as well with investigators obtaining a bullshit confession just to close a case. It's bad either way and should never be done, but it is.

When this personality gets an officer into the *"interview"* phase of the investigation, it becomes more like an *"interrogation"* of a criminal. If it weren't for certain rules that have to be followed in conducting internal investigations and interviews, these guys would be brow-beating the officer into a confession of some kind. Fortunately, these idiots are few and far in between and eventually are rooted out of *IA*, mostly.

Scene 4: Interviews - Truth & Myth

I want to cover something I've seen and heard other agency *Internal Affairs* do that absolutely pisses me off and is not allowed by my department's procedures and by US and Florida State Law.

How many times have you seen in a TV show or movie, and I will go back to this medium because it's where it is depicted both with some truths and lore, where an Internal Affairs investigator just shows up on a scene, pulls the involved officers aside, and begins to yell and interrogate them about the incident? Or they get them into the *interview setting* and go after them like they just killed someone, stole the offerings at Sunday Mass, or robbed bank, without regard for their rights and dignity?

This is not permitted, and we as employee officers have certain rights that are known as *Garrity Rights*. In *Garrity v. New Jersey*, 385

US 493 (1967), the Supreme Court held that Officers are not required to sacrifice their right against self-incrimination and cannot be compelled by threat of serious discipline, to make statements that may be used in a subsequent criminal proceeding; second, an officer cannot be terminated for refusing to waive his Fifth Amendment right to remain silent. *Gardner v. Broderick,* 392 US 273 (1968).

Therefore, if an officer gives a coerced statement, the statement is "protected," and cannot be used in a subsequent criminal prosecution. However, not all agencies follow this ruling and don't allow officers to properly defend themselves.

When we have to give a statement at *IA* as a subject officer, we are first of all entitled to the representation of our choosing. Whether it is an attorney from our union or a private one or representative, who will attend the interview with us and guide and counsel us, they are there to protect our rights and make certain that *IA* is following proper procedures. *IA* cannot interview us without our representative unless we waive that right.

Another procedure that is contained within our rights is being afforded ample time to review the charges, statements, evidence, and these days, videos pertaining to the case prior to giving a statement. If that takes all day then so be it, but we can see who is accusing us of what before we speak.

IA is a *"finder of fact"* only, and during their interviews are only permitted to ask relevant questions in a businesslike, professional manner, and not allowed to yell at and threaten us. If they start to do that, the interview is concluded and the union files a complaint with the department.

That bullshit we see on TV infuriates me and if some agencies are still treating their personnel that way, their respective unions or the officers themselves have to file complaints and/or lawsuits against their departments. Ask your questions and properly investigate but treat us with respect.

Internal Affairs is absolutely necessary, and it helps us stay on the right course. For those who think we don't police ourselves you're off base. We are investigated by not only our own departments, but by state and federal agencies, along with State and US Attorney's offices, as well as private citizens groups. The truth is the truth and it will be uncovered.

Sgt. (Ret.) Bert "Maverick" Gonzalez

Let the investigations run their course. We aren't the bad apples many think we are.

Act - 13 The Brass:

The Good, the Bad, the Idiotic & the Hypocritical

Scene 1: The Chain-of-Command

It has been said, *bureaucracy* is the only constant in the universe. I have to believe that's true because each and every organization needs one to function and survive.

Whether it's a business, a school, a hospital, the military, a local township, a family unit, or a police department, there' exists a need to organize daily operations and someone has to be in charge. Every organization has that person *in charge*. I think even alien civilizations would have them and suffer from some of the same ailments that we do.

In the private sector the head may be called the president or CEO, and those below her or him are department directors, managers and supervisors. In the military, fire and police, these are generally referred to by their rank and operational responsibilities.

For police, the head of the agency is called one of several titles: for city police it's usually a *Chief of Police* or maybe a *Commissioner* like NYPD, Boston PD, Philadelphia PD, and the California Highway Patrol. And all of these are appointed positions by the governor, mayor, or city council.

For counties, the agency head is a *Sheriff* elected by the people of the county. Florida has sixty-seven counties with sixty-six sheriffs and one appointed *Director* by the mayor and county commission. Guess who that might be? You guessed it, Miami-Dade Police, my department.

Back in 1956 the Florida Constitution was amended to allow Dade County to adopt a *Home Rule Charter*, essentially allowing the County to govern itself and in doing so, changed the position of elected sheriff to an appointed director of its police department, giving the commission total control.

This was both good and bad. The director, historically at least during my time, came from within the ranks. He worked his way up from being a *Silver Badge* (patrol officer), learning the job, through sergeant, lieutenant, captain, major, division chief, assistant and/or deputy director, to director, with some exceptions.

The *Director*, appointed to this lofty position is also under the control of the mayor and commission and doesn't carry the full authority of an elected sheriff. Meaning, he doesn't answer to the ballot box and can be dismissed by the mayor with cause at any time.

Thus, not every decision made for the department comes from him but from politicians. After all, politicians know so much about police work, brilliant! Makes you feel warm and fuzzy inside, doesn't it?

More of the good and bad aspects to this are that an elected sheriff may have never been a police officer anywhere, never having learned the job, and was elected because he or she was a politician, a lawyer, usually, or just popular for some other reason.

This could be disastrous for an agency. An aspect of having an elected sheriff few people outside of police work know is when a new sheriff comes in, that person has the power to look at the command staff and without cause, fire or demote anyone within that command.

That could be good or bad depending on the perspective of the officers below the commander. If they were good supervisors, then their dismissal or demotion is a negative. If they were terrible commanders, then seeing them go wouldn't be so bad. Just don't be in the crosshairs of the new sheriff!

The other side of this sword is someone from the outside could be appointed who has no ties to the department and owes no one, like in the case of E. Wilson Purdie, who was appointed in 1972 to *clean up* my department as it were.

According to those who came before me he was needed and began to bring our department more in line with the times. A change is coming however in that Miami-Dade County will once again have an elected sheriff commencing in January 2025. The voters decided to elect their sheriff again, returning power to the people instead of the politicians. Either way, there will always be pros & cons to how the agency head gets his or her job. The difference is *how* they command when they are *in* command.

Scene 2: The Good

I have worked for eight directors in my career. I started under Bobby Jones in 1983, who gave me my badge at graduation. I then went through Fred Taylor, Carlos Alvarez, Bobby Parker, Jim Loftus who was my sergeant for a spell in the Midwest District, J.D. Patterson who was my classmate in the academy, Juan "JP" Perez, who was my lieutenant at the Port of Miami station, and ended with Alfredo "Freddie" Ramirez III, who I have known for twenty-five plus years. I wished him much success before my departure.

The Good as I am calling it comes from those in command. I am referring to all the ranks within any department that hold the welfare of their troops paramount. Everything else falls in line after that.

Don't misunderstand, the service to our citizens is of the utmost importance as well and I am not diminishing that, after all that's what we're here for. But if you don't take care of your personnel and do your best to meet their needs, the latter will suffer.

Disgruntled officers mean poorer service and that hurts everyone.

Along with watching out for your troops comes the need to administer *fair* discipline. There will always be a need to discipline your personnel. We screw up quite often and that means getting "Ripped" as some agencies would call it. We call it getting "Written Up" or "Banged," and it *is* necessary.

Whether it's for a sustained discourtesy, missing court, yes that happens, dinging your patrol car in an at-fault crash, we do it all the time (nature of being on the road so much), losing equipment, poor performance—the officer/sergeant/lieutenant won't improve, notice I didn't mention captain or above—and severe violations of departmental rules bordering on nonfeasance of duty to the possibly criminal.

All of these things require discipline and as long as it's administered fairly, most officers understand the need for it. It's when the supervisor makes it a personal issue and looks for something wrong that the use of discipline is abused. I have worked for many supervisors up my chain-of-command who, if they could, avoided the use of formal discipline meaning it never went down on paper.

They preferred to bring you into a room or take you out behind the station, yell at you for a bit, and as long as you understood that you "*Screwed the Pooch*," the matter was over. When I made sergeant I used this method, it worked well, and we moved on.

A supervisor or command-level officer got the most out of their personnel when they lead from the front, not the back. His or her officers would follow them through any door at any time. If you showed you weren't any better than the personnel under you, you gained their respect. If you talk to them like human beings and solicit their input when non-critical circumstances allow, they will bust their asses for you. I've been fortunate to have worked for many supervisors like that, and in turn, did the same with my officers.

We've had some directors who would hold open meetings to allow personnel to voice their concerns about work conditions. In theory this might work, but too often unit or division commanders would hand-pick people to attend they knew wouldn't rock the boat, rendering these meetings useless.

These open meetings should be used to inform command of problems they can address. Some of our command staff did actually do that, but others just used it as facade and the issues were never rectified. Kudos to those who did this correctly, and shame on those at any level that didn't.

A great example of a commander who concerned himself with and was appreciative of his officer's efforts and hard work, was one I worked for as a young officer at Station 5 where I started my career.

He was the station commander Major Kermit Russell, the one we named the choir practice area after. He was on the job a long time and had been appointed as the station commander before my arrival there. He would walk the hallways and just say hello and ask how you were doing.

What impressed me the most was this; when we made a big grab during our shift or had some significant event occur, it was entered on the *Daily Incident-Log* which went to the major every morning.

Upon returning to work the next shift we would find a hand-written note in our mailboxes with the heading *From the Desk of Kermit Russell*, with an "Ada-Boy" or "Ada-Girl," which was delivered *by him*, showing his appreciation for what you did.

Those little notes meant a lot to us because it let us know the guy in charge was paying attention and was thankful for the effort. I would talk to him often and when he was trying to learn to speak Spanish, he chose me to ride with so he could practice. When I told him that I wasn't as fluent as many of my Cuban coworkers, he said ok, and we spent the next three hours talking about police work and the things he had done during his many years.

When my brother Pete was graduating the academy in 1985, I asked Major Russell if he would request my brother come to Station 5 with me, and he did. I was grateful and will always have great respect for "Kermit" as the older guys called him. Thank you Sir for your leadership and caring.

There are many examples of supervisors and command-level personnel I admire and appreciate their leadership and guidance. I have said as much to them and most know who they are. They have supervised and commanded well and fairly, and any organization would be fortunate to have them. I would like to mention them here but the list would be too long and conversely, by omission it would be obvious to those and everyone else who I didn't consider to be *"The Good."* I'll gladly leave that for a face-to-face.

Scene 3: The Bad

Where you have good you have bad. Anyone in any organization will agree and can name those off the tops of their heads without thinking about it. In any leadership training they will say that the number one reason people leave their jobs, or in our case ask for a transfer, is because of their boss.

This boss can be a sergeant, lieutenant, sometimes a captain, or the district or bureau commander. The reason I point to these ranks is because these supervisors most directly affect the majority of the troops. A sergeant has a squad, a lieutenant a platoon, the captain supervises the lieutenants, but the major affects the entire district. His or her policies can make life great or absolutely miserable. But make no mistake, an *asshole* at each level is awful, and it directly affects your daily existence.

If you were an asshole as an officer, chances are pretty good that trend will continue on your way up the proverbial ladder. Same holds true in the private sector. As you go up, you have more authority and therefore more room to increase and expand on your *asshole-ness* with less impunity. It isn't actually written that you have to be really nice to anyone as a supervisor, just not over the top disrespectful or blatantly unfair, though many get away with this.

I say it this way because we all know that rank usually gets away with much more and higher rank is usually protective of lower ranked supervisors.

But if you do act this way, your people are going to resent you and not come to you when they have a problem, and in police work we have problems all the time.

Thus, they will only show you *some* respect because of your rank, not because of you as a person. This can be detrimental to your ability to supervise and manage but you brought it on yourself Pal! And in speaking about problems and supervision, there is a little quip that I didn't come up with but is oh so true about police administration and dealing with problems; "The problem isn't the problem, your *attitude* about the problem is the problem."

Every business is going to encounter problems along the way, in police work it happens daily. Something is going to upset someone's apple cart, usually the supervisor's. I mean, that's what bosses get paid for, right, to supervise and address problems.

But how you react when a subordinate comes to you with a problem will make all the difference in how quickly and effectively it gets resolved. If you say to your officer, and it's usually officers with problems,

"Tell me what happened and how can we handle it," then together you *work the problem*. This would land you as a supervisor back in my previous *Scene 1 - The Good*. If you say something like, "God Damn It Gonzalez, What the fuck did you do" or "I told you not to get involved and cause me paperwork," (a popular stance by some lazy-ass supervisors) then you'll fit nicely right here in *The Bad*, because if this is the way you react then you don't deserve to be a supervisor at any level, period!

How you deal with your personnel and take care of their issues will set you apart from all others. It's a conscious choice.

When bosses treat subordinates as if they were inferior beings—ok let me say it, like shit—as if they don't know anything and employ the old adage *Do as I say, not as I do*, the deterioration of the unit begins and any semblance of productivity are all but gone.

One cannot demand respect or loyalty. Before long there is a mutiny and then *the* problem becomes *everyone's* problem. In a police department news travels fast and everyone will hear about what is going on with a particular supervisor on the other side of the County, especially in these days of social media, and then the reputation is cast in stone and no one wants to work for that guy or gal.

A Rebellion Story - Sort Of

I was on a squad in Midwest around 1990, and we worked afternoons but because we had a special task force operation going on we adjusted to midnights for about week. We had a tight unit but our sergeant was a complete and utter ass-wipe with no redeeming qualities that one could see.

Every roll call was a downer with this threat or that one, never a thank you from this guy and he was always looking for one of us to screw up. Sound familiar to some of you either in police work, fire, military or even the private sector? I know it does.

The station's command knew this was going on but couldn't or wouldn't do anything. We were so stressed out none of us wanted to come to work but we didn't call out sick, though we wanted to. So we decided we needed to relieve some of that stress. Since we were on nights when things slowed down a bit, and we knew our sergeant wouldn't come looking for us because he *never* came by our scenes to make sure we were ok.

Egg-Fight!

You read right. We were all doubled up and decided to duel it out using eggs as our weapons of choice. *Luis M.* was my partner and we started things off. Every night taking turns, each of us during patrol visited the Farm Stores drive through at SW 97 Ave just south of 8th Street, the famous *Calle Ocho.* We would buy about two dozen eggs and leave. Four different patrol cars would do this nightly, and I can only imagine what the clerk was thinking. Boys!

We would then set out to hunting each other in our patrol zone. We would do low speed passes on one another like we were on horseback in a jousting duel. *Whack!* Got-ya! We pelted each other with eggs every chance we got, and if you were an excellent shot and little lucky, you would get one in the car's window.

Nasty!

While you were on a call or parked at a coffee shop or other location, you had to keep an eye on your car because you were now the *hunted* with no escape. Moving was the best defense, but you had to stop at some point.

One night, two of the guys were stopped at a 7/11 off NW South River Drive. Luis and I were able to sneak up on them from the bridge next to the parking lot and found their Green & White perfectly lined up in our sights, elevated, at about twenty yards. What a target!

We began lobbing eggs at their car and one after the other found its mark. I would say we hit the target 6 or 8 times, splashing eggs all over the trunk and rear windscreen. The clerk saw what was happening and told our squad mates that "someone" is throwing eggs at their patrol car. We scrambled (no pun intended) to get out of there but we were both laughing so hard we tripped over the guardrail before making our escape.

This went on for about five nights and we had a blast. It also helped to open the relief valve on the pressure cooker we were all in. Now, I know it sounds like kids playing, but our acting out was as a direct result of the treatment by our sergeant toward us. I believe if we had a good work environment we never would have come up with this idea. Word to the would-be supervisor; treat your people well. As a whole, they deserve it and your life will be easier in return.

Scene 4: The Idiotic, Hypocritical, and the Police Ego

I and most of my colleagues don't begrudge anyone from aspiring to move up in rank. Most would want to become at least a sergeant or lieutenant if their life and career take them in that direction. Many don't seek promotion and that's ok. If you're comfortable where you're at, that's good. Many decide to make the leap up the ladder and in some police agencies you might start with the rank of corporal, but with most its sergeant.

Now you're *in charge* and *responsible* for a squad of officers you now have to *lead*, especially if you have a young squad. What you say, what you do, how you interact with them, speak to them, will dictate what your supervisory life will be like.

One of the things that absolutely frosted my ass throughout my career is watching supervisors of any rank, say, do, and dictate the most stupid policies and procedures for us to follow. Each agency has their manual, written long ago like the *Constitution* or *Ten Commandments*, evolving and amended as times and circumstances required. No need to reinvent the wheel, but some supervisors like to do just that because they feel the need to justify their existence and change the way we do things.

For instance, late in my career, I was running a specialized tactical squad assigned to our General Investigations detective unit, called *SET, Specialized Enforcement Team*.

We would go out and hunt the wanted bad guys for the detectives within the department as well as other agencies whose bad guys were in or close to our district. We also played with the Homicide-Gang Task Force on big warrant operations with the FBI and multiple other agencies.

We even did beach patrol on bicycles during the summer months at Haulover Park. Tough gig right? You officers who live and work in cold regions don't hate the player…I had this squad for four years at this point and we were very successful, were a tight team, and had a great rep around the department and other agencies, and a good time was had by all, until we didn't.

In 2016, our station commander retired, and we were assigned a new one. I knew this new major since we were fellow sergeants at a previous assignment.

During the many years that I was an instructor for Mobile Field Force (crowd control) operations, I helped him to succeed both as a sergeant and a lieutenant during the training. His first order of business was to disband my squad.

Now, we never had a cross word between us, but in retrospect I believe since I was the senior sergeant in the station, and quite involved with training and mentoring a good portion of our personnel over the years, people would follow me and therefore listen to me. I was known to express my opinion more so than others. Because of this, he targeted me specifically.

My lieutenant told him it would be a mistake to disband my squad because of the job we were doing. He didn't listen to him and the following shift change we were gone. I went back to a uniform patrol squad on the day platoon and now was handling regular patrol calls again. What confirmed my theory about targeting me was, a short three months later, he reformed my squad with all new personnel under another name. So there you go.

Now when this new major first met the detective unit, which wasn't until almost two months after he arrived, we sat in that meeting while he droned on for twenty-five minutes about all he had accomplished and how he had an undergraduate degree in organizational leadership etc., etc.

At the end of this first *meet & greet*, his last words to the group were; "I have a program, and if you don't get on board with my program I'll get rid of you." Very inspirational.

What do you think every detective in that room remembers about this meeting with the new major? Nothing about the first twenty-four minutes. It was his final comment and threat at the end that resonated with everyone. Is that how you meet your new personnel for the first time? I had never seen that happen before during my 33 years at that point.

So Major Andrew Compstat we'll call him, went on to reorganize the district, and implemented new procedures that emulated his very paperwork-heavy administrative style.

He instituted weekly "traces" as we call them, forcing all supervisors to spend a solid three or four hours per shift compiling statistics for him because he only lived on paper. This was his management style which didn't allow the sergeants to spend enough time properly supervising their squads because of the heavy administrative loads.

But wait for it; he mandated that each sergeant go by five, count'em five calls, to see what their officers were doing. What? Do hours of useless paperwork that by the way was never correct the first, second, or third time and was rejected, but then go out on the road with your squad.

You can't effectively do both.

Some junior sergeants took to telling their officers to take a traffic stop, they would then go by for a minute, and leave back to the station for more paperwork, then do it again just to fulfill the mandate. What a waste of time and resources. I didn't do it because I knew when I had to supervise my officers and I didn't need to be on top of them. I trusted them to do their job.

I went by on the more serious calls and death investigations as required, and you don't need to stifle your personnel. This guy was so bad in the way he ran the district our captain was the first to transfer out as she had had enough. Then the domino effect began and over a short period of time a good portion of the experienced supervision transferred out.

This major yelled at his secretary who is the sweetest, God-Fearing person you could meet and made her cry. He berated his lieutenants in the weekly, marathon Compstat (computer statistics) meetings and threatened them with their positions, all very senior and more experienced than he was, and didn't allow them to make personnel decisions for their own units.

He created his own point system for interviewing candidates for positions that was contrary to the department's own selection process and totally against policy. My very close friend and brother from another mother, Tom Gilligan, who was the station's Master Sergeant which is an administrative position, was not only given a veiled threat about his position, but he also accidentally found out from his replacement he was going to lose his position.

This is how this guy operated. He is the absolute Olympic Gold Medalist of Micro-Management. Life in the district was completely miserable for everyone. Remember how I said that the district Major affects everyone? Here it was. Shameful!

The PBA president asked to meet with me to find out what was going on at the station because of the dramatic increase in grievances they were receiving from our personnel. What does that tell you? So now it was my turn to try and get out.

I had put in to transfer to the Airport District every time our division chief asked for a name. Six months of requesting a transfer so I could finish my career at the Airport and in June 2017 I was again denied, so I put in a memo to see the director. I made it to the deputy director.

After I explained how I needed to get out, I spent the next forty-five minutes telling him about the work conditions at the station and no matter what happens to me, to please take care of the personnel at the station.

He sent me to the Airport, thank you very much, and he himself went to the station after our meeting to see what was going on for himself. Those bullshit traces were stopped, and eventually Major Andrew Compstat transferred out.

I went back for a visit to my old station and you couldn't believe how happy everyone was. It is absolutely unnecessary for this to happen, but it does more often than you know. Upon his arrival at his new command, the transfer requests immediately began. The same lieutenant I had in my old station under this guy had transferred out to get away from him, and as bad luck would have it, he gets him back again at his new assignment. He again transferred out. No matter where you work, your boss can make or break your work life.

A Stupid, Idiotic, & Stupid Again Story

In 1998 I was a new sergeant in our Northside District, the most violent district in our department. As you've read throughout my book,

I keep mentioning *Officer Safety* because it always comes first. I worked the 3p-11p shift and my Lieutenant, Charles Nanney, great, great boss, worked 2-10.

At 10 p.m. the midnight shift Lieutenant, Scott Linder would take over. I mention his name because he is deceased, not that I would care if he were still living because I say what's on my mind. This is a factual account witnessed by others, and it's my personal opinion that Lt. Linder was a *World Class Asshole.*

When Lt. Linder came on at 10:00 P.M., he tended to ride us pretty hard and held us over the end of our shift on a regular basis because of "calls holding,"

There are always calls being held but he was afraid he would look bad if we didn't clear them up quickly enough night after night.

So one particular night one of my guys, Alex M., raised me on the radio and on the point-to-point frequency (no dispatcher) told me he had a *"39"* with a warrant and needed to transport the subject to the jail but had no cage in his loaner Green & White. Our policy is a one-man unit without a cage will not transport prisoners, again officer safety.

I told Alex I would get someone else with a cage to transport and to stand by. Lt. Linder breaks in and says "Negative, Alex will transport. We have calls holding (again that) and we don't have anyone to spare."

I repeated that Alex did not have a cage and he ordered me to have him transport anyway. So I said "Negative! He's one-man, and he's not transporting alone."

Lt. Linder ordered me to meet him at Alex's location. While on scene, he ordered me again to have Alex transport the subject in his cage-less patrol car, whom by the way had a domestic and robbery past. I recited the officer safety violation again, and he yelled at me some more.

Not a good idea to yell at me. Again, I refused. He was so angry with me he took the prisoner and seat belted him in the front passenger seat of his unmarked, cage-less car and drove him to jail.

The look on his face was a Kodak moment, but I was not going to let one of my officers possibly get hurt because there were "calls holding" or because an idiot lieutenant ordered me to violate procedure. What I did get from Alex and the other officers on scene was a big thank you for watching their backs.

As I keep repeating throughout this book, officer safety comes first.

The next day he told Nanney, my lieutenant, he was going to write me up for disobeying a direct order. Nanney told him to go ahead but it would get kicked back immediately because *HE* was the one who violated procedure, not me. "Stupid, is as stupid does!" Thanks Forrest! He and others did crap like this all the time. No, I can't take that and I open my mouth. So be it.

Now let me go back to the saying *"Do as I say, not as I do."* Rank has its privileges, granted. But that only means that you can have longer lunches, maybe leave a little early, and do less work, fine. It doesn't mean now that you have rank you can disregard the book and do whatever you feel like or come down on people for doing or saying that same things you did before you got promoted.

There are those who forget where they came from which is an age-old adage, but it holds true no matter what line of work you're in. If your supervisor allowed you to say your peace when you were an officer, then why wouldn't you do the same for the officers that are now in your charge, instead of telling them just be quiet and take it? It doesn't set a good example and it breeds contempt. If you lay down guidelines then you have to follow them yourself. You are not above anyone and you should act accordingly.

A "Not-As-I-Do" Story

I was working in the Hammocks District in 1993. In case you didn't know this, selling merchandise on the roadside without a license is illegal in Miami-Dade County. It happens all the time and most of us don't want to bother with it because as the saying goes; "We have better things to do!"

But our platoon commander, *Lieutenant Roman Othello* let's call him, had a hard-on for roadside vendors and ordered the sergeants to have all of us either run off the vendors or issue them citations if they didn't leave or came back.

He's the boss so we did what he ordered, usually. So one morning I happen to come back to the station and my sergeant Bill S. told a few of us who were standing at the front desk the lieutenant had his favorite "Coconut Juice" vendor at Sunset Drive and SW 152 Ave and went

186

there every morning to get his shot of juice. Sergeant Bill knew this because the lieutenant made him drive him there every day, and he told us (me) with a purpose behind it.

As soon as I heard that I bolted and ran warp speed to Sunset and 152 Ave. I found the vendor who was also selling kids chairs and a variety of other things along with the lieutenant's coveted coconut juice.

I told him to pack up his stuff and never come back or I would arrest him. I wouldn't really but he didn't know that. The next day I was back at the front desk when Lieutenant Othello came in with my sergeant and told the desk officer, Juan, someone had run off his coconut juice vendor. Juan said "But lieutenant, a vendor is a vendor. And you told us to get rid of all of them."

The Lieutenant said, "But he was 'my' vendor." He turned and saw me and said "Gonzalez, I know you did it." Playing stupid I said, "I don't know what you're taking about, lieutenant."

My sergeant was standing behind him with this shit-eating grin on his face. "Not as I do!" uh? This guy was notorious for things like that and treated his people like crap. Do you think for a second that if he had taken care of his platoon I would have run off his vendor? Not a chance, but you reap what you sow.

I carried on this denial for years, but recently it came to my attention that the son of a lieutenant I did training with, Luis A., was Lt. Othello's son-in-law. I asked Luis to tell his son to tell his father-in-law it was me who ran off his coconut juice vendor. Sounds petty, I know, but treat your people well and they will give it back in spades.

EGO A Double-Edged Sword

A very important but sometimes dangerous trait we all carry is our *EGO*. We all have one. It's necessary to help us function, and it makes us or should make us want to be successful. It gives us a sense of self-esteem or self-importance. But sometimes that self-importance is carried too far.

In police work, like the military, having great authority over people can give you an overbearing personality which can lead to over-supervising, poor supervision, or bad decision-making based not on the facts at hand, but personal feelings. It can breed a sense that others are inferior to you, and you have arrived to show others "how it should be done."

As police officers, we are supposed to be in charge of the incidents we handle. Therefore, we have to order people to do things so we can gain control of situations. When you become a supervisor, you are now giving orders to those that give orders to citizens, and the trend continues as you go up in rank. That's how it works.

But sometimes some of our people become so full of themselves they think they are the end-all to police work. Ever work with someone like this? I know you have. I have an ego for sure, but I didn't demean anyone when doing my job, and didn't think I was better than thou just because I was a sergeant or a veteran.

I just knew more in certain areas and other folks knew more than me in others, and we worked together well. But for those who thought they knew better I had a real problem with them and sometimes called them out on it, regardless of rank.

Just because you have reached a certain station in life or in your organization, doesn't mean you get to treat people poorly and cast them aside as insignificant. Some supervisors are notorious for this.

I had a major at the old Midwest Station in the early 90s, call him Rodney Mc Goo, who was so full of himself, you would run into him at the station's front desk, say, "Good morning, Major," and he would literally ignore you and not respond in kind. WTF is that?

He did this to all the officers as he felt we were beneath him. He did it to sergeants as well as some have reminded me as of late as I write this book.

Well Major Mc Goo, I have news for you, no one really liked you and thought you were a pompous, egotistical, self-absorbed ass. I didn't say idiot because you are very intelligent. Idiot is reserved for Major Compstat, and I really wanted to tell you where to go when you treated us that way.

The only reason we didn't say anything is because we knew as a Major you would have taken retribution against us just for telling you the truth about yourself. Unfortunately, this is how these higher ranks are somewhat shielded from their own behavior, so we eat it. Same ole story. But I do hope to run into you soon.

I had a lieutenant at Station 5 early in my career who thought he was king. Let's call him "Lt. Ingemar Velasco" (Ingemar means Famous

God-and he thought he was.) He was an absolute dictator and questioned everything everyone did, even his sergeants. He was one of those that always looked for something wrong rather than praise you for doing something right.

He had his own policies for the platoon and we had no choice but to follow them. I was working on the Crime Prevention Unit, a squad that targeted higher crime *"hotspots"* as we called it, and as such we roamed the district as needed.

Out of the blue, Lt. Velasco orders our sergeant to restrict us to an area within a patrol area, with additional orders we couldn't eat or use the bathroom out of his designated area.

We, I, took umbrage with this as I could eat anywhere if necessary. I didn't use public restrooms when I had to sit down and think about it, other than the station's or my mother's home which was in our district. Would you?

So this trend with the cockamamie orders finally came to a head when I had a closed-door session with my sergeant to voice mine and the squad's concerns. Mind you, the platoon felt the same, but I was the martyr. I didn't know at the time that within a few short hours martyrdom would turn out to be the case.

During that meeting I told my sergeant exactly what I thought about our illustrious lieutenant, without holding back. Afterward, he ran right to him and told him what I said.

Needless to say after that we were not BFFs. I was difficult because of my outspokenness, but he rode me every chance he got. I get it, I hurt his feelings, but he could never say I didn't do my job exceptionally well and I wasn't the only one he rode.

He picked the most outspoken, aggressive officers to target and made projects of them. He took a dislike a little later to my partner Bill Duclo. Lt. Velasco is a big man, worked out in the gym. Most Latins back then had to have big biceps, it was a "thing," and he asked Bill for some "juice," steroids, because he thought Bill could get him some. Bill of course denied this, and later he got pissed at him too. This began his "stalking" of us on patrol. He would follow us to our calls and park down the street to watch us. At one call, a *"25 Silent"* (hold-up alarm) he parked down the block to watch us and when we reentered our patrol car, he came speeding up next to us on Bill's passenger side. Now let me paint a completely disrespectful but warranted picture on our part. We had roll down windows in our cars back then, archaic, I know. Bill and I looked at him and I started to back out. He motioned to us to stop and for Bill to roll down the window. Bill rolled his eyes and head, let out a deep sigh, and rolled the window down about two inches and said, "yes lieutenant?" He asked if the alarm was QRU (ok). Bill said yes lieutenant and rolled up the window. He again motioned to roll down the window and Bill again did the eye and head thing and rolled the window down two inches. This went on three times until I finally put it drive and we left. We informed our sergeant of what was going on and he told us to watch our backs because he was out for us. Why would a supervisor need to expend that kind of energy on the two most productive officers on the squad and perhaps the platoon, only because he didn't like us? That's some serious pathology going on, like Captain Queeg on the USS Caine.

Remember, I take full responsibility for my outspokenness, but I wasn't alone and this lieutenant did this to quite a few of us. If your ego is such that a little criticism really pushes you over the edge, then you first, need counseling, and second, maybe need a change in employment. I hope that no one has a supervisor like the ones I've mentioned because life is too short to put up with egos and idiots like these, but they will always be out there. Best of luck if you do.

Poorly Chosen Words

I have to mention an incident about one of our directors specifically because when this occurred, I was so enraged by the commentary which was completely uncalled for, that I filed an immediate complaint with our union, the PBA, to have the president address this with the director. This speaks to leadership and I will conclude this Act with some words on the subject, but first the incident. I am speaking about Director JD Patterson. Let me say up front that I went to the academy with him, had known him our entire careers of course, and when I needed a home and was being shopped around by a station commander at the time, he took me over to the Police Operations Bureau and I am forever grateful for that. But that doesn't excuse his public comments. On December 20, 2014, NYPD Officers Wenjian Liu and Rafael Ramos were ambushed in their patrol car while stopped in Brooklyn as revenge for the death of Eric Garner. May they rest in peace. But their assassinations began a series of ambushes against police throughout the country. This was happening frequently with no apparent end in sight at the time. Every September our union, the Police Benevolent Association, holds the *Fallen Officer Tribute* at County Hall, where there is a display of t-shirts hung with the name of every officer killed in the line of duty in Miami-Dade County. It is a very moving and sobering tribute. As is customary, the MDPD director attends. On this particular occasion in the wake of the police killings, Director Patterson attended and of course the media would interview him. He was asked about his feelings concerning the tribute, then his thoughts about the targeting of police in the US. After a few words about the ambushing of police he says and I quote; "The bottom line is the officers knew the job was dangerous when they took it."

Now the reality behind the dangers of police work; when we did take the job back in 1983, he and I, and every officer before and since, did know that there were inherent risks involved in this line of work. We knew that when trying to apprehend criminals there is a chance that we could be injured or killed because it was the job of the bad guy to try to evade arrest, and that sometimes they use deadly force to do so and win. You could be involved in a fatal traffic crash which in recent years was the leading cause of officer fatalities, but now its murder! Those are the real risks involved. But never, ever did anyone of us think that we would be either systematically or randomly targeted for ambush and assassination in the manner that was occurring in 2014 and 2015, and is still happening today, although to a lesser degree thankfully. This was a totally thoughtless, dispassionate, and careless comment to make, especially by the head of an agency. When you say things like this you're telling your troops that you are 1: Expendable and 2: you really don't care about them and that in and of itself is poor leadership. Perhaps privately you really feel this way, but keep your mouth shut when your comments will negatively impact your people especially since they had no responsibility in what was occurring. I was and still am very disappointed in my classmate's remarks. I found them very distasteful and saddening. JD, you should know better!

I am going to end this act with two last thoughts. First is a story from someone I have admired greatly throughout my life, Bruce Lee. Not only was he a great martial artist, in my view the best ever, but he was also a great philosopher, and this story from his book on philosophy which speaks to the ego of man, and how it is impossible to *know* everything. And for those that believe they do, understand that you may know a lot about some things, but

Sgt. (Ret.) Bert "Maverick" Gonzalez

someone knows more than you about others. As supervisors and leaders, you may have subordinates that will know more than you do. Listen to them, and always maintain an open mind and *know* that *you don't know* everything.

> *A learned man once went to visit a Zen teacher to inquire about Zen. As the Zen teacher talked, the learned man frequently interrupted to express his own opinion about this or that. Finally, the Zen teacher stopped talking and began to serve tea to the learned man. He poured the cup full, then, kept pouring until the cup overflowed.*
>
> *"Stop," said the learned man. "The cup is full! No more can be poured in."*
>
> *"Like this cup, you are full of your own opinions," replied the Zen teacher. "If you do not first empty your cup, how can you taste my cup of tea?"*
>
> Bruce Lee's Striking Thoughts

This last article is something I wrote as an Op-ed for our PBA at the request of its current president Steadman Stahl and was published in the December 2019 edition of the union's newsletter *The HEAT*. It's on *Leadership*, and speaks to what a leader should be, and shouldn't be. Some of it I have already outlined in this chapter because it was apropos to what I was thinking and writing, and for some time now these thoughts have guided me as the basis for my article. It may sound preachy to some, but for those who are in leadership anywhere, and to those who aspire to become supervisors and leaders in the future, I offer my views that I have learned over time by experience, trial & error and from those that mentored and taught me.

192

Leadership: What It Is. What It Is Not.

No matter what type of business you're in, the organization cannot survive without someone being in charge. That's called a bureaucracy, and those within it that make the decisions, we call supervisors. There is a hierarchy where one person is over another, who is over another, and over another, and yet another until you reach the person at the bottom that actually does most of the work. In police work, as in the military, we call that the *Chain-of-Command*. Contained within the chain are supervisors but few actual *Leaders*.

Leadership is that innate characteristic that separates those from the pack - those that others will actually follow into battle or, closer to home, through that door. What I have found throughout my 36 years on the job is that many make the mistake of believing that because they have achieved a certain station in their organization, becoming a supervisor, that that in and of itself makes them a leader. In achieving rank, as with making sergeant, there are those that believe that their officers will automatically follow them through that proverbial door. They won't if they don't believe in you. Because you took the test and have those stripes, that doesn't entitle you to blind loyalty. You have to earn it. The same holds true for the new lieutenants, captains, majors, chiefs, assistant directors and directors. Your subordinates will obey and follow your orders, to a point, only because they fear reprisal if they don't, and most orders are just part of getting the job done. Fair enough. But they're not doing it because you inspired them. That takes time. So how do you earn that loyalty?

First: You have to show your people that you are human, and in that respect, just like them. They may no longer be your peers as far as rank goes, but you are not now superior as a person and will still be prone to mistakes. You may have accumulated knowledge and experience, but don't ever act like you know it all because you don't.

Second: Don't talk down to your people. Engage them and ask their opinion when circumstances allow. If it's not an exigent situation where you have to issue orders as in an emergency, and one of your officers asks you "What do you think, sarge?" Ask them instead, "What do *you* think?" Young officers may not have the answer but *guide* them toward *that* answer and let them figure it out. You're including them in the decision-making process and that will pay dividends in the future.

The same holds true for every rank ascending the coveted corporate ladder. Allow your subordinates to make decisions and don't micromanage them if they are competent and most are. Did you like it when your sergeant, lieutenant, captain, or major micromanaged you? No you didn't. So don't be a hypocrite and don't do it to them.

Third: When someone comes to you with a problem, don't turn them away and push them off to someone else or tell them to figure it out on their own. They came to *you* as their supervisor and it probably means that they have exhausted every other avenue they know about how to resolve their situation. Whether it's work related or personal, help them help themselves. This will show them and everyone they work with that you care. Two things will happen here: 1) if you help them resolve their problem, you've earned their trust and that of those they will be telling about how you helped them; and 2) if you didn't help, you've alienated them and those same people they will be talking to in the first instance. We don't need social media to get the word around in a police station, do we?

Fourth: Don't berate your people publicly. If someone screws up badly enough that they need to be chewed out, do it privately and then if permitted, don't follow it with paperwork. Sometimes the chewing is enough and sends the message and both of you can move on. Is it correction you're after or humiliating someone? No one likes to be reprimanded and a public thrashing will obtain the opposite effect than what you are seeking. If you do it publicly, you've lost that person forever so word to the unwise.

I actually heard a high-ranking supervisor say to a group of officers and supervisors that he was meeting for the first time in his new command, that he had an undergraduate degree in Organizational Leadership. Impressive! Glad he went to college. He then went on to say at the end of that meeting that he had *his* program and if you didn't get with it he would replace you. All that the personnel in that room remember is his final ultimatum and nothing else. Good first impression. He then went on to violate everything I just talked about and is not liked and even less respected. If you think because you are in a command-level position or in any supervisory capacity for that matter that you can speak to your people in any way you choose and not expect

194

pushback you are dead wrong! Many will not challenge you because you are the boss. But rest assured that the salty, older veteran is going to reach that saturation point and will be coming back at you.

Fifth: Don't expect your people to do anything you wouldn't do yourself. In police work the officers do the work. They get the call, respond and handle the call, fine. That's the way it's set up. But let's start with your roll as the squad leader, the sergeant. Your job is to direct and guide them. But how do you do that? Bark out orders and tell them go in and take care of business? With some veteran officers that might be the case as they know or should know what they're doing and so treat them that way. With young and inexperienced officers that's a recipe for disaster. It is our responsibility as police supervisors and our mandate, to train the young Jedi Knights coming up under us and to show them the way. If you get your hands dirty with them they will take notice, walk through fire and follow you to the ends of the earth.

Several years ago at my brother's wedding, a North Miami PD officer came up to me and said he had known of me through my work at the Intracoastal Station and wanted to get some advice since he was about to be promoted to sergeant. Flattering to say the least and I was glad to help. He went on to say that he would give his upcoming new squad their marching orders and "cut them loose." I told him not to do that and he was surprised. I went on to tell him that his officers will be looking to him to lead them, from the front, not the rear. If you show them that you are willing to be the first through that door, the sergeant that starts his own case and finishes it, writes his own A-Forms and tickets, and doesn't dump any of his work on them, in time, they will do anything you ask of them. Issue orders as needed. Complete the missions as there will be many, and *LEAD* by example. So don't crack that whip from the rear. Take that whip, stretch it out behind you and tell them to hold on and bring them along with you.

And since I'm on the topic of doing your own work, never dump work that you don't want to do on your subordinates. This is particularly true in the case of some sergeants and lieutenants that think because they got promoted that the officers and sergeants below them are now their personal secretaries. They are not. Everyone in the chain has their own specific duties and responsibilities that come with that position and shame on you if you staff out your administrative work to a subordinate. Officers are busy handling calls or running down cases. Sergeants are busy supervising and guiding their squads on the front-line as they should be. Lieutenants should be leading their platoons and guiding their young sergeants without over-managing. They should be handling *their own* administrative duties without adding to their sergeant's workloads. Just because you got promoted doesn't mean that you don't have to work any longer and are R.O.D., *Retired On-Duty*. I have seen many a lazy supervisor and I try my best to stay away from them. They don't share my work ethic or sense of duty and I will not run in the same social circles with them because of that. That may sound harsh and even arrogant but I try to surround myself with people that are hard workers, loyal, and remember why we took this job.

Finally: Never tell someone "You work for me!" I absolutely hate that saying. It is widely used in our profession to denote that someone is under your supervision. I get that. But I have seen it used in a very negative and demeaning manner where some full-of-him/herself supervisor was berating and intimidating a subordinate and threatening them with discipline. For those of us that have rank, by all means do supervise, issue orders that are to be followed, and be responsible *for* those that we are appointed over. Unless you own the business, and none of us do in police work, then no one actually works *for* you. They are responsible *to* us. There's an enormous difference. Build your own business and you can say someone works for you all day if it will make you feel better about yourself. Having said that, we actually work for the public we are charged to protect. That's the job.

There is a saying that I read a long time ago from an unknown author that I have adopted as my own and use it below my signature on my email: *"Leaders are like eagles; they never flock together, you find them one at a time."* Be that *eagle* and others will want to fly with you. Let's be careful out there!

Heed the advice. It has been perfected over time by those that came along before any of us. Be the eagle that soars above the fray that leads and guides others. You'll be glad you did.

Act ~ 14 Police and Politics

Scene 1: Oil & Water

I had long planned to write a chapter on my opinion and that of most of my colleagues anywhere in the country, about the state of affairs between police and politicians, and so I write this in June of 2020 when the state of our relationship with the body politic is at the worst that I have ever seen it and perhaps ever.

For a long, long time there has been friction between police officers and those politicians that are elected in local municipalities that are charged with the management and budgetary oversight of police agencies. I have found that most politicians will publicly state that they support the police, and that police are necessary to protect the citizenry and keep the peace, but privately many of them curse and have little use for us until something happens.

For starters, many think that we are just a drain on the city's or county's coffers, and we are. Police agencies don't make money, we spend it. We are solely supported by tax dollars out of a municipality's general fund, whereas a fire department may have a "special taxing district" and obtain their funding through a separate source. We do cost a lot of money between salaries, health insurance, over time, and there's a lot of it due to the nature of our job. There're also the vehicles, uniforms, equipment, training, supplies, and the list goes on. But what politicians are really worried about is the liability we can cause them as elected officials if during the course of our duties something goes sideways and inevitably on occasion it does; again, nature of the job.

Politicians will say "we need to support our police," and I suppose many do, and in public hearings will argue for us and talk about how we stand between peace and anarchy. They will ask the head of the department what they need to keep crime down to a minimum and allocate funds to what the current needs are. But as soon as an incident happens, that support for the *Thin Blue Line* as we are referred to, falls apart because it is now their political asses that are on the line if they don't stand against us when the minority and a very vocal mob comes after them to punish us, then we see exactly what kind of support we get. Liberal leftist politicians don't like the police just as they don't like the military. They see us as a necessary evil that is overbearing and *Nazi-like* because of the authority we carry and would sometimes prefer that we didn't even exist as some do now in this current environment. If their political survival is threatened by something we did, then we are seen as expendable and all the weight of the political machine comes down upon us and even many within our own ranks in appointed-command positions buckle to the politics because their jobs may too be on the line.

There is politics everywhere and the low man on the totem pole is the one that suffers. We, like the military have a saying; *"The Shit Rolls Downhill."* If you are elected or appointed, you are going to deflect the *shit* and make it stick to someone else. That is the way the world works and nowhere is it nastier than in politics, especially when it comes to the police.

Scene 2: The Broad Brush

I have heard throughout my career people, politicians, news pundits (there's some experts) friends and family, and people in general when the topic comes up as it often does, that are not in my profession say that; "99 percent of all police officers are good." We get painted with this every time there is an incident somewhere in the country involving the death of a black man at the hands of the police. More on that later. I want to tell all of you to just stop saying that. Everyone sits on top of their little pedestal and looks down at us from on high when they say that and frankly, it's quite insulting. We are sick and tired of hearing it as if you have any fucking clue as to what it is we do, have to do, get told to do, and the shit we deal with as we do *it*.

First of all, we come from the same pool of people that all of you in your professions come from. You teachers, lawyers, healthcare workers, service industry, sanitation, plumbers, welders, mechanics, and everyone else including you politicians, though I think many of you politicians come into it looking for power and financial benefit. But you never, ever, hear anyone say that 99 percent of all politicians are good, or any other group for that matter. Never! And when we look at the whole picture of who is involved in more scandals where it either involves power, money, sex, drugs, or anything else? That's right, politicians. Someone in Congress or a city council or state legislature is caught ass-grabbing some intern, doing blow, taking bribes, insider trading, funneling or improperly using public funds for themselves. Yet, how is it that we police are always the ones described this way?

Another greatly annoying thing that *everyone* in any other walk of life, especially politicians as well as the *Cracker Jack Box* member of the *BAR* on a police scene does is tell us how to do our jobs. Yes, once again we have the only profession in our society where everyone is an expert on police work and somehow believe they are qualified to tell us how to do it. I go back to what I said earlier as if you had any idea what it is that we do. This notion that people think they can tell us how to perform our duties always comes from the person or persons that are the focus of our investigation; that person that may have committed a crime, a traffic violation, been involved in some breach of the peace, or comes from money and is therefore qualified to not only tell us what to do, but talk down to us as if we were beneath them or like a child being scolded. As a general rule, we never hear anyone say this about any other profession, do we? I have sat in county commission meetings and watched as those elected debate what we should and should not be doing, and how we should do or not be doing it. They are the elected officials of the municipality and have oversight responsibility of police, and of course a right to their opinion, but they should educate themselves by asking our department heads why we do things the way we do, and then come out to our training and especially, ride with us on patrol to *see* it for themselves, then they would better understand what and why procedures are in place, and then maybe would better qualified to address complaints and concerns from citizens as they come up, not whole heartedly condemn what we do. Don't worry; we'll give you a bullet-resistant vest to wear during your ride along so you can feel it! Police work is not like any other job in the world. We are the ones called upon to handle all the ills and tragedies in society that no one else can or will, and then you are going to second-guess everything we do? We're tired of it and it is blatantly unfair to all the women and men who wear the uniform. I'm so tired of hearing this that I think I'll get a fucking tattoo that says I'm one of the "99 percent!"

And on the subject of police reform; here is a nifty little catchphrase that is bandied about endlessly by those same politicians and academics who think they're qualified to "reform" us. In the past, whenever a municipality decided to "fix" their police department, they bring in someone from academia or, and this gets me, some high-ranking administrative agent from the FBI or some other federal agency. Somehow, because of their vaunted status as the world's premier law enforcement agency, these politicians believe that these former agents are qualified to render opinions on street-police work. They are not. They aren't cops and don't work the streets like we do. They are *investigators*, with all the resources available that most police agencies wish they had and don't, and that's where they excel. They don't answer calls for service or arrive first on anything unless they happen to be in the street and hear our call over the radio. We give them our radio frequencies for inter-agency missions, but unless they heard the call, they are not the First Responders, we are.

I don't want to take anything away from the agents that work the cases and go in harm's way. When they do have to arrest a bad guy, anything can happen and it has. They are brave and patriotic individuals that meet the challenge every day. But their administration leaves a lot to be desired as we've seen in recent years and they have tarnished the agency. I do know that the rank & file agents would prefer to distant themselves form their agency heads, but we and they are apples & oranges in the day-to-day operations, so no I don't believe that a former administrator is qualified to clean up a police department. I would like to be included in one of these "panels" on police reform so I can tell these people what exactly it is that we do. I fear though, that I would probably prefer to have root-canal after listening to them.

Scene 3: The Day We Became the Enemy

I was a police officer for thirty-seven years and in that time I have seen many changes in my life both as a person and as a cop. There were great times when we were revered by the citizens we swore to protect, and as such held in great esteem and when people met us on the street they thanked us for what we did. There were some down times as well depending on what happened in a police-involved incident somewhere here or around the country. The ebb and flow of these tides of appreciation and disdain came and went as most things in life, but now is a different time and it started on July 22, 2009. A few days earlier on July 16, Cambridge Police responded to a 9-1-1 call of a Burglary-in-Progress called in by a neighbor, and ended up arresting Harvard Law Professor Henry Louis Gates Jr., then President Barack Obama's former professor, for Disorderly Conduct. The charges were later dropped. Needless to say, it wasn't a favorable outcome for Mr. Gates and worse, for Cambridge Police Sergeant James Crowley who was the on scene supervisor. Whether you agree or disagree with the arrest of Mr. Gates, he was being uncooperative and failure to comply with police landed him in jail.

Now, 1: if he wasn't President Obama's former professor you never would have heard about the incident. 2: the reason you heard about it is because Mr. Gates called his former student to complain about the white police officer that arrested him. 3: Sergeant Crowley and his men responded to a call from a neighbor, they didn't just show up and arrest Mr. Gates. Police respond to calls; we don't make them up. 4: and what made the incident blow up as it were, was the press conference on July 22 where President Obama said that he "didn't have all the facts," he should have stopped right there, but went on to say that "the Cambridge police acted stupidly." When Mr. Obama uttered those words, he sent shockwaves throughout the country which would have long lasting effects that none of us could have imagined, and that's when we became the enemy.

If you don't have facts and yet still decide to opine on something that you know nothing about, then that makes you either careless or stupid. I can no more give an opinion on the *Theory of Relativity* than Einstein could tell me how to take down an armed, fleeing felon. If I started to explain Relativity to you, you would tell me to shut up because I didn't know what I was taking about. Unfortunately, no one in the president's inner circle told him not to say that about the police, which of course brings me to this; Mr. President, please tell me where you received all of your training on police procedure, your understanding of Massachusetts criminal law, and because you have a law degree doesn't mean you *know* the law if you haven't practiced specifically in that arena, and how dare you say that the Cambridge Police, meaning Sergeant Crowley, "acted stupidly!" You have no qualifications to say so but since you were the president that somehow relieves you of the responsibility to choose your words more carefully. It was careless and uncalled for and I think and hope that when you said that, you *unknowingly* and *unwillingly* began an ill-fated chain of events that would change the lives of police officers and their families for quite some time to come.

I know that this press conference and the presidents' words were completely out of line because in order to save face, the infamous *Beer Summit* took place where the president, vice president Joe Biden, Professor Gates and Sergeant Crowley all got together at the White House and hoisted some beers in a Kumbaya moment for the cameras in order to try and mitigate the damage. The president's words set back race relations and tainted police severely, but what I found most striking about the summit was its ending. When the foursome were walking down the White House steps, the president was leading of course, the vice president was next, but Sergeant Crowley was helping Professor Gates who uses a cane, to get down the steps. What a Kodak Moment! The "stupidly acting" police officer was helping the very person that he had arrested and was publicly and nationally admonished for actions by the highest authority in the land, while the author of those words was arrogantly walking ahead and not helping his dear teacher himself. Mr. President, did you ever really give a damn about Professor Gates or did you just use him to further your political agenda in disparaging police?

Scene 4: Police & Racism

So now I'm going to cover the hottest topic concerning police and everyone else in America, *Racism*. I am going to state my opinion in generalities and speak quite frankly on the matter and perhaps many of you will agree when I point out some things. I am certainly going to raise some eyebrows, appall some of you, really piss off others, but hopefully get everyone thinking a bit about our state of affairs.

There is no more divisive topic in America than racism. It's everywhere and nowhere. It's both blatant and in-your-face, or it's hidden and passive but it's there. I continually see it and or heard it either out on the street when I was working or on the TV all over the news on how police in this country are racist at every turn. Whenever there is an incident involving police and a black person, the race card is automatically thrown regardless of the circumstances surrounding the incident itself. Are police racist in America? Here is the question that occupies more airtime on the news other than the president, and I will answer it like this; are police racist, or is America racist? "But Bert, how do mean is America racist? I'm shocked and appalled that you would say something like that! Well, but, I have *black* friends," as the cliché applies. And it goes on and on. Are police racist, yes, but not how and to the extent that you might believe. But isn't everyone racist actually?

Birds of a Feather

So let me explain my thought process. I believe, and maybe some sociologists might agree, that we are not born to be racist or even prejudiced, and there is a difference in the two. We as children are raised by our parents in *their* enclave, and are influenced *by them*, by *their* belief system, and the beliefs of those around them that bombard us every day of our lives. When children enter school, they generally attend schools that have other kids that are from the same neighborhood, have parents that believe in the same things and those beliefs are reinforced again. We are a sum of all those influences and anything outside of that belief system is both foreign and frightening to us. Have you ever watched a group of small children at a playground where there is a mix of races and backgrounds and closely paid attention to how they interact with one another? They just see another playmate that is their size and likes to play on the same playground apparatus as they do. The same *Sand Box*. They see a "friend" and a "kindred spirit" even though they don't understand what those words mean, but someone like them that just likes to play. It is the purest form of human interaction there is, and there is no racism or prejudice involved. Just play time!

As children get older and start to better understand what words and actions mean, they begin to emulate their parents, their older siblings, relatives and friends, and if they see those folks talking and acting negatively against another people, albeit any race or background outside of their own, they too start to believe and act that way, and before you know it, we're raising another crop of racists and at the very least biased children and the cycle never ends. We all keep to ourselves and are afraid of anything outside of what we know, and the most obvious and striking difference between us is the color of our skin. And if we don't *learn* to understand the differences and similarities of others, we will never come out of our own nests and fly with the greater flock that is humanity.

My parents came to America from Argentina in 1959 and settled in New York City where my father worked for General Electric, a transfer from Buenos Aires. They settled in a neighborhood where everyone else looked like them wouldn't you know. At that time there were almost no black folks in Argentina, so my parent's first interactions with black folks came in the states. As they settled in, they were influenced by those around them, other white folks. So how do you think they began to think? Like other white folks of the time, black folks were not in their social circles and learned all the biases and fears that came along with that. As I grew up, I heard the "N-Word" everywhere, we all did. And in turn, we all used it. It was what we were ***TAUGHT*** to do, wasn't it? It's not inherent in us to hate, only to be afraid of something we don't understand or is different from us until we venture out and ***LEARN*** for ourselves how similar we actually are.

This *learned* behavior has been ongoing since man first formed tribes, villages, then towns, cities, states, and countries. This type of behavior is engrained in every culture and you can't tell me it isn't. Whites don't like blacks; blacks don't like whites. Chinese don't like Japanese, Indians don't like Pakistanis, Arabs don't like Jews, and the list goes on and on. Don't even get me started on religion. That's a whole other book. But let me not stop there; black folks are just as racist as white folks because everyone is afflicted by the same *Birds of a Feather* mentality as everyone else. I've worked with black officers that are just as racist as the KKK, so it's within all races to feel this hatred toward people that are different from themselves. It isn't a one way street by any stretch. And I will not be held responsible for the actions of slave traders, on both sides by the way, slave owners, and the Clan, because I had nothing to do with them, but it's a shame that I even have to mention it but somehow the cliché once again applies. We are *all* at-fault and we are *all* responsible for fixing it if we can. It happens across the board and no one is immune. Can we stop the cycle? Sure we can, but I fear given the charged environment we are a long way from reaching that end.

When people venture out into the world to make their own way and that generally means the workplace, they bring with them their own belief systems that have been engrained in them since they were children. Police are no different. Everyone has their own biases and prejudices and you can't erase that just because it's written in some SOP or company manual. Everyone, and I mean everyone, is going to believe what they believe and the biases are either going to be hidden or overt. How we act with others is the only thing we can control. Not until each of us learns not to hate because of the color of our skin or other differences, will we be able to move on. Some may not agree with me and that's ok of course, but you can't dispute that in the end, we are *products of our environment.*

Not a War Story - Just a Story of Humanity

I have a very close friend who is black, here we go again with the cliché, but it's what he said to me one day that matters. I was assigned at the Port of Miami and as the day shift sergeant I was responsible for overseeing all the overtime officers and sergeants that were assigned to work with us on a daily basis. We at the Port, trained everyone not permanently assigned there to assist us with all the post *9-11* security measures we had to implement. One of those sergeants is Allen Cockfield. Allen and I only really met when he started working the OT details with us and we began to spend a lot of time together. As our friendship grew, we rode motorcycles together and got to know each other really well. To understand how everyone has their own back story and what and how they bring it to the table, Allen would tell me about is upbringing. Allen and his seven sisters were raised in segregated South Carolina on the family farm in the 1940s 50, and 60s. His parents, James and Cecil Mae, were hard working folks with not much but each other and the farm. His father worked the farm, and Allen did as well, and they got by. At times, his father would sit on the porch with a shotgun to protect his family. Remember, it was the South. Something White Americans can't even begin to understand, but as Allen and his sisters were growing up, their father forced them to attend an all-white school so they could learn to interact with other kids outside of their race as Pop knew they would need to as they themselves eventually would venture out into the world. Allen told me that he as most of us didn't like anyone outside of his race but his parents tried their best to teach them otherwise. Eventually, Allen began to see that we are all pretty much the same and the hate dissipated. Make no mistake, Allen was treated like crap many times, even by some of the *Old Guard* within our own police ranks, but he never allowed that to become an excuse to act the same way. I was treated poorly at times as well because I am of Hispanic descent, so it was everywhere, just like out in the world. Either way it's not right, but we ourselves have to move on.

Here's what he said to me; we were on duty and heading to get something to eat and he was telling me his school story for the first time. He said that if his father didn't do that, he would not have learned how to accept people outside of his race (read enclave/feather) and he would never have had the pleasure of meeting me. Wow! Need I say more?

I have been fortunate that in my upbringing and the example that started me to change the way I thought, was meeting the *Big Brother I Never Had* when I was fourteen years old. At the soccer field signing up to play in 1976, I met Carlos Benitez who was twelve years older than me and had signed up to coach the very young kids. Carlos is from Puerto Rico and grew up in New York City. He is dark skinned and went through all the biases and prejudices that any person of color as is said, would have been subjected to in NYC of the 60' & 70s. He had to fight at every turn, something that I never had to, and he taught me what the differences in our lives were as well as the similarities. He was married at the time to Sandy, a white girl, and had two kids, Douglas and Heather. We became very close and along with my parents was the biggest influence on me growing up. I think sometimes and in some respects more than my parents. I learned from his life experiences and since I accepted *him,* for who he was, so did my brother Pete and my sister Marisa, and my mother Noemi who was from Argentina remember, loved him as a member of the family. Even my high school teammates liked Carlos, and when he wasn't working at Putnam Community Hospital as a nurse-anesthetist, he was practicing on the field with us. He was faster than anyone on the team and he was very young looking. So much so that our coach Marco Kirschner asked who the "new kid" was and is he playing for us? Carlos was super-fast but had little skills, so let's keep that between us. I ended up living with Carlos and Sandy and the kids when my family moved to Miami in the middle of my senior year in 79.' That's how close we were and I was and became in fact his "Little Brother," as he always referred to me as to his family and friends. Color was there, but it had no bearing on our friendship other than it was there, period! Both Carlos and Allen are like brothers to me and helped make me who I am today. I think it's safe to say that Allen and I can thank his father and mother James and Cecil Mae, and Carlos in part for our friendship today, and they all helped make us the persons and men we turned out to be. Maybe we could all take some cues from our experiences. What do you think?

So if we can't learn to accept one another for who we are we are never going to get passed this hatred in our country, let alone the rest of the world. We are all one people with differences but one nonetheless. So are police racist? Is America Racist? Are people everywhere racist? Weren't most of us at least inadvertently or in some instances purposely taught to be racist? Now it's up to us to break the cycle and I'm glad that I'm trying to be part of the solution by not allowing my kids to grow up with that hate and trying to influence those around me to do the same. In the end though, everyone has to decide what they believe, think, act and pass on themselves. You decide for yourself.

Scene 5: Manufactured Outrage

I tried to take you on a journey on how I see America and what our own ranks are when it comes to racism. Though we all bring our collective experiences and belief systems to work, you can't erase who you are or what you feel, and very few officers I have worked with outwardly show that they are or may be racist. Are there racist cops? Sure there are, but do they all act that way when interacting with people of color or another culture? And by the way, the term "people of color" was coined by someone else and is widely used so I'll use it to make some points. Some cops do act that way but the great majority doesn't. To say that every time an incident occurs between white police officers and "someone of color," is asinine on its face. The entire incident needs to be carefully examined, and of course there is plenty of time to do so after the fact, which is called *Monday Morning Quarterbacking*. Most all of these incidents whether they result in a death or not, are as a result of actions and reactions by both the subject and the officers and decisions made in a split second.

There are some incidents which there is little question to most of us as to the cause or the possibility of brutality by an officer such as the George Floyd case in Minneapolis. But what was the police department's policy on his use of force? And that case wasn't investigated thoroughly before everyone began commentating on it. No officer that I know has been trained to place their knee on someone's neck for that period of time, but was he? To most officers, this was an aberration and not the norm. But there have been so many others that on their face looked bad to begin with as I've been saying that many things police do look ugly; and no one likes "watching the sausage get made," remember that? Most of these incidents began with a complaint, officers respond, they didn't pick someone out of a hat, a person becomes the focus of the investigation, the subject resists and fails to comply with the officer's orders, an attempt to arrest is made or at least a confrontation occurs, it goes bad and deadly force is used. To say that racism was a motivating factor on the part of police is just plain ignorant. But every time something happens, we start yelling racism and the whole thing blows up. To use a pun, not every incident is *"black & White,"* but we do our best to make it into that, don't we? The activists come out of the woodwork, fly into town with their entourages, spew a bunch of hateful crap then blow back out of town to wait for the next one. They really don't give a damn about who died, they just want to stir the shit and make their money. These activists are living high on the hog, bolster their agenda and leave. The aftermath isn't their problem, it's ours!

A perfect example of this was the Ferguson, Missouri Incident in 2014. The activists only cared that a white police officer shot a black man, without waiting for the investigation to take place. The "Hands up, don't shoot" line was a bullshit lie as we came to find out by witnesses that were initially too afraid to come forward. Michael Brown first committed a strong-armed robbery, and when confronted by Officer Darren Wilson charged him failing to comply with orders, trapped and began to beat him in his own patrol car, and Officer Wilson having no alternative shot him. Brown was over six feet tall and almost 300 pounds, and I wouldn't have been able to handle him alone and might have shot him too. That's called "overwhelming odds," but that didn't stop the false narrative and outrage from ensuing. We had riots, and quite frankly some poor response from police but that is my opinion as an 18-year crowd control instructor. Nonetheless, the jumping-to-conclusions which has become an Olympic Sport, took place before all the facts were out. Michael Brown died, and that's tragic, especially for his family and we should all be saddened that a family lost someone, but that doesn't mean that the riots that followed and the racism picture that was painted again was warranted.

If you want to be outraged, why don't we talk about all the shootings that have been taking place in Chicago for instance and committed by black males on black folks. This has been and continues to be a national tragedy and disgrace, and innocent people and children are dying, but none of the activists say anything about that. Sharpton, Farrakhan, leftist politicians, and not to mention the "celebrities" that jump on the band wagon, not a peep! The moniker of racism is only placed on white police officers who were doing their job and the situation went sideways. Not on the criminals who are committing the shootings and murders. How is that even fair? But it isn't part of the narrative.

A Racist Traffic Stop - Or Was It?

A now retired colleague and friend of mine, Sergeant Craig Sciortino, was working what we called *Carol City*, an area of northern Miami-Dade County, before it incorporated as the City of Miami Gardens, a predominantly black residential and business area. Craig stopped a car for a traffic violation; taking a red light. The woman driver, who was black, accused Craig, who is white, of only stopping black people for anything, not acknowledging the violation she committed. Craig took this opportunity as a "teachable moment," as they say. He told the woman to stand with him on the corner and watch the drivers as they drove through the intersection to see if he was selectively stopping only black folks, and if he was, he would agree that is what he was doing.

So they stood there for a while and the woman watched as motorists, black motorists drove the intersection and blew the light. The woman had to apologize to Craig because she only saw black folks and no white folks driving through. Craig was just doing his job and she got stopped because of what she did, not because of who she was. There is a saying I like to use for several things but it applies here; "we have to fish in the pond we're in!" But few see it that way.

I Thought I Was Here to Help

In 2016, as tensions between police and black folks continued to grow, I headed out from the Intracoastal Station to meet up with my guys and go on patrol. I came across an unattended vehicle in the middle lane on NE 163 Street just passed the railroad tracks. I pulled up behind and engaged my overhead lights to block the vehicle so I could investigate. As I walked to the rear of the car, a saw a woman, a black woman, walking toward me from the gas station with a gas can in her hand. Ahh, the FBI would call this a clue. As she walked up I said, "I see you ran out of gas." No reply. I noticed the type of gas can she was carrying because I had the same type in the trunk of my Green & White and offered to help her with it because it had a safety spout that was difficult to manipulate. Her reply was a sharp "I don't need your help!" I was a little surprised but not picking up the clues yet. I didn't go to Quantico so bear with me. She put her keys and gas receipt on the trunk of her car, and the receipt was getting blown around so I grabbed the keys and placed them on the receipt. She then bit and said, "Leave my keys alone!" Then it dawned on me, she didn't want my help and probably saw me as the enemy.

I asked her "Oh, you don't want my help, do you?" And I got a resounding 'NO!' I said, "Ok," got in my car and left her in the middle of the road.

Even when police officers are helping a stranded motorist, they may still be viewed as the enemy simply because of their profession. I hope that the lady's family told her the cop was only trying to help her and she realized she was wrong. I hope.

This leads me to this; I know that many black folks believe that all police officers believe that all Black people are criminals. Of course that is an asinine but widely held belief. I think this lady was holding me accountable for perhaps a bad encounter she once had with an officer, yet we had never met.

Isn't it wrong to think that *ALL* of certain group believes either this or that? Isn't it just perpetuating another false stereotype no matter who it is? I was just trying to help someone as I have always done, but she never gave me the chance. We both walked away upset, the narrative continued, and nothing got resolved. Very sad.

Scene 6: The Choke Hold Myth

POLICE OFFICERS DO NOT USE CHOKE HOLDS!
Another part of this movement against police is the attempt and becoming successful I might add, is to remove an invaluable use of force tool we use known as the *ACTR*-Applied Carotid Triangular Restraint. I covered this in my chapter on *Use of Force,* but it is mistakenly and often referred to as a *Choke Hold*, which it isn't. Yes, we use our arms to encircle a subject's neck, but we applied the pressure to the carotid arteries on the sides of the neck, not the front of the throat where the airway is. The pressure on the arteries restricts the flow of blood and oxygen to the brain TEMPORARILY, rendering them unconscious for a few seconds so we can gain control of a violent person.

Like I mentioned previously in the book, you may know this better as a *"Sleeper Hold"* in professional wrestling, which is simulated for theatrics. We are trained to then immediately revive them *after* we handcuff them so we don't have to do this dance again. Everyone is now on this kick to "outlaw," yes outlaw this tool which has proved essential to ending a violent confrontation with little or no injury to anyone. Remember, police officers get injured in confrontations too. Of course, it can have negative consequences, but it is employed solely in violent circumstances, and who starts it? The subject or person with mental illness or on drugs, not us! The subject always dictates how we respond.

We have used this technique too many times to count where the subject was subdued without further incident or injury and arrested. If you take it away, be careful what you're asking for; as you will leave officers with no alternative but to A: beat the subject into submission using hands, fist, feet, baton, or any other weapon of opportunity in an all-out, drag-out fight. B: officers may have no alternative to go to deadly force when the subject gains the advantage and the officer is in jeopardy of being subdued and defeated. In every fight, there is at least one firearm involved (the officer's) which puts the officer's life at risk. Beating a subject and leaving lasting or permanent injuries is much worse that putting them to sleep for a minute, isn't it? So officers will resort more quickly to the firearm than before because in combat, there are no points for second place. You want to disband, disarm, and render police impotent. What you're asking for with banning the ACTR will lead to more deadly confrontations and then you'll be screaming about that. Remember that I and the entire law enforcement community warned you, but you know better than us how do police work. At least that's what you keep telling us.

Scene 7: Under Fire - Circle the Wagons

These incidents I have written about sparked a chain of events never seen in my time as a police officer. Like I stated, President Obama's comments about the Cambridge Police and others afterward, along with all the incidents following involving police and black males, led to what I'm certain were unintended consequences but occurred regardless; the specific targeting, ambushing, and killing of American police officers. Never have we seen this kind of malicious, hateful, vengeance aimed at our ranks, which makes it extremely *more* dangerous to wear the uniform and go to work. I understand many people who don't like the police, have been pulled over, even singled out sometimes because they were black or Hispanic, or for any other reason, but carrying out assassinations of police is way beyond what our society should allow, and it just makes the already difficult job we do even more dangerous, and it is fueling a powder keg that will eventually explode.

Do you believe police are going to sit back and continue to take it? Think again. Police are human beings with feelings, families, and lively hoods they *will* protect.

I have mentioned the ambush of NYPD officers Wenjian Liu and Rafael Ramos in 2014. This was in retaliation for Ferguson, starting a series of these ambushes around the country that continue to this day. The job of a police officer used to be held in high regard, and we had thousands of people applying to join up, but that's now changed in light of current events. Who in their right mind would want to be a police officer now? Recruiting is way, way down, and because of what's occurring to us around America, retirements are way, way up. Almost every day I get told "You picked the right time to retire!" I was even asked by a colleague over at Florida Fish & Wildlife if I had a crystal ball he could borrow since mine seemed to be working. Timing is everything and I knew it was my time even before all this anti-police shit and COVID-19 (read Chinese Virus) came to pass. But my son BJ, his wife Michelle, my niece Alina, and my friends and colleagues still working are of great concern to me naturally. If I am now asked by someone for advice on signing up, sadly I have to tell them not to. Before I was proud to endorse our profession, I can no longer do that in good conscience. I am proud to have been a Metro-Dade Police Officer, but it pains me to say now is not the time to become one. Go be a firefighter, everyone loves them. But when they're in the shit, who do they call? That's right.

Scene 8: The Social Experiment

In the wake of the death of George Floyd, America has lost its collective mind and everything has gone to shit, especially where police are concerned. One idiot officer did something no one I know of was trained to do, and the other two *See No Evil, Hear No Evil* idiots stood by and watched, and the world has been turned upside down and police everywhere are paying for it. Once again

"The Broad Brush." But we're here and dealing with the fallout. Cities are burning, murders are being committed, and homegrown terrorists are occupying our towns. And let me explain this to you idiots out there, most of these "protesters" as you call them, are shipped in from around the country who have nothing to do and are getting paid by leftist supporters to wreak havoc just because, and our history is being erased in the *"Cancel Culture"* being forced upon us. Our founders must be turning in their graves. Oh, that's right you want to erase the memory of them too.

What is absolutely astonishing and I guess I shouldn't be surprised, is this movement to get rid of us altogether. The *"Defund/Disband"* bandwagon the left is perpetrating, to include not only the activists that don't know what they are asking for because it will directly and negatively affect the people they say they are protecting, as well as stupid politicians who want to appease the tiny but vocal and dangerous anarchists and that's what they are, make no mistake about it. Mayor Bill "Comrade" De Blasio and the New York City Council voted to reduce the NYPD's funding by one billion dollars and canceled the upcoming academy classes and recruiting. Great move Bill! You already alienated the NYPD, but now you want to bury them too. You think by increasing funding to social programs will do the trick? Hey Mr. Wizard, and all the Mr. and Ms. Wizards out there in local governments, when you cut police funding the first thing to go is training. Yes, that very thing I hear politicians mention in the *Police Reform* narrative. "We need to better train our police!" Good, do it. Training is out the window because there won't be any funds for it, and no one will be able to be taken away from the road to go to training. Brilliant!

You are going to kill recruiting and force early retirements, Calls for Service response times will suffer and so will the people who need the police the most; those folks of "color" you say we mistreat and abuse. I heard the president of the Minneapolis City Council, Lisa Bender, say on a CNN interview, having the police respond to her home is a "privilege," meaning "white privilege" though she didn't come right out and say that, and having the police respond (to black folks calls-implied) could actually make things worse.

Are you fucking kidding me?

This notion that it is first of all a privilege for us to respond is preposterous. Second, when these geniuses say police "selectively" respond to calls, once again to calls from the "people of color," is so far away from the truth I can't believe no one calls them on it. By the way folks, Ms. Bender had Minneapolis Police Officers on overtime guarding her house during all the "unrest" in the city. Talk about privilege. Hey Ms. Bender, why don't you and your entire council go ride with the Minneapolis Police and see for yourselves where it is they actually respond to, not often to your neighborhood I'm sure, and what they actually deal with. You won't because it doesn't fit the agenda. So please go ahead and vote to disband your police force, hire social workers instead, and when the *9-1-1* calls start coming in, have one of your social workers go handle it. Maybe it will take one or two to get assaulted or killed to get your attention. But then again you're not the one going in harm's way, are you?

So let's proceed with the *Social Experiment* I have been suggesting for years now, since the Minneapolis City Council thinks they're on the right track. Pick any Friday night at 6:00 p.m. Have every police officer and corrections officer in America go home, and not come back until 6:00 A.M. Monday morning. Just over two days.

Let's see how America fares without police for just one weekend. While we do this, you politicians, activists and celebrities, let's not forget about you too, will be hiding in your walled compounds with your private security so you'll be safe, won't you? Everyone then go for a drive down any street in your city, take a stroll in the parks and beaches, and go shopping for groceries or clothes and home goods. Oops, take that one back because all the stores will be getting looted and burned. Go to your favorite eatery, oh, that one will be either looted or closed too, and try and have a normal, family outing in the meantime. No police to patrol and respond to anything, but since this is what you are asking for, let's go for it.

What will happen is it will be like the movie series *The Purge* but to a factor of 100. It will be a post-apocalyptic scene out of a *Mad Max* movie where there are no laws, no rules, and no peace. But this is what you want, so make it happen. You'll find out in a hurry who and what the police mean to a civilized society. As a

216

movie buff I'll say this; "You have no idea what it takes to defend a nation. You want me on that wall; you need me on that wall!" But let's not have any of us stand that wall for a while and see what happens. I know there are some Americans who despise and hate us and are doing everything they can to destroy our good standing with the rest of America. For those I can only say you don't deserve the police you have. Go live in another country where you think you have rights, say, Russia, China, North Korea, and closer to home Cuba and Venezuela, and find out how quickly you don't.

Scene 9: Media - The True Enemy

What many of us as a society don't realize is happening, is we are being manipulated to bolster the agenda of the extreme, leftist minority in this country. Now stop and think for a minute, do police officers really go out there with the intent to kill a black person during their shift?

"Hey Jose, what are you going to do today?

"Well, I haven't killed a black guy all month. I'm a little behind on my quota."

"Better get on it, Sarge is going to be pissed!"

"Ok, I'll get one right after coffee."

The utter stupidity that anyone one would believe America's police are systemic racists, ruthless killers, and instruments of brutality is beyond comprehension to the sensibilities of anyone I know. Yet, you are being fed it, day in and day out, by a small group of extremists whose message of hate is perpetuated by the media.

You see it on the news at every hour, pundits telling you what you should think and feel and to be angry with anything having to do with police. When one officer goes bad, fine, be angry, but with all of us? If you didn't hear it constantly on the news and watch the chaos ensue, you would be able to analyze the facts for yourself and see things aren't as they appear to be. The media is the faction keeping us divided as a nation because they are in the tank with the extreme left. They did it during the *OJ Saga*, the *Elian Circus* here in Miami, and continue to do it today. The news anchors of the past like Walter Cronkite and John Chancellor are spinning in their graves at what's become of their business. I go back to what I said in an earlier chapter; *if it bleeds, it leads, a*nd add *if it burns, it earns*. Think for yourself America, and stop being told how and what to think by people and factions who don't give a damn about you. It's destroying us from within and that's how every great empire has fallen. Let's not add the United States of America to it!

Scene 10: A National Disgrace

The absolute disaster that took place in Seattle is appalling to every officer in this country. Allowing anarchist to overrun any part of the city, especially a police station, goes against everything we stand for as officers, soldiers, and Americans. I and any and all of my fellow officers cannot believe the city leaders and I use the term loosely, ordered the police to stand down and allow this occupation to take place. But then again that's the *Left-Coast* so I shouldn't be surprised. Second, how dare the Seattle police chief, Carmen Best, go along with Mayor Jenny Durkan to allow this to occur! I know the mayor can fire the chief, but to allow this to happen and undermine the entire force let alone the good citizens of Seattle is beyond my understanding. What she should have done is bite the bullet and cleared out all the protesters' as everyone keeps calling them, and if she gets fired so be it, she would have been hailed as a hero for saving the city and the precinct, written a book about it, and gone on a speaking tour. I am pretty certain her officers have lost all respect for her. The other way to go would have been to arrest the mayor for allowing anarchy to overrun the city, and again she would have been hailed a hero. The actions of the mayor are a gross malfeasance of duty and responsibility. It took several shootings and the murder of a teenager and shooting of another for the chief to finally say enough! Easy to say now, isn't chief? The Seattle Police Department's motto is *Service, Pride, Dedication.* No one in authority upheld. I can tell you that we would not have allowed it to happen in Miami-Dade County. No fucking way!

I leave this act with a letter to the mayor of Seattle from my brother, Pete Gonzalez, who served alongside me and our colleagues for thirty years at Miami-Dade Police. Pete retired eight years ago as a dedicated officer and one of the best Crime Scene Investigators we ever had, and he proudly served as a Military

Policeman in the United States Army. His thoughts are from the heart and echo how America's police and I'm certain law-abiding citizens everywhere, feel about the Seattle debacle manifesting itself throughout America.

Pete's Letter:

Jenny Durkan,

Notice that I did not refer to you as Mayor. A Mayor is someone who leads their citizens, stands up for their rights, and sets policy for a better life. You have FAILED miserably in that aspect. If you haven't noticed, you're the laughingstock of the entire world. You're an embarrassment to the citizens of your city and this country. You allowed a hostile takeover of six of your city blocks and you did nothing to stop them. You call them patriots instead of anarchists. Now you want to negotiate with them instead of sending in the Police to restore law and order. This nation was built on rule of law. In case you didn't notice we have a constitution that was written by our founding fathers. You are allowing a group of terrorist thugs to violate the rights of the citizens still stuck in that *Autonomous Zone*. What a F..ing joke that is.

Thank god I am not a citizen of your city. I pray god watches over all the good citizens still there, because as of now, God is the only hope they have due to your failed leadership.

I watch the coverage from the news and online, and I can't believe that this chaos is happening to our country. I served three years in the US Army and I am beside myself watching your city get destroyed and you don't have the fortitude to resolve the terrorist takeover in an appropriate manner. For several years Antifa has been gaining traction in Seattle and now they secured a foothold. Hopefully, President Trump will send in several thousand troops and restore order. You're an incompetent liberal mayor that has no business to be the leader of a city. You should resign and let someone else clean up your mess.

This has never happened in a United States city other than the civil war. You will go down in history as a failed leader. Kids in school will learn in history how a city was occupied by Antifa terrorists and the mayor didn't stop them. She supported them.

Did you say it was going to be a "summer of love?" Good luck with that.

I can only imagine how many Seattle Police Officers are seeking employment with other police departments due to your lack of leadership. I hope they are successful. They had to abandon a precinct and I watch the police chief say it wasn't her call. It was your call, and it showed how spineless you really are.

You put the citizens in danger and I'm sure there will be more loss of life. You should be ashamed of yourself for allowing this to happen.

I know my sentiments reflect that of the rest of the country. Your term as mayor will be an example to the rest of the mayors of how not to respond to a crisis.

God bless the good citizens of Seattle.
Pete Gonzalez
Homestead, FL 33030

Act - 15 Sergeant

Scene 1: What is a Sergeant?

In every organization there is the supervisor for the front-line workers. Those who actually perform the work makes the beehive function and deliver the end product. Those are known as the *immediate supervisor,* and in police work that supervisor with few exceptions is the *Sergeant.*

He or she is directly responsible for overseeing, directing, training, evaluating, disciplining, and the overall care of those officers assigned to him or her while at work, and sometimes even off-duty. When an officer graduates the academy, he/she is assigned to a district or precinct and within that district to a squad. That squad is supervised and led by a sergeant.

It has been said the most important rank within a police department is the sergeant. Why? Because the sergeant is the closest to the officers in terms of the hierarchy of the chain-of-command, just like in the army. The sergeant runs the squad, the lieutenant runs the platoon, the captain runs the company (in police work a district or precinct) the major oversees the captain, and so on. But you'll have *some* individuals with higher rank who think they are the most important rank and person in the chain and can make life difficult for those below him. Sometimes we forget where we came from, buts that another story.

The US Army textbook definition of a sergeant is: *To train, discipline, and look out for the welfare of his troops.* Sergeants do all of that. But what does *Sergeant* actually mean? Surprisingly, most sergeants don't know where the name of their title originates and what its meaning actually is so here we go; the word *sergeant* comes from the French *sergent, which comes from the Latin serviens,* which means *to serve.* The sergeant serves his officers, as well as his supervisors. Loosely translated it means to "serve two Gods or two Kings; the one above you and the one below you." The one above is the lieutenant, and the one below is her or his officers. The sergeant is in between those two and it can be the most difficult supervisory position. Another word that means to serve is *Samurai*. So sergeants are in pretty good company, albeit a difficult one.

So being close to the officers makes you directly responsible for their actions, to a point, and allows you to have the most influence on them, both good and bad. The sergeant is the one supervisor in the entire chain-of-command who sees his officers every day, either at roll call or on the road. Officers can go days, even weeks without seeing their lieutenant, which again, could be both good and bad, and almost never see their captain or major because those are entirely administrative positions that involve the district's day-to-day operation and endless golf outings, I mean meetings.

You might only see those two command officers on a noteworthy scene that garners attention like a big shooting caper involving an officer, great loss of life, and unfortunately an officer injured or killed. But as an officer you would see your sergeant every day, and you should. As the immediate supervisor, the sergeant is responsible for responding to calls that may require direction and guidance, especially for the young Jedi Knights every agency has that need direct, hands on supervision. In the case of large scale incidents, perimeters have to be established and additional resources have to be called in to first contain and then manage the incident, like a shooting scene, robbery or burglary with subjects at-large, a hazardous materials incident or any one of a myriad of situations requiring command & control by a supervisor. This falls on the sergeant to begin handling them first until relieved by a higher rank. And that's if the higher rank wants to take over. Many don't and will say; "You're doing just fine. I'll monitor." Which, depending on the individual could translate to; "I don't really want ANY part of this."

When you see the *"As seen on TV!"* large scale incidents involving a great number of police personnel; those incidents are first managed by a sergeant. It is up to the sergeant to gain control of the incident in its very early stages, and control or lack-there-of will most likely determine the course and eventual outcome. Just like there are really exceptional and good officers as well as mediocre ones, the same goes for supervisors in general and sergeants more specifically. There are strong leadership types, and weak, passive types who can't or won't engage. It is no different in any other business but with us it could mean the difference between life and death. Fire Rescue and the military operate the same way. The decisions we make as supervisors can have profound affects whether done right or wrong, so we better get it right. The sergeant is the most visible symbol of supervisory authority for the police, and is recognized by the stripes on his or her sleeves. Sergeant stripes or *Chevrons* as they are officially called, are what everyone gravitates to, officers and civilians alike, and represent the authority on scene. Even the higher-ups will seek out the sergeant for a *SIT-REP (Situation-Report)* when they first arrive on scene, so the sergeant better have his or her proverbial *Shit* together. If you want to talk to the boss, speak with the sergeant, that's what they're there for.

The sergeant oversees what the officers do and don't do but cannot be there all the time. A squad can have anywhere from 6, 10 or 12 officers on it and the sergeant is responsible for all of them. Any officer could have a priority that requires their sergeant's attention and from time to time sergeants get spread pretty thin. Sergeants are also responsible for fielding complaints such as discourtesy and sometimes excessive force about their officers from citizens, do tell, and have to address and sometimes investigate the complaint. In the case of excessive force, those are automatically kicked over to Internal Affairs. If the *IA* investigation of any complaint results in a sustained finding, then it is the affected officer's sergeant who has the responsibility to prepare the disciplinary paperwork and trust me, no one likes to do that.

It is also the sergeant's responsibility to make certain his officers are performing well, and if they are not, to take corrective action by training them, sending them to more formalized training, and/or draft and implement a performance improvement plan. If an officer is failing to improve, then the sergeant may have to issue discipline to get their attention. Again, no one likes to do this but sometimes it is necessary.

Scene 2: Meet the New Boss, Same as the Old Boss?

When someone becomes a sergeant, they just went from being responsible for themselves to being responsible for a squad of officers, who bring with them various years of experience and levels of training, different skill sets, past histories, work ethics, and personalities. As a new sergeant, you just became a *Den Mother* to a group of people you may know nothing about and are now charged with their care. Depending on how much time on the job you have when you become a sergeant, will either help you or hurt you in this transition to the supervisory ranks, which is considered the most difficult of the job. Going up the chain from there is easier because you have already been a supervisor for a number of years before the next leap. Yesterday you were "one of the guys," today you're the boss. Now that you have become the boss, you are expected to be *"all knowing and all seeing;"* your IQ and knowledge level just shot up a few points, and when you're asked a question, either by your officers or by your own boss the lieutenant, you're expected to instantaneously spit out the answer to their satisfaction. For anyone who has become a supervisor in any vocation you know this to be false but expected.

First Day

When you meet your new squad for the first time, there are usually some congratulations on your promotion and welcome gestures to your new assignment, and when your new officers got the word you were coming, they reached out to people they know who may know you, to get the word on you. You better hope it was good or you're going in already from behind.

Now you have your first roll call with these folks and you introduce yourself and talk briefly, hopefully, about your experience and where you came from. Then you advise your people of what your grand outlook for success is and what you expect. While you're speaking, the following occurs though you are not even consciously aware of it, though you did tis yourself to *your* new sergeant in the past.

You're standing in front of your new squad with your *Velcro Stripes* (meaning you're on one year probation and a major screw up can rip them off) and looking into their eyes. What do you see?

225

The rookie on your squad is looking at you with "wide eyes" and thinking, "Wow! One day I want to be just like him."

The slightly older and more experienced officer is thinking; "I probably know more than this guy."

And the *seasoned & salty* veteran is saying what sounds like it's coming from a loudspeaker but is actually not coming out of his mouth at all; "Another rookie sergeant I gotta break in!"

All of this happens at your first meeting with your squad, and you're wondering if you made a good impression. That's natural for anyone to hope they did. On the other hand, you may have some newly promoted guy who doesn't give a rat's ass what you think. Those personality types will soon appear in all its splendor. After you cut loose your squad and send them on their way to begin patrol, your new lieutenant calls you into the office for *The Talk*.

Your new boss as a sergeant is the platoon lieutenant. He or she is charged with overseeing the entire contingent of sergeants and officers on any given shift; days, afternoons, midnights, and will now be supervising and evaluating *you*. Everyone has a boss.

In your first meeting he or she will tell you some of the same things you just told your squad, her experience, where she came from, and her expectations of you. These types of first meetings have taken place for centuries, well, decades anyway, and are part of the getting-to-know one another culture and traditions in a police department. So now you get sent on your way after the pep-talk, and onto supervising your new squad.

But wait, a memo has to be written on one of your officers who missed court or training the last sergeant didn't do because he went on vacation a week before your arrival, and now you have to do it.

"Yes mam, I'll take care of it."

Going on the road will have to wait a bit. "But how do I prepare this memo? I've never done one before. Shit!" And so your new life as a police sergeant begins. I can tell you this; every new sergeant says to him or herself within the first month, "Why the fuck did I do this to myself?"

The first month his tough because you're finding your way and everything is being thrown at you all at once, and you better have learned to juggle because that's exactly what that first month is, a juggling act. It does get better after you begin to catch your stride.

While the sergeant is the immediate supervisor of the officers in any squad anywhere in the department and should be out in the field supervising, guiding, and leading them, there are those pesky administrative duties that have to get done, and when the proverbial shit rolls downhill, it's the sergeant at the bottom with the catcher's mitt.

Sergeants have to prepare and/or approve the squad's payroll, review their reports, approve or disapprove leave and schedule vacations for everyone, then report back up the chain on complaints and missed assignments, schedule training, and what would come to be a favorite when I became a sergeant, prepare monthly and yearly evaluations.

Yay! Note the sarcasm in my words.

The most useless report sergeants prepare is the *"Monthlies."* If your officers are performing steadily, then how can you say every month, using different wording, Officer Gonzalez is performing to standards? If something really good or really bad happened, then you have some new material to write about, but the same thing every month, month in and month out is utterly useless and a waste of supervisory time.

So for my former department, Miami-Dade and all the rest, develop a better evaluation system like quarterlies instead of monthlies and stop wasting the sergeant's time! They can't be in the station tapping keys and out on the road supervising at the same time, and when something big does happen, the first thing commanders say is, "Where's their sergeant and why wasn't he on scene?" Stop! Remember when you were a sergeant and you said the same damned thing? Remember where you came from. Oh yea, some of you have forgotten.

Scene 3: Baby Sitting, Sometimes

What would a supervisor in any profession tell you is the most difficult part of their job? For us, managing a major incident where there is death and destruction? Nope. After a while as a police officer those incidents come pretty routinely and are handled quite easily, not all, but most. The single most difficult aspect to being a sergeant is dealing with personnel issues.

Sergeants basically supervise a den of lions which are usually full of Type A personalities who are used to being the one in charge on a scene, which is part of their job, but put them all in the same room (cage) and the sergeant has now become the *Lion Tamer*.

Each officer has a distinct personality and with those sometimes comes egos and an unwillingness to follow directions. When you have just one officer who may be referred to as a *"Supervisory Nightmare,"* it makes for a difficult time because Officer Jones keeps missing the radio calls, arrives late on back-ups, forgets to go to court, doesn't turn in his reports on time and has them rejected regularly, doesn't submit his payroll and screws up too, his uniform is always wrinkled and looks like shit, and he has domestic issues to boot. That is the "nightmare!"

We've all had them and it makes sergeants have to come down on their officers and throw their weight around, but when an officer acts this way and won't change, they bring it on themselves.

Another problem is squabbles among the squad itself. Two or more officers don't like each other, have bad blood between them, the squad thinks a member is lazy and not carrying their workload, and now you have a metaphorical *Jerry Springer* brawl taking place daily.

What a pain in the ass!

If the sergeant doesn't try to correct it or any of the other issues, it leads to dissent on the squad and no one is happy. This can get out of control and now it's made its way up the chain and everyone is involved. But it will fall back on the sergeant to fix. This cannot be tolerated nor should it.

"But wait Bert, you gave some of your sergeants a hard time." Yes, but only because I was vocal about some stupidity going on or having a weak supervisor somewhere in the wood pile, even my own, and I could never tolerate that. But I never, ever was told I wasn't performing in an outstanding manner. I was taught by the best, and if I do say so myself, became one of the best. You bet I gave a couple of my sergeants a hard time, but there was never a question about my work. Never!

Scene 4: Sergeant James "Pappy" Slack

As a young officer who aspires to become a sergeant one day, you look at those you consider to be good sergeants and watch them, learning from their actions, both the good and the bad traits, and you may say as I've said previously of the rookie officer; "I want to be just like him."

Him, for me was Sergeant James Slack, "Pappy" as we called him. More on that shortly.

In 1988 I was summarily transferred from the Southwest District to Midwest because of an ongoing battle with my lieutenant, Ingemar Velasco who I mentioned in my *Brass Act*, what a surprise, but he was an idiot that screwed with everyone who didn't kiss his ass, and he made stupid decisions all the time so it wasn't just me. I was just the first to be targeted, and since he was asshole buddies with the major, (not Kermit Russell who I spoke about earlier,) they solved their problem (me) with a transfer..

So be it.

I landed on Sergeant Slack's squad which was the midnight Field Training Squad. He supervised the FTOs who trained the rookie officers. We had our first roll call where he introduced me to everyone, and afterward we had *The Talk*. So I'm the new guy with baggage, and he told me right off, "I've heard some things, but I want you to know you have a clean slate with me." Wow! I didn't expect that, but he put me at ease. He didn't prejudge and was giving me a fair chance to prove myself. I hit the road and started working. During my first week there, I was doing some neighborhood patrol off Bird Road and SW 122 Ave, and as I'm driving down the street with headlights off, that's how you sneak up on bad guys, I looked at a stone wall surrounding a good-sized property and thought I saw a silhouette bobbing up and down on it. I decided to stop and watch for a while. Sure as shit, it was a bad guy who trying to burglarize the residence. Imagine my surprise. A *Cat Burglar!* I called in for the troops and we set up a perimeter. One asshole-bad guy in custody!

Later that same first week, a burglary had occurred and the bad guys fled in a "*22*," stolen vehicle, and I picked it up fleeing northbound on the Palmetto Expressway. "Chase! I've got them!" So I *Buford T. Justice'd* them for a little bit and they bailed out at NW 74 Street. I called in again for a perimeter, and after a while we rounded them up too. Pappy was on scene during the perimeter as a good sergeant should be, and he took me aside again and said after two big grabs in my first week he didn't see what the problem was with me. I said to him there wasn't a problem with my work, and when I told him who my lieutenant was he said, "I get it now." When you become "that guy" the officer or supervisor no one likes, your reputation travels far and wide, across oceans and mountain ranges, and certainly from district to district. He knew my previous lieutenant and added, "Say no more."

That week Pappy began to show me what kind of a supervisor and person he was, and from that moment on I wanted to be like him. Pappy held roll call every night, and back in 1988 there was no internet and very few law enforcement magazines, but that didn't stop him from finding information on officer safety practices, tactics, training, and he did his best to teach us to do our best. Pappy had military DNA that he brought to the table. He was an A-6 Intruder Bombardier/Navigator during the Vietnam War, so survival was paramount to him, and he made sure we could survive during the course of our duties.

He took us out to the firearms range to do extra training with him after our shift. I later rotated to day shift, but then wanted to become an FTO and went back to his midnight squad because of *him*. When we had rookies in training, Pappy would have us go out of service and into the warehouse areas and practice building searches and felony stops. Though I hated the midnight shift, there wasn't a single night I didn't want to go to work because of Sergeant Slack and the squad environment he fostered. He was fair, unselfish, giving and a caring person who ALWAYS looked out first for the welfare of his officers, and he trained and disciplined us when required, just like the textbook said he should. One of my squad mates who became a very dear and close friend David "Jester" Fariss and I, always did our best to live up to Pappy's expectations, and later on when we became sergeants ourselves, both said we wanted to be just like Pappy! Hands down, Sergeant James Slack had the most influence on me and was the best supervisor I ever had, and I learned and adopted his style and added it to my own to make me the sergeant I became. I learned from the best, and I became one of the best, thanks to him.

"Pappy, I can't ever thank you enough for the kindness and fairness you showed me at first, giving me the chance to show you the cop I was, but also the good guy I am. Your leadership, guidance, and tutelage made all of us better than we were and who we became. Thank you Sir!"

Scene 5: Maverick is Born

So you've heard me call Sergeant Slack "Pappy," and Dave Fariss "Jester," so where did these nicknames or *call-signs* come from. As I stated, I was kicked out of Station 5 and sent to Station 3 and assigned to Pappy's squad. This was in 1988, two years after the blockbuster, best all time *Guy* movie *Top Gun* came out. What I didn't know was the members of my new squad had adopted call-signs from the movie for each other. But the names were based on your personality and not just arbitrary. Dave was *Jester* because he had a jovial personality and nothing ever seemed to bother him.

Joe was *Viper* because he had a very outgoing way about him and didn't pull any punches, Rigo was *Iceman* because he was quiet and reserved, but could throw-down when needed. Marco was *Slider* because the name just seemed to fit, and Patty was *Mother Goose* for the obvious reason. She didn't get killed in a training accident by the way. And so where does *Pappy* come from since it wasn't in *Top Gun?* If you'll recall your World War II history, first with the Flying Tigers in China, then with the US Marine Fighter Squadron VMF-214 in the Pacific Theater, Major Greg "Pappy" Boyington was the commander of the *Black Sheep,* so that's what my squad was called and our leader was Sergeant James *"Pappy"* Slack.

So when I landed there they told me everyone was given a call-sign, and since I had gotten into some trouble at Station 5 and I came with a reputation for doing things my way, "You're *Maverick!*" and that's how I became known for the rest of my career.

First *Ofc. Maverick,* and later on *Sgt. Maverick.* It fit so well it became part of my personality, in a good way, mostly, and it is now the name of the company I co-founded with my tennis and business partner Mike Gokel, *Maverick Law Enforcement Products.* By the way, if you're interested in investing with us, please check us out at MaverickLEP.com. Come see what we have to offer. Just a little plug, it is my book after all.

So it depends who you talk to as to who I am. Those I didn't get along with will say I was arrogant. Those who got to know me or I supervised found out I was confident in my abilities and took care of those around me, especially the officers I directly and even indirectly supervised. I thank that squad of officers and Pappy for accepting me for who I am and allowing me to become part of a great legacy in the annuls of the Midwest District.

Scene 6: My Turn

In late 1996 after 13 years of being an officer and an FTO two times around in different districts, having done some plain clothes and undercover work and general patrol duties, I was bored and needed a change. I had seen some of those around me get promoted to sergeant and was told by others I should enter the promotional process. I also watched as some idiots I worked with took the test and became sergeants. This left the possibility I would have to take orders from them should they become my sergeant. Remember, I have no patience for stupidity. It's been said at every rank you attain you eliminate those you might have to work for. So I had several motivating factors in my decision, but the main one was I needed a new challenge.

As with all promotional tests, the first thing to do is of course study. In order to make sergeant, you have to break out the *BFBs*, or *Big Fucking Books* as we call them, and organize your study material, and there's a lot of it. In any large department, the manuals are extensive, and in addition to them you have to read up on laws, legal notes and bulletins that came out over the previous two years our Legal Bureau put out, and anything new that wasn't already in the book. Once organized, it's time to start reading through the most boring and dry crap you can imagine and try to retain it. My studying began while on-duty in Area 2 of the Hammocks District, where I would back into my friends Chuck and Margaret's driveway, and in between calls I would comb through the endless Blah, blah, blah of procedures. You would highlight things you thought were important and might be on the test. Well, you ended up painting

232

your notes yellow and it was a waste of time. I studied in their driveway and at home for about five months. I thought I had hit it pretty good and was ready for the written test in June of 97.' Or so I thought. Phase 1, the written test came and you needed a passing score of seventy-eight in order to move onto the next step of the promotional process for our department. I got a 78. Damn! I thought I nailed it. I must have suffered a brain-fart at test time. I'm pretty smart but I guess I just couldn't recall the material. But I made it under the wire and was scheduled for Phase 2 of the process. I guess it was like horseshoes and hand grenades; I got "close enough!"

The second part of our process was an interactive exercise where a proctor would read four scenarios to you and you would verbally state how you would handle each one as a sergeant, and you had twenty minutes to answer all four. You could take notes as they were being read and you can ask to have the scenario reread to you but that was it. The scenarios ranged from a tactical incident, to administrative, to a personnel problem, to an emergency or perhaps a sexual harassment case. This one is actually easy. From lessons learned, MDPD and Miami-Dade County government put procedures in place if an employee came to a supervisor with this complaint, the supervisor reports up the chain, and it's automatically kicked over to Internal Affairs for investigation. The sergeant who was initially told does nothing else which makes it easy.

While addressing the scenarios, you are being videotaped and your responses will be reviewed at a later time by a group of *assessors*. These folks are generally supervisors from other departments who come into town and review and score your responses on a scale from 1 to 7, and then blow back out of town. It's been rumored you want your video to be reviewed early in the day because near day's end, these folks are tired of watching hundreds of videos and the scores begin to slip. When MDPD has its sergeant test every two years, 600 officers will sign up. After the written test, there could be 300-400 who make it to Phase 2, so that's a lot of videos. But wait, there's more; Phase 3. This is the final part of the process where you have the *In-Basket* exercise. This means you have a pile of paperwork in front of you that you have to address as if you were a sergeant. Sergeants have quite a bit of this to do during their duties, so you have to *prioritize* the paperwork in writing and do it in two hours. No rush!

When the bell rang and we were done, a great weight was lifted and the pressure was off. Thank, fucking whatever you wish to add! It was over. A group of us headed to Longhorn Steakhouse on NW 87 Ave and had some beers with lunch. We commiserated about the journey and were glad to be done with it. The list came out in November, and while I was on patrol and had stopped into a K-Mart to get something to drink, a lieutenant friend of mine Pat Hanlon called me to let me know I was Number 30 on the list. Yes! I was guaranteed to make sergeant because anywhere from 70-100 will get promoted off any given list and those were good for the next two years. What I kick myself in the ass for was my 78 written score. At fourteen years on I had accumulated six Seniority Points, maxed out, to add to my overall score, and my scores on the oral exercise and In-Basket were 6s & 7s. I couldn't do any better there. Had I scored say 85 or 90 on the written, I would have finished No.1 on my list. I know it sounds petty and egotistical, but I wanted to do the best *I* could and *I* didn't. I have never gotten a score like that again on any test since. But, horseshoes I guess. I made it! By the way, this promotional process in Phases 2 & 3 was completely subjective, and your scores were based on someone's *opinion,* and we didn't really feel it was a fair process. A few years ago, the department went to a one-phase written test format, so doing well or poorly on that was fairer. If I had to do it now, I better retain that info.

On April 5, 1998, I got promoted and after a two-week delay, was shipped off to Northside Station. But before I left, another two of the best sergeants I've had, Wayne Gaskell and Kathy Engstrom, both told me it was good to get promoted to sergeant, the first rung, because you get to be part of the decision-making process. Mmmm. Made sense, so instead of taking orders and waiting for others to figure things out, now I could be the one doing the figuring.

I then reported to Northside and got my first squad on the afternoon shift, and another of the best supervisors I have ever had, Lieutenant Charles Nanney, became my supervisor. He was a "cop's cop!" We had *"The Talk,"* and he simply told me "I heard you're great cop." I replied in kind, and that was *"The Talk."* He cut me loose and didn't micromanage me. I kept him informed of things as they happened or came up, and he let me *be me*. We had a great relationship and he did teach me well, as I needed to learn how to be a sergeant.

My first squad was all rookies with the senior guy having only three years on. But these kids busted their asses for me and the greater good. So much so, that in 1999 Lt. Nanney wrote us up for a Unit Commendation which a uniform squad never gets. It's usually specialized units that receive this award. My first squad was great and I am forever grateful and proud of them for their hard work and dedication.

I went on to other assignments but making sergeant opened a lot of doors for me where I could mentor and influence others. I joined the Mobile Field Force (MFF) Training Committee in 98' and later became the senior instructor after having been mentored by those great instructors that came before me, like Sergeant Tim Adams, Sergeant Craig Sciortino, and Sergeant Rick Poling. They passed the baton to me and I am grateful to them for showing me the ropes. I have had the opportunity as a sergeant to instruct about 25000 officers and supervisors over the years in MFF, driving, Major Scene Management for supervisors, Crisis Intervention Team and some others. There have been so many great aspects to having made sergeant but the most rewarding one for me was getting to lead, supervise, and teach those officers directly assigned to me on my many squads over the twenty-two years I was a sergeant. I started with a completely rookie squad in 1998, and when I retired in February 2020 as "Sergeant Maverick" from the Airport District, I had the most senior squad in Miami-Dade Police. I came full circle, and I am proud of the work we have done. I was very content to remain a sergeant, though my wife Rosy kept pushing me to make lieutenant then captain, but that would have taken me away from what I enjoyed most; being in *"The Shit!"* The crazier it was, the better I liked it. So there!

There are sooo many more stories about being a sergeant, both good and bad, it would fill two or three chapters, but I will leave you with this; professionally, it was the best move I ever made. I have learned from the best, and the worst, and went on to be one of the best, I hope. Only those I supervised and worked with can judge me. My motto, which I adopted from an unknown author, and I used in a previous chapter came directly from my experiences as a sergeant and I will use it here again; *"Leaders are like eagles; they never flock together, you find them one at a time."* As a sergeant I became that leader, thanks to those who came before me.

The Best of the Best

Sergeant James *"Pappy"* Slack
Sergeant *"Tactical"* Tim Adams
Sergeant Bob Holden
Sergeant Jack Breen
Lieutenant Charles Nanney
Sergeant Bill Solen
Lieutenant Bob Waller
Sergeant Vicki Payne
Sergeant John Long
Sergeant Tom Linehan (RIP)
Sergeant Joe Hodges
Sergeant Ed Petow
Sergeant Larry Neill
Sergeant Jim Loftus
Sergeant Bob Paige
Sergeant Brian Williams
Sergeant Bob Diers
Sergeant Ruben Galindo

Sergeant Wayne Gaskill
Sergeant Kathy Engstrom
Lieutenant Bill Brink
Lieutenant Mauricio Rivera
Captain Carl Wright
Major Connie Cooper
Lieutenant Raul "Chewy" Martinez
Lieutenant Bobby Wilcox
Lieutenant Rafael Rodriguez
Lieutenant Tom Buchanan
Lieutenant Gordon "Chappy" Chapman (RIP)
Lieutenant Steve "Ski" Czyzewski
Lieutenant Manny Miranda
Major Raymond Melcon

My undying gratitude to everyone I worked for and who showed me how to be a good *Cop!*

ACT – 16 Court - Another Circus

Scene 1: How Court Actually Works

Another aspect of being in law enforcement is learning how the court system actually works and how to navigate this branch of the Criminal Justice System. Some of the cases we handle as police officers ultimately end up in the court system, whether it's a major crime such as a homicide, robbery, burglary, assault, or something as simple as a traffic infraction, and traffic court is the most common. There's a chance when we put pen to paper, or nowadays tap a computer keyboard, what we document will invariably end up in front of a judge or perhaps a jury, maybe. What many folks don't realize about our system of justice is when a police officer makes an arrest or issues a citation, it doesn't mean the case is over and the subject of the investigation is automatically convicted, sent to jail, or pays a fine. We are only the beginning of the journey for an individual who crossed swords with the justice system and it by no means ends with us.

Police will make an arrest, say a felony for Aggravated Battery, where the subject cracked a baseball bat across someone's head and put them in the hospital. We take the subject into custody, prepare the A-Form (arrest affidavit), deliver the subject to the jail where depending on the crime they can post bail, are denied bail, or have to appear in front of a judge to get bail, and from there the actual court process begins. Our A-Form and related reports go to the State Attorney's Office (SAO) or more commonly *As Seen on TV*, the *DA*, or District Attorney's Office in other states. This is where our reports are *"screened"* and a determination is made as to whether the charges will actually be *"filed"* against the subject. "But wait Bert, didn't you say the victim was hit in the head with a baseball bat and you have pictures and witnesses who saw it?" Yes, but that doesn't mean the SAO will file the charges.

It depends on how seriously the victim is hurt, (seriously! as in no shit) what the subject's criminal past is like, and what the SAOs case load is that month and if it's worth pursuing. The SAO doesn't like to waste it's time on cases where there is a chance the victim may not appear in court or if the case gets drawn out. The SAO will also talk to the victim and ask *if* they wish to pursue their case. Many times the victim doesn't want to, so it ends there. Domestics are the exception and the State will file even without the cooperation of the victim; thank OJ again. In a jurisdiction like Miami-Dade County which is very busy, and I get it, but they want slam-dunks if they can get them. This is part of the reality of making arrests and filing cases. We can do hours upon hours of paperwork following the arrest, processing the crime scene, impounding property, transporting the prisoner, and it may never see a court room. But "good work on the arrest."

A part of the screening process known as a *Pre-File Conference* is appearing in front of a screening ASA (Assistant State's Attorney) who reviews the case and makes the determination to file or not to file the case, hence the name *pre-file*. You as the arresting officer will give testimony under oath as to the facts of the case and may think it's a no-brainer, especially when you the officer was the victim of an assault by the subject, but then the SAO decides not to file the case. I can tell you unequivocally going back not too long ago, screening attorneys thought it was part of our job to get assaulted and hurt, trampled, kicked, punched, scratched, and even spat on. So imagine how an officer feels who got a few bruises in a fight from one of our pillars of the community, and the SAO says they don't want to go forward? It happens all the time and we have had to get our union, the PBA, involved in some cases to force the SAO to file the case.

A Not-So Flattering but Poignant Story

In the 80's under then State's Attorney Janet Reno, *Battery on a PO* (police officer) as we call it, was a very difficult case to get filed because as I stated, the culture at the SAO was very much anti-police, and getting injured was "just part of the job" as many in the office saw it. The officer had to be seriously hurt to get the case filed, so I guess we've come full circle in current times in America once again, but that was another chapter. So getting into arguments with the SAO was common and very frustrating. After all, the attorney isn't the one who was punched in the face.

So at one pre-file conference, one of my station mates was giving testimony and told a young ASA the subject ended up spitting on him and John H. (RIP) wanted the case filed. The ASA told John who was a veteran officer getting spat on was just part of the job and he wouldn't file the case.

John had had enough at this point in his career and stood up, leaned over the desk, and let the ASA have it right in the face! He then said, "how do *you* like it?" added a few colorful metaphors and walked out.

I guess the ASA was so shocked he didn't file a complaint. Not that John would have cared, but it speaks to some of the frustration of being a police officer. Again, I guess we've come full circle. When you are a new officer you don't understand this process and you question why it's done this way. After a while you learn to accept it and realize you are just one of *Cogswells Cogs* in this big machine and you are relegated to just turning your *Spacely Sprocket* and move on to the next case.

Scene 2: Raise Your Right Hand

Appearing in court early in your career can be very intimidating because you've had no experience in speaking in front of a judge or a jury, and now you're being asked questions by an ASA and a defense attorney, and even though you thought you knew the facts of your case, you have trouble recounting them under pressure. Out on the street you may have to make a quick decision on what to do, make the arrest, write down what happened, and then months or even a year or more has gone by and now you're trying to remember what occurred. If you didn't pull all of your reports and review them before trial, you're going to look pretty foolish on the stand when you can't remember what happened. This unfortunately happens quite a bit with younger. and some older, complacent officers who don't prepare. I don't know about you, but I don't like to look like I wasn't fully prepared and possibly lose the case. If it is a low-level misdemeanor case, not only are you inexperienced, but the ASA assigned to prosecute the case is also pretty wet behind the ears and just saw the case file the evening before or the same morning and isn't prepared either. So you have two strikes going in, and chances are good you're both going up against an experienced defense lawyer, who may have been a prosecutor at one time and knows how to exploit the weaknesses. So a bit of advice for all of you young Jedis' out there, whether you are in criminal court or traffic, review your reports and copies of your citations so you don't look the fool when testifying. Seriously!

First Court Story-Ever!

As I related in my earlier act on training, my first trial was of a DUI named Kendall Stover. A bad drunk and he was even drunk when he finally appeared in court. It was a slam-dunk arrest at the time my FTO Al Goodall and I had and thought it would be the same in court.

Nope! I was sooo nervous when the very experienced defense attorney asked me to demonstrate the *Roadside Tests* we had Mr. Stover perform on the night of; where I stood with my head tilted back and tried to stand straight, I swayed like I was being blown by the wind.

That attorney to his credit, made me look like I couldn't stand straight sober, and discredited the test and me, and we lost the case. I felt so bad and, of course, questioned how this could have happened. For Christ's Sake, he was drunk in court! But that wasn't when it counted. Juries can be fickle, and I looked bad. I swore I would never let that happen again.

One of the tricks I learned from veteran officers when giving testimony, besides trying to prepare, is to give short, to the point answers without a lot of adlibbing. When you answer only the question posed to you without elaborating, you can't have your testimony twisted around and confused, and it leaves the defense with nowhere to go.

Prosecutor: "Officer Gonzalez, did you respond to the defendant's residence on a 911 call?"

Me: "Yes."

Prosecutor: What did you see when you arrived?"

Me: "I saw the defendant's wife bleeding from the mouth."

Prosecutor: "Did she tell you her husband hit her?"

Me: "Yes."

Defense: "Officer Gonzalez, you said you saw Mrs. Rodriguez bleeding from the head, as if she fell and struck her head, correct?"

Me: "No, I did not."

Defense: "But you said she was bleeding?"

Me: "Yes, I did."

Defense: "So where did you say she was bleeding?"

Me: "From the mouth."

Slow and steady and that drives defense attorneys crazy when they can't trip you up to confuse the issue, and that's how you give testimony. There are times where you have to elaborate more of course, but when your answers are short and sweet, there's little room for interpretation. If you ramble on, it can look like you're searching for answers and that bodes poorly for any witness.

Court Battle: Counsel for the Defense vs. Officer N. Gonzalez

I was a young officer with about three or four years on, 86'/87' and was patrolling alone when I received a call of a *"3-17" (crash w/injuries)* that occurred on SW 92 Ave just south of 128 Street. When I arrived, and I was alone the entire time by the way (no one from my squad ever showed up, thanks a lot) I saw a scene where I thought for sure I had some fatalities.

The Set Up

The Scene: SW 92 Ave in this area is a sweeping curve to the left and slightly downhill. It is four lanes divided by a 200-foot-long median with palm trees (Miami-of course) every 20 or 30 feet. I saw three sets of trees broken in half with a Mercedes SL 350 (two-seater, convertible) on its side at the end of the median, with a kid trapped underneath it. "Shit!" Along with some good Samaritans, we were able to pull the kid from under the car, and miraculously he was only a little banged up.

The Investigation: I began to piece together this puzzle as it was a *One-Car Crash*; mmmm. What I learned was *Speed Racer*, the kid that was under the car and underaged, and two of his idiot sidekicks were at home bored, while Mommy & Daddy were out on their boat, and decided to take Daddy's Benz for a joyride and along the way and stopped at a Gulf Gas Station to buy beer. Yes, Mr. Wizard behind the counter sold *Speed* some beer because he was a big kid; more on that in a bit.

After the *Three Amigos* released some inhibitions, they wanted to see how fast Daddy's toy could go so with *Speed* at the controls, Idiot Number 2 in the passenger seat, and Idiot Number 3 seated in the small space behind the seats sideways and no seatbelts for anyone of course. He punched it west bound on 128 Street and when they reached 92 Ave they were doing roughly 80 mph.

But wait there's more; *Speed* decided at this point it would be a good idea to turn hard left onto 92 Ave. No, it wasn't. When he did, he put the car into a slide, went right over the median, hit the first palm tree, which launched the car into three rolls, ejecting the *Three Amigos* into the air, and somehow *Speed* ended up under the car at the end. How they weren't killed is beyond me.

When I conducted my interviews of *Dumb, Dumber, and Dumber* still, they all told me independently of their Sunday Drive around the park and how they wanted to see how fast the car could go. So folks, when you drive like a maniac like *Speed* did, your actions are willful and wanton with a disregard for the safety of property and persons, meaning you intentionally tried to drive that way, and in Florida that's called *Reckless Driving; FSS 316.192 (1)(a)*, which is a misdemeanor, criminal traffic offense, and is usually an arrest situation that requires a court appearance. So I issued the citation because *Speed* was in the hospital and waited for court. Oh yea, I had to call the parents of the three very lucky halfwits and tell them how stupid their sons were. Fortunately, they weren't death notifications.

Court Day

So now court rolls around for the driver and he shows up with Daddy and an older, high-powered lawyer. If you got the clue before where it was a Mercedes Benz SL and *Speed's* parents were out on their boat, then you know they had money. So as court goes, the calendar is called and the judge, Alphonso Sepe in this case, dispenses with the "Guilty" & "No-Contest" pleas to get them out of the way, leaving the "Not Guilty" cases for *"The Break."* This is where the judge calls a recess and the prosecutor meets with the defendants and tries to work out *"A Deal;"* meaning they'll reduce the charges and fines if the defendant agrees to plead it out without a trial. While we are on break, the defense attorney, smelling inexperience and perhaps fear on my part like a wolf, comes up to me and tells me I will never win this case and I should tell the State to drop it to *Careless Driving*.

Wrong way to come at me Spanky! I may be young but I don't scare easy anymore. He was trying to intimidate me because I was a young officer and as *Counsel for the Defense*, he pulled every trick to do so. Neither I nor the ASA wanted to drop the case but what I didn't know at the time was there was a big civil case going on behind the scenes.

The prosecutor saw the diagram of my crash report, and I can tell you I can draw. I took mechanical drawing in high school and my crash diagrams were detailed and elaborate. So she asked me to redraw it on a chalk board during lunch and we kept it hidden until trial. You want to fight a guerrilla war, so be it! Ambush!

Trial started and the prosecutor did her direct examination of me and I told Judge Sepe exactly what I saw when I arrived on scene, what we did, and what the *Amigos* told me. When we flipped the chalk board you should have seen the look on not only the attorney's face but Judge Sepe as well. Surprise! A Kodak Moment for certain. The defense attorney now had his turn on cross and he tried to twist everything I said with; "Didn't you say" "No I did not, I said…" and that's how it went for about fifteen minutes. He did his best to make me look like the inexperienced officer I was, but remember, after the early DUI case I lost, never again.

After *Counsel for the Defense* made some motions for dismissal, Judge Sepe said "Denied, Officer Gonzalez's testimony and evidence tells the story; guilty!" I was glad and relieved it was over and I had hit one out of the park!

The Bitter End

Almost three months later I receive a subpoena for what appeared to be a civil case. I looked up the case and retrieved all the reports, and wouldn't you know it, it was my *Three Amigos* case wrapped up in lawsuits. My notice for the deposition was at *Mr. Wolf* Attorney's office, so let's see what this is all about. When I sat down at the end of the conference table, Daddy's Counsel was at the other end, and seated around the table were six other attorneys representing the other two kid's parents, the insurance companies, and Gulf Oil, the beer distributor. One by one they asked me questions about the case while Daddy's lawyer stayed silent. Now I know why he tried so hard to get it dropped to careless driving so the others in civil court couldn't prove willfulness which translates to more $$$$. At the end one attorney asked me what the outcome was of the criminal case. All of the attorneys should have known before deposition; they didn't do their homework. But I looked at my nemesis and said, "Didn't you tell them about the trial?" He sheepishly bowed his head and said: "No." I then told the gallery his client was found guilty of *Reckless Driving*, and they all frantically started writing down notes. I found out later the suits were settled out of court. Enough said!

Scene 3: Who Wins, Who Loses?

Attending court can be an eye-opener if you have never been, and most people haven't unless perhaps they received a traffic citation and asked to have their day in court.

When we sit in the court room waiting for our case to be called and remember I'm telling you this from a police officer's point of view, the officers are generally seated in the jury box, with the overflow into one side of the court room which is usually configured like church pews, with most of the "defendants" seated on the other side.

The prosecutors are at their desk and podium, dressed in their new lawyer-appropriate suits and frantically looking at their case files, which as I previously stated they were probably seeing for the first time, and looking around the court room like meerkats for their witnesses.

The other podium is empty and that's where the defendant and their attorney will be standing when their case is called. As an officer on a case, you have to check-in with the prosecutor to let them know you're there, and trying to get their attention is sometimes difficult as "newbies" can be a bit lost themselves. The lower the court, the newer the prosecutor, the higher the crime, the more experienced the prosecutor.

The judge walks in and you hear from the bailiff those famous words, *"All Rise!"* You can almost hear the *Law & Order "Dun, Dun!"* He or she sits and *"Be seated."* They go through the calendar and as each case is called, the judge asks if the State is ready, meaning is the State ready to proceed to trial, and the prosecutor begins nervously calling out names of victims and witnesses to see if they answer, and then replies, ready, not ready, or pass. The defense attorney will then begin their part of the game by filing a motion for dismissal if the State wasn't ready, or files a continuance so as to drag-out the case, which always bodes better for the defense. The longer a case goes the chances are higher a state witness or victim won't be available or lose interest in testifying. Cases are dismissed all the time and, if they are low-level, nonviolent misdemeanors, no one cares. There are just too many cases and the more dismissals the better. But don't let the reason a case gets dismissed be you as the officer. Oh no! If a civilian witness doesn't show, so what. If an officer doesn't and didn't call-in absent with a reason, the SAO files a complaint with the officer's department and believe it or not, even if all the other witnesses on the case didn't show, we get in trouble for not attending. The other side of that coin is the SAO will keep you around in court, not keep you abreast of the case, and then hours into it when you try to ask them what is happening, they say the case was continued or dismissed without any regard for your time there. True, we get paid overtime to attend court on our off-duty time, but if you're a midnight officer, do you want to stay awake and in court all morning for no reason?

When I attended court, of course I want to win my cases, why make the arrest or issue the citation then? But what I have noticed over the years and decades is who actually gets justice and who doesn't. If you can afford an attorney and it isn't a heinous crime, sometimes even if it is, you will probably get off with fines and probation and may even get a dismissal. But if you're that poor bastard with no money and perhaps little education or have a language barrier and are standing at the podium with that deer-in-the-headlights look, you have very little chance of a favorable outcome. Even for a very minor offense these folks sometimes end up in jail because no one is there to defend them and I have to say I truly feel sorry for them. Money wins, no money loses. That has been the main complaint of our justice system and I believe in many cases it's true. The State is looking for the win, the defense is looking for the dismissal, and the defendant many times is left alone to fend for themselves. Justice has to be administered but administered with compassion. Sometimes compassion seems to cost a little too much.

We make the arrest and many times have to tell the State to reduce the fine or plead it down to something manageable for the defendant because believe it or not, the most compassionate person on that case *is* the police officer. We have to do our jobs, but that doesn't mean we have to bury the guy; we save those for really violent, asshole-bad guys. A nonviolent crime isn't really important unless of course the defendant keeps committing it, then the state has no choice but to seek jail because Goober isn't getting the message. Winning at all costs isn't how the system is supposed to work. We as officers get very frustrated watching the power struggles between the prosecution, defense, and the judge, and we are left on the sidelines sometimes wondering what the Hell we're doing there. Remember, all three are lawyers and are always right.

Late in my career and because I became somewhat "saltier" at this point, have had to dress-down prosecutors that had no regard for and treated us very poorly. Just the same, I've had cases with very experienced prosecutors who saw the "Big Picture" and know how to manage a case, with regard to all involved, including the defendant. I've also gotten along very well with defense attorneys who are in most cases, just doing their jobs and thank goodness they are. If you need one yourself for any reason, then you want a fighter on your side. That's our system with the good and the bad. Winston Churchill said—I'm a big fan by the way—"Democracy is the worst form of government; except for all the others." Our system of justice is a big part of that, but it's all we got, so we better make it work.

Scene 4: Got Integrity? Better Have It

When a person testifies in court, whether it's a victim of a crime, a witness on the case, an especially a police officer, the judge and jury have to find you credible and any hint of being untruthful, even withholding testimony or evidence, and you are done as a witness and you'll probably not only lose the case, but everyone in the State Attorney's Office, Public Defender's Office, judges and private attorneys will know you lied on the stand. Any prior cases you may have been involved in can be called into question, reopened and maybe even appealed and overturned. You do not want to be *that guy* and that reputation will follow you for years to come. Fortunately, this is rare, at least in my experience, but the point is make sure you sound and look credible when testifying in a traffic case all the way up to murder.

I have had occasion to see very good, mediocre, and very poor officers testify. Those who have a command of the facts of their case are bullet-proof and win their cases and garner the respect of those in criminal justice circles. Those who are ill prepared and sound like they're searching for answers, not necessarily lying, but can't fully recall their case, lose and are remembered for that.

The reason I am telling you this is because of my first trial experience and loss I encountered. I wanted to make certain I was one of those who were respected and yes, feared by the defense, and my cases were air-tight. I never lost a case due to my involvement ever again.

As I outlined, traffic court is the most common court appearance an officer will have unless they spend most of their career in a specialized unit like homicide, robbery, narcotics, etc. If you work the road and write tickets, traffic court is where you go. I did this for most of my career and still issued citations up to one month before I retired because this person was in dire need of an education for her driving habits. But early on I did quite a bit of traffic enforcement and went to court a lot.

A Court Story

I received a subpoena for traffic court at the South Dade Justice Center, a satellite courthouse, where I *was* the One O'clock calendar; just me for the whole two hours for thirty-six tickets I had issued in the months prior, and those folks decided they wanted their day in court. This is everyone's right to appear and have a judge decide whether you pay the fine, get the points, or are found not guilty or have the citation dismissed for some other reason. This is part of the game and it isn't personal unless someone makes it that way.

The calendar started and I was appearing in front of Judge Harvey Klein, an experienced and fair judge to all sides. I started with my first case, articulated the facts, the defendant said his peace, and "Guilty!" After one or two more, I had this case where I observed a gentleman swerve out of his lane on SW 137 Ave in what I deemed to be a dangerous maneuver. I had to turn around and wasn't able to stop him until a mile or so from the scene. He told me he had to swerve due to a bend in the road and another vehicle had cut him off.

Not being able to confirm his story from where we were, and because people lie to us, no kidding, I issued the citation, and sent him on his way. But I went back to the area to see what he was talking about since I now had my doubts about what I saw. After surveying the area, I decided he was correct, so I made my notes on my copy of the ticket and waited for court.

When his case came up, I told Judge Klein what had happened and the gentleman was correct, and I requested a dismissal of the case. Judge Klein kindly complied, and the gentleman thanked me in open court. Just about every case after the defendant plead "No-Contest," meaning they weren't going to say they were not guilty and contest my testimony, because I had shown myself to be honest and fair and display great integrity and no way would I lose another case, and I didn't.

The best for last: I attempted to stop a car on SW 122 Ave north of Bird Road just after dark one evening that had the left taillight out. Now before you go off by saying it was only a taillight, my intent then and always has been to inform the driver a tail or brake light was out so they may get it fixed, not to write the ticket.

If an officer didn't stop you to let you know, how else would you know your taillight was out? Right! So I light up this vehicle and the driver refuses to stop. My first thought of course is maybe it's stolen, the driver has a suspended license or a warrant, or was involved in something else. I follow it for about four or five blocks into the neighborhood and the vehicle pulls into a driveway. Mmmm. A woman gets out and asks what *my* problem is. Bad way to start. I explained I was only trying to let her know her taillight was out, and she should have stopped where I first initiated the traffic stop, not drive to her house because that's what she felt like doing. She gave me a really difficult time, and if you have ever heard stories about giving an officer a bad attitude on a traffic stop and how that usually ends up poorly for the driver, it's true. This was only a courtesy attempt to inform her and it was a lousy $15.00 fine back in the 80s, but she graduated and earned her diploma. Cite 1! I gave her the ticket and went on my way.

Now fast forward back to court day; her case was called well into my calendar; I was batting a thousand and she knew better than to contest it at that point. A lousy $15 bucks and half a day away from work that she brought on herself, but her arrogance drove her to go to court. She pleads "no-contest" and Judge Klein upheld the $15.00 fine and added $25.00 in court costs. Everyone has the right to go to court, but if you're found guilty there are added penalties for your day in court. Judge Klein said next case, and as my darling defendant was walking to the bench to await making payment, she said under her breath and I quote; *"You Son-of-a-Bitch!"* I heard it, and so did Judge Klein.

He said, *"Son-of-a-Bitch!* I'll show you a *Son-of-a-Bitch!"* Get back over here and give me back that file." Two people you don't piss off; a cop on a traffic stop and a judge in court. He changed the court costs to $200.00 and threatened to put her in jail for contempt. Then he made her wait until the end of the calendar to pay her fines after everyone else had finished. This all happened because she didn't feel like stopping her car when I lit her up so I could just inform her she had a taillight out. Careful what you say. After that day I never lost another traffic ticket in Judge Klein's court or any other for that matter.

Integrity means everything.

I'll end this with some advice for all parties involved in a case that ends up in court. If you're a defendant, you're entitled to your day in court. But make sure you didn't actually do anything wrong. If you did, you're wasting everyone's time and it will cost you. If you're a prosecutor, enforce the law with compassion where guidelines allow you to show leniency where appropriate, and slam the hardcore criminals as warranted. Also, police officers don't get paid to get hurt or spat on. If you think they do, then strap on a bullet-proof vest and go on some ride-a-longs for a better perspective. If you're a defense attorney, yes, most of your clients are guilty, defend them, but don't make it personal with the officers. If you're a judge, don't act like a defense lawyer and question everything the officer did just because you don't like the police, and believe me many don't. And last, if you're a police officer, know and understand your case, prepare yourself well, read all of your reports and citations, and enforce the law with compassion as well, because this whole thing begins with you. Do it right!

ACT - 17 "Point - 0"

Scene 1: Yes, We Get Free Food - Get Over It!

Over the centuries, yes centuries, there has been law enforcement patrolling the streets of *Any Town USA*, or country for that matter, whether it was on foot patrol, horseback, or as of the early 20th century, a patrol car, and sheriff deputies, town marshals, constables, officers and cops, have had to eat while on-duty just like everyone else.

The difference is in modern times with a police radio at hand, an officer may get a call for service in the middle of that meal and have to leave it sitting on the table; maybe he comes back later to finish it, maybe he doesn't depending on what he was called away for. I have been called away many a time and have had to leave my food never to taste it again. That's the nature of police work; emergencies don't care you haven't eaten, and we accept that as part of our profession. Few other jobs get called away, like fire and the medical field, but most everyone else who works gets to finish their meal.

On those occasions, the restaurant merchant is usually kind enough to either pack it up for us or keep it warm awaiting our return. And to those restaurateurs out there who take care of us, we are very grateful.

Because of what we do, there were eateries that gave us either completely free meals or a greatly discounted one. It is less often now, but very commonplace when I was a young Jedi. Much has been made about this over the years from those that believe we aren't entitled to a "free lunch" as it were, so let me set the record straight here. Except for that rogue officer who might demand it once in a while, 99 percent of us and here we go again with the percentage thing, don't expect it, and it is *offered* by the merchant to us in appreciation for what we do and greatly in part for going in harm's way for the community. We don't ask for it, but it is greatly, greatly appreciated by police and firefighters as well, for when they eat outside of their station houses, and accepted as a kind gesture on their part, and we call that *"Point-0."* Meaning the cost is zero. *"Point-5"* means 50 percent off, and so on. Every agency has that little clause in their SOPs that states we won't accept gratuities, and in general we don't. A *"Point-0"* or discounted meal is not really considered a gratuity and is not enforced by most supervisors or by the command staff. They got it too when they were on their way up and as long as it isn't abused nothing is said about it. Gratuities are considered as payment or gifts given for doing our jobs and leads to problems. Meals are accepted in the culture, always have been, and for the most part always will.

I have eaten in so many restaurants during my career where the merchant simply would not accept payment from us, not because we expected or demanded it and we would actually try to pay, but our money was no good for them. They actually *like* having us around, unlike some of those in this day and age who have signs on their doors prohibiting us from patronizing their establishment, but because it ensures they are safe, for the time being, and enjoy taking care of us because we take care of them. It is not an official quid pro quo, (there's one of those political hot-potatoes), but it does seem that way to the untrained, biased, or cynical eye. And a little side note to you baristas out there that think we're evil and won't serve us coffee; we'll find coffee at your competitor's place where they actually want us to sit and relax there. And your coffee isn't that good to begin with *Buck-a-Roo!*

There are some very savvy restaurant merchants that simply do it to have us there, not because they necessarily like us but because it's good for business and they aren't going to get robbed if their place is known as a cop hang out. And of course, human nature being what it is, we will gravitate to those establishments that take care of us because who doesn't want to save a buck here or there? We all do, especially if you are a young officer with no money just starting out in life. It's natural, but again appreciated. A note on accepting gratuities: There are gratuities and there are gratuities. Accepting pay or a car is a gratuity, no doubt. But accepting a cake from a citizen on Christmas who just wanted to say Happy Holidays and thank us for what we do, isn't a gratuity. But this actually happened at the City of South Miami Police Department in the late 80s, where a kind lady baked a cake for the fine officers of SMPD and dropped it off at the station's front desk, where the officer covering the desk that evening graciously accepted it on behalf of the entire department. You know what that officer got for accepting that Christmas cake? Fired! That's right.

The chief, and I wish I could recall his name, took the gratuity thing way too far and fired the officer for accepting a cake for goodness' sake. He completely misunderstood what the understanding of what is and what isn't a gratuity, and how do you think the woman felt when she found out her cake got someone fired? A cake! Bad call on the chief's part and I'm guessing he would have fired himself for taking a free cup of coffee. Stupid.

My Mickey D's Story

I've told this story so many times to friends and colleagues over the years because it was so poignant in my life. When I was growing up in Brewster, NY, a small town about sixty-five miles north of New York City, going to the Golden Arches was a treat for us because we didn't have one in town, and the closest McDonalds was in Carmel, the next town over. So when we made a run over there, my father drove my brother Pete and my sister Marisa and I, and we would usually pick up the food and bring it home. Sometimes the real treat was to eat there. Don't misunderstand, we weren't poor, our parents Norberto and Noemi made sure we had everything we needed and we were comfortable. Though I didn't get that mini-bike I wanted but that's another story. But going to McDonalds was just a fun thing we didn't do often, but what kid doesn't like going there?

As an athletic and always active kid, I had a voracious appetite and my favorite was *"Two all-beef patties, special sauce, lettuce, cheese, pickles, onions on a sesame seed bun!"* I loved *Big Macs* and to this day every two years or so I'll indulge myself. Gotta watch the weight! But back then when we went, I had two, count'em, two *Big Macs* and two cheeseburgers, nothing like a McDonalds' cheeseburger, a large fry, can't go without those, and an apple pie. I bet your mouth is watering about now, isn't it? Mine is too. But I had to get it while I could because the next trip was three or four months away.

So now I'll fast forward to June 1883 and being an in shape, 170-pound, rookie cop in the Southwest District. Part of your training, unofficially of course, is to learn where the restaurants are that "take care" of us, and in my district, Miami in general, there were SOOO many McDonalds everywhere! I couldn't believe it! I had never seen so many until I moved to Miami, and *ALL* of the Mickey D's in my area were owned by the same gentleman who loved Metro-Dade cops, and they never charged us for meal.

Each store manager had standing orders cops didn't get charged. So imagine me now with my *Big Mac* fetish; I was like a kid in a candy store. We would break roll call and if we didn't get a call right away, we would look at each other and say, "You hungry?" And off to the drive-thru we went. Not everyday mind you, but often enough. Our diets as young officers on the go all the time were for shit, but we were young and didn't know any better.

Over the course of the next year, my wife at the time, No. 1, was pregnant and I didn't realize every time she was eating I was eating too. Couple that with my propensity for a *Mac Attack* and by July 1984 when my daughter Cristina was born, I was 200 friggen pounds! What the hell? How'd that happen? Bert you idiot, it happened because you had access to free food and weren't paying attention. Ah, the double-edged sword of over-indulgence! You can bet over the years I learned, as did most of us, to temper our appetites and the kindness of the merchants with moderation. Don't get me wrong, I still had some fantastic meals over the years at the insistence of the restaurateur, but as I got older there were a lot more salads involved. I wonder why?

One of our cardinal rules when we took a *"12"* was to make sure you had money at the ready in case you were charged, and if you were, so be it. We were charged so infrequently it didn't matter, and we still went back to that restaurant, not because of the price but because the food was good and the folks were nice. So let me wrap up this little segment for those of you who would say we don't deserve or shouldn't get a free meal now and then; you're not the one who has to leave in the middle of eating to handle someone *else's* crisis, maybe get hurt doing so, work all night on a couple of cups of coffee because there was no time to eat, write a report while wolfing down that meal in anticipation of the next crisis that's coming, and if the merchants want to show their appreciation by taking care of us, then we have no problem with that and are forever grateful. So, you can just get over yourselves and show a little appreciation!

Scene 2: Cops & Donuts-Stop with the Jokes Already!

Over the years in movies, TV, and in person, everyone has had a good ole time with joking about Cops & Donuts, haha. Had a good laugh? Good. Everyone likes to make fun of us because they think we eat a lot of donuts, even our brethren over at Fire like to have a laugh on us now and again.

But while you're telling the donut joke at the party at the expense of the only cop in attendance for that cheap laugh you so greatly need, do you actually know where the whole donut thing started? Of course you don't, you just think it's funny and don't realize that you are actually making a *fat-joke*.

Yes, after a while it bothers us, so knock it off! In the meantime, let me enlighten you a bit, but first; "I was stopped by a cop and he asked me if I knew why he had stopped me? I said, because you thought I had the doughnuts?"

As I've outlined time and time again throughout my book, there are a few professions that require a 24-hour tour of duty, police work being the most prominent. Going back to the mid-20th Century, officers in many cities were on a *"foot-beat"* as it was called, and later began to transition to a patrol vehicle, and in both cases they worked the *graveyard shift*, midnights. You not only had crappy hours but had to manage to stay awake, handle your duties, write your reports, and if you walked a beat in cold regions, had to try to stay warm. During this early time there weren't a lot of places open at night like we have now in our 24/7, microwave, hurry up, on the go lifestyle, and the only places open were the local *Mom & Pop* coffee shops, where an officer could stay warm, get a hot cup of Joe to keep him awake, write his reports in relative comfort, and get a bite to eat. What was served in every coffee shop everywhere, especially at that time? You guessed it, donuts! Or donuts, as we've come to call them.

When you're tired, sleepy, hungry, and needed a boost, that little, sweet, tasty, full of sugar, *Crime-Fighting Power Biscuit* was what was readily available and proud to be of service. To this day, a midnight officer might indulge in some form of the calorie-rich, round delight as a necessity, and who doesn't love a good donut now and then? So when you saw a cop sitting in a coffee shop with a coffee by her or his side, maybe you also saw a donut and so the legend was born. This was born out of necessity and availability, not necessarily the deep, overwhelming desire for a donut. As we now know all these years and medical studies later, a donut is one of the absolute worse things you can eat, but we all do occasionally, and that's ok, but believe me, we don't eat them like the urban legend would have you believe.

The donut cliché' actually goes back further than just cops on the beat, and you'll have to go back as far as World War I for it, when Salvation Army volunteers served donuts to soldiers on the front lines in France, and in the 1920s, the Red Cross provided free donuts for veterans who were living abroad. So, go ahead and have a laugh, we're in pretty good company. And that's how we came to be forever married to donuts!

Scene 3: Having Coffee & Never Saw it Coming

So, having coffee is a safe and mundane activity, right? For most people it is and many actually go to their favorite coffee house to have a cup and catch up on some work as do cops. It is a perfect place for us to do our paperwork, I mean computer work now, and kick back a little while completing those endless police reports we have to write. Not so on the morning of November 29, 2009, at 8:15 A.M. for a sergeant and three of his officers who were doing just that. Sergeant Mark Renninger of the Lakewood Police Department in Washington State was meeting with his officers, Tina Griswald, Ronald Owens, and Greg Richards at the Forza Café, where I'm certain they met countless times before to meet and go over the day's events to come.

What happened next is what you may see only for a minute on the news but is as tragic as anything could be. Some asshole-bad guy who I won't name, decided he had an unfair life (his doing) and was going to take it out on the cops. Patrol cars parked outside anywhere is a telltale sign there are cops inside. This guy walked in and opened fire, targeting, ambushing, and killing all four officers just because they were officers. They were busy with their reports and I'm certain a cup of coffee, and never saw it coming. Fortunately, two days later Seattle cops found and killed this fuck, saving everyone from the long, sad story of his pathetic life that was everyone else's fault but his own. So, the next time you see officers having a cup and catching up some work, say hi and thank them for their service. A cup of coffee for us can be just as dangerous sometimes as stopping a car.

May they Rest in Peace

Sergeant Mark Renninger
Officer Tina Griswald
Officer Ronald Owens
Officer Greg Richards
Lakewood Police Department
E.O.W.
November 29, 2009
This *Cup* is for you!

Scene 4: Dunkin Donuts & "NBC"

By now you've guessed cops like coffee and a place to work away from the madness that sometimes, ok, many times is our profession. I was no different and you can say I took it to another level. My love affair with coffee started when I started my first tour on the graveyard shift while on my own in my rookie year, 1983 to 1984, in the Southwest District. For the same reasons I have outlined, I needed coffee to help me stay awake because like everyone else I was used to sleeping at night for my entire life and now I *had* to be up. My beverage of choice: *Dunkin Donuts*. Always has been, always will be. I would get my cup once or twice during the shift and wherever I was assigned, I had my watering holes scoped out. Occasionally I would have a donut, but what I really enjoyed was a bowl of their corn chowder and a hot corn biscuit with my coffee. It was delicious and it kept me going when all I wanted to do was sleep.

As time went by, I would handle calls and if it was busy, I would have to clear and go to the next one without being able to complete the report, and this is how most busy agencies work. After I was behind a couple or maybe I had a complex one, I would stop in at *MY DD*, walk to the back counter and sit down, lay out my reports, and the waitress who knew me from my many visits, would bring me my cup every time just the way I liked it. Everybody likes to go to a place where everyone knows your name, right? I did this so often my squad mates and even some of my sergeants knew where to find me. If I had to write a report or two, chances were pretty good I was at my local Dunkin. Remember, '*America Runs on Dunkin!*' and so did I. When my wife Rosy and I are out on the street or traveling on a road trip, we always try to find DDs along the way. And one little aside; after our blind date when Rosy and I met, I invited her out for coffee a few days later and guess where we went? You know…

I was so engrained in my enjoyment of coffee right after roll call both as an officer and a sergeant, I would convince my cohorts my coffee was better than theirs and they would go with me to DDs and it became our thing. I also established a rule with my two best, good friends, Sergeants Tom Gilligan and Dave "Jester" Fariss, called "*NBC,*" not the TV network but "*Not Before Coffee.*" This was our unofficial mantra we tried to live by meaning nothing was allowed to happen on the streets of beautiful, sunny, Miami-Dade County until we had our coffee. Though the public didn't always cooperate, N'est-ce Pais?

Everyone has one thing in their daily routine they enjoy doing that makes the day either start, continue, or end just a bit better and gives them a sense of peace, at least for a few moments. Mine and most cops, at least the older ones, like getting that cup of coffee and settling into the shift. Get it while you can folks, because you never know when you'll be able to get it again because that's the nature of our job. Go to your favorite watering hole, keep one eye on that front door, and have one on me! Oh yea, and in thirty-seven years of doing the wild thing, I almost never paid full price for a cup of coffee. That's the nature of our job too.

Trademark Dunkin

Act- 18 Active Shooter: The

Unfortunate Truth

Scene 1: To Own or not to Own

This topic is one of the most prevalent and controversial issues surrounding our society short of race relations, and it occurs too often and sparks more outcries on gun control and the 2nd Amendment than anything else.

I am in total agreement there should be some constraints on gun ownership and usage, because as we know, many folks are too inept, careless and reckless to own a firearm, which requires proper training and acquired skills. I am a proponent of gun registration only so when a firearm goes missing and/or ends up located in a crime, law enforcement can trace it back to find out where its journey started and perhaps find the bad guy.

I am in no way in favor of the government confiscating our guns as some politicians say they wish to do, given the opportunity. But there has to be a balance as a firearm can be as dangerous as driving a car in the wrong hands. Background checks of course, but that won't cover all the bases either. And asshole-bad guys don't abide by the rules and get their hands on guns on the street, and disarming the public only emboldens the would-be robber/carjacker, so people have to be able to defend themselves. Posted "Gun-Free Zones" only create a hunting ground for these animals because they know no one is going to fight back and police are minutes away. So if you want to have gun-free zones in your community, have at it. Just be ready to be the sheep to the wolves!

An acquaintance of mine, a doctor no less, who is a brilliant man and has loads of common sense, recently asked me my opinion on how to best arm himself for a road trip he was taking to the Midwest because he didn't want to stay in a hotel due to Covid-19 concerns, and thought he and his wife might pull over somewhere to catch a few Zzzz and continue on their trip. He is an older gentleman and said to me he didn't know anything about guns. Frankly, an honest admission but a smart one. I told him now isn't the time to try to learn.

I recommended some pepper spray with a high Scoville Unit count, (that's the "heat" measurement in the Chile peppers) 2-3 million range should do, and it's easy and effective to use should the need arise. By the way folks, don't let the manufacturers sell you on the idea of a civilian stun-gun. You have to touch your assailant with it and when you release the trigger or break contact, the little pain it causes is over, and the bad guy will just take it away from you and stick it where the sun don't shine. They are **not** police electronic control weapons, more commonly known by their trade name, Taser. They don't work, in my not-so humble opinion, and pepper spray is nasty, nasty stuff and I have never seen anyone get sprayed in the eyes and act as if nothing happened. Did I say Nasty? The best defense though is to use the right pedal in your car to get out of *Dodge*. But this speaks to what I said, many people think they want to own a firearm for "personal protection," but have no idea how to use one. Get the right gun for your needs and more importantly get the right training to use it.

Scene 2: The Shooter

Who is or becomes an active shooter and why? That question is continuously pondered by experts, academics, law enforcement, the medical/psychiatric community, politicians, and people in general. What makes a person go to these extremes where they are so deranged or enraged they want to kill mass numbers of strangers? I fear this question may never be fully answered, but there are some profiles that have emerged over time that describe the person as well as can be. They are usually white males, who have a history of mental illness or domestic violence, childhood traumas, have a specific grievance like let's say against the government, no kidding, have hatred and possibly racism issues, another surprise, suicidal ideations or are seeking fame by killing many and maybe going out in a blaze of glory when the police arrive. It is estimated 56 percent of these mass killers do commit suicide prior to police arrival. Good! The idea of getting into a gunfight is a bad idea for any officer, so if they off themselves so be it. Another way to look at this is they are selfish cowards, which they are by virtue of their actions, and don't want to give us the satisfaction of killing them. They usually leave a "manifesto" behind for law enforcement to find laying out their pathetic, unfair, "me-against-the-world" deraignment, and their plan on how they were going to carry out their killings. Some are so cunning, knowing the police will eventually find their home, they booby-trap the entrances and windows hoping to take a few cops with them. Crazy yes, but pretty savvy if you think about it. *One last time unto the breech!*

Whatever the cause or motivation, we know these are highly motivated individuals with their end goal to kill as many innocent people as possible and also know when the police arrive they very well might be killed themselves if they haven't already done it. There are countless studies done by doctors, universities and the FBI profilers and I won't compare myself to these far more educated persons in their respective fields in giving you the exact reasons and diagnoses because I can't; I'm just a "cop," without all of that formal psychological education.

But, as a cop, while the characteristics I've laid out above may be relevant *after the fact* in an attempt to understand these people, they are not at all important to me as the guy who would need to respond to one of these incidents save two; that they are *heavily armed and motivated* and their job is to possibly stop me from doing my job which is to stop them! All the backgrounds of these killers have and will always be analyzed, *after* they have killed and after I (police) have either stopped them or not. White, black, Asian, male, female, racist, separatists, religious extremists, was abused as a child, chicks didn't like him, didn't make the varsity team, lost money in the stock market (we all have), his mother didn't love him enough, or whatever the fuck is wrong with them, it doesn't matter. None of that matters to us in the heat of the moment and it certainly doesn't matter to the victims in the line of fire, does it?

Scene 3: The Police Response-Truth & Myths

The *"Active Shooter"* or now *"Active Killer,"* is a phenomenon that came into the American lexicon with a bang, pun intended, on April 20, 1999, at Columbine High School in Littleton, Colorado, where two students entered the school, heavily armed, and killed 12 students and one teacher. This is considered the "watershed" incident that began to change the way police responded to these types of incidents. Why "watershed?" Up until that time and for many years since, uniform patrol officers all over the country, when handling barricaded, armed subject(s) incidents, were trained to respond to the scene, assess there was in fact a barricaded subject inside, meaning the bad guy was in a structure, house, office, store, etc. and had the place under his/her control, and the only way to get to them in hopes of neutralizing the situation was to "breach" a doorway where said bad guy could easily ambush the entering officers.

In the '70s, the _SWAT_, Special Weapons & Tactics teams were first developed to address this and other types of situations. These officers were highly and continuously trained in breaching techniques utilizing weapons and tools the road patrol officer does not possess, along with negotiating specialists utilized in talking the individual(s) into surrendering, hopefully. These SWAT units were the most highly trained police officers anywhere in the country and they had to go through a very physically demanding selection process much like military special forces units and maintain those standards throughout their tenure on the teams.

So when the officers responded to Columbine High, they followed their training and waited for specialized units, i.e., SWAT. _This_ was the procedure for all departments nationally and the uniform officers didn't do anything wrong, per procedure.

Unfortunately, procedures in police work as in many other industries don't keep up with and are slow to change with emerging trends and circumstances. This was also the moment things began to change because it was the highest mass killing at a school up until that time. However, there had been many incidents that occurred prior to that time and in the dark days of less media coverage, with perhaps the most notable being the University of Texas at Austin shooting on August 1, 1966, where a former US Marine climbed the main tower on campus and began shooting at students below killing fourteen and wounding thirty-one. He was up there for ninety-six minutes until a policeman and civilian reached and killed him. Perhaps we can call them the first _"Contact Team,"_ and heroes for sure.

Since that time, and with my best estimation at the time of writing this, there have been 440 mass killings in the US, and most involved high-powered firearms. And with almost all until recently, police have set a perimeter and called for SWAT. Though the training has changed dramatically since Columbine, entering an active shooter situation doesn't always go as planned. I am speaking from experience here regarding the training and here's how it goes. I was an active shooter instructor for quite a few years through my involvement in the Mobile Field Force Training Committee, and year in and year out for several years consecutively, and on and off in the years following, we at Miami-Dade Police as did some other agencies, established what came to be known in the industry as *"Contact Teams"* utilized to address an active shooter. We changed our procedures from waiting for SWAT or SRT (Special Response Team) as in our case, to establishing teams of first responding officers to enter immediately. The first 3, 4, or five officers arriving would become the *Contact Team,* make entry *as a team* and not *alone* as individuals, and seek out the shooter or shooters by going toward the sound of the gunfire, confront and neutralize the threat, meaning kill the bad guys if necessary.

Our *only* mission was to go after the threat and nothing else. Even if we came across wounded persons crying out for help and who possibly could be saved if we rendered aide right there, we were to leave them to the *"Rescue Teams"* who would come in after the *Contact Teams* and evacuate the wounded.

Here is something everyone needs to understand about entering an active threat environment and wounded victims; we can't stop and render aide until the lethal behavior (the shooting) is stopped. Until we take out the shooter or he kills himself or gives up, helping others will just lead to police casualties as well as civilian because the shooter will see us focused on the victims and try and take us out. That's the cold, hard truth about finding victims and it will not nor should it change.

We trained and trained on tactics to move onto shooters both in the open and in buildings, and you can become quite proficient on your tactics *in training.* But what happens when it's the real deal? How will officers react? This has become a point of contention and criticism in recent years. During training where we would set up scenarios for officers to enter a room where the shooter is waiting for them and they know it, some officers have said to me, "I'm not going in there because I'll get shot!" And there is part of the problem. He may very well got shot at and perhaps shot, but his own personal survival instinct is kicking in and this instinct is the most powerful a human has; to survive, isn't it?

Say, you as a civilian are out at the mall or theater, and you hear gunfire close by, what is your instinct telling you to do? It's saying,

"Marcos, don't fucking go that way, are you an idiot? Go the other way if you want to live!" That is exactly what happens to most and even to cops, firefighters, and military personnel. The goal is to train that out of us and go toward the danger, and thankfully the overwhelming majority of officers do. But there are officers who will either hesitate or not go in at all.

Two edges to this sword here; on the one hand we might say he or she is a coward for not entering the active shooting environment *alone*, and we should fire them or indict them for "not doing their job damn it!" Or we can look at it as they may be completely terrified and are *unable* to engage. Remember what I said, the survival instinct for any animal overrides everything else. The *Fight or Flight Response* takes over and it is difficult to override.

This brings me to the most recent and tragic mass killing incident which was in our back yard here in South Florida; Marjory Stoneman Douglas High School in Parkland, a small suburb in Broward County just north of us. On February 14, 2018, Valentine's Day no less, a deranged former student entered the school with a rifle and killed 17 and left another 17 wounded. We can't express our sympathies enough to the families and human nature being what it is; you can only say to yourself you're lucky it didn't happen at your kid's school. Selfish? Perhaps, but human.

But my goal here is to inform and educate on how and why police either respond or don't respond in time. Broward Sheriff's Deputy Scot Peterson was purported to be the first police officer on scene as he was the *SRO* or *School Resource Officer* assigned to there. He heard the gunfire coming from Building 12, called it in, but he didn't make entry and this is where the beginning of the controversy lies. Adding to this was the lack of proper coordination and deployment of personnel, utilizing the *Contact Team* concept. What occurred instead was a BSO captain as the ranking supervisor on scene, attempted to set up a perimeter around the school rather than deploy contact teams. Way wrong move!

Just like you don't stop to render aide to the wounded, you don't deploy resources on a perimeter or anything else other than going in after the shooter, period! This *IS* the training and nothing else matters until the threat is neutralized. These two factors which caused an improper response, coupled with several others, could indeed have led to more deaths. I know the families feel Deputy Peterson's entry may have saved some of the victims and that is completely understandable, but this is unknowable after the fact.

Here's the rub though and some will get upset with what I'm going to tell you; per his training, Deputy Peterson didn't do anything wrong. Yes, I am saying he followed his training up until that time and didn't do anything wrong. So before you start cursing me and sending me to Hell, let me explain. All of the *Active Shooter* training up until Parkland was the first arriving 3, 4, or five officers as I have previously outlined, form up a *Contact Team* or whatever their jurisdiction calls it, and make entry *as* a team, not solo. We have never, ever trained, until now, to make entry alone on any type of police call where there was a potential for bad guys. If it was considered a high-risk call, a "two-man" situation comes into play and you wait for back-up. That's right; you wait for back-up. Would an *Active Shooter* be considered a two-man call? You bet it would and our training took it to at least 3, 4, or five preferably, which gives us a better chance of taking out the bad guy(s) and surviving the engagement.

Now, is Deputy Peterson a coward and should he or any officer have gone in alone? That will be debated for decades to come. I can only speak for myself and those I have worked closely with and know them and their thought processes when I say I, we, would have made entry. This doesn't mean I/we have no fear, of course we do. But I and many others have trained to the point where we can override fear and move toward the danger. Not everyone can, and that is human nature no matter how much you *Monday Morning Quarter Back* this or any other police situation. You can't make people face extreme danger if they mentally and physically can't move. But this training was and even continues today as the standard for many agencies. Miami-Dade Police and others have changed the response protocol post-Parkland, from waiting and forming teams to making entry by the lone officer. On paper, everything works well. In the real world not so much and there will be shooting incidents where sadly, this will happen again.

An Unfair Comparison

I'm going to lay out for you how there are stark differences and the public's expectations of society's first responders, Police & Fire. First, everyone loves a firefighter because when they arrive they are there to "help you." When the police arrive, something bad is happening and someone could go to jail. When you see firefighters shopping for their food at the store, you say "how nice." They think of a Dalmatian sitting on the firetruck, firefighters sliding down the pole to respond to a fire scene, and perhaps even the infamous *calendar* with buff firefighters. Some see an officer eating at a restaurant and say, "he should be out on patrol," or think he's eating donuts or just lives to screw with the public. We get to eat too you know. But here is the biggest contrast on how these two groups of heroes respond to any call regardless of the danger, and I will let my former commander at the Airport District, fellow motorcycle enthusiast and friend, Major Ray Melcon explain it in the best terms I have ever heard.

Ray was at his kid's school for a social gathering after Parkland. As is always the case for any cop, when people find out you are a cop and usually the only one at the party, the questions start coming. "You know, I was stopped once or whatever, and the officer gave me a ticket etc., etc., etc." Ok folks stop right there, you probably deserved it, but this happens all the time. So at this one event, Ray was approached by another parent who happened to be a lawyer. Stick to lawyering and leave law enforcement to us, ok? But this parent proceeded to ask Ray about his opinion on the Parkland tragedy and was looking to back him into a corner on his response. But Ray is a thinker and always carefully considers his actions and responses, which made him a great cop and an even better commander.

He told said parent/lawyer he would answer his question this way; when fire rescue responds to a fire call, they respond as an engine company where they have four firefighters onboard and one of them is a supervisor. When the *Rescue* unit responds they have three paramedics onboard and one of them is a supervisor as well. When the incident requires a multi-unit response, say an engine and rescue unit, you have a total of seven and two supervisors at all times. When they arrive, they will be gearing up in their turnout or bunker gear as they call it, those flame-resistant outfits, air packs for breathing, then lay out and charge their fire hoses, and after all of this is done then they enter the fire *as a team!*

If there is a fire in a building, have you ever seen a firefighter enter a fully engulfed structure with a fire extinguisher and do it alone? Let me answer for you; no you haven't and you never will. Fire never does anything alone, ever! Alone with a fire extinguisher is not the proper response nor is it the proper equipment for a structure fire.

So now we come to the police response to the active shooter. What the uninformed public, so-called experts and of course politicians who think they know better than us, expect from us is to arrive at an unfamiliar building, with an unknown number of subjects inside and their locations, shooting with unknown types of weapons, (the fire) and enter with a sidearm (fire extinguisher) and take out the shooters (extinguish the blaze), alone and without back-up and supervisors! Mmmm.

So what's wrong with these comparisons and expectations? Everything. Why does it seem a police officer is expected to possibly sacrifice himself by going against every survival instinct and police training procedure in his response to an active shooter or similar incident in scope and danger, and will be heavily criticized and possibly prosecuted for it if he doesn't go it alone and fire rescue isn't? Yes, the training has changed since Parkland where officers are now being told to go it alone, but will they?

In some cases they will and we can only hope when they do and confront the shooter or shooters they somehow prevail, though the odds will be against them. I'm afraid this issue will be with us for a long time to come and if officers are prosecuted for not going it alone, what will happen instead is the officer who wishes to first stay alive, and second, not be criminally charged by activist prosecutors, won't be the first on scene and will make sure they take the looong way around to get there. If you're not there you can't get in trouble, can you? Some of you may not like what I'm saying here but these are the cold, hard facts about these types of incidents and it will not change.

Here is another comparison and please pay attention here and note the stark differences once again. The most elite warriors in the world who go in harm's way on a regular basis meaning combat, whether in an active theater of war or covert operations, and are *never* alone; US Navy Seals, Army Green Berets and Delta, the Army 75th Ranger Regiment,

Airforce Para Rescue, US Coast Guard MSRT, British SAS, German GSG-9, Russian SPETSNAZ, and any unit of any armed forces along with every police SWAT/SRT teams, never do anything alone!

They train as a team for every possible situation, have the best training, weapons and tools at their disposal, and see combat and counterterrorism situations regularly. But somehow in America we expect a lone police officer to enter a similar threat environment our elite operators face and would never go it alone.

Rambo, though entertaining, *Master Chief* in *HALO,* and *The Mandalorian* from *Star Wars ("This is the Way"),* bad asses for certain but they only exist in video games and the movies but we are expected be just like them. Police Officers are no different from anyone else and will do what they have to survive. What is the answer? I don't know but I would like to be part of a commission to study the problem and lend my perspective as a *Boot on the Ground* with real-life experience instead of politicians and academics who think they know better. But understand human nature and the survival instinct will always prevail, whether you are a civilian, firefighter or police officer. You decide.

Top left Bert's Academy photo 1984.
Top right Bert's father pinning on the badge (photo by Pete Gonzalez)
Bottom Academy graduation photo BLE 84 Tough to the Core!

Sgt. (Ret.) Bert "Maverick" Gonzalez

Top left, the Green & White
Bottom, Bert circa 1995

Top photo, First Squad, photo by Lt. Charles Nanney
Bottom: Last Squad, photo by Captain Gina Beato

Top Photo: Pinning the badge on BJ
Bottom Photo: The Tradition contines.

Top Photo: Brown Bloods: A Family Tradition
Bottom Photo: Sergeant Bert "Maverick" Gonzalez Last Day
Photos by Cyrniphotography

Act - 19 Body Worn Cameras

(BWCs):

Smile, You're on Candid Camera!

Scene 1: You Want to Make Us Wear What?

Another phenomenon that has come into the world of police work, and with some fanfare both good and bad has been the introduction of the *"BWC,"* or the *Body Worn Camera.*

During the Obama Administration and because of those "questionable" police-involved shootings of black men (back to that again), there began a nationwide movement to outfit and mandate the wearing of BWCs by police. This started in Great Britain around 2005 (though I never heard of any controversies like here because they don't carry guns-generally. I guess they've been beating people to death with beer mugs), and so about 2014 this started to take hold in the US because of said shootings. It has been controversial to say the least, both by law enforcement and by the legal field and privacy laws themselves.

When officers in some agencies first began wearing them, like with any other mandate, it was received somewhat less than warmly, and with the stigma we aren't trusted to do our jobs and our word means nothing. To some in the activist world that's exactly what it means. "Don't trust the police at any level," and that's the perception. Remember the "99 percent" crap I covered earlier? Remember also the 2014 Ferguson, MO. shooting where the *"Hands Up, Don't Shoot"* battle cry began, based on a lie, was where the BWCs movement came about, and dismisses the 99 percent are good belief and brings it down to zero. Those same people who don't like us will never trust or all day long and that won't change. But those that are looking at the whole picture will say "yes, we know the majority of officers are good, but we have to capture all of their activity to root out the bad ones," so we started wearing cameras.

There were no laws until in recent years that actually mandated police wear BWCs, but many departments like mine, saw the proverbial writing on the wall that at some point we would be required either by executive action (mayor/governor) or by law, so in 2015, Miami-Dade Police began the long and arduous process of developing our BWC program, to include what type and testing, cost of units, replacement and repairs, training, when and where to turn on the cameras and when not to turn them on due to privacy issues, and the storage of those videos and how long we have to archive them. Yes, data storage of thousands of videos per day for just Miami-Dade for example, has proven to be the most costly component of BWCs for many agencies. It is easy to say by the head of an agency standing in front of a news camera "All of our officers will be wearing cameras starting on (pick a date), and any officer not wearing and using them will be disciplined!"

Implementing a program of this enormity is quite difficult and it took us several years to launch with an infinite number of problems early on. Like any new program for police, change and acceptance is slow, but eventually we came around and we did. *BWC-Festivus for rest of us!* Almost.

Scene 2: Resistance is Futile

As I stated, police are slow to accept change as are other institutions because as humans we don't like change! We become comfortable and set in our ways. Anything new tends to disrupt that and we are reluctant to accept it. In time, we slowly began to accept the BWCs as just another tool we have to use and we can't fight the political winds. As officers became more comfortable with its use, in turn, it actually became quite useful to us. I accepted it right from the beginning because of course, I had no choice. The department mandated it and that was that. But I counseled and encouraged my officers and colleagues to accept it and use it to our advantage as in when complaints are filed against us and the truth is all caught on video as I outlined in my act on *Internal Affairs*. When someone made a bullshit complaint and the officer's actions were captured on video, *IA* would first review the video, play it for the complainant, and then ask where the alleged discourtesy or action was. The complaint then went away because the truth was captured on *our* camera and that became a message to people if you're going to make a complaint against us, it better be the truth because most of the officers on scene will have a recording of exactly what happened.

Another unintended benefit for us was when we as supervisors had to write a *Use of Force Report*, we could review the footage and see exactly what the officers and the subject said and did, and it helped us piece together a very accurate accounting of what took place. Yes, BWCs may have helped reduce the incidents of excessive force and discourtesy by marginal officers, and I don't have a problem with that. 99 percent again, but good nonetheless. But when someone questioned what we did, which is all the time, there it was on film, I mean digital video. I'm dating myself again, but it's recorded for all time! So BWCs weren't as bad as we first thought they would be. *Locutus* accepted his fate and was assimilated into the *Collective!* For the time being…

Scene 3: Careful What You Wish For

As I mentioned, the BWC movement began because of activists claiming police were out of control and killed blacks as a matter of course. That concept is preposterous on its face, but out there nonetheless and with the help of the mainstream media that perpetuates this misconception. If you are a reasonable person you know, as with any other extreme ideas, it is not probable, possible, or even near the truth. But when police were pushed to wear BWCs by the powers-that-be who are manipulated themselves by the most vocal minority, we knew eventually the cold, hard facts and truth about what we do would be revealed for all to see.

> Police: "So you want to record everything we do so you can catch us doing something wrong, is that it?"
> Activists/Politicians: "Yes, that's right. You're all corrupt and you kill people."
> Police: "Ok, we'll wear them. But you're not going to like what you see!"
> Activists/Politicians: "Well, we'll just see about that!"
> Police: "Careful what you wish for because you might just get it!"

So after we started wearing the cameras and most everything we did was being recorded, the world began to see EXACTLY what police in this country did. Yes, there are times we did kill people because that's the nature of the beast. Police get into deadly confrontations and we have to defend ourselves and sometimes people die. Sometimes and all too often it's us. We do get into non-deadly physical confrontations where force is necessary and again, same beast. But the BWC footage also shows how many really bad, bad asshole people we deal with on a daily and even hourly basis, whom have extensive criminal histories and are not the pillars of the community as the public is led to believe, and how it's the subject who caused the problems that prompted the 911 call for police to respond in the first place. And after we arrive we then have to deal with the vitriol and vile crap they spew at us because they can, and it's all captured live!

Until we started using BWCs, all you saw was the smartphone-cam videos people used to record us and gave to the mainstream media outlets or uploaded themselves to their own social media accounts, *after editing*, so you would see what *they* wanted you to see and not everything that actually took place. Kinda unfair but that's the way the game is played. The police cams also revealed how uncooperative many of the people we encounter; again called to respond to and not just showing up on our own. The videos show the attacks on us and the vehicle and foot chases that ensue and the extreme danger we are put in, not by our choosing but it goes back to the beast.

In addition to all the serious and dangerous incidents we handle, the BWC also captures the selfless and caring side of police officers where we really live up to the long-standing motto of *Protect & Serve*. Officers are constantly helping out thousands of people daily, but you rarely see that on the news, don't you? The helping of an elderly person at home or at the store, playing with a child in their yard, rescuing an animal that trapped itself somewhere, or giving money to a homeless person or family such as my former squad at the Airport District did in 2019 when they found a family from Detroit stranded at the Greyhound Bus Depot with nowhere to go. Thank you to officers Jose Deleon, Isabel Soto, Dago Azcuy, Dayana Wilhelm and Scott Mc Bath. You exemplify what officers everywhere do to help out those in need. I wish the public could see and hear more of these heroic stories of what officers everywhere do, and not just the controversial ones the media is obsessed with.

When the public gets a look at what we *REALLY* do and have to deal with, they are shocked and appalled by the stark realities of what life out there is really like. I have said throughout this book life and police work are raw and unfiltered and most can't understand or deal with that concept. When you are told all we do is hurt and kill people, and then you see our recordings of police-involved incidents, you start to see how wrong and misleading the rhetoric is. Are there abuses? Sure, and there will always be because of human nature. But if you are honest with yourself, look at the data and evidence as those same activists started to, then you'll see the truth. And when truth hit the digital airwaves, those activists who railed against us began calling for the discontinuation of many BWC programs because the cam evidence didn't support their wholesale claims of abuse and corruption and that wreaked havoc on their agenda. *"Want the truth? You can't handle the truth!"* Yes, it's one of my favorite movie lines but it accurately dismisses the false narrative that has been thrust upon our profession. So to the activists, ignorant politicians and there are many, and to the generally uninformed, if you want to see what it is we do, go on a ride along with your local police department and if you do, smile, because *You're on Candid Camera!*

Act - 20 Millennials - The Next

Generation

Scene 1: Every Generation Says…

In every aspect of life, whether we're talking about humans, animals, sports teams, social clubs or institutions, there are generations of beings that make up the fabric of the organization. And in every organization there are generations of people and employees that span decades, from the *"Old-Timers"* or *"Dinosaurs"* as I came to be described, to those five, ten or more years behind, to those *"newbies"* just on the job in recent years. Police work is no different and each generation brings with it its own culture, interests, music, habits, language, and most importantly, their own work ethic.

In keeping with my affinity for *Star Trek*, I will describe myself and my contemporaries as the *Original Series-Captain Kirk and Mr. Spock*, and for the new officers who came on in the last ten or so years, *The Next Generation-Captain Picard and Commander Riker*, with the stark differences each have from the other. Every generation blames the one before, and every older one says the next one isn't as good. True and not true, to a point.

So I am going to both criticize and compliment mine as well as those that came *well* after us and speak in generalities because there's no such thing as 100 percent. No protests please, and if I hurt anyone's feelings, suck it up Cupcake; there's no crying in Police Work!

When I and my compadres started in the late 70s and through the '80s, we were referred to as that time's *"New Generation,"* and we looked at the older guys as the *"Dinosaurs,"* and each generational cycle does the same thing. Though we were new and young compared to those officers who came on in the late 50s, 60s, and 70s, we were all still *Baby Boomers.*

Many came out of the military and we were all raised in much the same manner, experienced the progress and cultural changes in *Post-War America*, and listened to more or less the same music. I was born in 61' but I listened to everything from the '50s on up; we went through the *Cold War* where we had atomic bomb drills in school where we ducked under the tables in the event of an attack by the *BIG RED BEAR*; yea, like that was going to help. We had vinyl records and 8-Track tapes, roll down windows, and were brought up to have the same work ethic. We learned if you wanted something you had to work for it as it wasn't given to you.

When we entered police work, you did what you were told, sergeants walked the earth as *TITANS*, and if you needed something you asked a senior officer and didn't bother your sergeant with it. This may sound harsh or even like the sergeant didn't want to talk to you, but it was a training tool that taught you to figure things out on your own and the last resort was to go to your sergeant; ok for the most part but there are limits. Most of us became self-sufficient and that was invaluable. You arrived at work on time, mostly. Early on there were times I had trouble waking up and on occasion was late, so I apologize to my sergeants.

I got better with age. When you got held over on overtime, you didn't complain as it was part of the deal you signed up for and you went home when you went home. When given an assignment, shush! "Go take care of it." And when you *Screwed the Pooch* as it were, you were more likely to get an ass-chewing that took care of the problem instead of a touchy-feely "counseling session," and that would be the end of it. You didn't cry about it and run to the union if you had your feelings hurt. If you fucked up, that was it, no excuses, take responsibility and move on.

We, for the most part, were not afraid to get into shit either. We looked for it! The crazier it was the more we embraced it. Maybe that was just a *little* stupid at times; more balls than brains, but that's who we were. But like I've said, most everything in life can be a double-edged sword. I can say with confidence my generation is also more emotionally detached and even a bit unfeeling at times. I can also say with confidence my son BJ is much nicer than I am and though I could always talk to people and diffuse most, he actually conveys more empathy than I do which in some respects makes him more effective at times than me and my cohorts. He likes most everyone, I don't. But my bullshit meter is better than his, so there you go.

Scene 2: You Want It When?

As I have outlined who my generation is and what our characteristics are, let me now move onto the differences with our young *Starfleet Cadets* and who they are *as we see* them. We all come into police work, the fire service, the military, and healthcare with a desire to serve; at least I hope everyone does. When you choose one of these careers you have to realize up front there are sacrifices you are going to have to make. Time off may not come the way you like. Shift work is involved, a hierarchy of command and taking orders will be your way of life and you'll hear "no" a lot so better get used to it. Rewards and promotion come slowly, and you are not going to get *your way* just because you want it. And when you don't get your way that's it and that's the way it's going to be. I'm not talking about being ill-treated as there are remedies for that, but you have orders to follow and you may not always like or agree with them but you better follow them.

With our younger folks, again, as we see them, there are some stark contrasts in their personalities where they 1: want everything now without waiting or having to work for it. For instance, we have the great benefit of having Take-Home patrol cars and when you reach your One Year Probation you become eligible for the car when one is available. We experienced budget shortages and cars were not available to all and you might have to wait an additional six, eight, or even twelve months to get one. This doesn't sit well with some of our younger officers and they march into the Station Control Officer's office and demand a car! This is where the word "no" comes in. Listen Spanky, there are others ahead of you and senior officers are driving around in cars held together with tape and rubber bands so get in line. You get it when you get it, but some will actually file a complaint with our union only to be given the same answer. Have patience, it will come, but many of the young'ns don't have any. They want the car, the new equipment, the big new house instead of a *starter-home,* the latest smartphone the minute it hits the stores, and this attitude trickles, ok sometimes floods into our job.

I won't criticize them for getting that new car because we all wanted one when we started earning a bit more. I got myself a new 1983 Ford Mustang, my third 'Stang' by that time, so I understand.

But I certainly didn't get the $500,000 home when I graduated the academy. They also want the transfer to that specialized unit almost immediately before they're ready and that has caused *huge* problems because they got there because they knew someone not because they earned it. This has happened too with my generation but now it seems to be everywhere and many who weren't ready find themselves kicked out or "asked to leave" the unit within months.

I also believe many of the younger generation have been given too much by mommy and daddy just because, and have developed an *entitlement* mentality which comes into conflict with a police organization, and when they hear "no" it causes conflict. But the conflict is theirs, not the department's. I heard *no* a great deal growing up because it was my parents' job to give us what we *needed* not necessarily what we *wanted*. As supervisors and senior officers it's our job to be like surrogate parents and do much the same. Ours is to teach and nurture but not give in to every whim or request.

Sup Man!

This will be a short piece of advice. I have had brand new, I mean new-car-smell-new, officers arrive at the station and begin their tour of duty, and when we passed each other in the hallway, I get "Sup Man!" "What did you say?" There comes a lax sense of decorum and protocol with some and if a senior officer, sergeant, lieutenant, or captain, crosses paths with you, it's; "Good morning Sergeant Gonzalez!" Not "Sup Man." Do we have to teach you to be respectful as well? So word to the wise young people, respect your elders, damn it! Nough said.

Cut the Umbilical Cord

Another stark difference and this has caused quite a few problems, is needing to call the sergeant on most every call before attempting to figure out what they have. In the age of cell phones, it is easier to call your supervisor on speed-dial, I mean *favorites*, than it is to work the problem. In prehistoric times, we didn't have communicators (mobiles) and only the police radio. Before you raised your sergeant you better have exhausted all other means to rectify the situation, and we were also careful what we said on the radio. As a newbie, you might think you have "A" when you actually have "B," so careful what you say. Now you just pick up the phone and say "Sarge, I have this, this, and that, and what do you think?" This occurs all too often and with a squad of 6 or 8 officers handling calls all shift, the sergeant is busy fielding calls instead of supervising. I learned very quickly and have counseled new sergeants when they get that call, to respond by saying "what do you think?" This is the only way the young officer is going to learn to work the problem.

When I get the call and given the *Reader's Digest* version of the incident, sometimes the *War & Peace* version I'll add, I already know what to do as I should. But if I give the answer outright then I didn't teach *Young Skywalker* a damned thing, did I? The age-old adage comes to mind here; *"Give a man a fish, feed him for a day. Teach a man to fish, feed him for life!"* And this is a difficult concept for many of our young folks to accept. They want a resolution now and in life and police work it just isn't that way, and I lay some of the blame on their parents, and the rest on the techno, instant-gratification world that comes with smart-phones, computers and the internet. Yes, the internet is a great tool, especially for research and shopping, but take a fucking history lesson why don't you? If you rely solely on this for knowledge and of course spelling, you're crippling yourself by always needing this crutch instead of *learning* what you should know.

Scene 3: Put Down the Damned Phone!

I don't think there is any other characteristic that defines the *millennial* generation more than the use of the mobile phone, or smart phone if you prefer. It seems to be surgically attached to their hands and they spend almost every waking hour on it, and if you were to take it away it would be like not letting them breathe. Don't get me wrong, once you take a leap forward in technology you can't go back. Ever see anyone with a beeper these days? Um, no. It's convenient and has connected all of us in ways we couldn't have imagined, and in some ways has made life easier no doubt but it has created other drawbacks as well. Do we have to spend all of our time on it? No we don't and we shouldn't. There's a time and place for everything and the mobile phone has its place as well. But it can't be 24/7.

I didn't get my first mobile phone until 1997 and back then you can make a call on it and that was it! Now you can do almost anything on it which is pretty cool, but it has become a monumental distraction, especially in police work, and this is the rub; If you're off-duty, play on your phone; *Face-Face, Stripper-Gram, Tweety Bird, What's Up* and *Snap,*

Crackle & Pop with your BFFs all day long if that's what you like as long as it doesn't interfere with your job! By the way, I personally don't reside in any of the so-called social networking communities as I think it takes up too much of one's time but that's just me. Have at it!

But you don't see the young folks or most anyone these days that aren't on their phone. Since they were raised with the use of mobile phones, it seems like it's a part of their very being and personality and detaching from it is impossible. While it is useful for talking to one another off-line while on-duty and discussing *"sensitive"* issues or planning out lunch, while handling calls it has become a major problem, not to mention driving. This can be dangerous as we and most departments if not all, have policies restricting phone use while driving.

Here's my beef; I have seen on way too many calls and tactical situations where the officers are almost completely absorbed with their phone instead of focusing on what's in front of them. They're running a *"3"* to a call and talking on the phone in their hand! It's difficult enough negotiating traffic running lights & siren with two hands, but now you're on the phone doing it. Stupid and dangerous Skippy. Can't it wait? I had a tactical team where I hired additional officers on overtime to work with my guys, and our focus was saturation patrols in high crime areas as well as locating and arresting wanted bad guys. So when you're walking up to a front door or setting a perimeter on a house with said bad guy inside, shouldn't you be focusing on the doors and windows where a little annoying thing like maybe getting shot from could occur or, should you be getting out of the car with the phone in your GUN HAND? Damn Spanky!

Well, this is exactly what I found many of our young officers doing. This is where, as a sergeant, I have to be *"That Guy"* and come down on them, which I didn't have a problem with as it's my job to do so, and if I chew a little ass and it saves lives, well then I've done my job. I did take two of our officers on a *"Come to Jesus"* meeting and talk to them for forty-five minutes about this. They are good people and becoming fine officers but their habits where going to get them hurt. This scenario has played out countless times I'm sure with other sergeants and their young charges everywhere, but it is absolutely necessary to re-focus *Young Luke and Rey Skywalker* on what is paramount when doing their jobs, staying alive. After our meeting, the officers understood as do most and they became much more aware of their surroundings and tasks at hand. Bravo!

Scene 4: There's No App for That!

So to make the phone issue die, using the phone in police work other than to call, text, spell-check, and looking up contact information for agencies and resources, there is no other use for it. "Well, what do you mean Bert?" I mean when confronting a bad guy, a Baker Act, a drunk-idiot, or a warring couple in a domestic, the phone is not going to have an app telling you how to handle it. This reminds me of a movie with one of my favorite scenes that speaks to this very issue, *Demolition Man.* The 1993 offering has Sylvester Stallone as the Neanderthal, freeze-dried cop from the '90s who gets thawed out in 2032 to deal with a super-criminal who was also thawed, Simon Phoenix, played by Wesley Snipes, because the cops of that future can't. The scene finds bad guy Phoenix at an ATM and six San-Angeles police officers arrive on their *Protect/Serve* call to confront him. This is where it gets good, or bad. The lead officer looks at his tablet device and speaks into it.

Cop: "Maniac is imminent, request advice?"

Tablet: (in a soothing female voice) "With a firm tone of voice, demand maniac lie down with hands behind back." (This instruction accompanied by a video depicting how the bad guy should comply-ah, no!)

Cop: "Simon Phoenix, lie down with your hands behind your back."

Phoenix ignores him with a nasty comment and look.

Cop: "Maniac has responded with a scornful remark."

Tablet: "Approach and repeat ultimatum in an even firmer tone of voice; and add the words, or else!" (Remember I said never to use those magic words?)

Simon Phoenix then proceeds to kick the crap out of the six officers, and then the pièce de resistance of commentaries from an officer watching live from police headquarters; "We're police officers; we're not trained to handle this kind of violence!" And there you have it.

Folks, the smart phone with all of its wondrous technology and capabilities will not show you how to do police work. Until the day arrives and the phone can render someone incapacitated by pointing a laser beam at them, I'm afraid you'll have to put it away and get your hands dirty for now. Don't let the distraction of the phone get you hurt or worse. Your *Facetime* can wait.

Scene 5: A Tale of Two Cities

As I've stated, the younger generation is more tech-savvy, and perhaps kindler & gentler than we Neanderthals, and that's ok, to a point. I've been called by some of my officers *"Gunny Highway"* and I should be sealed in a glass case with the label, "Break in the event of war!"

I'm fine with that because when you get into the shit in police work you *are* at war and you better see it that way, and by the way, you're welcome. But I also see the other side as I have described my son BJ and his contemporaries. There's a time and place for both, but when it's throw-down time stop talking and go hands on for Christ's sake! Here are two brief, contrasting stories of the *Old-School* and *New-School* mentality we see happening with some, not all, of our young squires;

Old-School

A couple of years ago our officers were working a University of Miami Hurricanes football game at what I still call *Joe Robbie Stadium*, home of the *Miami Dolphins*. If you have ever attended a football game, college or pro, you know it can get quite "chippy" with some of the fans, mostly due to alcohol. No kidding. At this particular game, a young female fan imbibed a little too much of the available spirits, and after a while was advised by our officers working the game to kindly exit the stadium. She didn't. So the flag was thrown by the referees (police) and she had to be shown the door and when refused to exit, several officers picked up her drunk-ass and carried her up the steps to eject her. During the carry, she struck one of our senior officers, a big guy for sure, and to his credit, he ignored the initial salvo. When *Ms. Hyde* didn't get the response she wanted, she hit the officer again. This time, *Old-School* gave it right back to her on the jaw, and she was out for the count, literally out! You never put your hands on a police officer, period! So you better be tough if you're going to be stupid.

New-School

Fast forward just a little that same year. Two female officers responded to a *Wendy's* in South District for a call of a male who was being disruptive and causing a fracas. He was tall, loud and out of control, and as is procedure, the officers attempted to talk him down. It wasn't working and he was getting worse and became threatening to the officers and the Wendy's employees. There comes a time in every encounter when talking doesn't work and you have to go hands on.

This guy was yelling, screaming, and walking freely around the kitchen area behind the service counter. The officers did not go after him and he was now trapping employees up against the drive-thru window. Do you know what is behind a fast-food counter in the kitchen? Knives and hot oil. Think that might be dangerous to the officers should the guy get his hands on either? Of course! When talking doesn't work as in this case, you cannot let the person have free rein and you have to engage to control him. The officers did neither and wouldn't even approach him.

The call went out for *"3-15s."* It always takes a few minutes, at minimum, for back-up to arrive, while the subject could injure someone at any moment. A male officer arrived, withdrew his expandable baton, and began using loud, verbal commands (as trained) as he swung at the subject.

The problem here was while swinging he was holding back as if *he,* the officer, was afraid to hit the subject. If you are going to go hands on, you go *all the way!* The decision to use force has been made and if you strike with a baton you strike-hard at non-vital areas with the intent to disable and subdue. There's no going back at this point. This was a classic case of, in my experienced and cynical eye as well as other veterans, of young officers who may have taken this job for the wrong reasons and are hesitant to engage when necessary. If you come into police work believing violence is not part of your new world, either perpetrated upon you or executed by you, then your career choice might have been ill-advised. This job isn't for everyone and the security, salary, benefits, authority and standing in the community, and physical wellbeing come at a cost and sacrifice. There can't be two more stark differences between the generations than these two incidents. Once again, nothing is 100 percent but the many *seem* to act like this.

Scene 6: Fresh Minds, Fresh Ideas

Now the news isn't all bad and I won't beat up on the kids anymore as I think I made my point, and there are very good things the *Next Generation* brings to the table. They are more open and compassionate than we are, they are tech-savvy like no one's business and where the technology fits they're experts at it. I have learned from my kids and some young officers how to use my phone and computer as I am truly dancing here with two left feet and one hand tied behind my back, really! They look at the world differently than we do and communicate better in general than we did. The world is changing rapidly due to advances in technology and they are more in tuned with it as well as the cultural changes taking place due to social networking and they accept other people more openly and are better connected than ever. We old-timers are a bit more reserved and don't open up quite so easily and display our feelings, so they have us there which is a good thing. Young folks in general research more and don't necessarily leap before they look which also good, mostly.

So there is a balance between the two, three, even four generations that are not only in our ranks but our society as well. We could all learn from one another as there is both good and bad in everything, that double-edged sword I keep mentioning, and learning also to understand our differences and similarities to boot. One of my former partners and close friend Sergeant Tom Gilligan and I tried to do just that, learn, by attending a training course called *Supervising the Generation Gap*. It was an excellent class and we learned a few things. There are some things we will always be set in our ways about as will the *Next Generation*. But my last piece of advice to the young Knights is; one day you *will* be the *Old Guard* and you *will* be saying similar things about your *Next Generation*. Trust me, you will.

I'll end this act with a short article my former lieutenant, Charles Nanney, who retired as a division chief. He sent it to the Miami Herald where he speaks about the next generation of police officers. It encapsulates what I've been saying here and as I've outlined, the news about our younger officers is good, and is a perfect example of how a supervisor stands up for his officers. Charles is and always was a defender of our people, discipline them when necessary, but always praising and watching out for them. This is leadership.

"What's our problem with cops?"

A lot of people, even other officers, criticize police officers. Every generation of officers declares, "They don't make cops like they used to!" I've said it myself. But the current group (late 90s) at Miami-Dade's Northside Station, especially my platoon, make us eat our words. These "real" cops are hardworking, highly motivated public servants who arrest criminals with a smile and love to work in the busiest and most violent district. Not only would I choose them over any platoon anywhere, but I would also go to war with them. They are a credit to their supervisors, the department and their community. May God bless and watch over them.

Lieutenant Charles E. Nanney

Miami-Dade Police Department

Authors Note:

I am proud to say quite a few of those young officers Charles is speaking about were mine. Great performance reflects great leadership. Thanks Charles, it was a privilege!

Act - 21 "19s" The Traffic Stop

Scene 1: "Do You Know Why I Stopped You?"

There is perhaps no more frequent police/citizen encounter than the *"19."* What do people and police officers do the most? Drive a car! People drive to work, school, the store, doctor, etc. and in most areas of the country you need a car to do most anything for modern living. It follows then spending that much time behind the wheel and human nature being what it is, many will commit traffic infractions either without realizing it, or drive anyway they want to because they just feel like it (read many in BMWs here). Either way chances are good if a patrol car or motor unit is around, you will get an officer's attention. By the way, "What is the difference between a porcupine and a BMW? The BMW has the pricks on the inside!" *(CH)* That's just me.

We get trained in the academy on how to conduct traffic stops because it is so important and paramount to our jobs. Patrol officers everywhere will conduct *"19s"* as part of their duties and will encounter a myriad of situations from the sublime to the terrifying (more later) and will hear every kind of excuse as to why the *violator,* as drivers who commit infractions are called, did what they did. An often-used investigative tool we use when we stop drivers is to ask them *"Do you know why I stopped you?"* This little question will generally set the tone for how the stop is going to go. If you are honest with yourself and us, you'll reply you were speeding, ran the stop or light, cut some one off, usually us, or whatever the infraction may have been. If you're truthful and apologetic and the infraction wasn't a serious one, then chances are pretty good you'll be let off with the infamous *"Warning"* and you're on your way.

If we're strictly talking about traffic violations, we didn't stop you because you didn't run the stop or red light, and our job in traffic enforcement is to educate and correct illegal or poor driving habits by warning, citation, or arrest (for criminal traffic violations) and the question is used to gauge your honesty and willingness to *self-correct* your behavior. Driving, for anyone, is dangerous, and if some are driving carelessly or recklessly it jeopardizes everyone's safety. Our job therefore is to correct behavior when possible. If in answer to the question you say you have no idea, then it's either you truly didn't realize you committed an infraction, and by the way, ignorance of the law is not a defense, or you're playing stupid. If you choose to do the latter, it will reflect not only in your attitude, but at the end of the stop if you'll excuse the parlance, you didn't "have it your way!" This isn't Burger King.

Scene 2: Attitude is Everything

You've heard it before; a good attitude in a traffic stop will garner you more sympathy and perhaps getting off. I always began my *"19s"* with a *"Good morning Sir/Mam, May I see your driver's license, registration, and insurance information?"* Just like they taught us in the academy and FTO phases and it's never changed. Then you the violator have the opportunity to comply with my request and understand it isn't really a request at all because the law in most any state states *upon demand* by a law enforcement officer you are required to provide said documents. Something many people forget is driving is a *privilege* and not a *right*, and it comes with mandates and requirements. If you ask me why I stopped you before I get to ask for your license, my answer always was *"I'll be glad to tell you after you provide me with what I asked you for."* This establishes the tone and who is leading this little exercise. You must comply, period. So don't make it anymore adversarial than it is.

Now come at the officer with *"Why the fuck are you stopping me?"* Or here's a favorite; *"Don't you have anything better to do than stop me?"* The short answer to Question No. 2 is, "No we don't." We're stopping you for that traffic violation you just committed and at that particular moment in space and time, you are our sole focus in the universe, and obviously from your less than polite response to us you needed stopping and reeducation concerning your driving habits. As soon as you give us an attitude for stopping you due to *your own* driving behavior and I might add for just doing our job, you just dictated how this encounter is going to go. And to answer Question No. 1, *"Why the fuck..."* well, you just fired the first shot and this will not go quickly and you will not enjoy it! The worst thing (verbally) you can do is go off on us with a colorful metaphor and that is a sure-fire way to graduate and receive your *"diploma"* for driving.

To further go into your stupid-ass questions as stated above, over time and gaining experience, we develop responses to those idiotic questions that sometimes may not be polite but remember, you fired the first shot. As to *"Why the fuck,"* we might reply, *"Why the fuck do you think I stopped you?"* (CH) Not condoned by police agencies but somehow appropriate in response to your stupidity nonetheless. And one I've used for the question *"Don't you have anything better…"* I've said, *"I'm not a very good officer so they have me doing traffic enforcement."* (CH) We are going to have a comeback for most anything you say, so why not be polite? You don't have to apologize, just don't be an ass-wipe and things will go well. We already witnessed the violation and if we weren't predisposed to issue a citation, your poor attitude now insures we will.

Scene 3: Excuses, Excuses!

As you can well imagine, an officer upon initiating a traffic stop might hear a myriad of explanations or better put, *excuses*, why the driver might have committed the violation or violations (plural) as many times there are more than one. I wish I had written them all down over the years because they would have filled a book by themselves. I think I'll begin with the obvious first one and this will be full of *(CH)*.

"I didn't know." Ok, maybe you didn't and that's fine. We will enlighten you. But after you say you didn't know and we tell you, don't argue you didn't do it when you just said you didn't know. Uh?

Here's one we hear all the time; "I'm late for work!" So is everyone else!

"I didn't see you back there." So it would have been ok if I wasn't back there?

"I'm not from around here." Stop signs must be different where you're from, mmm.

"I'm lost officer." Then going from the far-right lane across three lanes of traffic is ok in your state?

"I'm sorry officer, I knew I was speeding and you're only doing your job" Depending on how much you were speeding you might get off. If you were doing say, 95 in a 55, we're going to call bull shit on it and sorry isn't going to cut it. Passing cars like they were standing still should have been a clue as to your driving at warp speed Mario!

"I didn't know how fast I was going." So I can write whatever I want on the ticket?

"I pay your salary!" (A perennial favorite) Here's your tax dollars at work, sign here!

"It wasn't me!" Yes it was!

"I'm going to shit myself!" Ok, that's happened to me. You're free to go. Drive safely!

"But everyone else was speeding officer." I can only catch one fish at a time.

"We're having a baby right now!" I escorted them to South Miami Hospital.

"It's a medical emergency!"

"Ok, let me call Fire Rescue and they'll be here in five minutes.

"No wait, I was lying." Diploma!

DUI: "I only had five beers officer." Put your hands behind your back, moron."

And the best parting shot; "I'll see you in court!" Great! You have to take off work and I get paid overtime!

And the hits just keep on coming! People will be very creative when it comes to excuses about their driving. I once handled a minor crash on SW 152 Street where the road was wet and this young girl ran into the back of a van that had come to a stop. When I was issuing her the citation for Careless Driving/Failure to Control the Vehicle, she said and I quote: "It's not my fault, the car skidded!" Need I say more?

Damned Speedometer!

I was running radar one night on the graveyard shift and I lit up a Mercedes SLC, the small convertible, doing 83 in a forty-five. Beeeeep! The sound of the radar unit registering the speed of the target. The higher the tone, the higher the speed. I came in behind the Benz and pulled it over. When speaking to the 30-something driver, I of course, asked her *The Question*. To wit, she replied she didn't know how fast she was going. Now, when looking me in the eye, I told her she was doing 83 mph and I shit you not, she looked down at her speedometer. Couldn't help myself and said, "Now it says Zero!" She just looked up and smiled. Graduate!

A Little Quip on Stop Signs

I'd like to end the excuses I mean reasons, portion, and the less-than-wise remarks in this part of the lesson plan and talk about *"The California Roll."* You may have also heard this referred to as *"The Hollywood Roll"* or *"Hollywood Stop,"* but they all mean the same thing. Someone slowed and *rolled* through the Stop Sign having never fully stopped where they were supposed to. In some cases where there is very light traffic or perhaps in the wee hours we may not care, but it does give us a reason to stop you and check you out. But when you do the roll and say to us, "But officer, I slowed down," I will just offer this little story; an officer stops a car that rolled through a Stop Sign. Upon stopping the driver and informing him of the failure to stop completely, the driver says, "But officer, I slowed down!" The officer then takes out his baton and begins striking the driver and asks, "Now, do you want me to stop or do you want me to slow down?" *(CH)* Here ends the lesson.

Scene 4: The Passenger Seat Lawyer

There have been many times an officer stops a driver for a traffic violation and goes through the usual question and answer session, only to be interrupted by the driver's buddy who is a first- or second-year law student and begins practicing law prematurely without a license.

Upon the driver's license request, F. Lee Baily starts telling his driver pal he doesn't have to give us his license and it goes downhill from there. With a prominent law school here in our own back yard, *"The U,"* The University of Miami, we get our share of side seat lawyers who don't yet realize a little bit of knowledge is dangerous and are not yet qualified to give legal advice.

You see, as the driver/violator if you don't comply you are subject to more fines and possibly arrest for not doing so. Sidebar: My advice to some of the motoring public (you young folks mostly) as it's always been during these encounters, you should ask yourself if your not-quite-yet-lawyer pal is going to bail you out of jail or take the rap for you because of his ill-advised counsel? If the answer is no, then do yourself a favor and just comply. If you don't, again, this will not go quickly and you will not enjoy it. And by the way, we don't give a rat's ass who your daddy is or who you know. They're not going to take the ride for you either. Nough said!

Scene 5: Miami Drivers

So now I'm going to go a bit of a rant, so bear with me. I think I've earned it. Most cops around the country will likely say the people that live and drive there are terrible drivers; Miami is no different. I've got to say *I think,* and I'm not alone, we have some of the worst drivers in the country. I don't know what it is, but people here get behind the wheel and it's as if they are the only ones in the universe at that moment, and no one else matters.

You would think by their actions, they believe they own the fucking road and can drive any way they want. Well, folks in Miami or anywhere else for that matter, and I'll say it for my colleagues around the country, you don't! You can't drive, cutting other people off, speeding as if you are the most important person in the world that has to get there and you're God's gift to the highways. You're not, I repeat not, "An Excellent Driver" Rain Man! It's not about you and the rest of us don't revolve around you. It's about *all of us* on the road. You are just a tiny little piece of that but your actions can have an enormous impact on the rest of us should you decide to drive like an asshole and endanger everyone around you.

When I'm driving, whether it's in my personal vehicle or even when I was still driving my Green & White, and if I'm not on an emergency, I turn on my blinker, asking and advising I need to change lanes.

First, you're supposed to by law, second, I'm letting the drivers behind me know I need to come over and soon. My wife tells me no one is going to let you in. I hate hearing that but I won't change and sadly, she's right, most won't. You suck. I let people in all the time. What the fuck hurry am I in? None, that's what. I'll get there when I get there.

So what do many of our selfish drivers here do? They speed-the-fuck-up so I can't change lanes! Now why the Hell do you need to do that? Need to get to the next light or make sure you stay ahead of me for no damned reason whatsoever? It must be a competitive thing because I can't figure it out. If any of you don't let the driver ahead change lanes when they signal their intent to change, then all I can say is you're a dick! I don't know what else to say. And while I'm on this particular issue, if someone does let you merge in, enter the road from a side street or driveway, the least you can do is wave and say "Thank you" to the driver that let you in. Don't be ungrateful, it's bad form.

I do know it's not so much a *technical skill* thing because *most* anyone can learn how the mechanics work in order to drive a car. It's an *attitude* thing. How you are thinking, feeling, acting, and your outlook on life is what dictates how you are behind the wheel. Remember, driving is a privilege not a right. Nowhere in the Constitution of any state does it state Joe and Jane have a right to drive. Change your attitude behind the wheel and be courteous to everyone around you, you selfish prick! If this upsets you, then maybe I struck a nerve. Is it *you* I'm talking about? If it is, take a look in the mirror and become nicer behind the wheel. Maybe, just maybe you won't cause the crash that takes a loved one's life.

And another couple of things while I'm on my rant; ladies, wake the-Hell-up 10 minutes earlier and put your damned make-up on AT HOME! What is wrong with you? You can't drive while looking in the rear-view mirror and put on eye liner. You can't! I don't care what you believe about your driving skill. It's distracted driving even worse than being on the phone. Maybe to get your attention you need to tap the bumper of the car ahead of you and drive that applicator into your eye. Then maybe it will dawn on you.

And do some of you think you can put down the phone for ten frigg'n seconds while you back your car into a parking space? Apparently not! I've watched countless times people stay on that all important, I can't hang up, the president is calling me phone call, and put the car in reverse, back up one foot, put it drive, go forward one foot, back and forward, back and forward, taking as much as a minute to do something that should take FIVE seconds! PUT DOWN THE PHONE!!! I'm done! Woosah!

Scene 6: The Most Dangerous Thing We Do

After all the fun and games and humorous things we encounter on traffic stops is over, there is the much more serious and perilous aspect to *"19s"* most people are oblivious to, and I don't say that to insult anyone, I use the word because most people really have no idea of the danger. In police work, stopping a vehicle is perhaps the single most dangerous thing we do.

I'll explain.

When an officer pulls over a car, say for an apparent traffic violation or even suspicious behavior, that officer has literally no idea who or what is inside that vehicle, none! We may think we are just conducting a *routine* (there's that word) traffic stop for a taillight out or the *Hollywood Roll*, but the guy may have just committed a robbery, assault, rape, burglary, drug deal, theft, or even murder, have a warrant, and we have no frigg'n idea about it. To us, maybe we're going to issue a citation; to him, he thinks he's caught and now will try to take us out. Everyone has seen those *dash-cam* videos of officers being shot and shot at and otherwise jumped on traffic stops. Pay attention boys and girls, those are as real as it gets for us.

Think about stopping a vehicle, say a van, no windows or very dark tints, at night, and you're walking up to the driver's window. The officer can't see there are three or four people in there, perhaps three or four asshole-bad guys and there is nowhere to hide should they come out firing, nowhere! The best you can hope for is to try and run to another end of the vehicle while firing back. Why do you think you sometimes see an officer with his or her gun already in hand when approaching a vehicle? To give us a fighting chance, that's why. When someone pulls on you and your gun is holstered you will probably get shot. I've had my gun out so many times if I had $10.00 for every time I did I could have retired earlier.

More officers have died in traffic stops than in any other encounter. We talked about Active Shooters, rare, Domestics probably No. 2, but *"19s"* lead the pack. There is no more vulnerable position for us to be in. Think about the lone officer in maybe a rural area with back-up 20 or 30 minutes away, or a State Trooper, which in Florida the Highway Patrol officers are always alone. And up in central or northern Florida? Forget it! Always alone and have to survive on their own should it come to pass and it has; all too often.

304

Don't Do It!

What gets drivers killed by police when tensions are high and actions by the occupants are suspicious or downright dangerous? Failure to comply with the officer's orders not to move or go for what we think is a weapon. Plain and simple! When we say, *"Don't do it,"* why the fuck would you go for the weapon with a gun already trained on you? You will die if you do and that's happened just too many times. Then the officers are blamed for the stupid, stupid actions of some guy who perhaps would have just been arrested but instead decided to tempt fate. We are not going to let you *go for it* because we have to go home first. If you're stupid, then perhaps you decided to die that day.

Shootings, pursuits, bailouts and foot chases, fights, getting hit by other vehicles where the DUI is drawn to the red & blues or just not paying attention, have all resulted from the *routine* traffic stop. We have taken sooo many firearms off people in vehicles you would think collectively they could warehouse the military's armory. So when an officer is approaching your vehicle, especially in low-light conditions, you would do well to place your hands on the steering wheel where we can see them and comply with everything we ask. Your actions will dictate how easy or how hard it will go.

Simple Mistake(s)

Quite a few years ago a training film from a *Police dash-cam* video was circulated among agencies about a traffic stop that went so badly for the officer, she almost lost her life over it. Many others have, but this one was used as *what not to do* on our part so we wouldn't make the same mistakes, and to drive home the point about the perils of traffic stops and being alone.

An officer somewhere in the Midwest stopped a van with a really big guy driving who had his young daughter with him. As a matter of course for us, we run a check on your vehicle, your license, and you, to see if you're wanted for anything. Many arrests are made on warrants discovered on traffic stops, and this is another reason someone might act against us because they know they have the warrant, but we don't know that yet. So a check is run locally from that jurisdiction, as well as nationally through *NCIC*, the National Criminal Information Center.

This is a database for wanted persons all over the States. It's like Santa; it knows if you've been naughty or nice.

This officer ran the check on the driver while standing between his vehicle and hers, with him standing there next to her. (Mistake No. 1.) Between the vehicles is a very bad place to stand. The subject can push you into traffic or you can hit from the rear and become trapped between the two cars. While she wasn't paying attention (Mistake No. 2) the dash-cam audio picked up the driver saying he can't go back to jail; not with his little girl there while nervously pacing (a red flag) back and forth. He was walking around unsecured (Mistake No. 3). Always try to keep the occupants secured in the vehicle because from there it's more difficult to act against you.

Then while standing within earshot of the driver with her back turned, the dispatcher comes over the shoulder mic and announces the outstanding warrant the subject has; (Mistakes No. 4 & 5). Never turn your back and never let the subject hear the transmissions and here's why; the subject heard the warrant announcement and without warning, cold cocks the officer so hard he knocked her out. He got on top of her and repeatedly punched her shattering most of the bones in her face. He then tried to remove her sidearm from her holster but couldn't get it out because thankfully, her agency utilizes safety holsters with multiple retention systems to prevent just what he was trying to do.

What do you think he was going to do *if* he was able to get her gun? We will never know but trends over the decades have shown he probably would have shot her with her own gun, like what happened to my colleague Bobby Zore on Christmas Eve back in 1983. Perhaps she was inexperienced but quite a few mistakes were made that led to what could have been her untimely and senseless death. She survived and underwent many surgeries to reconstruct her face, but it didn't have to happen, but I fear it will again because officers will make mistakes and asshole-bad guys will be just that.

Scene 7: The Sovereign Citizen

There is a movement in the United States and Canada that the overwhelming majority in both countries doesn't even know exits, and that is the group that call themselves *Sovereign Citizens*. They are a collection of self-proclaimed anti-government, anti-tax, generally white supremacy-based/style *Kentucky Fried Idiots* that don't recognize most any form of government but come in all colors of the rainbow. The most extreme of these individuals have been classified by the FBI as domestic terrorists. Oddly enough, their doctrine only recognizes the *County Sheriff* as having the highest law enforcement power in the country, even over the federal government. Nice to know since I was a deputy sheriff, but I can tell you it doesn't hold true. So why do I mention these so-called *Free-People* in a chapter discussing traffic stops? Because police officers encounter these idiots behind the wheel all too often and they give us a very difficult time at each and every encounter and are hazardous to our health.

They refuse to either give us their license or be wise asses by holding it up against a closed window. They refuse to acknowledge our presence and authority, and just plain like to jerk us around. They don't refer to themselves as "drivers" in the usual sense, but rather say they are "traveling" and are free to do so without the constraints of any laws. I have even seen one of these so-called *citizens* in court read to the traffic judge a prepared statement about his sovereignty and how he doesn't have to obey any laws. It makes for an entertaining showdown in court to say the least.

I had one of those young officers I mentioned previously I hired to work with my squad, stop one of these idiots who played the game with her and refused to comply with any requests. The officer called me and I was on my way.

One of my guys, Big Mike J. got there first. When I say big, I'm talking 6'5" and intimidating to say the least. Mike attempted to reason with him and he asked what was going to happen. Mike told him his sergeant was on his way and didn't put up with any shit. Mike went on to tell him if he continued to refuse to comply and didn't come out of the car, we were going to break the driver's window, extract him through said window, and if he fought, show him the way to the hospital before jail. He gave Mike his license. But they don't all go this way.

Some of these *citizens* are hardcore and will fight at every turn. *Traffic Stops* are just the tip of the iceberg, but it all went to hell on May 20, 2010, when two West Memphis, Arkansas police officers stopped a father & son team of these *Sovereign Citizens*. The father first physically attacked one of the officers, then the son (of a bitch) got out of the van with an AK-47 and opened up on the officers killing one and mortally wounding the other. They were later located at a Walmart and a gun battle ensued with at least ten officers where finally these two fucks were killed.

These confrontational encounters occur every day with these kinds of anti-government types, and they make life for law enforcement particularly hazardous in addition to all the other perils of our profession. A word to the would be assailant of police; you may get some of us once in a while. Those are the odds. But we will never stop hunting you down and there are more of us than you!

Scene 8: One Last Thing

It's been rumored cops don't give other cops tickets. It's not a rumor, we don't. It's a little thing we call *Professional Courtesy*. This is given in most professions by colleagues to one another like doctors to doctors, lawyers to lawyers, politicians to politicians (no shit), state's attorneys and judges and so on, and most any other profession.

Colleagues take care of each other, or at least they should when permissible, and not writing another cop is one way we take care of our own. This goes for firefighters and military as well. Fire Rescue are the ones who respond to many of the same things we do and are the guys and gals who you're staring up at when you're down on your back and injured. They not only take care of the public but they take care of us, so professional courtesy is extended to them as well.

There are extreme circumstances where an officer or firefighter is just a flaming asshole and leaves the patrol officer with no choice. There's also the criminal violation that leaves no latitude, but for an infraction? Not a snowball's chance in hell! There is the cop that doesn't see the big picture and will write his own mother, but they usually learn quickly.

We have to take care of each other because in the end, we're the only ones we can truly rely on. When I have stopped a driver and found out it was a fellow cop or firefighter from it-doesn't-matter-where, I told him or her why and said have a nice day. It's not officially sanctioned by departments but we just don't do it, period! This may also extend to family, depending on how the family member treated the stopping officer. I have been asked to reach out and the first question I ask is how the wife, husband, brother, son, daughter, father, mother, uncle, aunt, or whomever, treated the officer. If they gave them a hard time, then as they say in New York; *"Fuhgeddaboudit!"* It goes back to attitude.

I once handled a crash with the at-fault wife of a City of Miami officer and she continually harassed me during the investigation. I mean she just wouldn't shut the fuck up! She was earning herself a diploma and after I presented her with it, she called her off-duty husband who responded. He asked why, and I gave him the why of her behavior. He apologized and told her to shut the fuck up!

When we can, we won't do it. So some may not like to hear it and scream corruption, "Russia, Russia, Russia, *The Code*, or whatever you want to attribute it to, but we don't and we won't. That's just the way it is...

Act - 22 So What is a Cop?

Scene 1: Who Are We

During my career, I've been asked by citizens what kind of person it takes to become a police officer. We sometimes seem *foreign* or perhaps *out of the norm* to some folks and they wonder what kind of people we are. Not necessarily an easy answer but let me offer my thoughts and attempt to describe for you who and what I am/we are, and why.

First, I think the aspiring police officer in most cases has an overwhelming desire to serve the public. I mean, how could you not since this is the basis for everything we do. In this regard, you have to be somewhat selfless because your service is about everyone else and not you.

If you, the officer-in-waiting don't feel this way, then perhaps this profession isn't for you. Seek life elsewhere because sacrifice for others comes with the territory. But back to my point; the person who becomes a police officer also has to have an overriding sense of right & wrong, *Law and Order* to put it another way. You watch the news, hear stories, and see how bad guys commit crimes and in many cases get away with it and you say to yourself, "If only I could do something about it!" Well, joining up is the way to do something about it.

That sounds naive and corny but when your young, you don't know any better and possess a pureness in your heart that unfortunately with time tends to fade because of the injustices you experience along the way. But wanting to *serve* is the necessary foundation of becoming a police officer.

Scene 2: Where Do We Come From?

We come from the same pool of people all of you come from. High school, maybe college, the military, and the work force where everyone else is. There is no special prep-school for law enforcement, just the normal vocations where people are. Though we would like to believe we, along with Fire and the military, all came from the *Planet Krypton*, and our mothers made us a cape and an outfit with a big *"S"* on our chests. It's not true; it should be.

Scene 3: What Do We Like?

We also have an overriding sense of action and adventure. I am an adrenaline junkie and I like the "action" and always have. But I'm not predisposed to jumping out of a perfectly good aircraft, which *Gunny Highway* said wasn't a natural act, so I have my limits. But out on the street? Bring it on! Most of us are like this because of what we do. Quiet and mundane one second, then insane terror the next.

We like sports just like everyone else. We have our own version of the water cooler and on Monday cheer or curse the Dolphins, ok, mostly curse, but get into it just the same as the rest of the country does with their teams. We like pizza, beer, wine, whiskey, ice cream, parties, BBQs, (boy do we!) cars, motorcycles, movies, TV, hobbies, and hanging out with family and friends. No different from you, we just perhaps need it a bit more to let off some steam. As a group, we're a good 90 percent conservative, meaning mostly republican. The conservative platform and ideals are more in line with our values but this should be of no surprise to most. We feel strongly about the Second Amendment and again, this should be of no surprise. I however, do feel there should be some limitations on automatic weapon ownership because there are just too many yahoos out there who shouldn't be allowed to order in the drive-thru let alone own weaponry, but that's just me.

Scene 4: And Speaking of Family

We go through life in the same manner and stages as the rest of you. We start out in our profession and after a few years, we get married and have kids just like you. Our outlook may be slightly different because we fully know what kind of world we are bringing our kids into that the public doesn't fully comprehend. And because of that, we are overly protective and stricter than most parents. We know too much latitude can lead to troubled kids and yet we fail at times. Some of the kids of officers end up in the most trouble. Perhaps this is their way of pushing back at us for being very strict.

But we do what we can to protect them, just like you. We love and cherish our kids and we hurt when they hurt. Our hearts bleed when they bleed, and we cry when they cry. Though we aren't very good sometimes at the relationship thing, by-in-large we are pretty good parents who go to soccer practice, gymnastics classes, ballet recitals, music lessons, parent/teacher conferences (those too), the doctor's visit and the emergency room. So how are we so different in these respects than all of you? We're not. Outside of police work, we're mostly all the same.

We have mortgages, car payments, credit card bills, groceries to buy, lawns to mow (I hate cutting grass) houses to fix and maintain, dogs and cats to take care of, birthdays and Christmas to plan for, vacations to go on, and the list goes on.

So what is a cop? A *cop* is you, because we come from and are just like you. We just do a job most of you either won't or can't do, and that's ok. Not everyone is cut out for police, fire, and military work, just like I wasn't cut out for the medical field. I entered pre-med in college and that was an F'n mistake! Chemistry? No clue! Got out before I failed it. But many of you are whizzes at it and I'm glad you are. I need you to take care of me when I go to the doctor or show up at the ER, which I've done often enough. So when you see me or one of my colleagues, please take a moment to ask yourself how he or she is and what dreams, aspirations, goals, burdens and pain they're carrying around with them while serving you. They are the same as yours, only we're wearing a uniform and a badge and gun because we are so desperately needed out there.

Scene 5: I am not a Robot

Some people think we are programmed to act a certain way, and we are, but that doesn't mean we're not human! Did you know we actually like to eat like everyone else? Why do I say this? Because some not-so-clear thinking folks have actually asked us in a restaurant, why are you eating when we should be out on the street patrolling?

The first time you hear this you're surprised someone would ask you this question and you respond politely and say, "Mam, do you eat when you're working? So do we," and you leave it at that. But after a couple of times of hearing this we might tend to now say "WTF?" "What's wrong with you?" I'm not exaggerating here. This actually happens. So if you see officers in a restaurant and want to say something to them, say "Thank you, and enjoy your meal." We appreciate that.

Scene 6: What is a Hero?

I'm going to first tell you what I, and most of my compadres, believe, is *not* a hero. The word *hero* is an overused term that usually describes some great feat of skill where the star of the team was able to reach down *against all odds* and score the winning touchdown, go yard in the bottom of the ninth, sink the 3-pointer at the buzzer, come from behind in whatever race, and pull off the *"miracle"* finish.

Then in the post-match presser, the coach says it was a "heroic" performance by No. So-and-so, to help the team snatch victory from the jaws of defeat. Then the sportscasters on ESPN and the local news jump on the bandwagon and for days and weeks and we hear them say it was a "herculean" effort and he/she was a hero.

Stop! A great performance on the sports field doesn't make you a hero, it makes you a great player, that's' it! I bet many athletes would agree with me here. While we all marvel at the athletic abilities of some of our team's players and other single athletes, we enjoy watching their sport to keep us entertained, but none of those guys and gals ever did anything heroic on that field.

I am a tennis player and while I want to play like Roger & Rafa and admire them for their skill on the court, their greatest contributions have come from their foundations. Bravo!

But some of those same sports heroes carry with them an even greater responsibility than we do. Our kids identify with them more than us because of sport, and yet many act like spoiled, privileged asses that have no responsibility whatsoever. A hero? I think not. Off the field is another story.

If one of those superstars opens a school, academy, or foundation for children, (Roger Federer, Rafa Nadal, Andre Agassi, Shaquille O'Neal, Dan Marino, Alonzo Mourning (three Miami favorites) Tim Duncan, Mia Hamm, Russell Wilson, and many others) and puts his or her money where their mouth is and creates scholarships to help underprivileged kids with just living better, then of course.

Many do and I don't want to take away from that and applaud them for it, but it's off the field, not on it where they get my vote. For those that have served in the military before their athletic abilities took them places, then again you have my vote. Those especially that play sports and attend the nation's military academies, Annapolis, West Point, the Air Force and Coast Guard academies. All of the cadets, not just the ones on the sports field. Those are heroes not by playing on the athletic field but the battle fields they will soon face upon graduation.

The best example of a football hero I can think of is Arizona Cardinal Pat Tillman. Not because he was a great defensive player and made the team *against all odds*, but because in the aftermath of *9/11*, he gave up a multi-million-dollar pro football career and enlisted in the US Army with his brother Kevin.

Before that he volunteered with Boys and Girls Clubs, the March of Dimes, and read and talked to students in schools in the Phoenix area. Pat and his brother Kevin are heroes! Pat gave up his life for us, regardless of the circumstances surrounding his death, and to me and many, many others, he *is* a hero for what he did *off the field*. So if you need a jersey number, it's *No. 40. May he and all of our fallen military rest in peace.*

My Heroes

Now I'm going to tell you what I think a hero is. I've already mentioned our folks in the military. Without a doubt they are. But the soldiers, sailors, coastguardsmen, airmen, and marines will tell you they aren't heroes because they came home. I understand, but I would argue for the men and women that didn't come back whole. They lost limbs, suffered severe brain injuries, suffered personal loss and PTSD *for us*.

Yes, they sacrificed for all of us so we could watch a game on Sunday, so to me they are heroes. My friend Tom Sr., whose son Tommy Jr. I wrote about losing at thirty-nine years of age, was in the US Air Force, Special Operations, during the Vietnam War. He was under siege at Nha Trang during the Tet Offensive and flew in and out of Khe Sanh under fire. He lost friends there and would be the first to tell you he's not a hero, but to me he is. Thanks Tom, and to all that served like my brother Pete for your service to our country.

Firefighters are another big one for me. They will go into a fire to find you and me, and I've watched them do this. They pick up the pieces when we screw up and tell you it's going to be all right. I was this close to becoming one, but I chose law enforcement instead. I have worked alongside these brave women and men my entire career, so heroes for sure.

My own colleagues bring up the rear on the usual suspects. Every single person, man or woman, color and creed, who puts on the uniform and ventures out into the unknown, day or night, are all heroes.

As with military and fire, there isn't a finer group of people that walk the planet as far as I'm concerned. I know some out there specifically despise us over the others, but you know what, whether you like us or not, we're still going to show up to *your* crisis, do our job, and go to the next person or group that doesn't like us either. That's just who we are. Heroes all!

But what about the unusual suspects you may not normally consider heroes? The obvious one to me, especially in the age of *China-Covid 2020*, are our front-line healthcare workers. Especially our nurses and doctors who face this threat daily with little regard for their own safety because they simply knew they had to.

Who else would do it? They face dangers we don't understand and could become sick or die as their patients have. Historically, doctors and nurses have faced some of the worst diseases that have plagued the planet, been in war zones taking care of the population, and give of themselves willingly so that we may heal. My niece Megan, my brother Pete's youngest daughter, is an ER nurse at one of our leading hospitals, and she puts it on the line every day, and goes home to take care of her kids. She and all the others are superheroes and deserve an *"S"* on their chests in their own right. Thank them the next time you run into one.

How about our teachers who go into their profession knowing they aren't going to make a lot of money, give of their own time and resources, and work to make our children succeed to the best of their abilities. Teachers are role models and should be treated as heroes as well. Thank you to all of mine. Even though I didn't always behave, do my homework, and you called to speak to my mother. I'll let it slide just this once.

But what about the good Samaritan, who is just a *somebody*, who went out of their way to help someone in need, whether it was an accident, terrorist attack or crime, or just did something to make a person's day better or even a life-changing moment when they didn't have to. A hero? You bet!

The most important hero has to be a Mom. To me, it's the toughest job in the world. My mom Noemi had her hands full with me, Pete, and Marisa, ok, mostly me and Pete, but a tough job at any rate. Dads, we're there too but bringing up the rear. Moms have it harder. I watch my daughter Crissy with her three kids, Andre, Yzabella, and Alexa, and my daughter Lauren with her daughter Olivia and it's no easy feat. They make it work every day, so do moms everywhere; you are all truly *Wonder Woman*!

Scene 7: The Thin Blue Line

First, what does this term stand for? It is seen and used everywhere but most people don't even know what it means? The *"Thin Blue Line"* is a term that typically refers to the concept of the police as the *line* which keeps society from descending into violent chaos. The *"blue"* in *"thin blue line"* refers to the *blue* color of the uniforms of most police departments. Blue is the most common color of police uniforms but there are several others.

Miami-Dade Police, my department, wears *"The Brown Gown"* as we've always called it because of the two shades of brown we sport. But sheriff's uniforms in Florida and other states are green and also tan. There are gray and black and white shirts as well, but we universally accept the blue line in describing us all.

This idea of the *blue line* is also a rallying cry for us to show our solidarity for our profession and for each other. Though we come from you and have lives like you, the *line* also separates us in some ways *from* you. Not to say we are better than anyone else, just different.

When you wake up in the morning and get ready for work, chances are pretty good, barring an accident or a plane landing on your head you are pretty certain you'll return home for dinner with your family. For us, before we walk out the door, we put on our uniform with a bullet-proof vest.

When I've left my house for the day's events, and I do mean *events*, I never knew if I would make it home that night. And it's even more freighting for our families because they don't know if we will make it home either.

As an officer, we accept the dangers and if you are gung-ho like I was, you embrace them. It's easier being on the inside than looking from the outside, trust me. At least we have control, mostly, where our families have none.

But the greatest difference in what makes us-*us*, is we will run toward danger when the rest of society is running away from it. Yes, we are paid to do that, and we're ok with it, but it is important that everyone understands that because of our predisposal to run in; we are wired a bit differently than you, and therefore, think and act differently too.

Many times and to our detriment; call it *hazards of the job* or being *scarred*, and soldiers are like this as well, this too makes us different in this sense. What you might cringe at we might laugh at (remember-*CH*), and what you might think is normal behavior for some we say it's crazy or vice versa.

When we get criticized and we often are, for being hard-nosed, uncaring, cold, accused of brutality, remember what it is we see on a daily basis. Not yearly, on TV in a drama, in a video game, but daily we see the absolute horrors humans can inflict on one another.

These *events* tend to leave marks, and we become somewhat callous, even to our own families. It's not intentional, but it happens. And because of what we see and do, and are therefore looked upon with disfavor from some in society; like politicians (a favorite of ours) very liberal academia, the media of course, and as of late some celebrities and sports figures, we will point out that none of you or them will ever have to deal with those things we have and become like us.

When the call comes in at 0200 of let's say just noises behind the building where you live or your back yard in suburbia, we respond. I want you to picture this; we have to walk down that dark alley not knowing if the noises were caused by a cat, dog or raccoon, or by a burglar or rapist, and if we confront a bad guy, what will happen. What will the bad guy try to do to us and how we'll react? Think we're scared? Sure we are, to a point, but we do it anyway because it's that thin blue line that separates good from evil. There are two sayings some us use to describe the biggest differences between us and the rest of society.

1-Be polite and courteous to everyone you meet and be prepared to kill them! It can and has gone sideways countless times for us where we ended up having to take someone's life because that's the nature of our job, not yours, but ours.

2-Understand some of the people you meet might want to kill you! This one comes from one of my colleagues Captain Mario Knapp. We all learn from one another and this as we know has happened too often over the years and will again. Again, the nature of our job, not yours.

My goal here was to hopefully help everyone understand who and what we are and why. As written, we have some very stark differences that make us who we have become, yet I hope you can see the vast similarities we share with everyone.

We are, contrary to popular belief, *human*. We are sons and daughters of society with a *calling*, to step forward of the line, raise our hands and swear, just like our brothers and sisters in arms in the military, who do it *over there* so we can do it *over here*. And our public safety partners in the fire service, to serve & protect *everyone*, day or night, no matter what. So the next time you see a police officer, say hi, and thank them, for standing watch over what separates us from total anarchy and for holding, *The Thin Blue Line*.

Act ~ 23 "06" ~ The Final

Transfer

Scene 1: What Do You Mean Retirement?

As you have read throughout my book, I have used our Miami-Dade County specific police codes to describe chapters and events, so you can "hear" in your mind's eye, or ear if you will, what we sound like when we're talking to one another.

I've also used our codes in our slang to describe the more humorous side of what we do. So this will be the last one; our *"06"* code normally means we are getting off shift or *transfer* as we say it; the *Old Crew* going home and the *New Crew* coming on-duty. Well now I am the old crew having gone home-permanently. I am of course talking about retirement.

When we started our careers at the tender ages of 20, 22, 25, etc. the last thing on the mind of a young police officer, firefighter, career military, and even a professional athlete, is retirement. Why would we even think about that while beginning this journey. We never consider the *R-word*. That is 100 years in the future in a galaxy far, far away?

We're having the time of our lives now, going from call-to-call, kicking ass and taking names, putting asshole-bad guys in jail, saving people, making friends and getting paid for it. We can't even begin to contemplate not doing it any longer because in our young careers and minds, we have no point of reference. How could we? We are mere *Babes in the Woods* without a clue.

Scene 2: The Old Man and the Sea

But what we do hear a lot of that eventually makes us think about retirement, is the older guys or *dinosaurs* as we call them, talk about their upcoming retirement and the desire to get the Hell out! When you're young, this is a foreign concept to you, but after you've had a few years under your belt along with some physical and emotional scars and listening to the veterans, you begin to realize there *will* be an eventual end to this journey.

We also start to look at those same veterans as being a bit *salty* and even disgruntled and can't understand why. Why? Because we haven't gone through, yet, what they've gone through. We haven't seen what they've seen, and we haven't been hurt like they've been hurt. But after a while you begin to understand what they *feel* even though it's so far off.

When you take the time to talk to a veteran and really *listen* to what they've been through, a clearer picture begins to emerge and when it starts to come into focus you say ah! I'm beginning to understand.

Police Work will kick the shit out of you if you let it and sometimes even if you don't. So many things can happen that impact you and have negative consequences later on in life and in retirement. The stresses of going from call-to-call, day in and day out, year-after-year. The horrors of what we deal with, the fights we get into, broken marriages, poor diets, not to mention the travesties of justice we experience in court, And the constant battles with our own administration where we have overbearing, micro-managing, ass-wipes of a supervisor or commander. All of these factors take their toll on any first responder or soldier, and the machine begins to break down.

A very senior officer I once supervised, or should I say learned from, when I was his sergeant, Gary Gable, once said to me we go through life with knapsack over our shoulder, and every day we put a little something more in it and carry it around with us. And the next day put another something more in it, and the next and the next, until that sack is soooo heavy we can't seem to move any longer.

Our profession will do that. Then it's up to us to learn, yes *learn*, how to start emptying the sack so it no longer weighs us down and we can move more freely about the country once again. This made so much sense to me I began to learn to let things go so I can remain healthy and once again enjoy what I was doing.

Everyone has their ups and downs in whatever their profession. The objective is to create an atmosphere that gives us mostly the ups. We've all gone through this and once you learn to navigate these waters it can be smooth sailing into the sunset. There will still be waves, but they won't be as bad because of your attitude toward them.

Scene 3: Plan Your Dive and Dive Your Plan!

In the early 80s when I started, we didn't have a clue about planning ahead for our retirement. That was something our parents did. We were just kids having fun and thought we had a secure pension at the eventual end that would take care of us. We did, to a point, but it is so much more complicated than that.

You had better start getting advice from people who have done it and professionals that can guide you. Investments, what's that? Exactly! You have to start learning how to do that but where do I begin? Fortunately, investment opportunities began to pop up in the form of IRAs and Deferred Comp accounts; more commonly referred to as 401s & 457s.

When you're young you have no idea what these things mean. As you get older these numbers become part of your daily lexicon and watching them grow in value becomes a spectator sport.

In Miami-Dade County, all employees are part of the FRS, Florida Retirement System, and will have a defined pension at the end with monthly benefits paid. The private sector is different and employees have to contribute to their retirement.

We have the additional 457s to invest in as a supplement, but we have to learn how to do that. So now as you begin to get older you start thinking about what it is you'll need to do to prepare for the end. Not easy for anyone. Some advice for the young officers out there; *Start early!* Begin preparing for retirement as soon as you get out of the gates. I've given this same advice to my kids and other young officers and they are doing just that. You'll be glad you did.

So, as your planning you say to yourself; "I've worked the overtime, off-duty jobs, worked on paying down my debt, helped my kids get started, learned to better take care of myself, stayed active, exercised, stressed less about bullshit, and started to see the light at the end of the tunnel as no longer a train." And when you're nearing the end, you hear the terms *Social Security* and *Medicare*. "What, what's that?" "You mean I have to plan and enroll in those? When? What?" Yes, those things as well. Why are they so important? Because we will need them to live later on...

Scene 4: Why Do They Get to Retire So Early?

One of the great benefits police officers and firefighters have is we get to retire earlier than most people. This is by design. The stresses our two professions experience can be exponentially greater than the average person. Think of them as *dog years*. All those negative things that happen to us take away years of our lives by comparison.

Studies show the life expectancy of a career police officer in the US is shorter than the general population. There are a many reasons for this as we face higher levels of cardiovascular disease, occupational stress, physiological stress from shift work, obesity (policing is often a sedentary job punctuated with bursts of physical activity) and hazardous environmental factors (getting shot at or attacked would qualify as an "hazardous environmental factor" I think).

Officers also face higher rates of various cancers and skin diseases. Suicide rates are higher among police as well. This is a whole other dynamic I'm not qualified to talk about other than to say too many of us at the end, due to illness or the new reality of not being on the job any longer is sometimes too much to bear, and some officers take their own life. Sad but true.

Officers also have a higher rate of depression and less sleep (due to shift work insomnia) than the general population. This is also true of anyone who works at night but couple it all the other factors we face and it creates a powder keg.

The general consensus from research is being a cop takes about ten years off your life. Think about that. We may as well be smoking three packs a day, drink heavily, and eat like shit, and that could add up to ten years. Oh, wait, many of us have actually done those things. Doesn't exactly make for a healthy retirement.

When I started in 1983, the stats indicated many police officers die within five years of retirement. Only five years! Now it's about ten to twelve years; a marginal improvement but still not good. That doesn't make for enjoying a long retirement with your significant other, does it?

But fortunately due to better education, nutrition, learning how to live better, the departments better training us, and of course modern medicine, this stat has been reduced.

But as I completed this act we were hit with tragic news. One of my colleagues, who I have known since the mid-80s and worked with as instructors within Mobile Field Force and Critical Incident Management training, passed away while still working in his mid-50s, Captain Gus Duarte.

He became the captain of the Airport right after I retired, so I didn't have an opportunity to work with him at the district level, but those who did enjoyed working for him. I have been retired three years since Feb. 8th, 2020. In that short time we've lost over fifteen colleagues (that I know of) not due to gunfire or assault, but to illness. One was in his late 40s, Gus 50s, and two 60s and one 70s. As I said and as an average, we live shorter lives than everyone else.

In just my first year of retirement we lost the following Heroes: Thank you for your service and may you all rest in peace.

Gordon "Chappie" Chapman
Norman Gregorich
Mike Duggan
Wiliam Decker
Gustavo Duarte

The pension system is designed to allow us to retire early, sometimes in our mid to late forties if you started at say, 20 and did twenty-five years. For us in the FRS, it was twenty-five years of service and then you're eligible to retire. By the time my son BJ joined eight years ago, the retirement was changed to thirty years, but you can still get out in your early 50s. Some municipalities around the country allow you to retire at twenty years, but you're at 50 percent pension, and may have to continue to work. I/we are fortunate for the most part, we work again if we want to. Unless of course your wife took **half** of your pension in the divorce, then you may have to. But retiring earlier gives us options, not to mention taking advantage of the years we have left to enjoy life after police & fire work.

Scene 5: I Never Knew I Would Be so Busy

I have heard throughout the years and almost to a person from my friends that retired before me, that they discovered when they retired they had so many things to do that has kept them occupied. All of those projects around the house (Honey-Do Lists) they weren't able to get to because they worked the overtime, Alpha/Bravos, off-duty jobs, taking the kids here and there, getting divorced and losing the house (if you lost your house you don't have to finish those projects, do you?) didn't have time to get to, and now they're faced with finishing, not to mention travel and new hobbies they never got to do.

This holds for most and that's a good thing because you need something to replace the job and all the activity that comes with it.

When you retire from police or fire, the *action* is gone and you need to replace it with something. Travel and projects can do that for you but it still isn't quite the same. No chases, running *"3s,"* perimeters, shootings, fights, riots, having coffee with the guys, nada. So staying busy with whatever is important.

For male officers, generally, we are waiting for our wives & significant others to retire from their careers so we can do some of those things together, but female officers have the same dilemma if their husbands & significant others retire later.

This is the case for me now. My wife Rosy and I didn't wait to do some of those things most couples wait to do in retirement. We've traveled significantly, remodeled our home, twice! Talk about stress. Bought and remodeled a condo for our eldest daughter Crissy and the grandkids, rode motorcycles, and have welcomed our fourth grandchild from our daughter Lauren and her husband Marcos as I write this.

So if I can give a piece of advice to anyone on enjoying your life, don't wait to retire to do some of things you want to do. If you can, do it now. Just do more of it when you're done leaping tall buildings in a single bound.

Scene 6: China-Covid 2020

I retired on February 8, 2020. Exactly thirty-seven years to the day when I started in 1983. I had the opportunity to book-end my career with the retirement option I chose. I planned for it and Feb 8 was going to be the day.

I felt I was done and made it happen.

On Sunday, February 23, 2020, I had my retirement party at a local joint, Pub 52 (a little plug) where the owner, being a fan of the police (rare these days) closed the place for us and we had a great time. My wife Rosy was in charge, and along with my daughters Crissy, Lauren, and daughter-in-law Michelle, invited everyone *I wanted* and pulled off a spectacular event.

I am proud to say those that could make it did, and the show was almost 180 people: many retirees themselves, along with folks still on the job. I'm forever grateful to Rosy, the kids, and all of my friends who came and several who came from out of town, thank you so much. Retired division Chief Charles Nanney told me having his party allowed him to have a sense of closure. He was right. I did and I am grateful for the friends and colleagues I have.

So now I begin my retirement and am planning to do some of those things I've wanted to for a while along with my life-long tennis addiction. Learn to play the drums, volunteer with vets, ride some more on my Gold Wing, oh yea, and grow my hair long along with a goatee.

What happens?

March hits and thanks to the fucking Chinese (government not people) we go into lockdown! Now I find myself sitting at home with nowhere to go in my new truck, except Publix for groceries wearing a damned mask, and everything else is closed. The tennis courts are closed, parks, restaurants, everything. No, don't think I'm crying about this; there's no crying in police work, or retirement, remember? "Additionally," as is said in police reports, our post-retirement trip to hike the national parks in California and Oregon was postponed due to Covid, and then in September postponed again due to the forest fires. Damned!

But these are just the facts mam, just the facts, and I/we have all been impacted but it just sucks when I finally call it a day, all of this happens. The real tragedy and I don't want to lose sight of it is, all the families who have lost loved ones to this *thing* and have been permanently hurt forever, my sincerest condolences. This is what's most important about this year and what has happened to the rest of us pales in comparison. My family and I are fine and I consider myself most fortunate.

After about eight weeks of this shit though I told my wife I'm going to Home Depot to get some supplies to work on a couple of garage projects because cabin fever had set in big time and enough is enough! I know many of you felt the same way and had to do something. Thinking this might be over soon, and then it wasn't, was an eye-opener. I now have an *ensemble* of masks I wear to make a fashion statement with. Ever think it would come to that? We're all in this together and we have to learn to live with this *thing* that has impacted us all, but I know we will get through this as we have everything else because in America, that's what we do.

Scene 7: Reflections

As I bring this book about my career and police work to a close, I can say I have had a great opportunity to reflect on my time on the job and my life. I have reminisced about all the great and not-so-great capers I've been involved in. The exciting and terrifying events we've been a part of. *The Thrill of Victory and the Agony of Defeat* we all experience. The great friends I've made along the way, and the friends lost too. I have been fortunate to have been trained and mentored by the *Best of the Best* and can proudly say I have become one as well.

I've had the privilege of having trained about 25,000 officers during my time as an instructor as an FTO & FTS, in Police Driving, as a Mobile Field Force Training Committee member, Critical Incident Management for Supervisors, and the Crisis Intervention Team in dealing with the mentally ill. Both as a senior officer and sergeant, I was able to become a mentor and have affected a great many careers.

I've saved lives, put real bad guys in jail, and helped countless people during my time on the job. I've met a vice president and a governor, I've coordinated security for US and foreign naval ship visits, TV and movie shoots, been trained to ride ATVs, police mountain bikes and jet skis. I have worked as security for Miss Universe contestants (not too shabby). Stood by and protected those exercising their right to protest and strike. And I have had the honor of serving with some of the best people our society offers.

Firefighters are called the *Bravest*, and Police are called *The Finest*, and both with good reason. As a police officer you wear so many hats you get to do a little bit of everything; and this job above all others is like that *Box of Chocolates…*

What doing this job has allowed me to do is provide a living for my family most of all. I raised three great kids, Cristina, Norberto II (BJ), and Lauren. I have my extended kids in Michelle, BJ's wife, and Marcos, Lauren's husband. Now I have four grandkids from Crissy: Andre, Bella, and Alexa, and Olivia Noemi just making her *Center Ring* debut from Lauren and Marcos. This job has also allowed me to meet, on a blind date, arranged by mutual friends Fernando & Maribel, my wife Rosy. Best move I ever made. While police work is a double-edged sword and it can cut deeply, it has allowed me and us (cops) to live good lives for the most part, and really learn to enjoy what's important because of what we've seen and experienced. Live is precious, so live it folks!

The Final Curtain

My colleagues and I have had a ring-side seat to some of the most amazing, hilarious, astounding, terrifying, tragic, WTF & Oh Shit moments you can imagine. We are involved in almost anything that happens in life, both outside of your home and many times inside.

When the world is going to Hell the ones who get the call are the police, with our brothers and sisters in Fire Rescue bringing up the rear to help pick up the pieces, and sometimes pick *us* up. I've often been asked, both while I was still working heading toward retirement, and now in retirement, if I miss it. I answer with an emphatic "Hell Yes!" How could I not?

I did this most unique of all professions for thirty-seven years, which is most of my adult life and carry all the medals and scars that came with it. I got out healthy and am now in that intermission between the job and moving on to the next *Act* where I am now a spectator in the stands. And as Captain Kirk said about our *Next Generation; "To their posterity we commit our future."* So true!

I have my son BJ to carry on in my place and he is doing a fine job. Most of my colleagues have said they will miss the clowns (us) but not the circus. I have a different take on it and always have; I took the job *because* of the *circus*. The clowns are all the rest of us and that's what has made it so great.

Stuff in the Basement

"Fighters Fight!" That's what Rocky Balboa said and that's the way I feel. I will always have the desire to do police work. It's something we all have to work out now that it's over. It's easier for some than it is for others. I know my time has come and it was the right decision to leave when I did, but I took the job for the right reasons, continued to do for those same reasons, and that's why I will always still, have the *"Stuff in the Basement."* I'll just have to keep it there and check on it every so often and remember why we did it.

I am proud to have worn the **Silver Badge** and been a **Metro-Dade Police Officer**, and that has allowed me to be one of the *Ring Masters* to a circus and all of its side shows few ever get to see up close. I can say without a doubt or regret, I will surely miss **The Real, Greatest Show on Earth!**

330

Act ~ 24 War Stories

Stories from the Fringe

The following is a collection of **War Stories,** *and all kinds of* **Just Stories,** from colleagues, friends, and family. As I've been saying throughout **The Real Greatest Show on Earth**, *a*ll cops everywhere have similar experiences and I've been telling you not only *my story,* but *our story*. They are true, personal, and come from the heart from each of my fellow *cops,* who graciously contributed to this book.

I will add **Author's Notes** after each for a personal touch. Read, enjoy, laugh, cringe, be horrified, shocked or astounded, but do try and *feel* what *they felt* as it was happening to them. You won't be disappointed. So, without further ado and appearing in alphabetical order, here are: **Stories from the Fringe**:

By Captain Tim Adams, Miami Gardens Police, Sergeant (Ret) Metro-Dade Police

Birth of a SWAT Team

The Miami-Dade Police Dept. (formally the Public Safety Dept. & then Metro-Dade) Special Response Team came from an early beginning as the Hostage Rescue Team (HRT) in the late 70's. The name was eventually changed to the Special Response Team or SRT, as Hostage Rescue Team was too confining in nature as to the overall mission of what SRT was to become.

The **HRT** was initially staffed by the 'pool system' whereby members were assigned from everywhere in the department, and from no particular district or unit. This was a totally unmanageable concept relying on who was at work that day, and conducting training was difficult at best.

This later changed to a *team* being assigned to each of the then six (6) districts. This was more manageable; however the training was still inconsistent even though the Director stated training would be allowed once a month. Not all the district commanders followed

332

the Director's memorandum, therefore some of the teams were under-trained and that can be dangerous given the specialized nature of the work.

Captain Richard Smith, then the Midwest District Commander, told me one day when I was the Acting Lieutenant and team leader of the Midwest HRT Team, he was going to a staff meeting, and as a fluke, (and some stones) I asked him to ask (tell) the Director if he would be willing to let me take all the district teams into our district, thereby alleviating the training issue and establishing a central command and base. Captain Smith did make that request and soon thereafter all six teams were assigned to the Midwest District, primarily as road patrol squads.

In 1980 I became the Range Master assigned to the Training Bureau. One of my primary assignments was to establish an *SRT School.* The first SRT School began in 1981 and has gone on to be one of the most prominent SWAT related courses in the country.

During this time period, SRT - related calls overwhelmed the Midwest District and greatly affected its patrol operations since team members had to leave their patrol duties in order to respond to a *call-out.* Due to the increase in drug related warrants, (the *Cocaine Cowboys* were quite busy) and hostage situations greatly increasing, the decision was made SRT should become a full-time unit; train and respond, that's it. The downside was SRT would have to downsize to four teams from six. SRT was then assigned to the Special Patrol Bureau, with two teams operational and two teams in training on a rotating schedule.

SRT has become recognized as one of the best and busiest teams in the country, having served thousands of narcotics warrants, hostage rescues, dignitary protection details to United States Presidents and visiting dignitaries, a Papal Visit, protecting the mayor (and family) of Miami-Dade County from active death threats from the Versace killer, and countless bad guy searches and apprehensions in backing uniform patrol units. I am proud to have been on the ground floor and to have served with the operators of SRT.

Mail Carrier Hostage Incident

On January 31, 2003, I was working in the Miami Lakes District as the Acting Day Shift Lieutenant (A/Lt.). A beep-tone went out followed by dispatch advising there was a hostage situation in-progress involving a postal carrier in the City of Miami Gardens. The department was contracted with the City of Miami Gardens at that time to provide police services before they established their current police department.

Some Miami Lakes officers responded to the area and quickly came into sight of the postal vehicle. I was already enroute and quickly became the Incident Commander of this rolling barricaded/hostage situation. A subject was in fact holding a female mail carrier at gun point, ordering her to drive around.

I requested MDPD Aviation and the Special Response Team (SRT). This was now a pursuit of sorts since the subject refused to pull over. However, they would stop or slowly roll through red lights and stop signs. The subject would suddenly have the mail carrier stop the vehicle so he could speak with a bystander along the circuitous route he was taking. The subject advised he wanted aviation to go away. The subject also threatened he would go to a school if the police tried to stop him. All schools in that region were put on lockdown.

Due to the live news coverage and interrupted television channel 'breaking news,' there were people lined up along the roadways waving as the mail carrier drove by. A true three-ring spectacle.

As we were driving around it became quite apparent that individual officers, especially from other jurisdictions, were chomping at the bit to stop the mail carrier vehicle. It was at this point I advised ALL units I was taking the lead vehicle position and NO ONE was to pass me or take any action without MY APPROVAL. As it was, every so often a municipal officer would pull alongside of me and ask what I wanted them to do. The answer was always the same, "Go back, I'll call you if I need you!"

During this incident I was continuously interrupted by telephone contact from the two district commanders and the two district executive captains. This became a hindrance to the point I had to advise the Brass I couldn't keep having the interruptions and run this incident at the same time. I needed my full concentration on a game plan with the SRT commander, who I was now in contact with as well as being the lead unit following the vehicle. Yes, a

COORDINATED GAME PLAN to resolve this situation was needed and we had to choose a place to make the stop with the appropriate resources in place. This situation as it was unfolding made this possible.

At one point the mail carrier drove to the front of Miami Norland High School and stopped. I made the decision if the subject got out of the vehicle by himself he would be immediately shot or run over by me. If he took the hostage he would be shot. Fortunately at that point he chose to drive on.

The subject attempted to drive into Miramar, a Broward County city just north of us, however Miramar PD was having no part of that as they had blocked off all lanes, both north and southbound on NW 27th Avenue. I had previously advised dispatch to forewarn the Broward Sheriff's Office and surrounding municipal agencies of the possibility he would try to come into their jurisdictions.

During this 'following' I was in contact with the SRT Commander collaborating on a plan to make the stop. His SRT units were now in the area and I advised all units to allow the SRT units in their individual cars, to pass and take up the lead vehicle positions. I determined we would have specific intersections blocked to force the subject to go south on NW 27th Avenue from County Line Road. The stop would be made at the intersection of NW 27th Avenue and NW 183rd Street. A *stop-stick (spikes),* of course from another agency (God forbid MDPD would have such a useful device) would be deployed to disable the mail carrier vehicle, so I had the intersection blocked off in advance for this plan.

The plan worked as devised and negotiations were now in play. I was now on foot surveying the inner perimeter as I was still the overall incident commander. I suddenly became incensed as to what I saw. There were civilians, supervisors and officers standing on the surrounding sidewalks viewing in awe at the SRT operation. Unfortunately, all of them were in potential lines of fire as the subject was armed. I had to yell at them to wake up and get the spectators back to areas of safety as well as themselves. I needed active supervision from the on scene supervisors. Just because SRT took over the mail carrier barricaded hostage situation, our job wasn't finished. We still had the safety of the spectators and SRT to maintain, as well as the inner and outer perimeters.

There were many accolades from around the country for how the situation was handled, ending with no one injured and the armed subject taken into custody. There was criticism from some; of course, stating they wouldn't have allowed the vehicle to drive around, and they would have immediately stopped it. I asked the same question each time I heard that; "Then what?" I received the same response each time....no response. When you can, slow things down and have a plan. Without a plan there is usually chaos and things spin out of control. The incident is *controlling you* instead of *you controlling it!*

Remember, BE PART OF THE SOLUTION, NOT PART OF THE PROBLEM, OR YOU BECOME THE PROBLEM ITSELF!!

Cocaine Cowboys & a Hostage Rescue

On June 21, 1985, at approximately 1037 hours as the team leader of SRT, I was requested by the Organized Crime Bureau (OCB) Narcotics to respond to 2900 SW 113 Avenue, in reference to a possible home invasion robbery.

Upon arrival I was advised OCB had information a home invasion robbery was going to occur at the noted location. OCB had set up surveillance and had observed three to four armed, Latin males enter the residence. The detectives became worried the subjects of the home invasion robbery were still inside the residence two hours after entering (YOU THINK!).

A second SRT team was requested and a perimeter was being established when the garage door suddenly opened, and two Latin males were seen getting into a light-colored van. I immediately ordered my team to simultaneously apprehend the vehicle and secure the occupants, while maintaining a point on the residence. A third subject was seen at the garage door and upon spotting SRT fled back inside. As soon as the two vehicle's subjects were taken into custody, SRT Officer Carlos Rosario was directed to announce, in Spanish, that all occupants in the residence were to come out with their hands up. The command was given a second time, at which time three persons exited the residence. It should be noted the first person to exit was in fact the third subject, who was now pretending to be a victim.

The other two persons to exit were the husband and wife victims. The wife advised when the initial two subjects were taken into custody and the police commands were given, those commands in fact saved their lives. The third subject had just placed a pillow over her head and put a gun to the pillow in an execution style manner. The subject, upon hearing what was going on outside then fled to the garage where he saw the SRT units and then fled back inside, having decided to now act as a victim in hopes of escaping. He then threatened the husband and wife to not reveal who he was.

Upon conducting a search of the residence it was determined the two hours spent inside prior to SRT being called, was utilized by the subjects to interrogate the victims, and to tear walls apart looking for drugs and cash believed to be there.

All's well that ends well, despite the two-hour delay!!

Author's Note:

Tim was the Range Master when I was in the academy in 83.' After I joined the Mobile Field Force (MFF) Training Committee in 98,' as a founder of MFF, he became a mentor and father figure to me. He Retired from MDPD in 2004, but we continued to teach Crisis Intervention Team training together, and in 2017 received CIT Officer of the Year (Tim) and CIT Liaison of the Year (me) together. We remain great friends to this day. He will always be "Sergeant Tactical" to me.

Feel Good Stories

By Lieutenant Alina Alvarenga, Miami-Dade Police Dept.

We Tried Our Best

I was an officer at the time riding two-man in the Hammocks District, it was a very busy day and we had just run into Wendy's to use the restroom and get something to eat. As I was leaving the restroom the call goes out of a *"3-44,"* of a 13-year-old boy who hanged himself. We ran out the door, jumped into the car, and started heading that way. The entire time updates were coming in from the dispatcher advising the boy was blue and CPR had been started.

When we arrived, I jumped out of the car before it was stopped, ran inside the house, and started doing CPR on the boy. I knew he was already gone, but I did everything humanly possible to bring him back. When Fire Rescue arrived, I wouldn't even let them take over compressions I was so amped up. When they finally took the boy out of the house I broke down in tears. It's the only time I have cried on a scene in fifteen years. I will never forget the mom sitting on the front lawn crying or what her boy looked like.

About a month later, the mom came to the station and gave me and my partner thank you cards with the funeral program inside. Even in the midst of her grief she still recognized we tried our hardest to save her son. I still have that card to this day and will keep it forever.

One Last Gift

As the Neighborhood Resource Unit Lieutenant I get tasked with everything under the sun. However, one of the greatest accomplishments of my career thus far was helping make a little boy's birthday extra special, as we were asked by the City of Miami Police to assist. This little boy had a rare brain cancer with a 1 percent survival rate, so naturally we pulled out all the stops. Along with Miami's units and our own Motor Unit, we gave that family the most special birthday celebration we could, which would turn out to be his last. We had all of our Motors, ATVs, and the Green & Whites, the City's horses, marine patrol, bike squad, the *PAL Bear,* and our very own helicopter. The helicopter hovered so low you could hear the pilot on the loudspeaker wishing the boy a happy birthday. Helping with the birthday celebration, and then seeing the pure joy on this little boy's face was one of the most rewarding things I have ever done or seen. So sad he couldn't grow up to share it with his own children.

We Made a Wish Come True

The Midwest District NRU was asked to participate in a *Make-A-Wish* celebration for a little girl with cancer. Her wish was to see snow but due to her health and the pandemic she couldn't fly. The *Make-A-Wish Foundation* reached out to us and requested our assistance at the last minute, and my officers went above and beyond even on such short notice. As a supervisor it is so incredible to see how much love and kindness the officers still have despite the negative media attention we constantly get. In fact, both the family and the *Make-A-Wish* personnel were blown away by our response. They said they never expected anything like that from the police. We had all the Green & Whites decorated with balloons and stickers from the *Frozen* movie. We had *McGruff the Crime Dog* on the back of a truck, the helicopter did a flyover, and the officers even threw marshmallows to pretend it was snowing for the girl. As a lieutenant it is so amazing to see the people who work for you have such big hearts and will go above and beyond the call of duty. Police work isn't just about taking the bad guy to jail. It's also about putting a smile on the kids' faces and making the community a little better.

Author's Note:

Lt. Alina is my niece. She followed in the family business; me, then my brother Pete her father, and her mother Sally, paving her own way and we're all very proud of her.

And We Thought We Did It

Story

By Officer Milton Arias, Metro-Dade Police Dept.

The Horror

My story deals with me driving home from the Metro Justice Building after a morning in court. This took place sometime in the 1990s when I was working midnights in the Kendall District. I remember how tired I was after having to go to court after working a midnight to 8 A.M. midnight shift and squinting as I drove home. I was traveling southbound on SR 874 in my marked police car when I observed what appeared to be a head-on crash involving two vehicles. I got on the radio, advised the dispatcher of the situation, and requested back up units. I was waved down by motorists and as I drive closer to the scene of the crash, I observed what I remember as three bodies on the ground.

These individuals had apparently been ejected from one of the two vehicles involved and were now lying on the roadway. I exited my vehicle and approached two female adults who appeared to be conscious. I then saw an infant female who was the third person lying on the roadway. I quickly approached her and it didn't appear she was breathing. I checked her vitals and there was no pulse. I began CPR on the infant and at some point Officer Lou Valdes, who was in my academy class, appeared on scene and helped me with the CPR. Fire Rescue arrived and examined the infant and told us she had a pulse and was breathing again. I remember the feeling of relief and accomplishment me and Lou had as we walked back to our police cars after all the other units arrived on scene and took over. The infant was subsequently transported to a hospital by Fire

340

Rescue, and I later learned on the television news she had sadly passed.

I remember the extreme loss I felt, but at the same time I know we did all we could to save her because of the training we had received over the years. A bit later, Lou and I received what we were told were the first ever, Life Saving Awards given by Metro-Fire, and they were presented to us at The County Commission Chambers by the fire director himself. It was a nice gesture by Fire and we greatly appreciated it, but would have preferred the little one had made it. It doesn't always turn out how we'd like.

Author's Note:

Milt was on that "Dinosaur Squad" I've mentioned I took over when I transferred to the Airport. He would become my A/Sgt. until I retired. He has a wonderful sense of humor and he kept roll calls light and funny each and every morning. I truly enjoyed our time together and he will be missed.

A Teaching Story

By Deputy Kerry Bathe, Homestead PD & Michigan Sheriff, (Retired)

Diploma or Not Diploma

While as a deputy on road patrol of a county in Michigan of 50,000 in population, I was called in to see the "Boss," meaning the sheriff. I was asked why I wasn't writing a lot of traffic citations. I then replied, "Are you saying I have a quota?" The "Boss" replied, "No, as we have a law stating we do not have quotas." He then stated he has seen where I make a lot of traffic stops at a particular stop sign area and I haven't written any traffic citations.

I replied, "What's my job?" I believe in teaching the public about laws as well as enforcing them when needed. I then explained I make the stops, identify myself as a deputy for the County, and asked if they knew why I had stopped them? They usually answer with "I didn't stop for the stop sign?" I then explain I could issue a traffic citation for a fine of $120 with an addition of two points on their driving record, and their insurance rate could go up or, they could go back and stop at the sign. So, "What would you like to do?" I'd say.

All would go back and stop at the sign they just ran, and when they drove passed by me they would wave with all of their fingers. Did I educate? Did I give that driver a different view of law enforcement officers? Will they relate their experience to others as something positive? I would hope so. I further explained when I did issue a traffic citation, and I call them diplomas, not citations, that they graduated and earned them. So they get a diploma and are sent on their way. I was told to go back on patrol without any further questions.

Author's Note:

Kerry and I met when my former partner Mal, who I wrote about in my act on losing a colleague. Kerry was Mal's FTO in Homestead in the late 70s,' and we became part of Mal's inner circle when he was on his deathbed. Kerry and I formed a bond that can never be broken.

A True War Story

By Officer Daniel Christie Miami-Dade Police Dept.

Oh No!

Friday, May 13, 2011

It was supposed to be a day like any other in my unit in the Intracoastal District. Go out, look for crimes being committed, and haul the offender in, blah, blah, blah. This day was a little different though.

It was Friday the 13th which is already surrounded in superstition. We just finished breakfast and if I'm not mistaken one of my squad members' total rang up to $6.66. The discussion over breakfast was about a particular individual who had been arrested the week prior, was in possession of multiple edged weapons, and had made serious threats against police. The threat was along the lines of "I should have killed you when I had the chance. The next time I will go for blood." We discussed how we should prepare a flier to send out to the district and surrounding agencies to inform them of this guy. Because we were on a special detail this particular day we didn't have the opportunity to get that done.

While patrolling, I happened to see what looked like a hand-to-hand transaction taking place behind a strip mall. It just so happened to be the same guy we were discussing at breakfast. I immediately let my squad know who and what I saw. We thought it best to have a few of us in place just in case things escalated, meaning went sideways. My sergeant was in the area and heard us discussing our plan to approach so he decided to park close by where he could monitor us. So now three of us approach this individual who is standing on the sidewalk.

I approach from the south, one approaches from the west, and the other approaches from the north. This guy looked at all three of us exiting our vehicles and for whatever reason, the focus was on me. I could read my partner's lips saying, "I told you!" The subject proceeds to reach behind the back of his neck and draw two long butcher knives from his shirt almost like a ninja. He then holds these knives over his head in a threatening manner while running toward me at full speed. All I could think of was, "OH SHIT!" Death is coming right at me.

I immediately began back peddling just as we were trained to create some distance while drawing my duty weapon. This guy was beginning to close the gap pretty fast and I was at a disadvantage by having to run backward. I raised my duty weapon giving loud commands for him to stop and drop his weapons but this guy just seemed to stare right through me. I could see what appeared to be hatred and anger in his eyes and I couldn't understand what I could have done to him. I mean, I have never spoken or dealt with this person before. I suppose it was my uniform and what it represented. This was all taking place in seconds.

When I finally realized words were of no use and this person was planning on killing me, I had no other alternative but to discharge my weapon. I can remember a quick double tap, and I could see the point in which my rounds hit center mass. The subject began to cover his chest at this point and stagger a bit but not fall. He was still on his feet continuing to close the gap. I fired several more shots which hit center mass again, and again he didn't go down. When I took the last shot he was within a few feet of me. I finally hit him in the middle of the forehead at which time all motor functions stopped immediately. His body dropped to the ground, arms spread out still holding the knives, and I can remember his legs being crossed. His body was positioned as if it was nailed to a cross. I just hoped after the last shot this guy would not be able to continue on.

When it was all over, I was so overcome with adrenaline and emotion I could no longer stand. I dropped down to my hands and knees in complete disbelief. My heart was beating out of my chest and all I could say to myself was, "What just happened?"

My sergeant at the time was in complete shock as well. I don't think he realized he was walking around with his gun in hand while pacing back and forth with his eyes bulging out of his skull muttering incoherently. It wasn't until another officer came along and pretty much told him in so many words,

"You need to get your shit together and take care of your officer." When the responding units arrived I can remember being escorted to my car and before I got in, I looked around and could see just about every officer working my district on scene along with the surrounding municipalities.

The sergeant who arrived would be the Incident Commander (IC) and responsible for the Use of Force came up to me and told me, "Good job!" He didn't mean it in the sense of GOOD, you killed someone. He meant it in the sense of, you identified a threat that had every intention of taking your life and you reverted back to your training and you neutralized that threat.

We always knew being involved in a shooting was always a possibility in this line of work. Realistically, no one wants to be the one to take someone's life. You have to live with it and in my case I think about it every day. I know there was no malicious intent in doing what I had to do. At that point it became about survival. All I wanted to do was go home to my family and I was not going to let anyone take that away from me.

Author's Note:

The sergeant Danny was referring to who told him "good job" and placed him in the car was me. I was to take over Danny's squad, the Priority Service Unit, the following week and he would become like a son to me. I recommended him for the Gold Medal of Valor which he was awarded and deserved. There is no "just another day" in police work. Danny and the guys walked right into it. He prevailed. He survived. He won! That's what we're all supposed to do. Good job Danny!

A Dog's Story

By Sergeant Allen Cockfield, Metro-Dade Police, Retired

Even Dogs See Black & White

I don't remember the date but around 4 P.M. one day I observed a boat leaving the area about a block away from my house. It was a very impressive boat with three 200 horsepower Mercury out board engines and painted in bright colors. It was a common occurrence because this boat left the area about the same time three to four times a week but would always be back in the yard the next morning.

I left home for work at 5:30 p.m. and headed north as I was the K-9 Unit assigned to work Northside District. As I was traveling north on SR 826 a K-9 unit was requested to respond to Oleta State Park east of Biscayne Blvd. and just south of 163rd street, in reference to a subject in a go-fast that ran aground into the park after a high-speed chase with federal drug enforcement officers.

Having a great tracking dog, I took him to the boat, which I recognized as the same boat I saw leaving my neighborhood earlier, and my dog immediately picked up a track and started running through the mangrove west from the boat. The dog ran a track for about 1/8 of a mile where he found a white male lying in the water with his head exposed. My dog, Cello, had never hesitated to neutralize a subject with a bite on whatever body part he could get to, but this time he licked the subject's face and didn't attack when the subject started to move away. Mmmm. I had to command the dog to stop the man and with more hesitation he finally did so. The subject was taken into custody and released to officers on the scene.

I was very concerned by Cello's behavior and had to figure out why he initially hesitated to take down the subject. I thought it might be because he might have been familiar with the subject but Cello had no friends. It finally hit me all the subjects he had apprehended were black and the only White person he had ever attacked was during training

347

sessions with the training sleeve involved. After talking to the unit's trainer he agreed Cello was associating working on the street with apprehending Black people and White people with training, which involved the wearing of a training sleeve. The sleeve was not present with the fleeing boater so in Cello's mind this could not be a person he was supposed to apprehend.

Racism is trained into our brains and apparently a version of it into police dogs as well, though they don't recognize the concept. In order to change things we have to retrain the racist brain and teach that doing things in a different manner is ok. Commanding Cello to stop the subject from fleeing told his brain it was ok to apprehend any subject even though his training had told him different.

Author's Note:

Allen is the sergeant I wrote about in my act on Police & Politics, where he and I were transformed by those who taught us about our differences. Allen has become my "Big Bro" and we are best of friends. Incidentally, he is the best K-9 instructor our department ever had.

A Good Story

By Sergeant Anthony "Tony" Corbin. Metro-Dade Police Dept.

Paying it Forward-Without Knowing It

I found it an honor to have been asked by my good friend and former partner, Bert Gonzalez, to contribute one of my *War Stories* for his book. I have been on the job now for twenty-five years; assigned to various uniformed positions and have experienced a great deal. For the first half of my career I was an officer and for the second half a sergeant. I've witnessed, experienced, or have handled hair raising calls for service, mind blowing acts of stupidity, and even some incredible acts of God. I have worked natural disasters, man-made disasters, critical incidents, major campaigns or events, been mobilized for civil unrest, and even faced the "End of all as we know it" during Y2K. I have acquired a new mindset as it relates to policing following the attack on our nation on September 11, 2001, and currently, I am learning yet another way of policing during this ridiculous year of 2020, where upon, the world has been affected by the COVID-19 pandemic.

I find it difficult to reflect back and try to recall my best story, or even a good one to recount. As for me, the memories just bury themselves deep inside until I'm with colleagues and we start talking about work. It's then the memories start to resurface. In fact, it's usually something about someone else's story that will jar my memory and I will recall an incident or a situation. But to be honest, any war story I have will sound like the rest.

There is one, however, that has always stood out for me and it happened during the first half of my career. I can recall it anytime and I think it's the best thing I have ever experienced. During the years I was assigned to the Hammocks District, I was dispatched to a particular residence on many occasions for heated domestic related arguments between a husband and wife. The wife had a young son, probably in his pre-teen years, and he was always a witness to the conflict between his mother and stepfather. I remember vividly the husband was a real son-of-a-bitch. A real freaking asshole. He knew just how far he could verbally abuse his wife and stepson and just how much he could turn the whole house upside down without breaking any laws. In fact, he knew the game.

He would cause an uproar, neighbors would call the police, we'd arrive and following an on-scene investigation, advised him to leave so he cools off. He never refused to leave and always left willingly. To this day, I can still see the terror in the eyes of the stepson. I always wished the husband had done just enough for me to arrest him to *really* get him out of the home for the night or even for a couple of days, just to give the wife and stepson a break and have some peace in their lives, even for just a moment.

Well, the day finally came and I was dispatched there yet again. And I know, you think this is the tragic end of the wife and stepson, but it wasn't. It was still very terrifying nonetheless for them. You see this time, the husband did just enough for me to arrest him when he had battered his wife by slapping her during this argument. This time he had too much to drink and went too far. I knew there would be some peace for this family on this day, for he was going to jail and would be there for at least the night.

Following that arrest, I never went there again. I would drive by on occasion, but never stopped in. Just drove slowly past every now and then to keep an eye on things. I have no idea how many times the police have been called to this home but, I can't believe I was the only one getting the calls there. I never had to respond there again.

Some years later I was attending court and was walking through the courthouse when I was approached by a young police officer who worked for one of the municipal agencies within Miami-Dade County. He asked me if I recalled this particular residence in the Hammocks District and all the domestic incidents I had handled there. I told him I did. He also asked me if I remembered arresting the husband. I told him I did. At this point, the young officer reached out to shake my hand and thanked me for bringing peace to *his* home. His stepfather never returned after I arrested him. He told me I was the reason he became a police officer. Definitely one of my best days.

Author's Note:

So things come full circle. Tony was a Public Service Aide in the Hammocks District and then became a police officer when I was assigned there as an FTO. Later at the Port of Miami, I became Tony's sergeant. Then later in Intracoastal, Tony had gotten promoted to sergeant and supervised my son BJ, and we worked together once again. And for my last two plus years at the Airport, we were two of the Day Shift sergeants, became partners, and were inseparable. The running tag line became "Where's there's one, there's the other!" "Coffee at "F.""

Fight Story

By Officer Jose de Leon, Metro-Dade Police Dept.

Let's Dance!

My story occurred in 1995/1996, when I didn't even have a year on the department. I was on afternoons, 2 p.m.-10 p.m. with the good days off, Tue & Wed. I and another rookie, Sandra G., had to double-up and ride as a two-man unit because there were no extra loaner vehicles which was a common occurrence. I'm not sure if it was the first call of the shift but I do remember the beep-tone and the comments: *"2-32"* Man attacking a woman on NW 27th Ave & 67th St." We start running a *"3,"* lights and sirens, and what felt like only a few moments later, our sergeant, Michael Fisten, took a *"3-15"*- arrival. We started from the old Northside Station and the call was close so I can remember getting there really fast! When we arrived, I first see a rather large, black male lying on the ground. I hesitated to advise the dispatcher of our arrival because I was mesmerized watching Sergeant Fisten slowly approaching the guy on the ground. Rookie mistake.

After what felt like an only a few seconds, I heard a commotion and as I looked up, I see the subject and Sergeant Fisten engaged in a physical struggle. I didn't know this at the time but the subject managed to grab Sarge's gun while it was still holstered. His holster was very basic and it had no retention system like they do today, and Sarge was fighting to retain his gun. I jumped out of the Green & White and ran toward them with my 10 inch flash light in hand which was my preferred impact weapon because I felt my PR-24 (baton) was too long and cumbersome. My academy class was also the first to graduate with the newly implemented expandable batons, but they felt gimmicky and flimsy. As I approached both men, the subject had his back to me and he had Sgt. Fisten wrapped up in his arms, completely covering him. I remember thinking to myself, "Perfect, he doesn't know I'm coming."

I raised my flashlight high and with everything I had, swung at the subject hitting him on the upper shoulder and neck area. My first reaction after hitting him was "Oh shit! I think I killed this guy!" After the strike, he quickly let go of Sgt. Fisten's gun and focused on me. I will NEVER forget this as long as I live; when the subject screamed at me "I'M GOING TO TAKE YOU TO SEE JESUS!" And it was then I realized this was real and the fight was on! As he now came at me, I saw just how big this man was.

As he approached me, I remember not hesitating and taking a running start and tackled him around his legs. I managed to slightly pick him up off the ground and then we both fell to the pavement. Sgt. Fisten, Sandra, and I now piled on top of this guy and tried to cuff him, which seemed like it took forever because of the fight in him. We were hoping additional units would arrive to help, and they did, but I'm not sure how they got there or even knew we were in the jackpot because I never got on the air to request *"3-15s."* Luckily though, they did.

We decided to Baker Act this guy because we thought at the time he had a mental disorder that made him violent. What we didn't know was he had taken a Speed ball; a mixture of heroin and cocaine before this dance, and while we were transporting him in the patrol car, he died. Just like that. Shit! We found out hours after his death from Homicide that his core body temperature was still 109 degrees. The drugs burned him up from the inside, and we couldn't do anything about it even if we had known. We got out with some bumps and bruises and were commended for our actions; Bronze Medals of Valor & Life Saving Awards for saving the women he had attacked, but they came at a price. Drugs, alcohol, mental illness or plain anger; same behavior, sadly, same result.

Author's Note:

Jose transferred to the Airport and was assigned to me. I can tell you he kept me on my toes with his keen wit and sense of humor, and always had us laughing. "Jose, what time is roll call?"

A Brave Brother's Story

By Lieutenant Carlos Devarona, Miami Beach Police Dept., Retired

Officer Gotsis - Part 1

Jimmy Gotsis was a rookie officer. He was assigned to an FTO (field training officer) by the name of Dave Hernandez, or *"Super Dave"* as he was known in the Miami Beach Police Department. The two Officers were paired up in the *North End* of Miami Beach. My name is Carlos DeVarona and I was the sergeant in charge of the two officers on this particular day.

I was sitting in the *North End Mini Station* entering statistics into the city computer (Actually I was playing solitaire). Officially, it was stats or taking a break. Officer Gotsis was assigned a crash involving a Miami-Dade County transit bus and a bicycle. On its face it sounds like a horrific accident, in truth, it was a minor one. The bus had slightly nudged the bike while moving over to the right. Still, the bike rider was lucky to escape with minor injuries. As protocol dictates, Miami Beach Fire Rescue was called to treat the injured, and a Miami-Dade Transit supervisor was called to view the scene. My department's Crime Scene Unit was also called to document the position of the bus and where the actual "hit" had occurred.

Gotsis was busy gathering information for his report as *"Super Dave"* watched his progress. Dave was an established crash investigator but in this instance his job was to monitor Officer Gotsis' progress as a rookie officer. As I sat in the office "doing my stats," two things happened simultaneously:

Officer Gotsis had the dispatcher contact me on the radio and the phone in my office was ringing simultaneously. I picked up the phone and asked the caller to hold one second while I responded to the police radio. Officer Gotsis was asking me if I could respond to the scene of the crash. He didn't want to ask me his question over the police radio where everyone could listen in. What I later found out was Gotsis was going to ask for permission to transport the injured bike rider to the south end of Miami Beach. Although she had minor injuries, her bike was not so lucky. The bike was a total loss and I'm sure the fact she was also a cutie in her early twenties was not influencing his thought process. Yea, right!

I told Gotsis I would respond to his crash scene as soon as I finished my phone call. *The Call,* was from the North Miami Beach Police Department, a city twenty miles to the north of our city.

The caller asked me if we had an officer named Demetrious Gotsis. Remember I said Gotsis was a newer officer and we all knew him as "Jimmy." I would later find out Demetrious was his birth name. The caller was telling me they had a 19-year-old drowning victim at Oleta State Park in North Miami Beach and found in the victim's back pocket was a typed note; *"In Case of emergency please contact my brother Demetrious Gotsis, Miami Beach Police Department."* I hung up the phone and left for the accident scene which was six blocks south of our mini station.

When a County vehicle is involved in a crash nothing moves until a County supervisor arrives on the scene to inspect the incident just like we do with our city's vehicles. Because a County bus was involved in the wreck the normal three lanes of south bound traffic was cut back to one lane causing a severe back-up. Seeing this and knowing I needed to get to Officer Gotsis as quickly as possible, I broke protocol. I turned on my overhead lights, activated my siren and drove southbound in the northbound lane. A no-no but I had to go. With traffic being blocked as it was it would have taken me at least ten minutes to travel the six city blocks. With the lights and siren I arrived in less than a minute.

Upon arriving at the scene I noticed Officer Gotsis approaching my vehicle. He wanted to ask me about transporting the accident victim. Before he could finish his sentence I stopped him. First, I told him what North Miami Beach had told me and asked him if he had a brother. I told him an accident had occurred at Oleta State Park and didn't tell Jimmy his brother had in fact died in the accident.

Demetrious "Jimmy" Gotsis is a very fit individual. His body fat is very low and is probably one of the best athletes our city has ever hired. What I saw next I never expected. Jimmy fell to his knees, put both his hands up to his ears and started screaming, "NO, NO IT CAN'T BE!

My mother was murdered a few years back. NO, PLEASE NOT MY BROTHER!"

Officer Hernandez and I both helped Jimmy to his feet. I turned to Hernandez and told him Gotsis had to be taken to Oleta State Park to identify the victim as possibly his brother who had drowned at the lake. I further told Hernandez to forget about our shift and to accompany Gotsis and aide him in whatever he needed, and to take as much time as Jimmy needed to help him get through this. With Hernandez driving, both officers left the crash scene without another word.

The Miami-Dade County supervisor had finally arrived as I turned toward the victim of the accident and asked her how she was feeling. She told me she was battered and bruised but seemed to be ok. She then asked me what had happened to Officer Gotsis. I told her his brother had also been involved in an accident at Oleta State Park. The victim tilted her head to the side and asked; "You mean the drowning victim?" She then started to scream, "NO, THAT CAN'T BE. I WAS THERE, I SAW HIM DROWN!"

I tilted my head in the same manner and asked, "What are you talking about?" She answered, "I was at Oleta State Park. That's where I was coming from on my bike ride and I was there when the helicopter arrived, and I was at the lake when they pulled him out of the water. I then left the park and rode my bike down Collins Ave. It's just too strange I was somehow involved with both brothers today. I can't handle this. It's too much of a coincidence." I agreed with her and got her a ride back to the south end from our ID tech. Unfortunately, the victim at the lake was in fact Jimmy's brother.

Officer Gotsis - Part 2

A few years later Officer Gotsis and I were both assigned to patrol the midnight shift in the south end of Miami Beach, what everyone knows as the famous *South Beach*. I had since been promoted to Lieutenant.

Sometime after midnight, a call went out over the police radio and the caller said he had heard multiple screams coming for the ocean but couldn't see anyone. It was pitch black and nothing was visible out in the water. Both police and fire were dispatched to the scene. After whatever time was deemed necessary and prudent, both police and fire hearing no screaming, began to clear the scene. The only person that stayed and listened was Jimmy Gotsis.

After about twenty minutes Officer Gotsis spoke into the radio. He advised the dispatcher; "I now hear someone screaming, I'm going into the water." He did not ask permission, he just found a passer-by, stripped down to his underwear and told the citizen on the beach to watch his equipment and soon other units would be responding quickly. I reached for my radio and told the dispatcher to tell Gotsis not to go into the water. My job as the shift commander was to monitor all of our officers. The dispatcher repeated what I said but didn't get a response. Gotsis was already on his way. I told the dispatcher to make sure that the Coast Guard and Fire Rescue responded to the scene ASAP!

The currents on the south end of Miami Beach can be treacherous. When units arrived at the scene, the officers first recovered Jimmy's equipment from the passer-by, and he pointed out the direction in which Gotsis was headed. There was silence out on the beach as all available units and Fire Rescue arrived on the scene.

At first, none of us could see or hear anything coming from the water. Fire Rescue was preparing some boards with which to paddle out into the ocean. Jimmy was then spotted bringing one victim back to the beach. Fire Rescue headed out to meet and assist him in the rescue. Jimmy had swum out to the closest buoy where he found the two victims hanging on. As Jimmy appeared on the beach I approached him. He was out of breath and ready to return to the water to rescue the second victim. I grabbed him and told him he would not be returning to the water, and Fire had all the equipment necessary to affect the rescue. Fire was able to rescue the second victim from the buoy. I was relieved and glad Jimmy was safe on the beach, but as his supervisor I was upset with him. Before I could get out another word Jimmy said, "You know why I did it, right Boss?" I nodded my head and walked away. What else could I say?

I could not have been more proud of what Jimmy had done. He did what was necessary. He broke all protocols about going into the water. He broke all protocols about leaving his equipment with a passer-by citizen who he didn't even know. He broke all protocols for not asking permission. Because of doing what was *right*, Officer Demetrious "Jimmy" Gotsis had saved two lives that night, all at the risk of losing his own life.

"I did what I had to do." I wrote Jimmy a *Letter of Commendation* and recommendation for *Officer of the Month*. He's a hero.

Author's Note:

Carlos and I went to the academy together and have been very close friends for thirty-eight years. Because of our "Brown Gown" uniform, Carlos always called me a Park Ranger. "Hey Boo Boo!"

A Welcomed & Not so Welcomed

Stories

By Sergeant Angel Dovale, Metro-Dade Police Dept.

A Thankless Job…or Is It?

In a 30-year career in law enforcement each and every officer regardless of their background, race, ethnicity, male or female, has been called everything in the book! We each have our various personal reasons why we became a police officer, but over all we can agree we wanted the opportunity to help or save someone. Furthermore, many of us can go through our long careers and never know if the actions we took actually saved any of the individuals we encountered. Just like anyone else in the world, we want to feel appreciated and be thanked once in a while. It's a comforting feeling that validates your actions and your drive that directed you to become a police officer in the first place. This story is not your typical *War Story,* nevertheless, I believe it's an important one given the chaotic state of how law enforcement is seen and demoralized today or second guessed when the management of a mental illness call goes bad.

In 1992, I recall being dispatched to an in-progress attempted suicide call with a gun. Because my district was an extremely busy one, I remember that only my sergeant, A. Franqui and I were available and dispatched. While heading to the call the dispatcher provided an update that the subject, a black female who was armed with a firearm, was being chased around the house by her husband who was on scene and on the phone with 911 operators. I recall driving in a southerly direction on Northwest 42nd Avenue from Miami Gardens Drive and arriving on the scene simultaneously with my sergeant. Although the house was located on a corner, we both parked about two houses away to conceal our approach since we had confirmation that the call being around much of a choice, we approached the area of the front door and identified ourselves. Suddenly, a male voice shouted from inside the house with a sense of urgency that the door was open and to come in quickly! Not knowing if we were about to walk into an ambush, my sergeant and I pushed the door open and swept the entryway and as much of the house as we could see from our position.

Having a clear sight path, we entered the house and followed the voice to the rear bedroom where the male was shouting for us to help him. As we approached the bedroom door entryway, I saw a female armed with a gun and crying. I also noticed the male was dressed in a Metro-Dade Fire Rescue Uniform.

We didn't see any rescue trucks anywhere, so we asked him who he was while ordering the female to drop the gun in very loud commands. The male identified himself as the female's husband. He said she's very upset because her best friend since childhood had just passed away the previous week. The female then stated she was very distraught but was even more upset since she believed her husband had been having an ongoing affair with her best friend! She exclaimed she wasn't sure if she wanted to only kill herself or kill him and then herself yet, but she was close to deciding.

My sergeant and I continued talking to her for some time after calling for additional assistance. We used anything and everything taught to us during training and managing these incidents. It seemed to work because our rapport with the woman convinced her to lower the gun to her side as we flanked her. As we did this, I looked at my sergeant's eyes which gave me clear direction of what we were going to do. Without a word said, my sergeant and I leaped forward and took the female down while disarming her. After quickly handcuffing her, we had an opportunity to talk with her and her husband in a less threatening frame of mind. I Baker Acted her and transported her to Jackson Crisis for evaluation and with that, I moved on to the next call.

Many months later as I sat in my vehicle completing an arrest form and parental juvenile release documents for a young boy who had been caught shoplifting at Walmart, a couple exited the store and knocked on my window. The woman, I first thought, was a teacher and one of my wife's coworkers. I motioned to them to give me a few minutes to finish my paperwork. Once finished, I approached the couple and after exchanging our hellos, I asked how I could help them. They looked at me and asked if I knew who they were. I said "Of course!" That she was my wife's coworker. They laughed and looked at each other and the woman, sporting a vibrant smile, replied "No." She asked me if I remembered the house on the corner of NW 42nd Avenue & 173rd Street. I pictured the area in my mind and at that moment I realized who they were. I can guess with my expression they knew I had just remembered them at that moment. And at that moment, I could see tears streaming down her cheeks as she said, "Thank you," as she expressed how grateful she was for what I had done for her when she was in the darkest place in her life, and how my actions saved her life! Not knowing how to properly react to that shocking moment, I stupidly replied something like "Sure, no problem." Idiot! She and her husband then politely asked if they could hug me and of course, I said "Yes."

This affirmation of our actions happened so long ago that even now I'm truly grateful to how wonderful that lady made me feel by having the courage to approach me. I can always say I truly helped and saved someone's life!

A Lack of Experience

This memorable story is no different to that of many other officers regardless of jurisdiction, and very typical of a junior, inexperienced officer in the Metro-Dade (now Miami-Dade) Police Department. After Hurricane Andrew had devastated Dade County on August 24, 1992, I spent nearly four months working 12-hour shifts; 6 P.M. to 6 A.M., and like in many areas of the County, we had none or limited power and were being hammered with an increase of home invasion robberies and other violent crimes. I was a rookie officer assigned to a very senior uniform squad, which meant I had to handle the highest workload, be the first to answer the radio, make more arrests, issue more citations etc., and I was really okay with that. I was happy to have a great job.

On an unusually cold night, I was one of many officers dispatched to a home invasion robbery somewhere in the area of Carol City, (now the City Miami Gardens). A very good description of the subject was provided by the victim and as the rookie, I had to get there first. As I headed south on NW 32 Ave from 199th Street, the dispatcher advised the subject was running in a westerly direction approaching 32nd Avenue.

As I reached the area I saw the subject crossing the intersection. I turned onto NW 191ˢᵗ Street in my 1989 Crown Victoria with roll down windows and overtook the subject. I quickly jumped out of my unit and with loud, verbal commands ordered him to stop. Amazingly he did! He was well over 6 feet tall and drenched in sweat, and very agitated because I had stopped him. He immediately shouted he didn't break into anyone's house! Not being a very experienced officer, I waited for the radio chatter to stop on our large UHF radios as I stood across my hood where he had placed his hands. As the radio traffic cleared, I asked the dispatcher to provide a subject description to prove to my subject he indeed was my home invader.

As the dispatcher provided the description, the subject immediately reached across the hood grabbing the radio from my hand throwing it down the street. I was lucky to grab him by his arm as he attempted to punch me, and the struggle began. Each time he attempted breaking free from me, I held onto him harder and harder in an effort to deflect his punches. As we fell on the ground, we each fought for our own reasons of survival. Ironically, even now I can clearly recall my thoughts of how in the hell I'm I going to call for help? My radio was on the ground because I was careless.

With each mutual strike, I became more resolute in that I needed to get my radio. At some point in the ground struggle, he gave me his back and I knew I had the advantage, at least for the moment. I then applied the *Lateral Vascular Neck Restraint* (LVNR) also well known as a *Sleeper Hold*, but since I had my thick winter jacket on, I couldn't achieve the proper arm positioning to effectively control him. Nevertheless, I refused to give him any slack and I dragged him across the roadway until I reached my radio. With the radio in hand, I called for help. I remember clicking the radio and quickly giving my unit designator, my location and shouted *"3-15!"* As I did this, the subject once again slapped the radio away from me. We continued rolling around on the ground and literally ended up halfway under the passenger side of my vehicle.

At this point all I could manage to do was hold on to him to prevent him from getting away or injuring me. Meanwhile, in the distance I can see headlights heading in my direction. Finally, my call for help was answered. As the lights came closer, I realized there were no accompanying red and blue lights or sirens.???

As I was wondering what was going on, the vehicle came to a stop. A female driver quickly exited her vehicle and began yelling at the subject and me that we're very lucky she stopped when she did, since she claimed not being able to see my marked police vehicle stopped across both lanes of NW 191st Street. She further suggested I should turn on my emergency equipment to avoid not being seen. Again, I must explain I was fairly inexperienced, and I actually apologized to her for my failure. Since that time with more than twenty-seven years on I would now have some choice words for her, but back to the story.

I tried to let her know I couldn't do anything at the moment about the lights since I was a little busy. I was still engaged with my subject. Just then, I heard the greatest sound in the world; police sirens coming to my aide. The female driver quickly jumped back into her car, backed up, and drove off in the opposite direction never attempting to offer a finger to help me. Thanks a lot! It didn't matter at this point because at least ten units arrived on my scene and helped me finally handcuff my subject. Amazingly, that was the first of five times I would have an encounter with that same subject. However, each time we made contact, I was more experienced and never allowed myself to be blindsided again. I was lucky to walk away that night with a great lesson learned, and I could never allow it to happen again.

Author's Note:

Angel and have known each other for over 20 years, and as the job does, it finally brought us together at the Airport at the end of my career, and I'm grateful for the time we had together. "Remember, you're an Airport Supervisor…"

A Between a Fence and a Hard

Place Story

By Sergeant Tom Gilligan, Officer, NYPD - Jan 1984 to Sept
1990, Metro-Dade Police Dept., Retired

Don't Turn Green, Don't Turn Green. Fuck!

It was within the first week of September 1990, the afternoon
shift (1600-0035) in the New York City Police Department's
Queens, 104 Precinct, for me and my steady partner Officer John
R. While in roll call our squad was informed about a dark, two door
car, occupied by a black male that had done several purse snatches
(theft from a person then) on Cooper Avenue between Cypress
Hills Street and 69 Street during the day shift.

After roll call was over, we loaded up our Radio Motor Patrol
(RMP), a Chrysler Grand Fury (what a great car for patrol) with
John driving the first half of the shift and me being the recorder (I
got to write the reports, yay). Being active officers as we were, we
decided to head down to Cooper Avenue to see if we could find the
perp.

After making our way to the area, we were headed east on
Cooper Avenue when low and behold, what did we see coming at
us traveling west, you guessed it! John flipped a U-turn to go after
him. But John didn't turn on the lights just then. The perp didn't
notice us as he stopped for a red light at Cypress Avenue. I told
John to pull up alongside the car. When he did, with my six shot 38.
in hand, I was able to lean out and point it at his face. As I was
giving him commands, he was complying, until…. the light turned
green. Fuck! And the chase was on!

He took off north on Cypress Avenue and for what seemed
like a lifetime and while holding on for dear life (we were not

wearing seatbelts) and neither of us getting on the radio, and after multiple turns to lose us he pulled into a Waldbaum's Supermarket parking lot at 454 Wykoff Avenue in Brooklyn, the neighboring borough.

As the car was trying to exit the parking lot John cut him off. He now tried to drive backward through the chain link fence. He was successful for a few seconds, but then he backed over a metal fence pole getting hung up and the car stalled. We got out of the RMP and ran toward him as he tried to restart his car. When we got as close as six feet the car started, and he began driving right at us.

John was able to sidestep the vehicle as he was further out of the vehicle's path. With not much room between me and the fence, I started back peddling to get clear, but I slipped on a patch of oil and down I went. "Down Goes Frasier!"

The car drove between me and John, but he didn't see me and thinking the car had run me over, started shooting at him as he was fleeing the parking lot. After getting on my feet and seeing John shoot, I shot too! John was relieved when he saw me and said, "I thought he ran you over." Luckily, he didn't. The perp ended up driving through the fence and disappeared. A few seconds later a New York Fire Department crew that was at the Waldbaum's doing the shopping run, in their words said they "Saw the whole thing," and came over to see if we were injured.

Now the fun part; raising our sergeant and asking him to respond to our location. Once he arrived, we told him what happened and the Fire crew along with a few other witnesses that were in the parking lot confirmed our account of the shooting. Now it was back to the precinct for the paperwork and telling our story once again to our Police Detective Unit for their follow-up.

When we returned for our next shift one detective told us the car was found abandoned in Brooklyn on the day shift. Then when returning to work after our RDOs (regular day off), officers from another afternoon squad told us the same male had done more purse snatches and was picked up by one of their units but fled again. This time though, he crashed into the entrance of a cemetery within the precinct. He fled on foot into the cemetery and attempted to hide. Aviation was requested, which in 1990 was a rarity, and along with other officers he was located and taken into custody. Streak ended! All this for snatching purses.

Author's Note:

Sgt. (Ret.) Bert "Maverick" Gonzalez

Tom and I first met at the Intracoastal District in 2010. We quickly realized we both thought alike, and our lieutenant said we must be brothers because we drove him crazy. We became partners and life-long friends and had our "NBC" every morning.

A Jack-Rabbit Story

By Lieutenant Jose "Gonzo" Gonzalez, Metro-Dade Police Dept.

The "Black Andrew Cunanan"

This caper is the one I tell the most stories about. After everything was said and done, I dubbed him the "Black Andrew Cunanan." I can't remember his name or the exact date but here goes...

I was a RID (Robbery Intervention Detail) sergeant at the time, and my squad, the RID-120's, worked the 10a-6p Shift. I received a phone call around 9 A.M. telling me the Beach was working a big caper and RID was requested to assist. Once I arrived at the Beach station I was briefed on current events that had occurred the night before. Let's start from how this case developed.

This was a homicide where a young 17-year-old boy who worked in a movie theater on Miami Beach was strangled and killed. Apparently, the subject saw the victim as he was working and took interest in him and called the movie theater later and left his phone number for him to call back. The subject disguised himself as a female and said that she was interested in meeting up, and after several text messages back and forth they set up a meet location. It's unclear how the "31" went down but they met and the male victim ended up dead from strangulation. It was too early to tell if he was also "33'd." Beach detectives do a workup on the phone number the victim was in contact with last, which led them to a "QTH" on the beach where the apparent suspect lived. As detectives approached the building the subject spotted them through a dark screen mesh, he had disguised himself as a women and distracted detectives just long enough so he could jump out of the 2nd floor window. The subject ran and a foot pursuit ensued.

A perimeter was set up and the subject knocked on a first floor door where a mother and her 14-year-old son lived. The subject advised the mother he needed to borrow her phone because he had gotten into a fight with his girlfriend and he needed to call the authorities. As the woman walked inside her apartment to get the phone the subject followed behind, went to the kitchen and armed himself with a knife.

The subject held the mother and son against their will the entire night in order to elude police. During the night the subject tied up the mother and locked her in a closet. He then turned his attention toward the young boy whom he sodomized all night at knife point. He also poured Clorox around the front door to throw off the K-9's scent. Sometime during the early morning he called the Beach PD landline and made another distraction phone call saying the subject they were looking for was at a nearby Starbucks and he was armed with a gun. Even though the perimeter was broken down hours before he did this as a precaution. He was then picked up by a male friend in a vehicle and was able to escape. His downfall was he took both victims' cell phones.

Once we finished the briefing the hunt was on. Although we did not have a description of a vehicle or a complete subject description, we had a B/M in his 20s, with tattoos on both arms. We were hoping eventually the victims' cell phones would turn on and at approximately 2 p.m. our prayers were answered. One of the cell phones turned on and it was pinging off a tower in North Miami. The US Marshall's Trigger Fish along with the County's Trigger Fish were able to pinpoint the cell phone to a B/M fitting the description, who was sitting on a bus bench by the K-mart at 10700 Biscayne Blvd in the Intracoastal District.

My RID squad was able to locate and detain the individual and interrogate him. It was later learned the subject was the person who originally picked up The Subject the morning of the getaway. He added the subject bad guy we wanted gave him the cell phone for helping him out, and he was located in a motel just up the block and provided his clothing description. Good, more to go on. The subject was supposed to be wearing orange shorts and orange sneakers. Better. My squad responded to the motel and made entry into a room where the subject was crashing. He was GOA! We missed him. We issued a BOLO and the hunt was on again. A deputy from the US Marshall's Task Force spotted the subject walking a few blocks away from the motel and a foot chase ensued. He was able to scale over a very tall wall into a new apartment complex. I immediately responded to the last location where the subject was seen jumping over the wall, and a huge perimeter was set up by RID & Beach detectives.

My thoughts were this guy was going to force himself into an apartment like he did the night before on the Beach and repeat his MO. There was no way that was going to happen because I organized a search party and we were going door-to-door looking for this guy until we found him.

As Aviation and K-9 arrived, I recall looking toward the entrance and making eye contact with the K-9 officers in order to direct them to me which was where the subject was last seen. Suddenly, I hear glass breaking above me and as I look up I see an elderly female flying out of a 3rd floor window and slam to the ground. I immediately say to myself, he's in that apartment and as I worked my way to where I can see the front door, I spot him exiting the 3rd floor apartment, however he had changed clothes, again! This guy's slick. Now he's wearing a blue and red polo shirt and a blue Kango hat. The chase is on again and he runs to the far side of the building and jumps off the 2nd floor balcony. That's where Detective Freddy Trillo spots him in the center courtyard and gives chase with Detective Dustin James as his back up. He attempted to run toward the front exit and was met with a hail of gunfire from Detectives Jesus Pacheco and a Beach Detective. The subject was pronounced DOA on scene. I immediately went back and administered aide to the elderly female who lived but suffered multiple broken bones and a torn spleen. Lucky!

The story, I later learned, was that the elderly female's A/C had broken and she put in a call for maintenance. When the subject knocked on her door she thought he was the A/C repair man she was expecting. What are the odds? When she opened the door the subject forced his way in and armed himself with a butcher knife. The woman ran into the back bedroom that belonged to her adult son who was not home at the time. The subject pursued her into the room and began to strangle her until she became unconscious. He then put the knife down on the bed and proceeded to look through her son's closet for clothes to change into. The woman regained consciousness and when the subject noticed her getting up he grabbed the knife and began to walk toward her. This is where she felt she had no choice but to jump out of the window in fear she was going to be stabbed and killed. In all, a great job by everyone involved to apprehend this guy. It was a mission!

Author's Note:

Gonzo, no relation, and I worked together many years ago and have remained friends throughout, even though the job takes you away from each other. He is the epitome of a cop. On the day before Thanksgiving, 1999, I was back in New York for my 20th reunion. Gonzo, from NY originally, and I ran into each other in a NYPD clothing shop next to the Empire State Building. What are the odds?

Some Real CSI - Miami Stories

By Officer Pete Gonzalez, Metro-Dade Police Dept., (Retired)

"Damn! I Didn't Think of That!"

I was working in our Crime Scene Investigations Bureau and in November of 2002 we responded to a double homicide, where two teenagers were found bludgeoned to death. The victims were boyfriend and girlfriend. Apparently, the male victim's cousin came to the house to help them paint. Something set off the cousin. He grabbed a baseball bat and began to brutally beat the victims to death. The male victim was found just inside the front door with his head smashed like a grape. A mirrored wall was next to the front door and it was completely covered in blood, and cast-off blood spatter marks from the bloody baseball bat were all over the walls, floor and ceiling. The female victim was found lying on the kitchen floor and bloody shoe prints led from the front door to the kitchen. The female victim had also been brutally beaten with the bat.

A dining room was located east of the kitchen and was used as storage. The dining room table was at the far east end of the room, and a bloody handprint was on the floor behind the table. Apparently, someone knocked on the door and startled the subject who hid behind the table and transferred his bloody palm and fingerprints onto the floor.

The police were notified a short time later and the subject stated a black male broke in and killed the victims. Back then we used 35mm cameras and I photographed the bloody palm and fingerprints with several rolls of film using an oblique lighting technique to capture the print from all angles.

The photos of the prints were positively identified by our Latent Examiners as belonging to the subject, and of course the blood matched the victims. I guess he didn't think about that!

Miami Bonnie & Clyde

In March of 2004, a boyfriend/girlfriend duo were on a crime spree and attempted a purse-snatch at a large shopping center at the corner of SW 8 Street (Calle Ocho) and 67 Ave. A 76-year-old (I think that was his age) security guard detained the male subject after he had snatched a purse from a victim, while his female accomplice was waiting in the car.

As the security guard detained him a crowd gathered and held the male subject for him. Remember, the security officer was in his 70s. The female subject pulled up in the car and her partner told her to run them over! I guess he figured that was a good escape plan. The female accelerated and struck the security guard and the male subject. The security guard became wedged underneath the car as the female sped toward the exit. She exited the parking lot and headed south on 67th Ave. She then drove west along SW 12 Street, which is the street along the south side of the shopping center. Witnesses behind the car could see the security guard's feet flailing under the vehicle as he was being dragged. Apparently his leather pistol belt caught something on the undercarriage and kept him wedged under the car.

She proceeded west and then turned north on SW 70 Ave. and then east on SW 8 St. The victim security guard became dislodged just east of SW 68 Ave. Unfortunately, the security officer was dragged 4,238 feet. A mile is 5,280 feet, so it was a substantial distance. The back half of his head was missing because it was ground off by the pavement as he was dragged. Blood and tissue marks were visible on the pavement along the entire drag distance. That would possibly be the longest crime scene we've had and it would have to be secured during the entire investigation.

The female subject then turned back into the shopping center (?) to the area where she struck the security guard and was taken into custody. The male subject suffered serious injuries when she struck both of them with the car. Both were tried together and convicted. Crime spree over!

The Long Arm of the Law

In April of 2006, a three-year-old Haitian female was abandoned on a street in the City of Miami, and of course it was a big news story. Her mother was nowhere to be found and a description of her vehicle was broadcasted on the news. A few days later, a mechanic recognized the car. He had just bought it from a Haitian man and so he called police.

Crime Scene units responded and found large amounts of blood in the car.

A week or two later, a US Customs & Border Patrol (CBP) officer took his son fishing at the canal located along the 18-mile stretch, as it's called, heading into the Florida Keys from southern Dade County. The canal was approximately 740 feet west of US1.

While fishing, the CBP officer's young son spotted something in the water, but the father couldn't see it and dismissed it. They returned to the same spot the next day to fish again. And again, the son spotted something in the water, but this time the father was able to see it and called police.

Suspended approximately a foot under the water was a pair of feet floating near the surface. We responded along with our Underwater Recovery Unit, (Police Divers). The divers entered the water and recovered the body. We identified the body as the mother of the abandoned three-year-old. Her boyfriend, who is the Baby Daddy, killed her in the car, dumped her body in the canal, and then sold the car to the mechanic. The victim had seventy-seven pounds of barbells tied around her neck which held her head against the bottom of the canal but allowed her feet to float upward. After being in the water for some time, the dark pigment of her skin had faded and she appeared to be a Caucasian woman. Her body was so severely decomposed, her torso was barely attached to the lower portion of her body. She had a tattoo on her leg and by the tattoo we immediately knew who she was. We later discovered the boyfriend fled to Haiti.

A family friend of the victim felt he needed to do something, so he flew to Haiti and at the airport he spotted the subject. He told the Haitian Police the subject was wanted for murder in Miami. Fortunately, the local police detained him and the US Marshals were contacted, verified the subject was wanted, flew to Haiti and extradited him back to Miami.

Stupid is as Stupid Does

In June of 2012, police received a call from an 18-year-old black male who said he found his boyfriend dead in his apartment.

Right from the get-go red flags were waiving when he told us the story. He claimed he was using the victim's car since the day before, and on this day he went to KFC and picked up two meals, then returned to the apartment only to find him dead.

The victim was in his late 50's, a white male, was found dead in his kitchen. He was naked but wrapped in a blanket, had been bludgeoned and strangled to death, and we found ligature marks on his neck. Blood drops lead toward the bathroom and some appeared to have been diluted to some degree with water, possibly an attempt to clean them up.

Did I say red flags?

Diluted blood stains were also found in the bathroom sink, bathtub, on the shower head and on the shower knob. We also found the victim's car was cluttered with the belongings, and a thorough search of the car revealed a UPS receipt from the day before. The 18-year-old was questioned and released because we had nothing on him at that time. The victim's credit card statement was checked, and we discovered the 18-year-old subject used it the day before to buy a camera valued at over $500, clothes at Walmart, and the UPS store. Flag!

The UPS package was intercepted by police and found inside the box was the camera the subject bought, the clothes from Walmart, the victim's laptop, and the bloody clothing the subject wore during the murder. The subject mailed the box back to his own residence instead of throwing away his clothes. It never went to trial. He took a 25-year plea. You can't make this shit up!

Forensics Don't Lie

In May of 2011, a body was found burning in a farm field west of Krome Ave. in the agricultural area of Dade County. I believe the victim's brother knew something was wrong; his brother was missing and he called police to a warehouse off Bird Road (SW 40 Street).

I'm not sure what happened then, but a search warrant was obtained and the search revealed evidence someone was killed inside the warehouse. The victim, we learned, was tied to a group smuggling weapons to the FARC (Marxist Guerrillas) in Colombia. They were cutting up metal sawhorses and using them to hide weapon parts so they could be shipped from the US to Colombia. The warehouse had an office in the front with a door, and an overhead garage door next to the office which opened to the warehouse bay.

A wooden table was located in the center of the warehouse and bloody drag marks were found next to the table leading from the interior office door area toward the overhead garage door. Bloody hand marks were found on the bottom of the table leg where the victim tried to grab the leg as he was being dragged. The drag marks ended in the area just south of the garage door. This is where the victim was loaded into a car. The crime scene also revealed two casings and two projectiles in the warehouse. An orange Home Depot bucket was found and inside the bucket were a bloodstained machete, and a pair of Playtex style gloves were turned inside out, and blood stains were all over the outside of the gloves.

The scene and investigation led to arrests and the case went to federal court where the subjects were convicted. We tied the subjects to the crime scene and murder because their DNA was found inside the Playtex gloves, and the victim's DNA matched the blood on the outside of the gloves. Forensics can be a Bitch!

Author's Note:

So this time, we are related. Pete is my younger brother. After serving as an MP in the US Army, he immediately followed me on the job. He spent twenty-three of his 30 years in the Crime Scene Investigations Bureau and is one of the best Crime Scene investigators we ever had. He didn't wear a smart blazer, fancy sunglasses or drive a Hummer. But if it was his crime scene, rest assured, he was going to find you!

A Bravery & Cowardice Story

By Officer Norberto "BJ" Gonzalez II, Miami-Dade Police Dept.

I Couldn't Believe It!

It was February 4, 2017, the start of my midnight shift. An ordinary start to the night. After roll call at the Intracoastal Station, I was prepping the car with my rookie partner, who was a former marine, and checked in for service. I remember thinking that night the weather was perfect! A little chilly, not too cold, not hot, just right. As soon as we checked in at approximately 0030 hours, we received a request to assist our K-9 units, Miami-Dade, and help out the Miami Shores Police Department with a perimeter, where they had set up for an armed robbery subject. Me, having about four years on the department, just coming into my own, and recently having transferred to a midnight squad was eager to work, and we made a B-Line straight to the scene.

As we were leaving the station we felt a positive energy the night would bring and were joking about it on the way as usual. My partner and I arrived there in about five minutes and responded directly to the briefing location where K-9 Officers were prepping for the search. The senior K-9 officer instructed us on which routes to take, expecting us to walk with K-9, but to our surprise a Golden Beach PD K-9 Officer responded, which would change the course of events to come.

The Golden Beach officer advised it would be his first perimeter and wanted to get his new dog some experience. Miami-Dade allowed him to assist and briefed him on his search route. As my partner was the rookie, he volunteered to search the backyards with the new canine and his handler. The instructions were to search each residential backyard as I paralleled through the rear alley at their pace. And just like that the search began, slow, steady, methodically, house by house. Now, even though I had only been an officer for a short amount of time, it felt as if I've done this 100 times before, and in actuality, we're so busy here I have. It was *just* another perimeter; regular, ordinary, like every other one before.

You've probably heard the term *routine* before. A term law enforcement officers frequently, but incorrectly, use as we've come to

375

find out. And it's a term I have now come to hate. As I patiently waited for our new K-9 buddy and his inexperienced handler to finish searching each assigned back yard, we became somewhat annoyed as it seemed in each backyard they searched, the dog would grab hold of some loose object like a toy, and the handler would have to pry it out of its mouth. The handler didn't seem to have any sense of urgency as to getting the dog out of play mode and into work mode. I know sometimes the dog wants to play, but this behavior was a little over the top.

About 10 or 11 houses into the search and finally approaching the last two, I noticed from the alley at the rear of the residence there was a structure attached to the back of the house; a permanent concrete shed with a broken window with the door cracked open, so I made it a point to let the K-9 officer know as well as my partner who was walking with him of what I found. Up to this point nothing had changed and everything seemed normal, even though we were coming to the last house and the odds are the subject had to be in this shed or house. It still didn't feel any more tense than usual. As a matter fact, it felt more relaxed; another mistake sometimes made in our profession.

I can specifically remember the address; 10674 NE 11 Court. Mmmm. The K-9 handler enters the small structure with a holstered weapon and two hands on the lead of his dog. And as my partner attempted to look through the broken window, I lost complete sight of the both of them.

As they entered the structure gunshots erupted. I can still remember the rhythm in my head. All six shots in sequence with the last shot coming a beat and a half after the initial flurry. The handler comes running out holding his right shoulder and behind him was his dog with his tail between his legs.

My partner, the former marine, quickly back-peddled out of the shed and as the Golden Beach officer exited, my partner got between the subject and the officer shielding him from more shots. I began to yell "Get them out of there! Go around the house," as I held point, and my partner walked the wounded officer to the front of the residence with the dog trailing behind. As my partner got the officer to the front of the house to relative safety, he got on the radio and broadcasted the house number to let all the other officers on the perimeter know exactly where we were and requested Fire Rescue and back-up.

I'm in the backyard by myself now calling for officers to condense the perimeter and join me in surrounding this house. At this point, I have my gun and flashlight pointed directly at the door. I began asking again and again for Miami Shores officers who we were there to help to come and help *me* now. I remember being really calm for a couple of minutes considering an officer had just got shot in front of me, but that quickly changed as I realized no officers were coming to help. None!

I'm looking down the alleyway and there is a Shores officer wearing a ballistic helmet and holding a long gun, standing behind a light pole taking cover three houses away from me. It seemed as if he was looking at me but not responding to my call for help. Insane I know. He was better equipped than I was—having and rifle—I just had my handgun and a flashlight, yet he still didn't come to help.

I looked down the other side of the block and there is a Shores unit in an SUV looking my way, and he was standing there as if nothing was happening. So, needless to say but I will, my frustration is getting worse as I found myself cursing at the officers over the radio. This was very stressful and it pissed me off, and all I can think about was not breaking eye contact with the door and that I might have to kill this guy; this unknown monster that's lurking in the darkness. A boogie man of sorts.

I knew this situation in my career could come when I was signed up to be a police officer, however, I was hoping a situation like this would *never* come where I might have to kill someone. A long-standing nightmare of mine, and it was actually happening now in-the-flesh! Was I scared? Hell yeah! But now actually being in the situation, I was more angry and frustrated at the fact the police officers whom I rushed to help are not rushing to help me. Kinda made the incident much more frightening in hindsight. I'm still standing there asking for units to come help while maintaining point with my firearm and flashlight lighting up the entryway. About five minutes into the stand-off my flashlight goes dead. So now I'm down to my gun light and if that fails, this guy might try to exit the shed and I'll lose sight of him, maybe leading to me or another officer getting shot down the road.

It was actually fortunate for me that my flashlight died because it made it a bit easier now that I didn't have to use two hands to do two different things. I remember radioing for help one last time and advising my flashlight had died. After the radio was silent again, no back-up, again, I stayed there for another 15 minutes just waiting. Waiting for anything. Either for a gun fight or for help. As time went on, I was feeling more and more tense and it's weird because you usually start feeling a little more comfortable but in this case being solo just got harder. My body was tired and my mind was exhausted but my focus increased as time went on. It's very hard to explain.

What I couldn't believe was with of all these police officers in this neighborhood, not one was coming to help me. When I started this job I knew what I was getting into but I took comfort in knowing that other people were going to be there with me; they were going to go into that house with me, and together we're going to fight the fight. So this lack of back-up was very surprising to me. Am I scared taking a traffic stop? Yes. Am I scared of going into a house? Yes. Am I scared responding to a call? Yes. But our chances of survival as police officers increase dramatically if we do it *together*.

When people need help we go no questions asked, but when we need help who comes to help us? If we don't help each other no one will. So back to the story. Approximately twenty minutes go by now and an officer from my squad, a former soldier who has a big mouth when he needs to (let's call him Frank) arrived, and all I heard was him asking a Miami Shores officer who was hiding behind the light pole fully decked, "Where's the party at?"

There was silence. Frank later told me the Shores officer was pointing his rifle directly at *me*. Then Frank yells, "Why the fuck aren't you over there"?

Frank runs over to my location and sees how tight I am. He points his shotgun in the direction of the shed which is only about fifteen feet away and tells me "I'll take it from here man, relax."

I immediately felt a huge load fly off my shoulders. I have never been so happy to see anybody. I remember him telling me a couple of times "It's ok to leave, you get some rest." And I told

Frank, "I'm not leaving until this is finished; this guy shot one of us! He can't hurt anybody else, not tonight." About a minute later one of our rookies that had started four months earlier arrives and rushes to our location. Frank was on my left and the rookie on my right, and it wasn't until that moment that I realized those two Shores officers didn't come to help earlier.

Now that the cavalry had arrived they wanted to come and help out. Real fucking brave! All were a bunch of veteran cowards! Anyway, as angry as I was I didn't lose focus and we stayed on point for about another three hours never having put my gun down continually pointing it at the shed until SRT arrived and took over the inner perimeter. All of the other officers cleared, and I stayed on the outer perimeter for another six hours, where I was able to catch my breath.

At this point I am so angry at the Miami Shores Police Department I found myself wanting to confront every fucking officer on the perimeter and punch him right in the face.

However, my sergeant was ordering (begging) me not to since there was media all over the place now. I respected his wishes and knew it would have been unprofessional, but I was so pissed! We waited for the stand-off to end, and when it was all said and done the subject had shot himself in the head. Fuck him! A self-inflicted gunshot wound and just like that he took the easy way out. He was a coward too! I remember a couple SRT guys came up and asked me if I had shot my gun thinking that I took him out. I didn't, but in some small way I wish I had.

This night was the most stressful night of my career thus far, and this experience woke me right-the-fuck up. I've seen cowards before here and there, but never so many in one group. I will forever despise those officers on scene that night and they should be ashamed of themselves. I hope no officer ever has to go through that again.

The officer who got shot was very lucky that night. The shot in his arm went through and through, and his vest stopped the round from going straight into his upper back and into his spine. My partner didn't wait for Fire Rescue but ran him straight to the hospital. We *all* got a little lucky that night, and we left without anybody from the Miami Shores Police Department taking our statement or even saying thank you.

Now fast forward two years later. That same Golden Beach K-9 officer that was shot just happened to be in the same training class as me. He didn't remember me but I knew exactly who he was. He was with a group of officers and was telling them about the incident from February 4th.

I heard him say how he went into the shed *by himself* and got shot, and then my partner ran away in fear for his life and left him alone in there. I don't know what it was about that night, but Miami-Dade County's *Finest* (and I don't mean MDPD) were MIA.

It didn't surprise me he was lying to this group of cops so I let him finish his little story. As soon as he finished I jumped in and set him straight, which is not in my nature as I'm a reserved human being. I made it clear to every officer he was lying to, and anyone within earshot, that his stupidity and inexperience almost got him killed, and it was my partner he was trashing, and without hesitation got in between him and the subject as he ran away from the fight. *Mr. K-9* left training early much to my satisfaction.

To this day, a couple of the officers who backed me up that night from *my* department are still some of my best friends on this planet. Those others? Well, I guess sometimes that's the nature of the beast. Stay safe.

A Case of Mistaken Identity Story From a Dog, Insult to Injury

It was January 14, 2021, my eight-year anniversary of being on with the Miami-Dade Police Department. I was now assigned to work in RID, Robbery Intervention Detail, a specialized unit out of the Robbery Bureau, which focuses on high-profile robberies and in the apprehension of some serious bad guys. On this day, we were working in our Northside District where we have the highest rate of violent crimes. A few hours into the shift, we were breaking for lunch and enroute to a seafood restaurant when a vehicle used in an armed robbery was spotted by one of our rookies in the unit, and it didn't take long for the driver to start fleeing, and the chase was on!

There were two subjects inside of a white Cadillac CTS who had just robbed a 70-year-old man at gunpoint. Real asshole-bad guys as my father would say. We were slamming on the gas and cutting corners trying to catch up to the rookie who's calling the chase. The driver of the fleeing Caddy only lasted about three minutes before he crashed into another vehicle and just like that the chase was over! But as usually happens, it was a really bad crash but luckily the innocent civilians in the other car were ok. Close one!

The bad guy driver bailed out of the wrecked Cadillac and to my shock, failed to attend to the injured civilians. Just kidding! These guys don't care about anyone but themselves, naturally. Let's pause for a second just so I can paint a picture. The Cadillac was completely totaled as it jackknifed into the other two vehicles and a light pole. However, sometimes the energy in the universe syncs up just right and a *Big Bang* called karma just appears out of the ether. Turns out, the second subject who robbed the seventy-year-old (who could barely walk by the way) was the passenger in the Cadillac, and was pinned inside of the vehicle with a broken sternum as well as a fracture for every rib he owned. Too fucking bad; I mean, poor guy. A rare case of immediate justice though. Miami-Dade Fire Rescue pried him out of the Caddy and transported him to the Ryder Trauma Center. Now back to the bailout.

The rookie who spotted the car began running after the subject as the rest of us were still trying to get there. The rookie chased him down the block but lost him as he jumped fences through some backyards. Subjects like this are frigg'n jackrabbits and hard to catch. Being out of breath, he was unable to set up to start setting a perimeter; a "box" as we call it. Up to this point, he had done a good job on calling everything over the radio. So as I arrived a few seconds later, I saw the crashed vehicles and kinda remembered the direction they were running from his transmissions. I took over setting up the box and I made it about eight blocks wide. HUGE! as perimeters go but necessary to contain an animal like that until we can gain control and begin our search. Luckily, we had just enough people for the perimeter because two of our platoons were working the detail.

About a minute later, the entire neighborhood was on lockdown with an armed robbery subject on the loose but contained. And that's the important part, *contained*. Nobody wants a guy like that preying on the weak and to be on the loose. After about twenty minutes holding the perimeter, our K-9 units and aviation responded and began prepping to work the scene. Around that time, the subject at-large just so happened to cross the street running eastbound right in front of me about midblock which was lucky and great! Because now an eight-block perimeter can be brought into a one block perimeter, narrowing our search area and increasing the odds of capturing the armed subject. Pretty boring for you so far?

Well, the next five minutes would drastically change the immediate future of my life and career. Let's continue. I advised all my brothers and sisters of the *hot-block*, and K-9 began working the sweep. Only this sweep felt a little rushed. K-9 units we're running straight to the 2nd and 3rd house on the block where I saw the subject run into, but searching the wrong side of the street. They didn't hear all the radio transmissions, and something felt off. I yelled at the K-9 officers from a distance to get their attention and directed them to the correct side of the street. They quickly adjusted and ran across the street and began working the block where we thought the subject was. Rarely, have I seen K-9 running as they are usually reserved and methodical during their searches. I spotted the K-9 sergeant working his dog with his back-up officer, and they walked up to a wrought-iron gate that had arrowhead shaped spikes on top. I see him trying to figure out a way to get the dog over the fence, which they train to do and when qualifying for K-9, have to be able to pick up an 80 lb. dog just for this reason. But this was too dangerous given the spikes on the fence's top rail. His back-up officer, (K-9 without his dog) then jumps the gate and is now searching the backyard by himself looking for the armed subject. This was one house south of where I last saw the subject run.

The sergeant left the gate area and went to the other side of the residence and back to the street in the wrong direction. I was watching all this from my perimeter point and didn't want to let a one-on-one confrontation happen with the lone K-9 officer and the subject. So I ran toward the lone officer while calling for another officer to take my spot on the perimeter. As I closed in on the house the officer yelled "He's back here!" Now at this point the sergeant was with his dog moving to another residence just north of us. As I heard the officer yelling he was confronting the subject, I ran from the street passing the sergeant, and his dog launched at me and tried to take a bite. Lucky for me, the sergeant had him on the lead. In case you didn't know, police dogs that do man-work (tracking) don't know the difference between good guys, that's us, and the bad guys, that's them, and only respond to their handlers. The dog thought I was a bad guy because I was running.

I ignored it and ran to the iron gate area where the lone officer was. I can now see the officer is ok, but he is holding the subject at gunpoint in the back yard. So I started to jump the fence to get back there not knowing the K-9 sergeant had come up behind me with the dog and on a "loose" lead. As I was scaling the gate, the dog jumped up at me (again thought I was a bad guy) and bit me in the right calf, and as trained to do, pulled me down with his weight. This threw me off balance while on top of the gate, and when I fell downward, I impaled my right hand right onto one of those arrowhead spikes on the gate. Now that fucking hurt! As the dog released my leg, my momentum climbing flipped me forward and into the backyard, while tearing my impaled hand off the spike. I fell onto my back, got up quickly and began walking to the officer with the subject at gunpoint. It appeared as the subject saw what happened to me and when he saw all the blood, got up and ran again jumping the fence and into another yard.

The officer gave chase right behind him, but as for me, I knew I couldn't jump any gates again in my condition. My right hand was bleeding profusely and I couldn't pull my trigger finger or move my thumb, much less grab anything. With blood pouring out of my hand like a water fountain, I asked my partner to get some bolt cutters. I wasn't really paying attention to him and suddenly became light headed. I went down on one knee and waited for our guys to open the gate. My sergeant radioed for Fire Rescue to respond in emergency mode, and attempted to kick the gate open. Fast forward; he gets the gate open, Rescue checks out my hand, and my partner drives me to the Ryder Trauma Center, where the crashed bad guy was taken. Just my luck but that's the best place to go in South Florida, maybe anywhere, for traumatic injuries and he qualified. So did I.

But most importantly as I saw it at the time, the asshole-bad guy was caught and arrested. Let's hope he gets convicted and sentenced to several years in prison for the victims he's terrorized. But in Miami-Dade County, that may not happen, no matter how good of a job we did on the arrest and paperwork. We'll see! That's a whole other story though.

Now driving to the hospital, I can rewind a little bit. My emotions were disappointment and anger when the injury first happened. Disappointment, because it seems every time I've been injured on the job, no matter how minor or major, it was because of another officer. Never fails. And anger because now I'm going to be out for who knows how long. But, as they say; "Shit Happens!"

Now I'll bring you back up to speed and move on quickly from here on. I arrived at Ryder Trauma Center and the staff didn't make me wait at all. I walked right into a room and the doctors actually left whatever meeting they were in and came to treat me ASAP, which was really good to see because it seems the consensus in the media is the majority of the public hate the police. I know it's not the "majority," just the vocal "minority," but it was certainly not the case at this hospital. They treated me like a king, and explained everything to me after the several tests, x-rays, cat scans, etc. The bad news was I had several tendons completely severed during the impalement and surgery was imminent and necessary.

That night they did a little open-hand surgery and sewed my tendons to the top of my hand so they wouldn't snap back into my forearm then sent me home. The next day I'm awakened by a phone call from my Lieutenant, who's checking up on me as well as referring me to a surgeon at the University of Miami Health System. Dr. Patrick Warren Owens, Chief of Hand & Orthopedic Surgery. A quick back story; my current major was involved in a serious motorcycle crash a few years ago, in which he lost both of his legs. He almost lost his arm but for Dr. Owens who was able to patch him up and save it.

My lieutenant and the Major called Dr. Owens, and he saw me in between surgeries. My wife Michelle, who is one of our robbery detectives by the way, drove me to Coral Gables to see Dr. Owens, and I didn't wait long. Doctor Owens checked out my hand and told me he feared there might be nerve damage. Because of this, he didn't want to wait a week for me to have surgery, which was what the worker's compensation (Risk Management-again, another story) recommended. He and his staff fit me into the schedule after the surgeries he already had that day.

After a bit of arguing with Risk Management, my surgery was approved. Thank you Bean Counters! I tell Michelle I'm going right into surgery and she's pretty bummed out because she can't be there with me due to Covid restrictions. But what a tremendous staff and team Dr. Owens had. They stayed about four hours past shifts on a Friday night just to take care of me. It's a debt of gratitude I can't ever repay. Surgery was a success! My dad asked me later what the doctor said about the surgery. I told him he said, 'It was a piece of cake!'" That's confidence! I was sent home with prescriptions and now for rest and recovery. If only it were that easy.

I get home and wash up a little with Michelle's help, and off to bed. Only I couldn't sleep at all. The nerve block was wearing off and the pain was getting more and more severe. My wife is sleeping in the same bed and my body won't stop shaking. I'm trying everything not to wake her up, but my breathing is loud and deep, and my body was shaking out of control. And after a couple hours of that she woke up.

She tried to make me more comfortable, but it just had to run its course I guess. I can say without a doubt, it was the worst pain of my life. It was two or three hours of more shaking until I finally passed out. This pain was actually worse than when I impaled my hand. This would be the pattern for a while to come. Fast forward a couple weeks when I see the doc for the follow-up, and I find out I was supposed to start physical therapy the week prior to this appointment. The sooner the better! The doctor's staff sent all the necessary paperwork and prescriptions to the Workers Compensation adjusters who failed, of course, to do their job and set up the therapy as I needed to get back to work as soon as possible.

Like you, I have a wife, we have a house, bills, and I kinda need to get back to work. Although I am getting paid while convalescing, it's not my same salary. It's at a lower rate; not to mention the overtime and off-duty jobs I'm missing out on. But you would think Risk Management would be competent enough to get you the best health care in a timely manner so as to get you back to 100 percent as soon as possible. This isn't the case at all and mine is not a unique story. This happens all the time, and employees have to do battle with them.

This could have been a career ending injury. If I can't use my hand, I can't shoot my gun, and so how am I supposed to be a police officer? It's the only line of work I've ever wanted to do. So after a few days of calling the Risk Management adjuster and arguing with them to just do their jobs and approve my therapy at the Hand Institute, that specializes in these types of injuries, they instead try to send me to some sub-par therapy practice that's in some shopping centers close to my house. Unbelievable!

So more phone conversations, horrendous arguments, and nastiness on behalf of the case workers; only now it's two weeks after I was supposed to start. I'm hoping I can get back to work soon, but as I write this, I've only been cleared for light-duty. Michelle has been holding it down and taking care of me as well as doing most of the chores around the house. I try to get some things done while she's at work, but it takes ten hours with one hand. Frustrating.

The public may not realize we can get hurt in a blink of an eye if we aren't 100 percent focused in our line of work, and unfortunately these types of incidents happen all the time. I'm just waiting on the bench for now. "Put me in, Coach!"

Author's Note:

You may have guessed by this time BJ and I are related; he's my son. He chose to follow in my footsteps and the "Family Business" like his uncle Pete, Aunt Sally, and cousin Alina before him. He has turned out to be one Hell of a Cop. And has now been promoted to sergeant.

The time I "unofficially" supervised and worked with him in Intracoastal was the best time of my career. I couldn't be prouder of him.

A Who Is It? Story

By Chief Alan P. Graham, Retired

A Modern-Day Sherlock Holmes Mystery

While assigned to the Community Policing Unit of the North Miami Beach Police Department, I also acted as the department's PIO, Public Information Officer. As the PIO, I was the person who gave interviews to the news media representatives about our police activities and events.

One day, one of our Traffic Homicide Officers, Steve Stewart, came into my office, and told me about a traffic homicide case he was working on for the past few days. He needed my help to contact the news media to help identify the elderly victim who had no identification on him when he was struck by a car and killed.

The idea was to go to the Miami-Dade County Medical Examiner's Office, take a photo of the dead victim's face, and get the news media to air it on television during the evening news broadcast. Hopefully, someone might recognize the photo and contact our department. Unfortunately, the victim's facial injuries made this idea unpalatable. No can do.

So, I started thinking like one of my favorite sleuths, Sherlock Holmes. I went to our department's Property Room and inspected the personal property of the deceased. Inside the evidence bag was a set of keys and a money clip with seven dollars. On the outside of the money clip were two engraved letters, "ER." That was all I had to go on. Not much. *"Watson, we have a case. Come at once if convenient. If inconvenient, come all the same."*

I put on my thinking cap. Officer Stewart had given me the location of the crash site, which was the 1000 block of North Miami Beach Boulevard, and the victim was killed while crossing the street. I looked at the keys on the key chain. No car key. The only keys on it looked like regular house keys. I deduced the crash victim might have lived in the neighboring residential area and had been "on foot" crossing the street when he was hit by the car. *"The game is afoot."*

The keys intrigued me. I needed help from a locksmith to give me some information about the keys. So I went to a local lock company and spoke to one of their salespersons. I asked him if he could identify the keys for me and what kind of locks they might open. One key turned out to be a standard mailbox key, another was a standard door lock key, but the last key he looked at turned out to be a "factory-controlled" key. These types of key are commonly used to open exterior apartment or condominium doors. The key companies who make them also maintain a record of the names of the buildings they are made for. *"A good detective knows every task, every interaction, no matter how seemingly banal, has the potential to contain multitudes."*

I found out if I contacted the key company headquarters, they could give me the name of the building that purchased this particular key cut. However, getting this information from the key company could take days to weeks to obtain. Not such a good idea but a possible fallback position. *"Contingencies Watson, contingencies."*

Armed now with "key" information, (pun intended) I set out to do a "grid search" of the neighborhood in the immediate area of the car crash. There were a bunch of apartment and condo buildings just north of the crash site, so I started with them. After several tries at the exterior doors of some buildings, and to no avail, I came up next to the exterior door of an apartment building just two blocks from the crash site. I put the "factory-controlled" key into the lock and gave it a try. To my surprise, the lock opened. Unbelievable! *"We balance probabilities and choose the most likely…"*

Once inside, I made my way to the building's office where I found the building manager. I asked her if she knew of any residents whose initials were "ER." She thought for a few moments, and said "Yes," it could be Ernest Roth." She told me that she hadn't seen him for a few days and he lived upstairs. *"We balance probabilities and choose the most likely. It is the scientific use of the imagination."*

I went upstairs to Mr. Roth's apartment and using the key that looked like a standard door lock key, I placed it into the lock. Sure enough, it fit and turned to unlock the apartment door. I announced myself and entered the apartment. It smelled musty. I noticed some bread had been left out on the dining room table and it had curled up from being dry. Not a good sign. I started looking around.

When I entered the bedroom I saw an elderly woman in the bed. She did not look well. I told her I was a police officer and asked her who she was. "Tess Roth" she replied. I asked her "Where is Ernest?" She told me he had just gone out to Publix to go shopping. I knew that was three days ago. I learned Tess had been in bed for the past three days. No food, no medications, and no Ernest to take care of her.

I called in the cavalry. Got Miami-Dade Fire Rescue on the way and requested my dispatcher to get Officer Stewart to my QTH (location). While I waited for help to arrive, I found Tess's medication bottles on the nightstand next to her bed. I called the physician who prescribed the meds and he said to "Get her to the hospital immediately!" When Fire Rescue arrived, off they went with her to Parkway Hospital's Emergency Room.

The next time I saw Tess, she had been transferred out from the hospital to a local nursing home and I went to visit her. She looked much better and was glad to be alive. I visited her on a regular basis for the next year until she passed away.

Thank you, Mom and Dad, for making me read novels as a child, and falling in love with Sir Arthur Conan Doyle's character, *Sherlock Holmes. "When you eliminate all which is impossible, then whatever remains, however improbable, must be the truth."*

Author's Note:

Alan and I met, guess where? At the Dunkin Donuts on Biscayne Blvd. when I worked in Intracoastal. Dave and I had our coffee every morning, and Alan and Doc Hal sat next to us. Hearing each other talk we realized that Alan was a Retired cop, and he and Doc were kindred spirits. After that, we met every morning, NBC permitting, discussing life, politics (always) and have been good friends ever since. See, police-coffee time leads to many things; great friendships and great stories!

The War Story of War Stories

By Officer Mario Gutierrez, Shield 1856 Metro-Dade Police Dept., Retired

The Incident!

My story, which I sometimes refer to as *"The Incident,"* happened on an October night. It was a Tuesday, the 29th day of the month in 2013, at approximately 1910 hrs. It had been a quiet shift for me for the most part. I was assigned to the Motorcycle Unit as a *Motorman and* was attached to the Airport District. I worked the afternoon shift, which was my favorite shift for the majority of my career. It was my favorite because it was busy and I enjoyed the pace of it and the time would go by fast. Since my main duty was traffic enforcement in and around Miami International Airport (MIA) this night and just before it started getting dark, I switched from my assigned Harley-Davidson Road King Police "Scooter" as we called them, to my Green & White Police Dodge Charger. I switched because the people driving around at night at MIA don't see the bike and I didn't want to end up as a hood ornament, hence, the switch to the car.

Anyway, during my patrol I entered the *Shell* gas station which is located on the corner of NW 42 Ave. (also known as Lejeune Road) and NW 25 St. I backed my car into the far NE corner of the gas station property in order to observe the intersection for traffic violators. This is known in police jargon as *"Sand Bagging,"* not something glamorous like chasing speeding violators, but necessary at this location because this one in particular was dangerous to motorist and pedestrians.

In fact, the following day after *The Incident*, a pedestrian was hit and killed by a car at that intersection. So, while I was sand bagging, my cell phone rang and it was my wife Laura calling. I was distracted for a bit from watching my surroundings while talking to her, so I didn't see what was happening on the opposite side of the property at the farthest fuel pump, and because my vision was blocked by other cars at the pumps nearest me.

Before I get into *The Incident*, I want to share with you the background of the *dirt bag* (as he will be referred to) that walked on to the scene that night. I am not going to say his name so as not to immortalize him in any way. I am only going to refer to him as the *dirt bag*. So this dirt bag entered the country illegally (what a surprise) and was in California at the time he committed the murder of an innocent person. I was later told this by the Homicide Detective that would investigate my case. He told me that an innocent man while walking, crossed in front of this dirt bag's path, when he suddenly and without provocation, pulled a knife and stabbed him to death. He was arrested and charged with murder, naturally. He was found unfit to stand trial due to the court finding him insane. Right.

So the court in California committed him to an institution for the Criminally Insane. California being a *Sanctuary State* (you can already guess my opinion on that) did not attempt to deport him. It should be noted this is the first of many failures in the system that was designed to protect us. After six months California, in their infinite wisdom, released this murdering dirt bag back onto the streets. He already had an extensive criminal history by this time and as he traveled around the country working his way down to South Florida, he was arrested multiple times by different police agencies, and every time the jurisdictions (courts) not the police, kept releasing him back onto the streets. Again, note the continued failure of our immigration system, our federal government, and the court's in dealing with this and many other murdering dirt bags' illegal statuses.

The dirt bag eventually arrives in Miami and while loitering around Bay Side, he attacks another male and stabs this guy in the neck. See a pattern? This victim fortunately survives the assault and the dirt bag gets arrested and charged again. The victim didn't show up when this case was called for trial, so the dirt bag was again released and not deported. The system failed to protect us once again, and a few weeks later he ends up at MIA.

He is spotted by one of the officers patrolling inside the terminal. The dirt bag was loitering and causing a disturbance and harassing customers in front of the *Subway* restaurant. He was promptly arrested without incident and taken to DCJ (Dade County Jail). Two months later, while I'm on the phone talking to my wife, the dirt bag enters the Shell gas station.

Surveillance video cameras belonging to the gas station recorded the entire *Incident*. The dirt bag is seen walking westbound on NW 25 St. as he enters the south side of the property, while I'm parked on the north side chatting on the phone with my wife and don't see him. He is wearing a ball cap, backpack, camouflage T-shirt, tan pants and white sneakers. Video shows him lifting a large, heavy, three-foot circular diameter steel cover protecting the valve system to one of the three, underground, 8,000-gallon fuel storage tanks on the south side of the station. He is carrying a white plastic bag from which he retrieves a red blanket. He is seen on video attempting to ignite the blanket on top of the valve system but fortunately for all of us is unsuccessful. He now walks away onto NW 42 Ave and heads northbound. Just before he leaves the perimeter of the gas station, he returns to the property, actually walking across in front of my marked cruiser, and approaches several newspaper dispensers in front of the store. He opens the one requiring no money and removes a stack of the local *New Times*. I didn't see this.

He now returns to the open port and this time he is able to start a fire inside the port on top of the valves. I can now see from my vantage point a large cloud of billowing smoke which my mind starts to process as a threat. One of the vehicles partially blocking my view moves away and I see the dirt bag grab one of the nearest fuel pump hoses and stretches it out toward the fire in an attempt to douse it with more fuel. He was unable to do this because the pump was not active. I told my wife "I gotta go!" and I threw my phone down on the floorboard of the front passenger side of my cruiser. I quickly drove the short distance to the front of the store near the emergency fuel shut off switch that is installed in every single gas station.

I exited the vehicle and punched that switch, shutting everything down. My mind was trying to process what I was being confronted with and later in the video, I can see exactly where I hesitated slightly, and when I was processing and trying to come up with a plan. I now make a mistake; I didn't get on my radio to ask for help, so I inadvertently insured I was alone. Honestly, processing what I was seeing frightened me and I realized I had to stop this quickly before the gas station blew up! So the radio never entered my mind.

My plan was to quickly take the dirt bag into custody, place him in the back of the cruiser, evacuate the gas station and surrounding area, and request the fire department come and secure the place. I could see the dirt bag's hands and they were empty; he had no visible weapons. Now, because of the magnitude of what was occurring I have been told by several people who sit in front of a monitor and watch the videos, and by the way, are not in any way experiencing stress or risking their lives, what I should or could have done, or what they *would* have done. I don't get upset because I realize people are generally like that and have opinions. Until it's them!

They weren't there. I was. So it fell on *my* shoulders. These were the cards dealt to *me*. I had to confront it, deal with it, and overcome it. By myself and *ALONE!* I faced it and took it on. I accept that. I was all that stood between this dirt bag and the disaster he was going to cause. I had a plan…

My plan, since to my mind he had no weapons in hand, was to deploy my ECD, (electronic control device) or what is commonly referred to as the *"Taser."* Something happened or rather I did something unexpected. Let me explain. Every night at home when I removed my gun belt, I would always remove my service weapon (Glock 21.45 cal.) and my Taser from the gun belt, along with the cartridge case containing the darts, wires and the compressed gas which is attached to the front of the Taser. I always separated them from the ECD because it was my way of making the ECD as safe as possible while at home. I would then place the separate parts on the top shelf of my closet, and this was my routine every night for several years. I am right-handed and I always used my right hand to draw the ECD from its holster which I carried on the left side on the gun belt (cross draw) as designed.

So now under extremely high stress, I drew the ECD with my right hand and my mind, reverting to "muscle memory," REMOVED THE CARTRIDGE from the device rendering it combat-ineffectual. Meaning, I screwed up! I extend the now useless device, point it at the dirt bag, who is crouched over the fire at this point, and I fired it. All it did was arc. When I realized what I had just done, I quickly turned off the device and reattached the cartridge. I again point the ECD at him and fired. Now remember, I am very close to him; I estimate approximately 4 or 5 feet, and he was crouched and wearing a backpack which I didn't see due to being focused on his hands. *Hands* are what kills officers.

As I fired he started to stand and turn to his right toward me, body bladed to me, when one dart hit him and the other missed, so the Taser didn't work. What happens now is very spotty in my memory and I can only remember fragments of what occurred. I will share with you what I remember and also what was seen in the actual video recording. Some of what I remember is not in chronological order so bear with me.

The dirt bag produced a large, 9-inch serrated blade knife and a large flat-tip screwdriver. He held one in each of his hands and he rushed me whirling his hands quickly in the air as he tried to stab me. I do remember seeing the weapons as he came at me, so I tried backing up to create some distance. Backing up is a "fine motor skill" maneuver. I was under high stress and couldn't get back fast enough and my feet failed to keep up with my body, so I fell onto my back. I remember falling backward and my training instinctively kicked in on how to break my fall from all those repetitions back in the academy. I immediately brought my knees up to my chest and kicked out at the dirt bag, but missed. He flanked me to my left and pounced on me with the knife and screw driver.

The video shows me on my back, him on my left on his knees over me and his knife skittering several feet away. He drops the screwdriver next to us, and starts fighting me for my pistol, which is in a *Safariland-SSIII* triple-retention holster, and I reverted back to my handgun- retention training. I keep my right hand on the weapon pushing it into the holster and keeping my right thumb over the retaining strap. I use my left hand to strike him numerous times while he bends down and viciously bites my right thumb, filleting it open from the first joint down its left side to the nail bed and exposing the bone. I felt nothing, No pain. I was more scared that he might get my gun. My hand remained on the gun and I would not yield. This entire time I'm still trying to process what's happening.

I remember being shocked and confused because things are happening *extremely* fast and the conscious side of my mind is struggling to keep up. This is where I have been told by our Police Psychologist Dr. Scott Allen, my brain kicked into survival-mode and started processing what was happening to me, and it does not record into the memory center of the brain, it just reacts. It uses whatever it has in its "filing cabinet" which for me was twenty-one years of the finest police training the Metro-Dade Police Dept. had to offer.

In the video, I later see I turn over and crawl forward on my knees toward the knife which had skittered away a few moments ago, when he reaches back and picks up the screwdriver he dropped. He has total situational awareness and knows where everything is. He never looked to see where the screwdriver was, and just reached for it and started stabbing me across my chest and stomach. The stabbing I do have a memory of. I now have "tunnel vision" and can't see him. All I see is the hand with the screwdriver stabbing me and remember being frightened, which caused me to think to myself "I'm going to get hit in the heart, lungs or liver and I'm going to be killed!" At this moment, a thought crossed my mind and I thought of my family, my wife Laura, my daughter Crystal, my sons Gabriel and Andrew, and my granddaughter, Adilyn. They are everything to me and the thought of never seeing them again angered me. It was really more rage than anything I've ever experienced and I have never been so angry! I was so *pissed*, this guy was trying to take me away from them.

The video shows me crawling toward the knife and picking it up with my left hand. My right hand is still protecting my holstered pistol while he's stabbing me, and he's is still trying to get at it.

I quickly come across from my left side pointing the knife toward him. He's standing behind my right shoulder and while still on my knees I stab him in the chin and in the upper part of his left chest. To this day I have no memory of this. I found out later while at the hospital recovering, during a phone call from a brother officer I had stabbed the guy. I was shocked because again, I had no memory of it.

The video shows no reaction from the dirt bag when I stab him, and it shows me dropping the knife, rolling onto my back, bringing my knees up to my chest and quickly striking him in the chest with both feet, effectively knocking him back. At this point my conscious memory returns and I remember him sitting on his ass just at my feet and me having all the time in the world now. It's like everything just stopped. So now I reach for my pistol. I didn't know it at the time but I had a dozen stab wounds in me and a mangled right thumb. The most severe wound was on my right triceps; a very deep 5-inch gash. Also at the time of *The Incident,* I was under a doctor's care that had me on a blood thinner which made the situation even more grave, because I was unknowingly bleeding to death. Now, as I drew my pistol the video shows him reaching back and without looking, grabbing the knife I had dropped.

He got up off his ass and was coming at me again! This time, from the hip, I quickly fired two rounds striking him. I knew I hit him because I saw his face change. His forward momentum from his lunge carried him on top of me. His head was just past my right shoulder, and his left shoulder neck area was exposed to me, so I quickly brought my pistol over and pushed the muzzle against the nape of his neck. I remembered angling it as to not shoot myself should one of the rounds punch through and hit me, and I then fired another three rounds into his chest cavity as fast as I could finally killing him. I was told the three rounds went through exploding his heart, lungs and cutting his liver in half.

Now, what I have been describing sounds like a long, drawn out fight, but in reality from the time we began our "dance" the whole thing lasted thirty seconds! In thirty seconds the dirt bag swung his weapons at me over 20 times. He struck me 12 times and bit my thumb. I fired an ECD, transitioned to a knife, stabbed him twice, transitioned to a pistol, and shot 5 rounds at and into him striking him five times, all in thirty seconds.

As I now roll out from under him, I crawl forward looking for my handheld radio which I had lost in the fight. I also lost my glasses and without them everything is very blurry. I find my radio but not the glasses and quickly transmit the call for help, *"Motor 81, 3-15!!! NW 42 Ave and 25 St. I've been knifed and I shot the subject!"* As I await a response, I quickly check myself looking for any bubbles on my chest where I was stabbed, which would indicate a hit in a lung, and I also looked for dark blood indicating a hit in my liver

(First-Aid training). Negative results! Good. I now look at my thumb and the flesh is hanging off it, and I can see the exposed bone. So I simply put the torn flesh back in its place as best I could, and I press my thumb to my chest to apply pressure. Still no response to my *"3-15"* request, so I transmit it again. Nothing. I realized my radio had switched channels and since everything was blurry, I couldn't see what channel it was on. I tried counting clicks with the channel knob, but the radio was slippery from all the blood, so manipulating it was a quite a challenge.

One of the employees of the gas station comes out and sees what is before him. I look at him and he has that look of shock on his face. I also see that because he's in shock, he freezes up and is of no help to me. I tell him to stay back and not to touch anything because it's a crime scene. I am trying now to protect the scene and not disturb the evidence for the investigation to come. Again, reverting back to training. On video, you can see this employee walking to his parked pickup truck, which was a good sixty feet away, enter the truck and retrieve a cigarette, lighting it, then calmly walking over to the port with the still burning valve system and peers inside. Fucking brilliant! Amazing what people do! At this point my frustration with the radio is growing and I find myself looking over at my Green & White and thinking to myself, "Mario, get your ass up, get in the car and drive yourself to the hospital!"

I now remember the *red button*. Our radios are equipped with a little red button on top and when you press it, it transmits your signal to everyone on the frequency and the dispatcher can now *see you* (your radio signal) on her screen. It's for emergency use only but understand we are cops and we sometimes hit the button accidentally, then we sound sheepish when we tell the dispatcher that was accidental. So no one wants to do that because we think it makes us look unprofessional. I have inadvertently trained myself *not* to touch the damn red button so as not to look like an idiot, but NOW I needed to use it.

I hit the red button and transmit my *"3-15"* again. She sees and hears me this time and puts out the call for help. The *"3-15"* tone is a distinct, high-pitched tone which alerts every officer on the frequency a transmission is coming that an officer needs help, now! She puts out my location, and just east of me a couple of blocks away are two officers getting some Cuban coffee. They are Officer Juan Leon, who was also assigned to the Motor Unit, and Officer Chris Garcia, who at the time was assigned to a regular patrol squad and later joined the Motor Unit, and is a former Homicide Detective. They arrive quickly at my location and the video shows them exiting their vehicles with their weapons drawn approaching the scene. Of course, guns out; good police procedure. I yell at them that there is a fire and we need to put it out! Officer Leon sees my condition and transmits an *Officer Down* call and requests Fire Rescue.

I want to share something else here before I continue. Five years before when I arrived at my new assignment at MIA, I had to go through several administrative procedures. One of which was obtaining a SIDA (Airport Security) badge in order to work as an LEO at the airport, which is federal, TSA policy. As I walked into the terminal, I spot Juan on a Segway and I remembered him from when I was a TA (Training Adviser) at the police academy. I asked him for directions on where to go, and Juan said he would take me there. In casual conversation, I mentioned I was on a prescribed blood thinner and half-jokingly told him if anything ever happened to me not to wait for Fire Rescue, to just throw me into a Green & White and take me to the hospital. Chilling!

On this night, five years later, Juan remembered what I had told him. He quickly got me to my feet and walked me to the passenger side of his unit. The door was locked, and in the recorded radio transmissions, one of us had an open mic, I heard myself say "It's locked I can't open it." I start thinking about shooting out the window because I *have* to get into this car and get to the hospital! Chris sees what is happening and in the video, you see him run quickly to the driver's side and unlock the doors. Also, during this whole *INCIDENT* and unbeknownst to me, a tow truck driver actually witnessed what had was happening to me and started recoding it with his phone as he was east bound on NW 25 St. He pulled into the gas station, exited his truck and while hiding behind the front fender continued to record it on his phone. He never tried to help in the prevention of the attempted murder of a police officer! He never even attempted to call for help on his phone, and just recorded the events which he later sold to a local news station for money. What-a-motherfucker! These are the citizens we serve and protect, sometimes with our lives.

As I start to get into the patrol car, I hear a voice behind me yelling "Hey! Hey! I have it all on video!!" I turn and see him holding up his cell phone still recording. I enter the unit and Juan gets us the Hell out of there. In the video you can actually see the "concerned tow truck driver citizen" enter into camera range for a brief second.

A bit later, the Homicide Detective on my case, along with Juan and Chris, had a "chat" with him, then his employer. When his bosses at the tow company heard what he did, or rather didn't do, they fired him. Good for them! The detective also spoke to the news station in question and had the video removed. I've only seen it once and can no longer find it on the internet. When Juan and I left, Chris stayed behind to handle the still volatile situation, risking his life to preserve the station, the people around it and the crime scene. I want to sincerely thank him for that.

While riding with Juan to the hospital, I decide to break protocol and tell Juan what happened. We are trained not to talk to anyone when something like this happens until we speak to an attorney in order to protect ourselves legally. Remember, I am now "The Subject Officer/Shooter" and the dirt bag is "The shooting victim." Screwed up I know, but that's how its termed. But I felt at the time if I were to die someone has to hear what happened *from me*. So I said to Juan "Hey dude, if I die you have to let them know what happened." I quickly tell him what I remembered and tell him to let my wife Laura know I love her. Juan yelled at me to stay awake and to tell her myself!!! He was driving like a mad man and got me to the hospital in three minutes! Other units from different agencies blocked the on-ramps to the expressway on our way to the hospital and we had no traffic and a clear road all the way to the Jackson Memorial/Ryder Trauma Center. Once there, I exited the vehicle and there was hospital personnel waiting just outside the doors with a gurney. I remember the nurse's eyes as she saw what I looked like, and they were as big as saucers! And this was a trauma nurse who has *seen it all*. I got on the gurney and me being me, told her "Patch me up I'm bleeding."

They worked fast and stabilized me. I was told they put five pints of A+ blood in me. My best friend and fellow Motorman Chris Rutledge went to my home on a *"3,"* picked up Laura and brought her to me. She never left my side. She is an outstanding "Cop's Wife," as she has had to put up with me and everything I have been through throughout my career. I love her dearly.

I was in the hospital for a few days before being released. The dirt bag had no communicable diseases so I got lucky there. While leaving the hospital and because of what I had done and hadn't realized, was the amount of coverage my *Incident* was getting. I asked Laura to get me out of the city, so we left and stayed in a nice hotel in Naples, Florida on the Gulf Coast. There is a saying all South Floridians vacation on the west coast, so we headed there.

She tended my wounds, taking pictures on her phone and sending them to the doctor as needed. She was in constant contact with the doctor who kept an eye on me remotely which was very nice of him to do. When I returned home and along with my attorney, I gave my statement to Homicide. I could only tell them in my official statement what little I actually remembered. Afterward and unofficially, the detective told me what I had done. My jaw hit the floor, as I had no clue of the details of what occurred. To this day I don't remember most of it. I do have a copy of the video and I see what I did, but it has never jarred anything in my memory. Later on, I was honored for my actions in adverting tragedy. I received numerous awards; the highest being from President Obama in an awards ceremony at the White House. He presented me the *"Presidential Public Safety Medal of Valor"* hanging it around my neck. Afterward, we shook hands where he passed his *Presidential Challenge Coin* to me. That was pretty cool.

I have been told by some of our police trainers at our Training Bureau it is very rare for a police officer to be involved in one-on-one, hand-to-hand, combat to-the-death with a subject. They also told me when encountering a knife wielding assailant, cops have a 50/50 percent chance of survival. They said some cops get to their guns and survive and others don't. So the odds were even in my case according to the stats. I didn't know any of that, not that it would have mattered at the time. All I knew was I had to stop him and he pissed me off!

After *The Incident*, I continued protecting the citizens I have always served in Dade County for five more years. I then Retired quietly and without fanfare. When I turned in my police credentials at our headquarters and officially Retired, I simply walked down the hallway and out to the parking lot without anyone looking my way or even noticing. I got in my pickup truck and drove away. I now live quietly and in peace with Laura until I leave this earth. Thank you for allowing me to share my story.

You can see the video at the below links: This is what can happen in *Police Work!*

https://www.youtube.com/watch?v=SJ251pv1GzA
https://www.youtube.com/watch?v=sOMtNu3WpBY

Author's Note:

Mario and I knew each other in passing over the years, and we briefly worked at the Airport together before his retirement. I knew of his INCIDENT, and reached out to him to ask if he would tell his story for us. He graciously and wholeheartedly agreed! Mario did what he had to do to prevail, and he is a hero in my book, and should be to all of us. I call his story, The War Story of War Stories! Now you see why. Thanks Mario. Enjoy retirement. You deserve it…

A You Never Know What

Stories

By Officer Mike Kelly, Metro-Dade Police Dept., Retired

It Was - a Quiet Drive to Work

On October 12, 2011, I was driving in my marked police unit heading south on the Florida Turnpike just passing the exit for Hollywood Blvd, in Broward County. As I'm not yet in Dade County where my *superpowers* work, I'm usually relaxed, and not "officially" required to take police action out of my jurisdiction. All that would change in a few minutes, however. As I continue to travel southbound on the turnpike, I notice a single engine aircraft very low, off to my left side. The aircraft suddenly turned in a westbound direction and rapidly began losing altitude. In my mind I thought, "He's not going to make it to the airport." Those familiar with the area will know a small airport (North Perry) is just west of the turnpike. The aircraft then crashed across all north bound lanes of the turnpike. When I saw that, I said to myself, "Ok, holy shit!"

Luck was on my side as I was able to get to the break in the center median, activate my emergency equipment, and drive south in the northbound lanes to the downed plane. As I got to the aircraft, I noticed it was a single engine turboprop, could see two crew members in the cockpit, and the aircraft was leaking fuel from its wings. Ok, here's the part where the lovely South Florida drivers really show how bad they are. One lane was somewhat clear for the cars close to the downed plane to get away from the hazard of the leaking fuel, but NOOO!, some motorists chose to get out of their cars and start filming the scene. I yelled a few choice words at them to clear the scene and was then able to block traffic. As I was dealing with this mess, the pilot was able to slowly exit the aircraft, and I could see he was in pain and had facial lacerations. I asked if he shut off his electrical and he replied he did.

Now I focused on the copilot who was injured and still in the aircraft in the right seat. The impact created an opening in the fuselage that I used to enter the aircraft and I was able to see the copilot was semi-conscious and complaining of back pain. I asked him if he was able to get out of the aircraft with my help and he told me to get him out of there! Ok, I know we're trained not to move someone with a possible back injury, but with the increased fuel leaking and the strong possibility of a post-crash fire, I was not going to leave him there so moving him was the only option. Dealing with his back injury will have to come later. We slowly made our exit from the aircraft and I helped the copilot to safety. It seemed like it took forever for Fire Rescue to arrive due to the traffic situation, but they did and transported both crew members for medical care and put foam down to mitigate any fire. Talk about *"Holy low flying airplane Batman!"*

Damn, That Was Close!

Ok a little "Oh shit" one for you. I was riding a one-man unit in the Central District of our county, I guess around 1994 on the afternoon shift, when I heard a *"3-30"* dispatched close to where I was (around NW 95 Street and east of 22 Ave). The dispatcher advised the shooting was in-progress with one person down and the shooter still on scene. A few moments later I was on scene and advised the dispatcher as I'm slowly approaching the area.

I see from about 50-60 yards to my south, a male down on the ground and another male armed with a handgun standing over him. As I'm exiting my unit I'm already withdrawing my handgun (Sig 226 9mm) and obtaining a sight picture while yelling for the guy to drop the gun. This guy then proceeded to fire one round at me that luckily went over my head. "Oh, shit!" As I'm on the trigger taking up that long double action pull to take a shot, the subject throws the gun down, and then got on the ground. I ran up to him and held him at gun point until some *"15s"* arrived. Ok, I put cuffs on this guy while yelling at him, then discovered the guy who I saw on the ground was not shot. What? Here's where it gets interesting.

My gunman was coming home and observed the other guy peeping into a neighbor's window, so he decides to play cop and confront this peeper and while doing so, he shot in the air or the ground, don't know, to scare the prowler who was probably scared shitless at this point, then made him lay on the ground.

A neighbor saw this and of course called in the shooting. This would-be cop told me after shooting at the prowler, his gun was in *single action mode* (I think he had a Beretta 9mm) and when I suddenly appeared on the scene, he was startled and had an accidental discharge of his gun, at me, which luckily went over my head.

We later go to court and the guy actually asked the judge if he could get his gun back. Ballsy! Thankfully, the judge denied his request. Oh, and his mother did thank me for not killing her son.

Author's Note:

Mike was on the "Dinosaur Squad" at the Airport when I became their sergeant. He has a great sense of humor and a world of experience. He was four months from retirement at that point, but I enjoyed having him on the squad for that short period of time. A flash in the pan!

A How'd That Happen Story

By Officer K. King, Metro-Dade Police Dept., Retired

Just Dumb Luck

I was a fresh-faced rookie and been out on my own for about two weeks working mids in the Northeast District. My first call (right out of the box) was a Sexual Battery. I arrived, issued a BOLO, notified detectives, took the report, and checked back into service for the next one. At about 3 A.M. while on *routine* patrol it starts to rain and I'm getting sleepy. So I decided to go to NE 163 St. & 6 Ave to the Krispy Kreme for a much needed coffee break.

While enroute, I reach the intersection in front of the Krispy Kreme and dozed off. I wake up abruptly while driving northbound through the intersection. First reaction....*Slam on my brakes!* My unit starts to spin uncontrollably, and after many spins I come to rest in the parking lot of the KK, in a parking space directly in front of the front door. Damn!

It should be noted however, I never regained control of the unit and when it came to rest it did so on its own. Talk about being lucky! I didn't hit anything and I couldn't have ever parked it that perfectly even if I tried. Well, I exit the vehicle shaking like a leaf and entered Krispy Kreme.

Upon entry, a guy bolts from a table and runs toward the restrooms. That side of the shop had no exit so he runs into the men's bathroom with nowhere to go. I look at the clerk and she shrugs her shoulders and says, "What's his problem?" I said, "I don't know but I'm gonna go find out." I enter the bathroom and cuff him (Officer Safety procedure) and then start questioning him. He breaks down and confesses to my earlier Sexual Battery. Talk about *Dumb Luck!*

I make all the notifications and the same Sexual Battery detective responds and looks at me in awe for the great catch, and then I transport the subject to the detective's office. My squad thinks I'm some kind of *Super Cop* until I tell them how it happened. I get an *"At-a-Boy"* in my file for my stellar police patrol techniques in the apprehension of a dangerous subject. That's police work!

Author's Note:

Sgt. (Ret.) Bert "Maverick" Gonzalez

Kenny and I never had the opportunity to work together as he was north end and I was south. But as I've been saying throughout the book, we *all* have stories to tell…

A Never Saw it Coming War Story

By Officer Carlos Labrada, Metro-Dade Police Dept.

Kings Creek Condo Shooting

January 13, 1998 was the first day of Shift Change (every 3 months) for the Miami-Dade Police Department. I was able to stay on the same shift, so my schedule didn't change.

Toward the end of the shift tour that day, I received a call from Officer Ivan Advincula who had been bumped off my shift and went from the afternoon to the midnight shift. He asked me to cover his *Off-Duty* job at the Kings Creek Condominium complex since his new schedule no longer allowed him to work the midnight to 4:00 A.M. slot. I agreed to cover it for the *easy* four hours.

After my regular shift ended at midnight, I checked in for the off-duty at Kings Creek and got my paperwork from the community office. They always left the paperwork in the mail slot of the office door for the assigned officer. The paperwork consisted of an *Off-Duty Voucher* and a sheet of paper with information on incidents during the morning and afternoon hours in the complex.

The shift started out as normal. I completed a canvass of the complex then stationed myself in the parking lot of the small shopping center on the property. The shopping center was located off the main road that cut through the complex from SW 88th Street and 79th Avenue to 82nd Street and 87th Avenue. This location offers the best view of all traffic entering the complex since the parking lot entrances to the apartment buildings are closed with heavy metal chains except for two locations on Camino Real. Easy enough.

After being in the parking lot of the shopping center for a time, my friend Enrique Ermas called and asked if I wanted some Cuban Coffee which I of course accepted. He showed up sometime later with the coffee and we sat in my car drinking and shooting-the-shit. During our conversation we started hearing what sounded like fireworks going off in one of the apartment buildings. The sounds seemed amplified because the apartment buildings for Kings Creek are square with a center courtyard, so the echo amplified the sound.

I assumed at the time someone was setting off fireworks as a prank to get the police to respond. I told my friend to wait for me in the parking lot while I go and investigate the source of the fireworks. Since the parking lots of the building were closed with the chain, I couldn't cut through the lots and had to go down Camino Real the long way around to check the buildings. While I was on my way, the sounds had stopped but after I had checked one building, I saw one of the apartments was on fire. I made my notification to the Kendall dispatcher to start Fire Rescue and more units.

The building on fire was on the north side of Camino Real that backs up to the State Road 878 Expressway. The apartment on fire was on the top floor in the southwest corner of the building. Since I was on the south side of Camino Real in the parking lot of another building, I had to go onto Camino Real to get to the building. Again, the long way around.

In hindsight, I made the mistake the fire department always advises police not to do: "DON'T PARK THE POLICE CARS IN FRONT OF A BURNING BUILDING!" Needless to say I parked on the swale in front of the building. While I was putting the car in park, I felt something hit the right side of my face and when I passed my hand on my face I saw it was blood. At that moment I knew this was not just a fire, but someone was shooting.

I got out of the car and took cover on the driver side of the car. Since the police car was a Chevy Caprice and was nice and wide and the only thing I could use as cover at that moment. I was trying to determine the location from where the person was shooting but when I looked up toward the building I didn't see anyone on any of the floors. Not knowing where it's coming from is terrifying. A few seconds later I heard another shot and then heard something fall behind me. I glanced behind me and saw my friend Enrique was lying on the road with a hole in his head where he had just been shot. I knew immediately from the wound he suffered he would not survive and he wasn't moving.

I looked back toward the building and saw a shooter on the 4th floor, pointing a rifle down toward me. I then returned fire with my handgun and the subject retreated into the building. The buildings here in Kings Creek have four exits, one on each side of the building. I had to move to another cover position to be able to see the three sides of the building (front, left and right sides).

I crossed to the south side of Camino Real into another parking lot and took cover behind a parked car and updated the dispatcher of the situation and location of the shooter. While on the radio another shot rang out and my leg gave out from under me. When I looked across the street to determine where the shot came from, I saw the subject on the passenger side of my police car aiming the rifle at me. He was about fifty feet from me. I returned fire and the shooter retreated toward the building.

[Being shot did not hurt; I believe because of the adrenaline coursing through my body at the time. I did experience an incredible thirst though].

I advised the dispatcher of the shooter's movements and I heard the police sirens approaching in the distance. I turned my attention to my leg and since I could not see how bad the injury was, I decided to use the shoelace of my boot as a tourniquet. The leg felt at the time like it was only attached by skin. By this time, the Cavalry was arriving in the area.

While I lay on the ground of the parking lot, a funny thing happened, at least it was funny to me; a police car pulled up next to me as I laid on the ground and I thought it was one of the responding units even though it did not have its emergency lights on. As it stopped next to me, I was surprised to discover it was Officer Fernando Castillo and he was not in uniform. He asked what happen to me and I told him I was shot in the leg. I can't remember his exact words but I do remember it was a one or two-word response. He then drove off.

The next thing I remember is a Miami-Dade Fire Rescue truck pulling up next to me and while in the truck, the fire lieutenant was arguing on the radio with what I believe was Jackson Memorial Hospital staff where the Ryder Trauma Center is with the best docs, and I think he wanted to take me there. Almost all cops with serious injuries are taken to Ryder. But he was being instructed to respond to the nearest hospital since I did not have a life-threatening injury and so I was taken to Baptist Hospital literally three minutes away.

Sgt. (Ret.) Bert "Maverick" Gonzalez

While I was at Baptist, one of the homicide detectives came to see me and told me the subject fled on foot when he heard all the back-up units coming. He tried to hide near the expressway. He ran out of bullets and gave up. What a tough guy! No more ammo and now he's a pussy. As it turned out, he suffered from a mental illness and had gone off his meds. My friend is dead and I was shot because some guy couldn't keep it together. This happens more than you know.

Author's Note:

Carlos was my corporal and A/Sgt. when we in the Police Operations Bureau together. I could rely on him 100 percent to handle things when I wasn't around, and we've been friends ever since. Carlos is a hero!

A Winds of Hell Story

By Officer Robert "Bobby" Longworth, Metro-Dade Police Dept., Retired

Hurricane Andrew

It was August 23rd, 1992, and *Hurricane Andrew* was coming. I was a cop, working Sunday from 7a to 3p, but the people of Dade County were becoming a bit.... well crazy! And this is my story:

We were held over until 5 p.m. because of the impending hurricane. After work, I tried (in vain) to find anything to board up my house, since the stores had long been out of boards. I finally "borrowed" scrap wood from a nearby construction site using pieces stuck together to cover my windows. After working on my house until about 10 p.m., I was called and told to show up for work by eleven. Alpha/Bravo was starting. I was paired with Officer Joyce Hood and we patrolled until the winds began blowing too hard for our own safety about 2 A.M. We finally took refuge in a Metro-Dade Fire Station on SW 147th Ave. and 48 Street.

The storm's fury finally hit with all its might and believe me it was a real gut-punch! Officers at the station were trying to get some sleep, and some did. I couldn't. The winds topped out at over 200 mph and when you've heard people say it sounds like a freight train, it's true! It's a frightening sound. At about 7 A.M. when the winds had died down to about eighty miles an hour, I called my house to see how my wife, her grandmother and our four children were holding up. My wife replied curtly the house wasn't doing too well and she had to go! Joyce and I were using her patrol car for the shift and I advised her of the conversation I just had with my wife, and then added I was taking the car and going home; she was welcome to come as well, but *I was* going!

Off we went driving through the hurricane, winding our way through streets almost entirely blocked by debris, trees and the like. We drove south on SW 137th Avenue, and as we passed Tamiami Airport, it looked as if it had been bombed. The only planes visible were strewn about in pieces. The many buildings that had once lined the taxiways were gone. The airport was about a mile from my house. While I was originally just worried, now pronounced fear was setting in.

411

We turned west onto SW 152 Street and came across 5-6 electrical poles blocking the road completely. These weren't little wood-log poles, these were the 90-foot tall, six foot wide concrete ones. Panic began to erupt in my mind as I turned south toward home (now about 1/2 mile from my house) and noticed a woman waving her arms frantically at us, so we stopped to assist her. Her family was still inside her house which had been blown down around them. After getting them out of the rubble, I turned to go back to my car and continue home. I then find the woman putting her two children in the back seat of my patrol car, ages about 4 and 6. I asked her what she was doing and she screamed at me "What am I suppose with them?" My stunned response was, "What am I supposed to do with them???" I told her to find a neighbor that was not as bad off as they were and to make do! What else could I do in that moment? I had to get to my family.

The further we traveled south; the worse things became. All westward roads were blocked, and then *all* roads were blocked. I tried to traverse a field that appeared to be passable, only to have my patrol car get stuck in mud. Joyce and I were now on foot. The winds were still at hurricane strength and we tried to hitch a ride with other passing (dumb) people trying to get home, including another police car, but every vehicle soon had flat tires from the debris. I came upon a bulldozer and intended to "commandeer" it to get me home, but it was padlocked. Damn! I momentarily considered shooting the lock off but figured a ricochet would probably hit me and I didn't want to die in a field. Hell, I made it through what would come to be the worst hurricane in history, so shooting myself didn't seem like a good idea. We walked on and were finally able to pick up a ride from a big 4x4 truck.

We finally made it to my house around 11:30 A.M. Once there, we found my house fared far better than any of my neighbors, and most of them had congregated at our home. We spent about an hour feeding everyone peanut butter sandwiches. Joyce was anxious to get home too, so I started off in my car intent on getting her home. I got less than a block from the house before I too had two flat tires. Joyce eventually had a friend pick her up, and I didn't see her again for months. She apparently made it home to her own catastrophe and decided she couldn't face going back to work.

Our house had three inches of standing water, and everything in the house was damaged and soiled with water, debris and glass. After cleaning up for hours, the department again called and ordered me/us to report back to work by 8 p.m. My mind was numb from being up for two days as well as the stress overload, but I did as ordered and left my family to fend for themselves.

At the station, I told my supervisor there was no way I could work as I hadn't slept in days. My friends Bert Gonzalez, and Cpl. Waters decided to take me under their wings for the next twelve hours. We rode as a three-man unit with me sleeping in the back seat. One of the few memories from that night is hearing Bert yell out "LOOTERS!" I awoke startled, jumped out of the back seat and looked around but had no idea where we were. As Bert and the Cpl. chased looters, I offered to stay behind to secure the car. LOL

The next day I told my wife to take our four children to her mother's house. I told her I would see her.... whenever.

Author's Note:

Bobby and I began riding together right after "Andrew" had hit us. We spent months working 12-plus hour shifts, first conducting rescues of citizens and our own officers who themselves were trapped in their destroyed homes. Traffic control, fights, crashes, everything! It just became worse after the hurricane. If you felt Bobby's stress while reading his story, imagine how we all felt going through it.

A But for the Grace of God Go

I War Story

By Lieutenant Raul "Chewy" Martinez, Metro-Dade Police Dept. Retired

Angel on my Shoulder

I truly believe God protects his humble servants; *Matthew 5:9 "Blessed are the peacemakers, for they shall be called the children of God,"* and I will go to my grave with this belief. I also believe those of us who wear or wore the *Shield* have a special calling and as such are granted certain unexplainable foresight and presumptions others simply just can't comprehend. Let me explain.

My name is Raul (Chewy) Martinez, and I am a thirty-year retired Police Lieutenant formerly with the Miami-Dade Police Department. I have worked and commanded many divisions and sections in my thirty years, and the case which I'm going to cover happened while I was a sergeant in our Narcotics Bureau. The following is a true story; and I am writing to the best of my recollection, of what transpired during that month in November 1998.

As I recall, it was a routine day for being just another day in the lives of police officers. I remember one of my detectives knocking on my office door requesting to talk. Of course, I asked him to enter and have a seat. It should be noted here I will use fictitious names for this story, to protect those who may not want to relive what transpired that week. Joe was one of my most productive detectives and laziness was not one of his faults. This saga started on a Thursday, November 6, 1998, and Joe was asking if we could get our hands on some cannabis as he had a potential buyer on the line. That's right, a potential buyer and yes, we, the

414

Police, sell dope. You see, we try to burn our candles at both ends by taking off not only the buyers, but we like getting the sellers even more. As a routine procedure, I prepared the paperwork necessary to obtain some grass from our lab, and by the afternoon I had five pounds of the best *Jamaican Gold* money can buy in my office safe. The deal was going to happen the next day so I secured a safe location to conduct our business with the bad guy.

The following day, a Friday, the deal didn't materialize as so often most narcotic cases don't, and I started my paperwork to return the grass to the property room for return-impound. You see, we are in the police business and I just can't keep 5 lb. of weed lying around in my safe past the 48-hour limit per our SOP. As it turned out, Joe told me his contact, a *CI* (confidential informant) contacted the bad guy and the deal was now set for the following Monday. Now let me put forth a disclaimer here; I would rather take a near fatal beating before I violate a departmental SOP, but laziness got the best of me that Friday and the weekend was looking sweet. So I kept the dope and figured we would do the deal on Monday and I'll explain it off to my lieutenant.

I have to admit over the weekend I thought about the weed sitting in my safe, and yes, I was aware I was violating SOP, so I'm figuring I had a duty to the department and was feeling a little guilty. The start of the workweek finally came around and I was looking forward to meeting with Joe to resolve the issue of the weed. When Joe arrived, he was excited and said the deal would happen that night and we were going to meet the bad guy as planned and go forward. At this point I must tell you; I was feeling a little concerned about this deal but didn't voice my thoughts to anyone. That little voice in my head was telling me to be aware....

I'm going to step away from my story for a moment and talk about that little voice in my head. You see as I've mentioned before, I truly believe God affords all officers a little extra oversight and we get these "vibes" from time to time that we sometimes ignore. In this case, I was warned more than once, but greed got the best of me and it almost caused a tragic outcome.

That evening Joe met with me on the road and explained the deal had fallen through again, but his *CI* had another person interested in purchasing our dope. Of course, I said it was off and came back to my office in the morning to return the weed. The next day, all was ready for the weed to be returned when Joe arrived. To try and convince me the deal was going forward, he called his *CI* in front of me and put him on speaker. Let me explain here the majority of *CI's* used by law enforcement around the country, all if not 99 percent, have alternative motives for working with the police, and as long as we recognize that we take everything they tell us with a grain of salt and try to verify all of their shenanigans. Although, this day my little voice was still telling me not to do this deal, and I cannot for the life of me understand why I decided to go forward with it Tuesday.

That evening, Tuesday, we prepared for our meet with the bad guy and as in all narcotic encounters, I made sure that extra protection and detectives were in place when we met this alleged dope dealer. As it turned out, and please note as most dope deals go, and after several attempts to verify the target had "hard-cash" in his possession to do the deal, the negotiations fell through as the *CI* could not verify the money. That was the last straw, or so I thought, and after getting pissed off at Joe, his *CI*, the bad guy, and the rest of the scum that dwell within this low-life narcotics world, I took our weed and returned it to my safe back in the office and headed home for the evening.

D-DAY

Thursday, November 11, 1998

I can't begin to tell you how many times that little voice in my head had warned me not to do this deal. So when I arrived at my office that afternoon I was prepared to return the already late narcotics back to the Department. I arrived at work and my lieutenant was waiting for me to accompany him to a meeting with the boss. I figured he found out about the weed in my safe and he was going to put a foot up my ass in front of the Major. As it turned out, they presented me with a commendation for me and my squad for our production from the previous month.

Naturally, I felt a little guilty thinking about that weed, but I was very proud of my folks and the effort they had always given me. After the meeting I headed back to my office and of course, as destiny always dictates, it was a little too late to return the dope. That evening Joe called me and said he was enroute to meet another potential buyer with the *CI* for the dope. Because of that little voice, I emphatically told Joe not to go to that meeting and to just send his *CI* to verify the money. Joe told me he would not go and would telephone me once the funds were verified. Sure enough, Joe called me after a two-hour wait and the deal was going to happen.

Knowing I would have to set up a location for this deal, I went to our *Bureau Log* only to find our undercover business location was being used that night by another Bureau supervisor. What do I do now? And of course *Angel's Voice* as I call it was getting louder telling me to cancel this deal. As it turned out, a friend of mine from another department called me and offered his location for this deal. I want you all to know I've never set foot inside this place and I was relying on my buddy to help me out with this dope deal. Don't get me wrong, I've done many deals with this other department and our teams have always worked well together, so I was confident this location was going to be all right for what we wanted to do, though I was busy convincing myself; "What could go wrong?" Early that evening, I met with my sergeant friend and we headed over to his location. After I inspected the locale, I was confident it would meet our needs and we would be safe. I contacted Joe and told him where he was to set up this meet with the bad guy, and the deal was going forward.

I suggested my friends' squad and my squad all have dinner together that night and discuss how this deal was going to happen. After hearing everyone talk, I started to feel a little better about doing a deal in a place where we have never trained. My *Angel* was going nuts, however.

THE LOCATION

That evening after dinner, my buddy took me to his undercover location so I could get oriented with their layout. I could see right away their location was much less tactically sound than ours and again I began to doubt this deal. Now I have worked several deals with this other team, and I was very familiar with all the detectives. I saw right up front I was going to have to put one of their detectives as the lead-entry on the take down team; a concept I was not fond of because it meant I was placing my guy's life in their hands.

Again, my *Angel* was going nuts.

Shortly after we were at this location, the rest of our team joined us for the operational briefing. I side-barred with Joe and told him, in my most serious of faces, I was not happy with this deal, especially with the new location we've never worked. Joe told me he had been here before and felt very at ease with the layout and that they (other team) have the entry point position. Again, you know my *Angel* was going nuts, but we pushed on.

I finally agreed to the plan as laid out but insisted on two points: First; my team would comprise the rest of the "stack" in the take down team, and Second; I was going to be inside as team leader; a move that goes against our departmental SOPs and I was sure my lieutenant would object to.

THE OPERATIONAL MEETING

As per our SOP's and plan, we met before the actual deal was going to take place. This is routine in all dope deals, so everyone is on the same page if something goes wrong. At the end of the meeting, I dropped my bombshell which I was certain would cancel the deal. I told my lieutenant I needed to be on the inside as we've never used this facility before and I was a bit nervous about the deal. To my surprise, the lieutenant said it was ok for me to handle the inside and he would take the cover teams on the outside, and the verification meeting with the bad guy. Again, my *Angel* flipped, as I could not believe the lieutenant was going against SOP. The deal was going to move forward. Joe made a control-call to his *CI* who by this time was with the target. All was verified including that the *CI* had seen the money to buy the dope. This made me feel a little better as with most deals no one ever shows money. We set up the outside meeting close to our inside location, and the lieutenant moved out with the cover teams to set up in advance of the bad guy's arrival.

THE OUTSIDE MEET

As a point of reference and to bring you all on board, these outside meets are very routine in narcotics deals as they give us the chance to meet the bad guy, and most importantly, to verify he *is serious* about buying dope and not ripping us off. We take this opportunity to get *a feel* and mostly look at that money. As it turned out, I later learned my lieutenant being a very old-school cop, had set up the cover teams too far from the actual meet site.

This is very important for two reasons: If something went wrong, by the time the team reached the undercover detective it would most likely be too late. And second, most bad guys bring counter surveillance to every dance, and the bad guys like to set up away like the lieutenant had done to see what was coming and going in the area. This would have burned the protection teams and expose the undercover to undo harm. On this deal, just so you can get a visual, the lieutenant set up his teams across the street from the meet location which was across six-lanes of traffic and a 12-foot median separating the east/west lanes. If something would have gone wrong at that meet site, Joe was on his own as the teams would have never been able to reach him. Of course, I learned all this later. Lessons learned, and God was on our side that night.

As planned, the bad guy showed up in an Infinity Q45; I know I'm dating myself, and with an expired paper tag no less. I'll explain the significance of that at the end. Joe saw them pull next to him and he exited his vehicle and walked up to the car. As told by Joe, the bad guy was driving with an unknown male sitting next to him in the front seat, and Joe's *CI* was seated behind the bad guy in the car. Joe introduced himself and the bad guy immediately asked to see the dope. *"Not so fast brother…before you see the dope, let's see the cash!"* Of course, the bad guy dicked around, and Joe's *CI* told Joe he saw the money and they were ready to go.

It's very important at this stage to point out something. Per our departmental SOPs, no dope deal will go forward without the detective verifying the money. This is done to avoid potential rip-offs, but Joe violated this policy and I'm here to tell you what happened, along with his SOP violation, could have very well saved Joe's life. Let me explain…If Joe would have insisted I'm quite certain this bad guy would have shot Joe right there in the parking lot. Thinking the dope was in his car, he would do the rip and drive off. And what I told you before, the cover teams would have been too far away to see weapons or take any kind of preventive actions.

Joe again confirmed with his *CI* about seeing the money and asked the bad guy to follow him to his place of business where they could do the deal in private. The bad guy agreed and drove to my location where I lay in wait. Folks, as an old cop let me tell you this bad guy was very arrogant in all his dealings with Joe. I say *old cop* because I've done hundreds of these types of deals, and this one was *TOO* smooth for my taste. Think about it, would you follow a guy you've never met, to a location you've never been, with $500.00 cash in your pocket just on his word? I didn't think so, so we as cops must take all of this into account as we go forward in this bizarre world of narcotics. I got the call from the Lt. they were coming at me so get ready…. *"Don't worry Lt., I was more than ready."*

THE MEET AT THE OK-CORRAL

By the time Joe arrived with the bad guys at our location, our take down team was ready. They were walking into the office; which we were all viewing on closed-circuit monitors, and Joe entered first, followed by his *CI*, then the unknown male, last followed by the real bad guy; the *shooter*. As they entered the room I was transfixed on that monitor, as it was the only lifeline I had to Joe. What caught my eye right from the onset is the shooter stood in the doorway of the office and looked around. He didn't enter all the way in as any normal person would have done. He looked up/down and side to side. This of course caused my RED FLAGS to go berserk. They all finally entered and Joe sat behind his desk with the shooter standing in front of him. Joe's *CI* never sat down and the other unknown male took a seat next to the front door. Joe pulled out the marijuana from the desk drawer and placed it on top of the desk. The dope was wrapped in plastic and ready to go to a friendly buyer. After some idle talk among themselves, the shooter asked for a scale to verify he was getting five pounds as promised. Not being *our* location, Joe had no scale and told the shooter he didn't have one. The shooter at this point asked to test the dope, and Joe offered him the package so he could cut into it. The shooter cut the bag, put a little sample in his left hand, smelled the dope, and told Joe this was fine. He also told Joe he had to go to the car to get his money. This too is against our SOPs. Allowing an unknown bad guy to walk out and retrieve something from their car is a huge *no-no* for the simple fact in our business, walking out and coming back usually spells *RIP OFF* and in all rip-offs that means the use of a firearm.

Here is the point of my story, and **YES, I BELIEVE IN GUARDIAN ANGELS;** as this mutt walked over to the door and put his left hand on the doorknob, and I remember thinking to myself this was weird how he reached across his body instead of using the closest hand; his right, to simply open the door. Turns out, he was pulling his gun from a hidden pocket with that right hand, and I was the only person in the monitoring room that saw this; well, me and my *Angel*.

At that very millisecond, I ordered the team to take down this piece of shit because every fiber in my body told me this guy had a gun even though I hadn't seen one yet. I'd like to bring you closer into the reality of how quickly a police officer must make a life-safety decision in cases where officers use deadly force.

The second I ordered the take down I remember the door to the room opening where we were standing, and the first detective leading the entry stack into the room assumed a one knee kneeling position using the door frame as cover, and I remember seeing; not hearing, him firing the first shot. The second detective in the take down stack jumped out into the open, and later testified he had no target acquisition and wanted to see what was occurring in the room. As this detective exposed himself, the follow-up investigation revealed the bad guy was able to get off a round from his handgun, missing the second detective's mid-section. It also revealed the round hit the wall next to the detective and was later found outside on the sidewalk after penetrating the wall.

His ANGEL was watching him that night as well, because one inch closer to the officer and we would have been attending his funeral. By the time I entered the room the bad guy was still standing with a gun in his right hand and looking in my direction. At this point I raised my firearm, pointed centered mass, and readied to fire. As I prepared to fire, I remember seeing the back of *Detective Jane's* head which was in front of me in the line of fire and coming into my view. I waited, for a split second, until her head disappeared out of my line of fire and took my first shot.

Every law enforcement officer in the country who takes firearms training learns about a psychology-based theory called *Fight or Flight*. This states when confronted with personal harm, you will either fight meaning become involved in combat, or take flight, meaning escape the situation in order to survive.

What they don't tell you is how *in-tune* you become when you feel you are about to get hurt. The best way for me to explain this is to liken this to a movie. If you've ever seen *The Matrix*, you'll remember how

Keanu Reeves moved in slow motion and was able to dodge bullets. NO, I'm not saying you'll dodge bullets, but I'm here to tell you your survival senses are so keen, that everything around you seems to move in slow motion. In fact, in your mind you can't move fast enough to get going. Therefore, all policemen have dreams (read nightmares) about firing our weapons and either our bullets fall to the ground when they exit the barrel, or we just can't fire fast enough to stop the threat attacking us. I know every cop that reads this understands.... As I prepared to fire my second shot, again, I saw Det. Debbie's head this time pop up in front of my gun then disappear. I was able to fire my second round as I saw the bad guy run out the door.

SIDE-NOTES & PERSONAL OBSERVATIONS

Before the bad guy ran out of the office, he had been shot 29 times. He made it to his car in the parking lot and expired on the sidewalk next to his vehicle (its adrenaline that keeps you going). During this whole ordeal, I never heard a single shot even though as a group, we fired thirty-six rounds. I remember my lieutenant saying later; *"Shit, it sounded like WWII in there!"* The psychologists call it *auditory exclusion*. I personally know I struck the subject twice because I saw my rounds hit him. During the gun battle, I could see the slide on my Beretta cycle to the rear and eject the spent round, and saw it fly in the air with smoke coming out (this is your body's amazing survival abilities to take note of everything around you as your fighting to survive).

CONCLUSION

SPEAKING FROM EXPERINCE, I can honestly say the majority of police officers will never fire their weapons in defense of their lives. We do our jobs with the belief in our oath of office of saving life, not taking it. During the portion of my career I was assigned to Narcotics, I was unfortunately involved in two shootings. This is something I think about every day, because even though this guy was going to kill my detective, the killing of another human being gives no personal satisfaction.

The follow-up investigation revealed several flaws in our Standard Operating Procedures. First, if Detective Joe would have asked to see the money for the deal as outlined in our SOP, he most likely would have had to fight for his life at that point as the fake money this guy brought was only a couple of twenty-dollar bills rolled up with newspaper. My lieutenant was too far away to have made a difference in saving my detective's life. Last, I recount this story with every class I've ever taught and continue to teach today. As it turned out, the bad guy's car had an expired tag. I mentioned it earlier. Why is this important? Let's say this was a regular drug deal (no cops involved-just bad guys) and this guy had just killed two of those guys for this pot. As he drives down the road at midnight, a lone police officer pulls him over for that expired tag. What do you think this guy is thinking after just having killed two other guys? That's why I teach every police officer, NEVER TAKE ANYTHING FOR GRANTED. Safety first, second and last! And of course, PAY ATTENTION TO YOUR *ANGEL!* He will never let you down. Stay safe my friends. #BLUELIVESMATTER

Author's Note:

Lt. "Chewy" as everyone calls him was my Lt. in Crime Scene for a short while, but when asked by the department to develop & spearhead a new training program for sergeants & lieutenants that became "Major Scene Management for Supervisors," he reached out and recruited me and several others from the Mobile Field Force Training Committee to join him as instructors. Chewy is one of the best instructors I've ever been around, and he made me a better one. I thank him for his tutelage and friendship over the years. We are all better for having worked with him. By the way, his son "Chewy Jr." followed in his footsteps, and they are another Father-Son Legacy duo of the job. Thanks Chewy!

A Split-Second Decision Story

By Sergeant Daniel Narcisse, Miami-Dade Police Dept.

When is Anyone Ever Prepared?

You have to brace yourself and do what it takes to make a split-second decision that can either be life or death.

That Friday could have taken a turn for the worse. As the dispatcher is asking for units to clear for a *"2-29A"* (Robbery-Armed), I was just explaining to my ride along that a regular day can go from 0 to 100 instantly. I was enroute to locate a burglary subject when the call came in. As I was driving I acknowledged the dispatcher and advised I would be responding. Lights and sirens came on and I headed into the unknown.

As I began to drive, I told my ride along "See how quickly things can change." I proceeded to the call, took an arrival, and attempted to locate the subject along with fellow officers who were responding as well. While trying to locate and asking the dispatcher to repeat the description of the subject, I was flagged down by a female who pointed out the alleged subject who had committed the armed robbery. He was sitting at the patio of the Three Palms Café on Biscayne Blvd. eating with another woman.

As I exited my vehicle my gun immediately came out of my holster. I approached with back-up units and ordered the subject to the ground. As I gave him commands to do so, he ignored me and proceeded to eat his pastry. I again gave commands to get on the ground, and again I was met with non-compliance. At this moment, I holstered my weapon, grabbed the subject by the arm and directed him to the ground quite forcefully. The subject began to physically resist by trying to defeat my control over him. I, along with my squad mates were holding him down on the ground when he began to start pushing up and place his hands under his chest so we couldn't handcuff him. The resisting continued until one of the guys delivered a drive-stun with his Taser to gain compliance.

Again, we were met with resistance and another stun was delivered. The resisting ceased and he was taken into custody. As we began to bring him onto his feet, I started my search of his person to locate a firearm, which he didn't have. Shortly after, I called my sergeant at the time, and said "Sarge, you need to respond, we just got into a Use of Force." As we waited for Sarge to arrive, I began to think how bad this could have turned out if he did in fact have a gun. Within fifteen minutes Sarge arrives and begins his supervisory investigation for the Use of Force.

After attempting to talk to the subject, Sarge was met with a refusal of a statement. After a bit of time passes the subject asks to speak to Sarge. This is when we discovered the caller was an ex-girlfriend aiming to get even with the subject because he was with a new girl. Just think if in fact he had a gun and the level of fear an officer can feel when these situations turn deadly, just because someone wanted to get even. We could have killed this guy over a "lie." When it was all said and done, the gentleman, who got it the worst of it was made whole and let go, and the instigating ex-girlfriend took the ride for lying to us. Just think...

Author's Note:

Danny's Sergeant was me. I supervised him and his squad mates and he became like another son to me. I worked with his father Louis. Danny says he had two fathers; Louis who raised him in life, and me who raised him on the job. I am honored. He has since made sergeant and has become what his father would have wanted. Very proud of him.

Mistaken Identity & an Unlucky

Miss Stories

By Officer Adejimi "Jimi" Obadeyi, Miami-Dade Police Dept.

Again, What are the Odds?

One day, late in my shift while working the Intracoastal District, I responded to a Chase Bank on Biscayne Blvd. regarding a white, Latin male attempting to utter a fraudulent check. The subject's description, as given by bank personnel, was a male subject wearing a brown shirt and blue jeans, common enough but a decent description to work off. As I and Officer Shirley J. from my squad approached the front door to the bank, guess who comes walking out? You got it, a white, Latin male wearing a brown shirt and blue jeans. With my gun drawn and at the low-ready position, I gave the male verbal commands to get on the ground and place his hands behind his back. This is a bank and it could have been a robbery for all we know, so the gun comes out. The male said "Fuck you! I ain't getting on the ground!" He refused to comply with my orders so now we have a problem. What is he going to do? I didn't see any weapons on the guy's body, but that doesn't mean he didn't have any. After a couple more attempts to order him to the ground which wasn't working, I holstered my firearm, grabbed him, and forced him to the ground and handcuffed him. Enough screwing around with this guy!

After I put this guy down, a branch employee came outside and told us we had the wrong guy. What? He matched the description, so what went wrong? I told Shirley to pick this guy up and uncuff him as I entered the bank with the employee to find the apparent subject. After I took the *real* subject into custody and secured him in my car, Shirley and I explained to *Mr. "I ain't getting*

426

on the ground," what had happened and we were working on what the bank called into *911*. He didn't want to hear it and complained of pain in his wrists to my sergeant, Norberto Gonzalez who had arrived on scene. The male advised he had a prior wrist injury and had had surgery. Part of Sergeant Gonzalez's job is to field complaints and try to make someone "whole" as we call it when a case of mistaken identity like this occurs. Sergeant Gonzalez offered Fire Rescue repeatedly, but instead of accepting medical help and our apologies, he just wanted to argue. He continued to state we had no authority to order him to get on the ground, and he has no obligation to comply with our orders. A note here: if we sense danger, like in this case and you're an unknown to us, you better comply with our orders. People have been shot and killed for not complying and making sudden movements toward us. He eventually left the scene prior to Rescue's arrival. It's over now, so we thought.

About seven years later, Shirley and Sergeant Gonzalez told me the guy was trying to sue us because we put him on the ground and insulted his dignity. He went through six attorneys before one would accept his case. I was never subpoenaed to appear in court regarding that suit. I wonder why?

Damn, He Missed!

In 2010 I was working days in the Intracoastal District when I received a call of a possible suicide where a male may have shot himself. I of course responded in emergency mode, and when I arrived I discovered two of my squad mates, one male and one female, were both in front of the residence pacing back and forth. They appeared to be in shock due to what they saw prior to my arrival. Mind you, they had taken an arrival approximately 4-5 minutes before I got there but didn't advise on what they found. I saw an SUV backed into the driveway on the left side of the residence as I pulled up and noticed the rear passenger side door was ajar, so I walked toward it to investigate. When I approached the vehicle I discovered a white male laying on the driveway in a fetal position. I then looked over and asked both officers if they were OK? They didn't respond to me.

Miami-Dade Fire Rescue had arrived with me and went immediately to check on the male lying next to the SUV. Rescue signaled to me there was a problem. As I approached them I discovered a shotgun in between the male's legs, with the barrel pointing up toward his head. I apologized to the paramedics for the shotgun not having been secured before they arrived as it is our responsibility to make any scene safe for them to operate. This should have been done by the other two officers who'd arrived before I did. I then secured then shotgun in the trunk of my patrol vehicle. I was livid!

Since it was my call and I was responsible for securing the scene, I began to direct the other officers on scene to set up a perimeter utilizing crime scene tape, including my sergeant, Norberto Gonzalez, who arrived shortly after I did. I was now in control of the scene, despite being the junior officer. The other two officers were well senior to me but couldn't do anything. Oh, and I almost forgot to mention, the male had apparently shot himself and was still alive!

The victim, as we call people who attempt or commit suicide, shot half of his face off. Some of his facial matter was in the tree that hung over the driveway. Thank God that guy didn't use that shotgun to shoot anyone else on scene. Hence, our requirement to secure any firearms we find. His estranged wife responded to the scene and was angry with him. Not because he had shot himself, but because he didn't do it correctly! She exclaimed, and I kid you not; "You can't do anything right. You can't even kill yourself right!" The irony here is she worked for a plastic surgeon. Gives you the warm fuzzies, doesn't it.

Once the scene was settled and Fire Rescue transported the victim to the hospital, I advised Sergeant Gonzalez I needed to address the squad at roll call because of what the other officers didn't do prior to me arriving. These were huge mistakes and I needed to speak my mind. The following day at roll call I addressed the squad as a whole, regarding the way the suicide call went. I expressed my displeasure with the handling of it prior to my arrival, as well as while I was on scene. Officer safety was my main message. Not removing the shotgun and properly assessing the victim's condition jeopardizes police and fire personnel on scene and can't be allowed to happen. I plan to make it home to my wife after every shift, by God's grace. A little help by my fellow officers would go a long way toward that end.

The male officer apologized to me for his role that day, and I accepted his apology. However, the female officer never did offer any apology and I haven't spoken to her since. That was 2010.

Author's Note:

Jimi was on my new squad when I arrived in Intracoastal in August of 2010. As he said, he was one of the junior officers, but after a short while, I made him my A/Sgt. He was mature and professional, and a good cop. I saw something in him I could come to rely on. In October 2020, Jimmy was promoted to sergeant and is now leading like he did that day on scene. Well done, Jimmy!

Sgt. (Ret.) Bert "Maverick" Gonzalez

A I had No Idea Story

By Officer Al Perez, Metro-Dade Police Dept., Retired

You Just Never Know

It was 1997 and I was going through a divorce—like most of us in our profession—and decided to be that angry guy and take all the money out of the bank to spite her. My area of patrol was Sunny Isles in the Northeast District where my bank was. I decided to walk in to make my withdrawal hoping it would be quick since I was in uniform and on-duty. I pulled up and parked on the west side of the building because the parking lot in front was full, and as I was walking up to the doors I had a second thought the bank might be too busy, so I turned and went back to my patrol car.

While I was sitting in the car still parked in the lot, I get dispatched to a hold-up alarm to the bank I'm parked in! I thought to myself, "What are the odds so let me play this one by the book." I creeped along and hugged the wall and did a quick peak inside the bank; this is where the term *"pucker factor"* comes into play. For those that are not familiar with it, it means your asshole gets real tight due to fear, hence, the "pucker." There were no customers or employees in the lobby, so I got on the radio and advised I had a bank robbery in-progress with hostages.

I went into training mode and drew my weapon, asked for back up but later I didn't remember having done that. I took cover behind a concrete pillar while aiming my six shot revolver at the front door, and there they came, two subjects holding bags of money with weapons in their front waist bands. Shit! At this point I heard a shotgun rack as Chuck and Jerry pulled up. Upon spotting the police, the two subjects went back inside and then we surrounded the bank. Suddenly, the west doors open with the subjects surrounding themselves with all the hostages, just like in the movies, but this was *real*. Luckily, one subject panicked and started running. The sounds of the sirens never sounded so sweet, as I knew the Calvary was on its way!

I jumped over a wall and chased this guy on foot but lost him the area. Sunny Isles isn't the best place to do a crime and I knew we would catch him. The subject I was chasing was caught by Ofc. Al G. hiding under a car, and the other idiot decided to jump into the Intracoastal Waterway. Note to criminals: if you can't swim don't jump in the water. This actually happens a lot. He tried to swim across to the other side which is the City of Aventura. So after he went under a few times he finally gave up. Well, we got those two in custody and transported them to the FBI office, where we discovered the non-swimmer had a handcuff key taped to his butt crack. Pretty savvy. I discovered there was a third subject I never saw who took a hostage in a carjacking. Jerry told me later this guy was aiming his gun at me as I was chasing his partner. I never saw him.

The next day I realized I had broken my foot jumping the wall and would need therapy, but that's were my life changed. I told the therapist my story and she prayed over me. Well, I didn't think much of it at the time till the next day when the FBI called me. They asked me if I was at the bank just before I got the alarm call. I told them yes I was, and they informed me the bank surveillance camera shows someone (me) walking toward the door and two of the subjects lying in wait, apparently ready to ambush him. Now I'm not the most religious guy in the world but I knew someone was looking out for me that day and had bigger plans.

I've worked with the greatest guys and gals and the *Best cops Ever!* After that day, I became a better father, friend, cop, and shortly thereafter I met the love of my life and was the happiest I had ever been. Oh yea, and I bought my 9mm Glock after that too!

Author's Note:

Al and I crossed paths many times during our careers, but we finally got to work together when he transferred to my squad in Intracoastal. Another kindred spirit to say the least. Good police!

A Not Your Basic Instinct Story

By Officer Frankie Rivera Metro-Dade Police Dept., Retired

I remember going to take the promotion exam for sergeant and I was so nervous that day. I put on my suit and drove to the testing site which was the Criminal Justice Building of our local college, Miami-Dade Community. This part of the three-part exam was a proctored oral interview on camera. You sat in front of a proctor and while being videotaped responded to four scenarios as if you were already a uniformed sergeant. The department never gave us dress guidelines, but everyone knew they'd be on film so they wanted to look their best.

I walked into the building and got in a short waiting line to be assigned a number that would identify me when I sat down in front of the camera. As I waited in line, I looked to my immediate left and saw a wooden classroom door, and immediately adjacent to it was a 6-inch wide pane of safety glass that stretched the entire height of the door.

I could see people in the room, most likely the group of exam takers scheduled for the hour before I was. I thought to myself, "I wonder if I know anyone in the room?" I decided to lean toward the window and I peeked inside. At the front of the room, facing the door, was a woman wearing a knee-high skirt, she was well dressed albeit a little rough looking. Maybe after a few beers…Anyway, she was paying attention to the person speaking to the class of exam takers, and suddenly she turned and looked at me while I was looking at her through the window, with her body facing me. Without warning, the woman opened her legs wide exposing her panty hose! Suddenly, it hit me... This was a male officer I knew well who worked with me for years. Damn! Let me shake that off!

I finished my oral exam and when I was leaving I noticed the command staff from my district station was there. There were high-ranking people who you didn't see very often, so something happened. Apparently, the college called the department to let them know one of their male officers was there wearing woman's attire and they came to investigate one of their own. I found my friend outside and asked him why he was dressed like that? He said he had no aspirations of getting promoted but didn't think it was fair women were getting promoted faster than men.

His thought was to "play the part" and dress to the nines, and just maybe he'd get promoted or at least send the department a message that affirmative action wasn't fair to those who worked hard to get promoted. He had spent more than $500 to get prepared and clothed to look professional. Needless to say, the department wanted to relieve him of duty on the spot, but command was advised not to do so by our legal advisers for fear of a retaliatory lawsuit. They allowed him to take his exam and the following test had a "gender specific" clause as a dress code requirement. Message sent!

Author's Note:

Frankie and I were partners way way back in the day at the old Midwest Station. We rode motorcycles together and still do to this day. We came across some folks that have had us laughing thirty years later. "Guantanamera!" "Are you ready?"

A Sad Story

By Sergeant Frank Rodriguez, Metro-Dade Police Dept., Retired

One of Our Own

On April 27, 1990, I had been assigned to our K9 unit for about eight years and had just finished my shift at 2 A.M. A short time later, the Communications Bureau Shift Commander activated all our pagers indicating we were to respond to an officer involved shooting in Northeast District. The entire K9 unit raced to the scene and assembled at the corner of NE 158 St. and 8 Ave.

I remember the tension in the air as we suited up while being updated on the description and direction of travel of the subject by Officer Lewis Velazquez, who had last observed him and was able to keep him contained inside the perimeter. We were told one of our officer's had been shot during the traffic stop of a stolen car. Two other subjects were already in custody and a lone, W/M shooter fled in the car, bailed out, and ran westbound on NE 158 St. toward 8th Ave. The canines seemed to all be highly agitated and barking as if they were alerting on the subject's scent nearby.

After we were given our search assignments by our K9 Unit commander, we paired up and started to search the houses east from the corner of NE 8th Ave. Almost immediately upon starting his search, Officer James Reddy advised he had the subject under a car at the corner house. He requested I respond to his area so we could surround the subject with two canines. We ran to the area where my partner, *"Bear"* immediately lunged under the car and dug his teeth into the subject's back as he attempted to cling to the car's undercarriage. He was no match to *Bear's* 80 lb. and powerful jaws. The subject cried out "I surrender, I surrender" several times and begged for the dog to release him. *Bear* dragged the subject out to the middle of the roadway where he was cuffed and searched. The subject was later identified, but I won't immortalize this asshole by stating his name, as the shooter.

The subject was subsequently transported to *Ward-D* with dog bites and a gunshot wound to a bicep from the earlier traffic stop. He was convicted a year later and received the death penalty; he is currently on *Death Row.*

During our After-Action briefing, we realized all the canines had actually been alerting on the subject's scent as we had assembled a dozen feet away from his hiding spot under the car at that corner house. Had it not been for the quick actions of the Northeast District officers establishing the perimeter, the subject was only one house away from breaking the western perimeter.

Sadly, a little while later we learned the officer didn't make it. Officer Joseph Preston Martin, 28, was a four-year veteran of the Metro-Dade Police Department and son of Homicide Lieutenant Larry Martin. Officer Martin had a wife and two young children.

24 years later my son, daughter and nephew joined MDPD and were assigned to that same district, now called the Intracoastal District. We will never forget that night.

Authors Note:

Frank and I worked together in the Police Operations Bureau and were Mobile Field Force Instructors together as well. Our kids went to the academy together and are proudly carrying on our legacies.

A Tried to Tell Him Story

By Sergeant Christopher Rodriguez, Miami-Dade Police Dept.

He Should Have Listened

The year was 2018. I was assigned to the Intracoastal District, (formerly Northeast District) General Investigations Unit (GIU) Person Crimes Squad. My assignment function consisted of investigating, as you might have gathered, person crimes, ranging from atrocities such as attempted murder and aggravated battery down to stalking and threats.

How do I describe the day? We've moved away from using wording such as "just a regular day" in police work, because there is no such thing as a regular day, or the ever so common "routine traffic stop" lingo, as there is nothing routine about law enforcement. Let's just say it was another hot, sunny day in South Florida.

I walked into the station, greeted everyone as I always did and placed my belongings down at my desk. My partner, Detective Alejandro Machin, or as we called him, *"Macheen,"* was at the nearby coffee table making his ever so popular Cuban coffee.

This was our ritual; we walked in, greeted everyone, then talked shit as all cops do, while Machin prepared Cuban coffee to be served to the station. Alex finished making the coffee; I chugged down the black liquid equivalent of gold and sat down at my desk to view my case assignments for the day. Just as I opened the case file, my sergeant walked over to my desk and asked me about the status on a particular case, saying command staff was *inquiring* about the developments. That's a euphemism for "We want to know now!"

The case involved an elderly woman and two toddlers that had been falsely imprisoned and forced to endure a nightmare in a vehicle. A young mother had backed her vehicle into a parking spot in front of a local market, walked into the market and left the vehicle on with the air conditioning while her elderly mother and two small children sat in the back seat.

Two, young unidentified male subjects jumped into the car, put it in gear, and sped off. Just one problem; the elderly mother and two small children were still in the backseat! After realizing their crime wasn't as perfectly thought out as they had thought, both of the subjects, *"unsubs,"* panicked. The subject driver crashed the vehicle into a Stop Sign, and both unsubs jumped out of the car and fled on foot. The elderly woman and two toddlers were located and thankfully without injuries.

Machin and I drove over to the mother's residence and interviewed her and her elderly mother. The elderly mother remembered both unsubs were young, black juveniles and the unsub driver was wearing a white undershirt, but she couldn't remember much else. I asked if the subjects left anything behind when they ran and the young mother said the subject driver left a sandal and a green sweater in the car. Awesome news! I was going to have something worthwhile to process for possible DNA and the vehicle for fingerprints. I asked where the vehicle was so we could process it, but to our dismay, the young mother said the incident was so traumatizing she had traded the vehicle in already, and someone had thrown all of the evidence in the car out. Our hearts sank. We lost our crime scene and the best possible chance at identifying the perps. Back to square one.

Machin and I, along with other detectives and our sergeant, scoured all nearby locations for witnesses and camera footage that may have captured the incident. We caught a lucky break. We spoke with a man who'd been standing outside of a gas station near the incident location and asked if he knew anything about the incident. The man said he didn't witness the incident, but he remembered seeing a "kid" that wasn't from the area standing around the gas station earlier on the day of the crime. The man gave us a description, saying he was a young, black male, probably about 14 or 15 years old, and he was wearing a white under shirt with a green sweater hanging on his shoulder. Bingo! We have two separate descriptions linking the subjects to the crime. The man did not want to provide his information to be a witness for the case and subsequently left.

All right, we're getting somewhere now. We have a good description and a possible time frame. Now it was time for the fun part, researching hours of camera footage. No cameras nearby captured the subjects entering the vehicle, only the car speeding away on the street. At some point I noticed a subject matching the description standing in front of the gas station entrance door for thirty minutes or so. The footage was grainy and pixelated, but clear enough to see a young, black male wearing a white under shirt with a green sweater hanging on his shoulder.

The footage quality was awful and there was no way in Hell we were going to be able to identify this perp with this footage. Fast forward, literally, and we caught a break; the unsub walked into the gas station only one time, and although his face was still hard to see, it was a much better picture. The quality was decent enough to put out on a *"Need to Identify"* flier.

I got a call the following day from another officer who told me they think they know the unsub in my flier, but the picture was too grainy to be certain. What stuck out in the officer's mind were the sandals the subject was wearing. They were a very distinct pair of expensive brand sandals, and the officer remembered the subject from a past case and he had very specific taste in apparel. Talk about a long shot! But we'll take it.

Machin and I head out to the possible unsub's residence for a *Hail Mary* interview to see if we can squeeze a confession. We had nothing to prove it was him. The picture quality was terrible enough that he could have denied the entire thing and a good defense attorney would have ripped the case to shreds. Machin and I arrived at the residence, knocked on the door, and the unsub's mother answered. We introduced ourselves and explained the reasoning for the visit. After some friendly convincing, the mother allowed me to speak to her son. Let's call him "Kyle." I fed Kyle every lie in the book. I told him I was sent on behalf of the County Commissioners to investigate the crime he committed, and that I had a 100 percent conviction rate, and I loved going to trial because I never lost. Kyle didn't budge, he stuck to his guns (lie) and said, "That wasn't me dawg." The nail in the coffin came when I showed him a picture of himself grabbing the handle of the gas station entry door, and I said "Well look at that, you left your fingerprints and DNA all over the handle. You forgot to wear gloves before you stole that car. And guess what, the fingerprints and DNA match from the car you stole and crashed."

Unbeknownst to Kyle, a gas station handle would be impossible to process for DNA or fingerprints, and don't forget our crime scene, the victim's vehicle and all the evidence in it, was gone. Kyle saw the picture of himself and I'll never forget it as he took a big gulp and his eyes lit up, and his jaw clenched. Kyle started sweating and twisting his hair. I pointed out the sweating and hair twisting was an obvious sign of fear and guilt and reminded him he's going to jail one way or another, and lying will only be an extra charge that his mom will have to pay for when he bails out. Hell, I told him it was a felony and at that point Kyle finally broke down. He gave me a full confession (and for the would be defense attorneys out there, Kyle was read his *Miranda* rights).

Kyle told me he committed the crime because he was trying to get into a new street gang after having left a previous one. I told him he was going to get killed in the streets if he kept playing with gangs, especially since he was trying to leave one gang and join a rival one. I tried to give Kyle some advice that his time would have been better spent playing sports and hanging with the right crowd at school. He smirked and didn't seem to value my advice. Good talk. Kyle was arrested and transported to the County Jail. The following day, Kyle's accomplice turned himself in and gave a full confession because he wanted "Street Cred," so we obliged him. Well folks, like I said, Kyle didn't seem to value my advice and it became all too apparent he didn't because he was found executed with a gunshot to the head before we could even go to trial. If only Kyle had listened to me.

Author's Note:

I listed Chris' story out of order here. You could have guessed Chris is Frank's son, and I've had the pleasure of working with him at Intracoastal before I transferred. He's a fine young man and just made sergeant, following in his father's footsteps. Way to go!

Comedy of Errors Stories

By Sergeant Nelson Rodriguez Metro-Dade Police Dept., Retired

I Wasn't Prepared

Back in 1996 I was working on a Monday-Holiday, not sure but I think it was Labor Day. I was the GIU Sergeant at Bay Ops and left a little earlier to gas up on the way home. I was assigned a marked Chevy Caprice without a cage and was driving North on NW 27 Ave approaching 79 St. The dispatcher was requesting all units *QSY* to *Channel D* because of an issue with the primary frequency, and when I was in the process of changing channels when I saw a heavy set, black female run onto the middle 27 Ave to flag me down. She advised a robbery was in-progress at the shoe store located on the SE corner of 27 Ave and 79 St. (don't remember the name). I was in plain clothes and had spent the entire day doing paperwork in the office and only had my gun on me. My handcuffs were in the trunk and my handheld radio was in the glovebox. Good place for them!

I immediately advised the dispatcher and gave her my *QTH* and sped into the parking lot. As I was pulling in, two black males in their late teens maybe early 20s, came out the front door and one was armed with a handgun. I couldn't see if the second one was armed. Upon spotting me, they fled south around the building. I gave the dispatcher a description and direction of travel.

I drove out and went to the trailer park next to the shoe store which was separated by a wall. Upon turning west in one of the trailer park streets, I saw the armed black male had left the shoe store and was running by one of the trailers. I jumped out and took him into custody at gunpoint. At least I had my gun on me. I walked him to my vehicle and pushed him under it so he couldn't run since I didn't have handcuffs or my handheld. Once at my vehicle I was able to notify the dispatcher of my location. Shortly thereafter a marked unit came and took over the prisoner. A Central District unit handled the robbery and I went home. I later learned the subject's weapon was recovered in the field next to the trailer park and the second subject was also arrested.

Lesson learned: ALWAYS be ready. Have your gear readily available no matter what you are doing, especially if you are in a marked vehicle. I was too complacent and got lucky.

A Little Internal Affairs Humor

I was working *IA* at the time, when an Intracoastal District sergeant requested an investigation to find who came into the men's bathroom while he was sitting in a stall answering the call of nature. He saw a pair of black shoes come up to his stall and a pair of non-descript hands came over the top of the stall and snapped a Polaroid picture of him sitting on the throne. The phantom photographer then exited the men's room.

Investigation Results: The sergeant retracted his complaint and the investigation was stopped before it started when he realized that only more humiliation could result from having to interview any and all males working that day who may have gone into the restroom. *"Pick Your Battles"* comes to mind.

Another Intracoastal supervisor called and requested an investigation to find out who laced chocolate cookies with a laxative after several people suffered the effects (movement) from eating the cookies. The cookies were in the kitchen with a sign posted on them by the owner stating "DO NOT EAT!" The baker (a sworn officer) had been the victim numerous times, of having his lunch items eaten/taken by others without his permission.

Investigation Results: No investigation was conducted since the owner clearly posted a warning for everyone *NOT* to eat the cookies. Additionally, there no more complaints of people's food being pilfered.

Author's Note:

Nelson and I met when I was a port sergeant, and when preparing security plans for US Navy ship visits, Nelson was the Police Diver sergeant and did the dock sweep dives for us. We went on to teach Mobile Field Force & Major Scene Management together and found out the other rode motorcycles as well. We've been riding ever since.

A Cut the Head Off the Snake

Story

By Sergeant Mike Santos, Metro-Dade Police Dept., Retired

Operation Boulder Boys

It was a routine homicide. If you can call the taking of a life by one person of another routine. It was around late 1991 in the *Scott Housing Projects* of *Liberty City*, where a young black male was gunned down while sitting inside of his vehicle. Several weeks had passed when the Homicide Bureau receives a call from the FBI. The *routine* homicide turned out to be anything but that.

I spoke to the FBI who told me they were working a violent group of drug dealers in *Scotts* responsible for several murders and shootings in the County and in the City of Miami. I was then detached to the FBI for a short period that would eventually turn into three years.

The FBI agents involved in the investigation were young, enthusiastic and had their hearts in the right place. To this day and almost 30 years later, we have remained personal friends. The Metro-Dade Police Department also detached an experienced narcotics detective who was by far one of the best and most competent investigators I ever met, and the best undercover detective I ever saw!

Our investigation uncovered a structured, organized, and violent group of crack cocaine dealers. Starting from the street-level crack sellers to the lieutenants that brought the "Bomb" or the amount of crack to be sold that day, and those who collected the daily cash from the sales. The organization had an enforcer who used violence often and when needed, at the orders of the head of the organization.

The FBI used a *Continuing Criminal Enterprise (CCE)* for their investigation. This is a *RICO (Racketeer Influenced and Corrupt Organization Act)* for narcotics. It allowed us to document and use previous crimes such as murders and shootings where the victim didn't die, and narcotics trafficking and other crimes against the organization. Under the *CCE* statute, everyone from the head of the organization to the lieutenants and enforcers could be charged. After a long and tedious, almost 2 years of investigation, thirteen federal indictments were handed down to take apart this violent group of individuals.

Prior to the arrests, the FBI sent all the agents and investigators involved in the case to the FBI Academy in Quantico, Virginia. We were there for a week for nothing but shooting our weapons, tactical scenarios and building searches. This was playtime and we really enjoyed it.

The Takedown

It was impressive. The very large conference room at the FBI office in Miami was full of agents and investigators. FBI SWAT teams were flown in from different locations for a very organized operational plan, and interview rooms were set up for all thirteen arrestees. The FBI planned everything to the last detail. I was on the takedown team for the main enforcer for which we expected possible violence. The main enforcer was being lured to a long street where there was very little to no traffic, thinking if it went sideways we could mitigate any civilian casualties, and an FBI sniper was assigned to cover us. Any potential violence by the enforcer would be taken care of by the sniper. In the end however, after we stopped the vehicle with the enforcer, surprisingly, he surrendered without a shot being fired. As a matter of fact, all thirteen persons were arrested without using force and no shots were fired at all. A good day all around!

The Trial

Federal court is a lot different from state court. None of the nonsense you see in State court is permitted. Attorneys normally don't raise their voice or are disrespectful like I have seen many times in State trials. The assistant US Attorney (AUSA) assigned from the beginning of our case was a real pro. A go-getter and sharp as can be.

At the end of the month's long trial, all thirteen defendants were convicted on a variety of crimes. The three main players were charged and convicted adding two homicides in furtherance of a continuing criminal enterprise. It was the first *Federal Death Penalty Case* in the

Southern District of Florida for a law that became known as the *"Drug Kingpin"* statute. I am proud to have been a part of it.

Author's Note:

Mike and I first met in 1989 when I had my In-Custody Death on that cold night. He was the Internal Affairs detective who responded.

We later ended up at the Port of Miami, post 9/11, as two of the three "Port Sergeants." We had a great time working together, and because of our efforts with others of course, in implementing the new security procedures, we received the first ever, "US Coast Guard Meritorious Service Award" given to local law enforcement. We are very proud of the work we ALL accomplished. "Hey Snapper-Head!"

A Pursuit Story or Two

By Sergeant Craig Sciortino, Metro-Dade Police, Retired

In Hot Pursuit!

It was 1984 and I was working midnights in Northwest District, and was in the area of NW 135 Street and 27 Ave. The dispatcher came on the air and advised a Central District unit was in pursuit of a light-colored Toyota involved in an armed robbery in Miami Beach. Miami Beach PD initially started the chase but fell off once they got into the County and the Central unit picked it up.

The vehicle was northbound on NW 27 Ave. approaching my district. I stood by and joined the chase at NW 135 St. and was the secondary chase vehicle behind the Central unit. We were traveling at about 65-70 mph, and there was no chopper available at that time.

We continued northbound toward NW 199 St. closing in on Broward County. The two officers in the Central unit advised the dispatcher if we went into Broward County they were not going to be familiar with the area, as most of our officers lived in Dade County at the time. I was one of the few at the time who lived in Broward, so I advised I would take over as the primary chase vehicle and the Central unit can switch to secondary. We continued northbound into the City of Miramar still traveling the same speed. The subject vehicle continued north into the City of Davie. As you can see we were moving pretty quickly through Broward County and traversing city after city.

We continued north and now entered the City of Plantation. At University Dr. and SR 84, a Plantation police officer was standing in the center median; why I don't know, and as the subject vehicle passed him it at speed, it appeared as if he threw something at the vehicle but I couldn't make out what it was or why. The vehicle abruptly veered from the left lane to the center lane but continued northbound. At Sunrise Blvd. we entered the City of Sunrise. As you can surmise, Broward like Dade has many smaller cities within it, and we were running from jurisdiction to jurisdiction, but we started it so it's ours until we decide it's not.

So as we approached Sunset Strip and University, Sunrise Police had many police vehicles set up at the intersection with their lights on. It appeared as though the subject got confused and ran into a civilian vehicle stopped at the intersection. We all immediately exited our vehicles and ran up to the subjects *extricating* them from the car, while Sunrise Police took care of the civilians. The two subjects sustained injuries (too bad) and were transported to Plantation Hospital. Inside the subject car on the front seat was a brick, and we could see the windshield had been broken. It appeared the Plantation officer, in trying to stop the subjects, threw a brick through the windshield, however that didn't stop them. We don't normally throw bricks at vehicles, but maybe I missed that one in our SOPs. We also recovered a gun and a purse with the original Beach victim's belongings. Got them!

The subjects were in the hospital under guard and a Miami Beach Detective responded to charge both with armed robbery. Along with this, a Davie Police officer responded as well and issued four tickets to the driver. Got to get those traffic violations in. It was a long chase however, other than the subjects being injured in the accident, no officers were injured and no County vehicles were damaged. A Win-Win for everyone.

And We're Off Again!

My second story begins in 1990. I was a sergeant again, working Northwest District although it was now called the Miami Lakes District; another city incorporation we policed. It was the midnight shift and I was stationary at Dolphin Stadium on NW 199 St., sitting in a driveway. I observed a vehicle westbound on 199 St. as the street was well lit, and I saw an arm coming out of a back window. I then saw a gun in the subject's hand and then a muzzle flash as well as hearing the shot. I didn't know if they were shooting at me or not however, I immediately got on the radio and advised of the situation. In addition, I activated my emergency equipment and the chase was on! They approached NW 27 Ave., with the light red, but blew right through it and continued westbound with me tailing. As we approached NW 37 Ave. they turned south bound, and at this point we were moving at about 60 mph. We continued on when they were beginning to slow down at the apartment complex located at NW 183 St. This place was infamous for subjects fleeing police and baling out of their cars, and then running into the apartments where we would lose them. Kinda like cockroaches scurrying into the walls. Knowing this was their M.O. and watching them drive right alongside the building I wanted to prevent them from reaching their bailout point, so I positioned my vehicle against the passenger side of their vehicle, preventing them from opening the door as I pushed them into the building. This also preventing them from opening the driver side as well; I basically pinned them against the building.

By the time the back-up units arrived, I had them trapped in their car and we took four bad guys into custody and recovered two guns. The only damage was to the left, front of my vehicle where I *guided* them into the wall. My Lieutenant at time was Irv G., and it was his opinion the subjects drove *into me* in an attempt to evade. Ok, I'll go with that. More bad guys in jail. Another Win-Win!

Author's Note

Craig was one of the senior Mobile Field Force Committee members when I joined the group in 1998. He led most of the training and took me under his wing. Craig groomed me and when he retired he handed over the training reigns to me. I am grateful for all he taught me and for his friendship. Though for the first two years he kept calling me Sergeant Reyes.

A What Was That Story

By Lieutenant James "Pappy" Slack, Metro-Dade Police Dept., Retired

Thought I was Good

I was working 8A-4P in Central District (now Northside), and been on about eight months, so I was too stupid to know what I didn't know but figured I was God's gift to PSD (before we became Metro-Dade). I was riding a two-man car and my partner, who shall remain nameless, had about two months less time than me. We were a good pair though.

I was driving and we were southbound on NW 22 Avenue near 54 Street where the Caleb Justice Center is now. Back then there was a two-story apartment building. Just as we got to the entrance of the parking lot of this building, we heard two shots. My partner, who had a clearer view of the parking lot yelled "In there!" indicating the location in the parking lot. I whipped the unit into the lot and there was a male standing about thirty feet away, directly in front of our unit. He was standing over another male who was lying on his back. I was able to see the male standing had a gun in his right hand.

He was with his back to us and don't think he was aware of our presence. I slammed the car into park and immediately got out, drawing my weapon as I did so. I took up a position behind the car door and yelled "Police, drop the gun" or words to that effect. Now the guy with the gun, did what was the most natural thing, and also the worst thing, to do; he turned around to see who was yelling. As he turned it looked as if he was raising the gun toward me and I fired my revolver. Bang!!!

Now I have to stop here and explain a couple of things. At that time, 1972-73, PSDs issued sidearm was a four-inch barrel, Smith and Wesson, Model 15 Revolver, great gun. Our duty ammo was a Remington 180 grain round nose "Lubaloy" rounds, not a

448

great cartridge. However, at that time the ammo used for qualification and training was 148 grain wad-cutter reloads. There is a considerable difference between those two types of ammo, both in recoil and muzzle flash.

When I fired my revolver (the first time I had EVER fired it since I qualified in the Academy) the ball of fire that came out of the barrel was huge; so large that the thought crossed my mind the revolver had blown up! The recoil was also unexpected and the muzzle was at about a 45-degree angle when I involuntarily cranked off a second round.

Now, while I was acting like *Wyatt Earp*, my partner had the presence of mind to get on the radio and let folks know what was going on (someone was thinking). As it happened, just about halfway through his transmission I pulled the trigger. The sound of that shot went out over Central frequency and deafened my partner (remember I was crouched behind the open driver side door). The dispatcher, (God bless ALL dispatchers), hit the beep-tone and sent everyone in the district on a *"3-15"* (she may have also sent the cavalry, the USMC and the Third Fleet for all I know).

While all this is happening, the subject, probably awed by my outstanding display of skill and Police Authority, dropped his gun, fell to his knees, and threw his hands in the air. At first I thought I'd shot him, but nope, I missed. During the investigation it was determined that based on where the subject had been standing, my first round had missed his right ear by a couple of inches (Ya gotta remember: sight picture, sight alignment). The second projectile entered low earth orbit and has never been see again. (I'll be honest, for several weeks afterward I was afraid I get a call from Hialeah PD to ask me to stop by and chat about a stray bullet that killed someone west of 37th Avenue).

The subject had shot and killed his next-door neighbor (the two shots we heard), because the subject thought, wrongly, his wife had been sleeping with the victim. As far as I know he is still in Starke, living or dead.

It took several months but eventually everyone stopped calling me *"Quick Draw."*

Author's Note:

"Pappy" was my sergeant I told you about in the act about being a sergeant. Absolutely the best supervisor and mentor I ever had. I credit him with teaching me how to be a good cop, and what my future successes would be as a sergeant.

In the movie, "*The Man in the Iron Mask*," in the final battle scene as the leader of the Musketeers Capitan D'Artagnan lay dying, his second, Lt. Andre, said to the man that had run him through; "All my life, all I EVER wanted to be...was him!" That's how I feel about Sergeant "Pappy" Slack. Thanks Pappy!

A Real Tough Guy Story

By Sergeant Tony. V, Metro-Dade Police Dept., Retired

Until an SRT Team Comes Thru the Door

It was the early eighties and I was assigned to the *Special Response Team (SRT)*. One of my first Arrest Warrants was for an individual wanted for several murders and drug dealing. There's a rumor he was the basis for one of the bad guys in the movie *Scarface*. He was allegedly going to put up a fight, and we feared a huge gunfight would start when we tried to arrest him.

We met at 3 A.M. for the briefing. In attendance was MDPD narcotics officers, Federal agents, lots of brass and us, SRT. Because of the expected threat level for this mission, we used two SRT teams. One would take the first floor and the other the second. As we always did, we put together the plan on how to assault the structure, breach, and affect the arrest. Tensions were high because of *Tony Montana*.

Just before sunrise we convoyed to the residence. We surrounded the house, and the command was given to go in.

I was the door buster on the team. My job is to get the door open fast! I had a sledgehammer and pry bar with me. I noticed the house had a wooden double-door that opened in. Good. I ran up, jumped and kicked it opened! (I got Lucky). My job then changed; I became the point-man for my team and we had the upstairs, so leading the team we ran up.

As I reached the landing, I was met by the suspect. I was prepared for a shootout instead; this so-called badass pulled a *Bin Laden* and was holding his own daughter in front of him as a human shield. We separated them and he was placed under arrest without incident.

There were several guns in the bedroom. All were confiscated and sent for ballistics comparisons. He could have come out with them; instead, he chose to come out with his daughter. Real tough guy, LOL!

Author's Note:

Tony and I met long ago. Would teach Mobile Field Force together and he would train me to ride a Police Mountain Bike. He founded the

Sgt. (Ret.) Bert "Maverick" Gonzalez

program. We ride motorcycles together to this day. Him a Harley, me a Gold Wing. And the rivalry continues...

A Final War Story

You have read stories from my family, friends, and colleagues, and though I've shared with you many of my stories throughout the book, at my wife Rosy's suggestion, I wish to close **Stories from the Fringe** with one last story from me, which could have been a pivotal turning-point in my career and that of my partner at the time, Officer Gary Burkholder, who also happens to my son BJ's Godfather. Had this incident gone sideways, it's very possible that this book would have never been written. So if you'll indulge me one last time, here it goes.

What If!

It was Wednesday, January 7, 1987, at approximately 2130 hours in the Southwest District. It was a cool night and it had been mostly uneventful up until that point. Gary and I were heading to the barn to transfer at 2200 for the night (I was driving as usual), when the dispatcher came on with the emergency beep-tone, *Beeeep, "Attention all units, a 2-14, man at the door with a gun!"* The address was given and wouldn't you know it, we were about a minute away as the house was on SW 114 Street, and we were on SW 112 Street. We were due to get off but knew that we would be passing the responding units on our way to the station, so we decided we better go.

There wasn't much more information from the dispatcher so we of course were cautious, and at about two blocks away as we were trained to do, I cut the headlights and approached in stealth- mode. I also parked just east of the house, not in front (that's a no-no) and we formulated our plan. Gary would take the east side of the house and I would take the west and head around back. So here is where that *policeman's intuition* kicks in. If you'll remember back in the book I called it my *Spidey-Sense*, but it's the same thing. That inner-voice that tells you to-do or not-do something. This night, it told us we shouldn't go to the front door. That's where the man with a gun was supposed to be, and at least out front I didn't see anyone.

I low-creeped it on the street past the front and went to the west side. As I worked my way around, I couldn't see anything through those windows, so I went around back. I was able to carefully look inside through a large picture-window and see the living area. I first noticed a 12 gauge shotgun lying on top of the couch. Ok, that's not good. I then looked at the front door and saw a subject (the *56 year-old* as I called him) standing at the front door peering out through the *Peep-Hole,* holding what we later learned was a .30 caliber carbine rifle. Ok, that was worse, but I didn't panic, my pucker-factor was under control, mostly, and I quietly called in to the dispatcher that we had an actual *Home-Invasion Robbery live and in-progress,* and so that Gary and the responding units could hear what I had. The bad guy didn't know I was there but he was waiting.

I continued my creep towards the kitchen, sliding-glass door, and stopped. I peaked in and much to my surprise I mean shock, the *18 year-old* subject as I called this one was right at the glass looking at me looking at him, and he was holding a semi-auto pistol. In my mind I said Shit! I saw the look on his face and I knew he said Shit! Now the pucker-factor was full-on and I was trying to figure out what the fuck to do! He ran back inside somewhere and I needed to find cover now. There was a low, about 18 inch high concrete fire-pit about 15 feet back from the kitchen door, so I ran for that and got really small behind it. I called it in and I could hear Gary just east of the kitchen doors say "Shit!" too. There were shits all around but no giggles.

As we were trying to figure out what the hell to do next, the *"32 year-old"* in a blue suit appeared at the glass door. We now knew we had at least three, asshole-bad guys to deal with, great! He saw me lying down behind the pit and was trying to tell me that everything was ok by his hand gestures and mouthing "Its ok." No it's not, but I'll go on. Suddenly, the entire family that resides there came out of a room adjacent to the kitchen in their pajamas. Things were getting *"Curiouser & Curiouser"* as *Spencer: For Hire* would say. They were mom and dad, two kids, and grandma, or should I say *Abuela?* Mr. *Blue-Suit* was trying to push them back and they were pushing him towards the glass door. Since I didn't see any weapons in his hands I broke cover, I know, you don't have to say it, and was yelling at him to come out with his hands-up but he wouldn't.

It was a stand-off for a minute but then all of a sudden, *Abuela* reaches under and unlocks the sliding-glass door (very slick) and the husband pushes it open and together, the family pushes *Blue-Suit* right out to me! Now your mine motherfucker! I grab him around the neck and put my gun to his head and use him as a possible shield in case the other two decide to join the party. While I drag him to the east side of the house, Gary runs from the corner and snatches up the family and takes them to the house next door out of harm's way. The cavalry is arriving and I turn over *Blue-Suit* to them and retake my perimeter position. Asshole Bad Guys 2 & 3 are still inside.

Sergeants arrive and take control, and after they hear what we had, set up a proper perimeter and called our Special Response Team (SRT) and negotiators. SRT arrived and took over the inner perimeter and I was relieved. I didn't know it at the time, but one of my future partners in the Midwest District, Frank Moreno, was on the team. You might remember him from the fight with the 18 year-old on steroids I wrote about earlier. Moving on. The negotiators well, negotiated with the other two, and after about two hours they gave up. Frank would later tell me when we were partners and recalled the story, that they basically told the bad guys that if they didn't give up, SRT would breach and kill them. They gave up. There were more guns inside, some drugs, and we found cut *zip-ties* in a kitchen drawer that the family was initially tied up with, but when the bad guys knew we were there, cut them off so that it would look to us like the family was ok. Nice try!

Detectives responded and began their investigation and later learned that these *Kentucky Fried Idiots* actually hit the wrong house. The house they wanted was the one to the east with the high fence and surveillance cameras everywhere. You'd think that was a clue. Nice going morons. You couldn't even get the location right!

Now we go to court a week later for the bond hearing. Each defendant was represented by counsel. The prosecutor prepped me before hand and we were off! He asked me to tell the judge what occurred while the three counsels-for-the-defenses tried to trip me up. I recounted what I saw and pointed to each bad guy and said exactly what each did and where. When counsel tried again the judge said that was enough, that my testimony was clear and accurate and he remanded them to custody without bond. A slam-dunk thus far, or so we thought.

Two things here. The State Attorney's investigation revealed that the two older subjects were old-hat at committing crimes. The 18 year-old was a new recruit to the game. But what got our attention the most, was that the 56 year-old was part of a high-jacking crew where after they jacked a truck on the highway, he was the tail and if a trooper stopped the truck, he was to drive by and take out the trooper. That's a real *Asshole Bad-Guy!*

The other thing that occurred a few weeks later was that *Blue-Suit* managed to escape custody from Dade-County Corrections at the facility known as the *Stockade*. Now I wonder how that happened.

A few months later we found out that he was located by police in Costa Rica, and that he "resisted arrest," and somehow flew out of a 5th story window. He didn't die, too bad, I mean good, and was extradited back to Miami in a full-body cast with a broken arm and two broken legs. He wrote some threatening letters to the judge on the case, and he received *Life*-plus two 25-year sentences, and the other two pillars of the community got 25 years each. This finally brought the saga to an end.

Gary and I were awarded *Officers of the Year* from a local Rotary Club for this caper, which was a great honor. But imagine if one or both of us ignored our training on how to approach, and of course, our *policeman's intuition* and went to the front door. Fortunately, the world will never know. But we know. By the way, the original dispatched-*911* caller for all of this, was *Abuela*. She saved us all!

Volume II?

I want to thank all of you for taking the time to read **The Real Greatest Show on Earth**. Especially my fellow police, fire, and military *Brothers & Sisters in-Arms*. I would like to invite you to submit your own **Stories** for a possible sequel to this book, where I can tell *your personal story* as you lived it. You never know, it could end up in a TV show or movie.

Please visit my website at:

Bertscopbook.com

and tell me your story!

And one last thing:

"Let's be careful out there!"

Sergeant Phil Esterhouse,
Hill Street Blues

The Last Word

For the families and friends of those lost Serving, Protecting, and Defending.

Epitaph
by Merrit Malloy

When I die
Give what's left of me away
To children
And old men that wait to die.
And if you need to cry,
Cry for your brother
Walking the street beside
you.
And when you need me,
Put your arms
Around anyone
And give them
What you need to give to me.
I want to leave you
something,
Something better
Than words
Or sounds.
Look for me
In the people I've known
Or loved,

And if you cannot give me
away,
At least let me live on your
eyes
And not on your mind.
You can love me most
By letting
Hands touch hands,
By letting
Bodies touch bodies,
And by letting go
Of children
That need to be free.
Love doesn't die,
People do.
So, when all that's left of me
Is love,
Give me away.
I'll see you at home
In the earth

About the Author

Bert "Maverick" Gonzalez retired with the rank of Sergeant from the Miami-Dade Police Department in Miami-Dade County, Florida, after 37 years. He served in numerous capacities as a patrol officer, plain-clothes surveillance & narcotics investigations, seaport and airport operations, dignitary protection details for vice presidents, a governor, and visiting heads of state. He coordinated security for naval and cruise vessels and TV and movie shoots.

One of the most important aspects of his career, as he would tell you, was having the privilege of being an instructor and mentor to 25,000 personnel during his career in the areas of Field Training, Mobile Field Force, Police Driving, Seaport Security, Crisis Intervention Team, Major Scene Management for Supervisors, and the Police Academy. Bert was most passionate about mentoring young officers and sergeants, serving his community, county, country, and his brothers and sisters in Brown and Blue.

Bert was often told by folks he encountered that he should write a book about what he'd seen and done, so he did. *The Real Greatest Show on Earth* describes what he—and cops everywhere—do every day and what they mean to a civilized society. In addition to the book, Bert has started a podcast, *Sgt. Maverick, The Podcast, All things Police Work, Politics & Life.* More of the unfiltered truths of police work.

His lasting legacy and what he is most proud of is starting the *Family Business* of police work. He was followed by his brother Pete and his wife Sally, their daughter Alina, Bert's son "BJ" and his wife Michelle. The *"Brown Bloods,"* if you will.

In addition to Bert's tennis addiction, he and his wife Rosy love to travel, hike national parks, ride motorcycles, and are expecting their fifth grandchild. So the journey continues…

About JEBWizard Publishing

JEBWizard Publishing offers a hybrid approach to publishing. By taking a vested interest in your book's success, we put our reputation on the line to create and market a quality publication. We offer a customized solution based on your individual project needs.

Our authors' catalog spans the spectrum of fiction, non-fiction, Young Adult, True Crime, Self-help, and Children's books.

Contact us for submission guidelines at

https://www.jebwizardpublishing.com

Info@jebwizardpublishing.com

Joe.Broadmeadow@jebwizardpublishing.com

www.ingramcontent.com/pod-product-compliance
Lightning Source LLC
Chambersburg PA
CBHW062110020426
42335CB00013B/909